ORGANIZATIONAL AND WORK
PSYCHOLOGY

Charles Seale-Hayne Library
University of Plymouth
(01752) 588 588
LibraryandITenquiries@plymouth.ac.uk

22nd International Congress of Applied Psychology Kyoto, Japan, 22-27 July 1990

Proceedings Volume 1

ORGANIZATIONAL AND WORK PSYCHOLOGY

Editors:
J. Misumi
B. Wilpert
H. Motoaki

LAWRENCE ERLBAUM ASSOCIATES, PUBLISHERS
Hove (UK)   Hillsdale (USA)

Lawrence Erlbaum Associates Ltd., Publishers
27 Palmeira Mansions
Church Road
Hove
East Sussex, BN3 2FA
U.K.

British Library Cataloguing-in-Publication Data

A catalogue record for this book is available from the British Library

   ISBN 0-86377-276-5

Cover by Joyce Chester; illustration by Professor Kimura
Typeset directly from disks supplied by the Editors
Printed and bound in the United Kingdom by Redwood Press Ltd., Melksham, Wiltshire

Contents

1990 ICAP COMMITTEE

IAAP Officers

President

Claude Lévy-Leboyer

Past President
Edwin A. Fleishman

President Elect
Harry C. Triandis

Secretary General/Treasurer
Charles J. de Wolff

Local Organizing Committee

Hiroshi Motoaki — *President Local Organizing Committee*
Jyuji Misumi — *Chairperson, Local Organizing Committee*
Tadasu Oyama — *Chairperson, Scientific Program Committee*
Yasuhisa Nagayama — *Secretary General*

Munehira Akita	Naosuke Itoigawa	Yoshiaki Nakajima	Sadao Sugiyama
Masaaki Asai	Sumiko Iwao	Nobuo Nakanishi	Takehisa Takizawa
Kazuko Asakura	Tomio Kinoshita	Seiichiro Namba	Bien Tsujioka
Hiroshi Azuma	Sonoko Kuwano	Akira Nishioka	Kikuo Uchiyama
Haruyo Hama	Takeshi Mamiya	Hiroshige Okaichi	Michiaki Uchiyama
Toshitsugu Hirano	Toshiaki Miura	Yoshito Okamoto	Yoshitake Umeoka
Akira Hoshino	Fumio Mugishima	Toshio Sugiman	Yuichi Yamada
Hiroshi Imada	Yasuhiro Nagatsuka	Chizuko Sugita	Kazuo Yamamoto

Sponsored by

The Science Council of Japan. *President:* Jiro Kondo
The Japanese Psychological Association. *President:* Takayoshi Kaneko

Supported by

Public Health Research Foundation. *President:* Masamitsu Oshima

Foreword

The present work is a record of the research reports presented at the 22nd International Congress of Applied Psychology, which was held in Kyoto in 1990. The content ranges from opening speeches to keynote addresses, symposia, audiovisual and poster presentations, and workshops. All these categories of contributions are classified into a number of subject areas.

The proceedings have been compiled in three volumes:

Volume I : Organizational and Work Psychology
edited by J. Misumi, B. Wilpert, and H. Motoaki

Volume II : General Psychology and Environmental Psychology
edited by B. Wilpert, H. Motoaki, and J. Misumi

Volume III : Social, Educational and Clinical Psychology
edited by H. Motoaki, J. Misumi, and B. Wilpert

Because of budgetary considerations and other difficulties the decision to publish the proceedings was made only after the congress had ended. We are now pleased, however, to present the *Proceedings of the 22nd International Congress of Applied Psychology, 1990*, the completion of which is a tribute to the contribution and understanding of all the authors and associates whose work is contained here. Our thanks go to the editorial team of Professor Bernhard Wilpert of the Berlin University of Technology for the excellent result, which has exceeded our expectations. Part of the difficult task with which the members of his group were burdened consisted of collecting over 500 manuscripts, sometimes by repeatedly urging the contributors to submit their papers by the deadline. The large participation of non-English native speakers, which in some cases necessitated the partial rewriting of some of the papers, made their job even more difficult. This monumental work has required of Professor Wilpert and his team more than a year of hard work.

We are also indebted to Lawrence Erlbaum Associates Ltd., Hove, U.K., especially Ms. Rohays Perry who has been instrumental and helpful throughout the publication process.

Last but not least, we also extend our sincere thanks to all those who have directly or indirectly contributed to the production of this work. We would like to express here our gratitude to many Japanese companies for their wholehearted assistance. Without their financial support and Prof. Wilpert's cooperation, this project would have never been realized.

Our hope is that the Proceedings will, even if modestly, contribute to the progress of applied psychology in the world.

Japanese Editorial Committee

Note of the Executive Editor

The 22nd International Congress of Applied Psychology was held in Kyoto, Japan, July 22-27, 1990. The purpose of the three volumes of its proceedings is to document the breadth and level of contributions made during that memorable event. Altogether 1,867 scholars and practitioners of psychology from 48 countries throughout the world participated. The actual work of the Kyoto Congress comprised 34 opening and keynote addresses, 117 symposia, and 493 poster contributions, 11 audiovisual presentations, and 15 workshops.

Despite the delay in the decision to publish the Congress Proceedings, we are proud to have been able to include more than 80% of all contributions made in Kyoto. The process of obtaining the more than 500 contributions that are now documented in the three volumes of these Proceedings entailed, among other things, contacting the main author, requesting their willingness to cooperate, checking on submission deadlines, sending out reminders, acknowledging receipt of contributions, language editing, standardizing the format of contributions, sending specific queries to authors, integrating corrections, scanning and retyping papers, and proofreading.

Wherever possible, formal opening and keynote addresses are included in full. All other scientific activities of the Kyoto Congress (symposia, poster papers, workshops, and audiovisual presentations) are documented as summary reports, with credit being given to the authors involved. The contributions are divided among the three volumes roughly according to the affinity of subdisciplines. In the effort to balance the relative size of the respective volumes, however, certain compromises had to be made. Within each of the three volumes, thematic affinity was the criterion guiding the decisions about the sequence of the contributions. An index of all contributors whose names appear in the three Proceedings volumes is contained in an appendix to each volume.

The executive editor is often faced with tricky decisions. In some cases, redundancies, references, or figures had to be deleted from a contribution because space was lacking or because the respective author(s) were unable to respond to queries in time. In a very few instances a contribution had to be omitted altogether, because we did not receive a publishable manuscript within the publisher's deadline. Furthermore, the ability to express oneself in English varies considerably throughout the world. Hence, English editing was often unavoidable. This process was based primarily on the 3rd edition of the American Psychological Association's publication manual, M. W. Fowler's widely used *Dictionary of Modern English Usage*, and, of course, the author's own responses to our queries. If a particular editorial decision is contrary to an author's intentions or hopes, I apologize in advance. To do justice to everyone in such a complex project as these Proceedings is a difficult art.

Nothing would have come of this project within the given time constraints without the unrelenting commitment and devotion of my collaborators—David Antal, with his precision and mastery of the English language: if a certain degree of consistency in style has been achieved throughout this publication, it is largely due to him; Ljerka Cuvaj, with her organizational skills and self-reliance; Hans Maimer, with his computing competence; and Ulrike Wiedensohler with her innovative mind, untiring assiduousness, and executive skills.

Bernhard Wilpert
Berlin, December 1991

Presidential Opening Addresses

PRESIDENTIAL ADDRESS :
THE ORGANIZING COMMITTEE OF THE 22nd
INTERNATIONAL CONGRESS OF APPLIED
PSYCHOLOGY

*Professor Hiroshi Motoaki, President of the Organizing Committee of the
22nd International Congress of Applied Psychology*

Madam President, Professor Claude Lévy-Leboyer, Distinguished
guests and Members of the International Association of Applied
Psychology, Ladies and Gentlemen. On behalf of the Organizing
Committee of the Congress, I take great pleasure in welcoming all of
you to Kyoto today for the opening of the 22nd International Congress
of Applied Psychology.

Although it has been publicized on several occasions, I would like to
emphasize again the significance of this 22nd International Congress.
We face today, what I believe to be an unfortunate consequence of
modern civilization. We are witnessing an enormous stagnation of
human and social sciences accompanied by a tremendous development
of natural sciences and technology. This has produced an overwhelming
imbalance between these disciplines.

Humans today live in an era of dramatic social change. At this time,
there is no doubt that natural sciences and technology are of great
material benefit. The quality of everyday life has been enhanced, two

examples being the standard of living and the standard of education. At the same time, however, people see these social changes as a source of conflict and dispute. The difficulties arise not only within individual countries, but also between the nations of the world. Society is now forced to deal with such hazardous events as environmental pollution, the destruction of ecological systems, overcrowded urbanization, and ever increasing interpersonal and intergroup differences. Many people encounter discrimination in socioeconomic status in areas such as educational opportunities, property, earnings, and individual needs.

These conflicts, disputes, and hazardous events, which occur among many nations of the world today, correspond to psychological pains of individuals and manifest themselves in many forms, such as anxiety, frustration, annoyance, and hopelessness.

I believe that applied psychology is a discipline that can advance scientific understanding of human behavior. From the perspective of psychology as a "science of human behavior" active practices to solve these personal, social, and national problems can be developed. In order to implement this universal problem-solving, it is my opinion that psychologists from all over the world should join together to conduct closely related collaborative research.

This is the first time that an international congress of applied psychology is being held in the Orient. I feel that the 22nd Congress can prove to be of great significance.

I hope that the 22nd International Congress of Applied Psychology will also provide an opportunity for Eastern and Western psychologists to exchange their views freely and discuss their mutual research interests thoroughly. Through this kind of endeavor, the current congress will make its proper contribution toward greater peace and prosperity in the world.

More than 2,000 psychologists from many different countries are attending this congress. It is truly an honor to welcome so many participants and I sincerely hope that all of you will be able to return to your countries with many worthwhile results and insights.

I should like to close with an earnest wish for everyone: that your experience at this congress leaves you the most precious of memories of rewarding personal interactions with many different psychologists from around the world. May your stay in Japan be a most enjoyable one.

WELCOME ADDRESS AT THE OPENING OF THE 22ND INTERNATIONAL CONGRESS OF APPLIED PSYCHOLOGY

Itaru Watanabe, Vice President, Science Council of Japan

Professor Claude Lévy-Leboyer, President of the International Association of Applied Psychology, Professor Motoaki, Chairman of the 22nd International Congress of Applied Psychology, Distinguished Guests, Ladies and Gentlemen.

On behalf of the Science Council of Japan, I take a great pleasure in this opportunity to speak to this great gathering of psychologists from more than 50 countries for the opening of the 22nd International Congress of Applied Psychology. The Science Council of Japan is an organ covering all scientific fields in the cultural, social and natural sciences division. We have been working to contribute to the progress of science by sponsoring many international congresses in Japan and by delegating Japanese representatives to international congresses held overseas. We do this because we consider international scientific exchange to be one of our most important duties.

We are holding the 22nd International Congress of Applied Psychology in cooperation with the Japanese Psychological Association. It is a particular pleasure to have this chance to meet with so many distinguished scientists from all around the world and to attend your lectures and presentations.

The International Association of Applied Psychology was organized in 1920, and this congress in Japan is the first of its international congresses to be held in the Asia-Pacific Regions. I am truly happy to see the increase in membership and the expansion of issues addressed by the organization over this period of time.

Applied psychology is concerned with wide array of human activities in a broad range of fields, including not only education, but also politics, economics, labor, religion, medicine, and health. I think that, in the midst of today's continually accelerating developments in the natural sciences and industrial technology, we must make an era of spiritual affluence to follow these materially affluent times. The natural sciences and other fields, too, are moving from physical to more spiritually-based investigations.

My sincere wish is for the many scientists gathered together here from around the world to be able to discuss numerous issues and arrive at sound results in applied psychology. I earnestly hope that all of you will find your participation in the congress worthwhile. Finally, I hope that each of you from abroad will enjoy your stay in Japan. I believe that this congress will be truly memorable for you through personal contacts with fellow scientists, and I hope that you will learn more about historic Kyoto and Japanese culture.

REMARKS OF THE PAST-PRESIDENT
INTERNATIONAL ASSOCIATION OF APPLIED
PSYCHOLOGY

Edwin A. Fleishman

This year marks the 70th anniversary of the first International Congress of Applied Psychology, sponsored by the International Association of Applied Psychology. That congress, organized by Edward Claparedi, was held in Geneva, Switzerland, in 1920 and comprised 17 participants representing 8 countries. During this coming week, our 22nd Congress will be held in this magnificent congress center. This is a congress that promises to be memorable occasion.

First, there is the scientific program, which is outstanding in the representation of topics and the quality of speakers and participants. Second, there is the hospitality of our Japanese hosts and the cultural environment and beauty of Kyoto, which should enrich the experience. Third, there are the social activities and plans for informal interactions among our colleagues, beginning with the reception that follows and the other events and field trips planned throughout the week, where we will meet old friends and make new ones.

I have had the privilege of working closely with our psychologist colleagues on the organization of our past congresses in Montreal, Munich, Edinburgh, and Jerusalem. Each congress has its own unique character and excitement—and its own surprises. The present congress in Kyoto promises to be very special. During the past five years, I have had the opportunity to work closely with our Japanese colleagues, who have undertaken the enormous task of organizing this congress for us on so generous a scale. I have seen first hand their hard work and dedication to the task, their commitment to excellence, and their attention to every detail.

They have honored me by inviting me to be part of this beautiful opening program, where my primary role is to introduce Professor Claude Lévy-Leboyer, the current president of the International Association of Applied Psychology. She has been president since 1982 and was vice president during my term as president from 1976 to 1982. She also served as the editor of our journal, Applied Psychology: An International Review. She has worked tirelessly to further the Association's goals of increasing scientific and professional communication among psychologists around the world.

She has been able to do this despite her many scientific and professional roles. Since 1968, she has been professor of work psychology at the Université René Descartes in Paris. She has been director of the Institute of Psychology there from 1976 to 1981 and in 1981 became vice president of the university. She is the author of a variety of books in organizational psychology and in environmental psychology. She has received many honors for her contributions and just recently was awarded the Legion of Honor by the French government—the highest civilian award in her country.

And now we can add our own modest award in recognition of her contributions to psychology. lt is my pleasure to introduce Professor Lévy-Leboyer and to present her with the Distinguished Service Award from our Association, the citation for which reads: *To Claude Lévy-Leboyer, President of the International Association of Applied Psychology 1982-1990, for Outstanding Contributions to the Advancement of the Profession of Psychology Internationally.*

PRESIDENTIAL ADDRESS

Claude Lévy-Leboyer, President of the International Association of Applied Psychology

Psychologists are often involved in prediction. We keep predicting the performance of people in their future jobs, the intellectual abilities of children, social life in new buildings, and the usefulness of psychotherapy or teaching methods, to mention just a few cases.

Organizing a congress is also a challenge involving a large measure of prediction, at least for the IAAP officers. Looking back at all the congresses I have been associated with, I could take a piece of paper, divide it down the middle, and write on one side events that were predicted and on the other side those that, for better or worse, were not expected.

In the case of the present congress, we did expect our Japanese colleagues to be hard working, dedicated, and never satisfied until perfection is achieved. We did expect Kyoto and the Congress Hall to present a most beautiful and refined environment. We did expect this congress to be an exceptional opportunity for psychologists from the Asian part of the world and colleagues coming from other continents to meet.

The Congress program as well as the list of registered members shows that all this has been more than fulfilled.

But, being ignorant and prejudiced *gaigins*, we underestimated our Japanese colleagues in their utmost courtesy, their respect for others' opinions and cultures, their skill in using the unsaid and the implicit to convey a message, as well as their concern for the aesthetic dimension of life. Moreover, as psychologists accustomed to considering motivation an individual characteristic, we could not help but admire the value our Japanese colleagues give to collective achievement.

These five years of collaboration have been an experience of an exceptional quality for the IAAP officers. For this, for hosting this congress, and for succeeding in shaping what will be remembered as a unique moment in the history of the International Association of Applied Psychology, I wish to thank most warmly Professor Motoaki, President of the Congress, Professor Misumi, Chairperson of the Organizing Committee, and Professors Oyama, Nagayama, Itoigawa, and Hama. I wish also to ask Professor Motoaki to convey my thanks and appreciation to all the members of the Japanese Committees.

This congress is not only unique from a cross-cultural point of view. Its success is also a sign of the dynamism of our field and of its powerful development. There is a good deal of proof that the importance of psychology is growing: the increasing number of our students, the variety of the fields to which psychology is being applied; the ever increasing number of books and journals in this field, and the fact that all the important new social issues require research on their psychological aspects.

Such is the case with the issues tackled by psychologists doing research on attitudes and behaviors as different as those responsible for AIDS or for the warming of the earth's climate. I could cite many other examples of topical issues—the psychological effect of unemployment, communication problems due to the development of information technology, evaluation of the effects of drug therapy, psychological factors in antisocial behavior, and the study of cognitive processes involved in the use of new technology just to name a few. Simply look at the congress program and compare it with the programme we had in Montreal sixteen years ago. None of these topics was on the agenda.

Those of you who have traveled in Eastern Europe in the last few months know that psychology is gaining an important place, for psychologists have been asked to tackle problems like worker motivation and consumer behavior in countries entering a competitive way of life.

This is sure proof that our field is in a healthy stage. But we must also be aware of the potential dangers brought about by rapid development. On such a pleasant occasion, I am not going to play the Cassandra and paint a black picture of our future. I would like simply to use a cognitive approach and describe the consequences of our success on what I would call our inside identity and our outside identity.

First, our inside identity. Applied psychologists work in very different environments. They must learn about these specific settings, their values, and the various roles played by the people they have to deal with. Some of them tend to become more familiar with the environment itself than with psychology, the results being that they lose a holistic representation of psychology and do not have enough opportunities for discussion with colleagues. The danger, for psychology, is to burst out into a number of subfields and thus lose its identity. The danger for psychologists is to give up the idea of a common training, a common language, and the ability to benefit from progress in other subfields. This issue is so critical that a round-table discussion in this congress is devoted to the unity of psychology.

Second, outside identity. As I have said earlier, the expertise of psychologists is sought, more and more frequently, when new social problems arise. When we are called upon, we react as any scientist would in similar circumstances. We plan research, assess methods, and ask for time in order to build tools and validate techniques. But other people, without any psychological knowledge or scientific wisdom, offer bright promises and miraculous methods. Psychologists should be aware that people much too often confuse validated methods and proven theories with "dummy" psychology. We should take this danger seriously and devote more effort to informing the layperson of the differences between charlatanism and psychology built on a scientific foundation.

Why do I mention these problems here and now? Because they cannot be dealt with by individuals. If there is a lesson we should learn from the Japanese culture and way of life, it is certainly the role and power of collective action.

We need the support of large associations. Even if we belong to networks focused on our field or limited to our region, we need the common perspective contributed by their federations. This is why the IAAP now has a divisional structure. We also need the visibility offered by publications. This is why we are increasing the number of our publications. We need to take part in meetings where we can compare our work. Above all, we need the strength born of international gatherings where psychologists work together to build their identity, their culture, a common set of aims, and a common ethic.

Throughout my eight years as IAAP president, I have tried to emphasize the importance of this large international organization covering all fields of applied psychology and the key role played by its world congresses. Your presence here shows that you share my beliefs.

I wish you all a very successful congress as well as a pleasant stay in this beautiful and hospitable country.

JYUJI MISUMI, CHAIRPERSON OF THE LOCAL ORGANIZING COMMITTEE

On the behalf of the people hosting the 22nd Congress of the International Association of Applied Psychology (IAAP) I would like to express my sincere gratitude to all the participants and their families who have come to Kyoto. There are some 1,800 of you, including over 800 non-Japanese participants, and your presence here shows that the Far East is not far anymore. It is a great pleasure to have you here.

No event held on this scale could be organized without assistance from many quarters. Given the stiff competition represented by applications for more than 30 international conferences this year, we have been very fortunate to have our International Congress of Applied Psychology (ICAP) co-sponsored by the Science Council of Japan and the Japanese Psychological Association. Moreover, 50% of our budget has been donated by industrial organizations. Without this generous support, I doubt that we would have been able to start.

I also owe thanks to the IAAP officers, our colleagues from the Japanese Psychological Association, and the invaluable cooperation of many psychologists from almost all parts of Japan for the fact that we have been able to complete the preparations for this congress. As indicated in the program, we now have 117 symposia, 30 keynote addresses, 500 poster presentations, and good number of workshops.

With the 21st century just around the corner, the world is experiencing rapid and dramatic change, especially in the socialist societies in Eastern Europe. Today's most important problem is how to make macrofactors in social systems, institutions, and organizations work effectively in conjunction with such microfactors as individual or interpersonal relations. In Japan, psychological phenomena used to be regarded as trifling, as phenomena incidental to social systems. What was important was the system or the organizational structure itself. From both the empirical and theoretical points of view, there was thus a tendency to underrate the importance of the psychological approach. But now, the redefinition of the social dimension in micropsychological terms has emerged as an important problem for social science and social practices.

One of the misfortunes in modern civilization is that the natural sciences and technology are advancing at an ever faster pace while the human sciences lag so far behind. The consequence has been an enormous imbalance between these two spheres of knowledge.

In my view, progress in civilization does not always result in a better society. Of course, as already discussed by Professors Watanabe and Motoaki, progress in the natural sciences and technology has brought about material benefits, raised living standards, enabled a life of leisure, and increased life expectancy. At the same time, however, it has contributed to environmental pollution; urban overpopulation; inequitable distribution of wealth and income; interpersonal or interorganizational confrontations, conflicts, and disputes resulting from changing public needs. Progress has thus also posed a threat to the safety of the biosphere. It is against this backdrop that the overall re-examination of the political, economic, educational, and cultural aspects of our lives from the human point of view is necessary.

Seen in this light, whether in a socialist or capitalist society (although such classification has already become archaic), psychological or microsocial science and the perspectives it gives on the relationship between individuals, groups, and organizations, will, in my opinion, become increasingly important. The significance attached to individual viewpoints will grow. The days are long gone when applied psychology was confined to mere application of principles elucidated by general psychology. In this sense, the word "applied" has lost its literal meaning. It is like the old clothes outgrown by the child. Problem-solving in today's society is a complex science comprising basic and theoretical research in psychology as well as practical, engineering-oriented, and clinical approaches. Given the compound nature of psychological problems in modern society, an interdisciplinary approach has become common practice.

In terms of the history of world civilization, the Asia-Pacific region is one of the new frontiers. It is thus all the more significant that this is the first time that the IAAP Congress is being held in the Asia-Pacific region. Much is not yet known to the world. It is true that Japanese products (cameras, cars, etc.) are familiar to many people of the world, but not much is known about Japanese culture and society.

As you know, Japan is a small island country. Until recently, it was a densely populated, agricultural society. To survive, the Japanese people had to work hard, growing rice. Nature was not considered as something to conquer but rather something to conform to and coexist with. Today, this tradition is being destroyed by industrialization and urbanization. It is my belief that modern civilization must be steered along a path that will lead humans to find a way of not only eliminating war but also coexisting and living symbiotically with nature, even if it means restricting industrialization. The human race's symbiosis with nature, a relation that Japan's agricultural society has traditionally maintained, should be extended to cover the entire world. I consider that this is a role to be played by psychology as a human science from a general point of view.

Last but not least, Kyoto is one of Japan's oldest cities, a site where many of the vestiges of ancient Japanese culture can be seen. In the vicinity of Kyoto there is another ancient city, Nara; Japan's second largest industrial and commercial city, Osaka; and the world-famous port city, Kobe. In Kyoto, you have the advantage of being at a very convenient place where you can see both the new and the old Japan at the same time. In addition to your active participation in the congress, I hope you will also enjoy travel around the area.

ON THE INCEPTION OF AN INTERNATIONAL CONGRESS

J. Misumi

The International Association of Applied Psychology (IAAP) formed in Paris in 1920, constitutes one of the oldest international psychological associations. Until today, however, no full-scale IAAP meeting designed for research reports had ever been held in the Asia-Pacific region. It was eight years ago that I received several letters from IAAP directors suggesting that Japan apply to host the 1990 IAAP congress. Because the number of IAAP members in Japan was limited and because the Japanese currency (Yen) was appreciating drastically against the U.S. dollar at that time, organizing such a huge event as a congress seemed next to impossible for us. We also expected difficulties in raising enough funds to cover the cost of the congress here. Owing to all these factors, we were very hesitant about seeking to host the 1990 IAAP congress.

There are twenty psychology-related associations in Japan today, but it seemed absolutely necessary for the largest of them, the Japanese Psychological Association (JPA) to participate in the effort. After all, any international congress to be held in Japan would make little sense unless a large number of Japanese psychologists were included. However, two factors made it rather difficult for the JPA to join in an IAAP congress as a host. First, unlike the IUPsyS, which is based on a corporate, or collective, membership, the IAAP is made up of individual members. As an organization, the JPA therefore could not be an IAAP member. Consequently, there was no clear reason why JPA should join an IAAP congress as a host. Second, there was no guarantee that we could raise the necessary money to cover the cost of an IAAP congress.

I started exploring the possibility of having a group of psychologists in the Kansai area host an IAAP congress alone in case we failed to enlist JPA participation. I broached the subject with Professors Nagayama and

Itougawa of the School of Human Sciences at Osaka University, to which I belonged. They immediately concurred in my proposal. We subsequently held meetings with professors from universities in Kyoto, Kobe, and Osaka to ask them whether they would agree. They did. Although they explained that there would be difficulties, they responded with "Let's try it." Thus it was that we declared our candidacy in Acapulco.

At the time, the JPA was not very enthusiastic about holding an IAAP congress. Only Professor Motoaki, the JPA president, expressed support for staging one in Japan. Even after we came out on top in the vote taken in Acapulco, the JPA remained cool to the idea. Although I concluded that we, the Kansai group alone, could manage to host an IAAP congress, I decided to abandon the idea of having it in Japan. I was afraid that if it were to take place in the Kansai area, the young and active psychologists in Kansai would have to be so involved in all kinds of preparations that they would not have enough time left for academic work. I then flew to Paris and met IAAP President Lévy-Leboyer, who unexpectedly accepted all my requests. First, she agreed that one additional IAAP executive member would be named among the incumbent JPA members. Second, the IAAP would write a formal letter to the JPA, requesting that an IAAP congress be held in Japan. This correspondence led to the nomination of Professor Tadashi Oyama as an IAAP executive member. Thanks to the good offices of Professor Mamiya, the JPA then started to move.

In the meantime, the Science Council of Japan decided to become a joint sponsor, thereby laying the groundwork of the Kyoto IAAP congress. However, this does not mean that the Kyoto IAAP congress was handled by the JPA and the Science Council of Japan. In Japan, any large-scale organizational activities require a sort of double management—an official organization and a working-level organization. The substantive activities involved in the Kyoto IAAP congress were not handled by the formal sponsors, that is, the Science Council of Japan and the Japanese Psychological Association. Formally, these two official organizations were sponsors, not working entities. While expediting the process of the congress, we also organized a preparator committee comprising working-level psychologists centered on JPA members. All the substantive activities involved in the Kyoto IAAP Congress revolved around the executive committee, organized with the Preparatory Committee as its nucleus.

What was the "merit" of these official, nonworking sponsors? First, JPA as a formal sponsor made it possible for JPA members to become members of the in-group formed to accelerate the activities leading up to the Kyoto IAAP Congress. As a result, as many as 944 Japanese psychologists—a number far in excess of our original expectations—registered as participants despite the fact that many of them were not actually members of the IAAP. Moreover, because the Science Council of Japan also became a formal sponsor, we could be provided with a certain amount of funding by the central government. This fact encouraged some private corporations, too, to make substantial monetary contributions to the Kyoto IAAP Congress. All these factors contributed to making the Kyoto IAAP Congress a reality.

In all fairness, it must be pointed out that Kyoto IAAP Congress owes many of its substantive activities to the Kansai Group of Psychologists, especially Professors Nagayama, Itoigawa, Nakajima, Nakanishi, Nanba, and Yoshida; Associate Professors Sugiman and Miura, all the other research assistants from the Faculty of Human Sciences, Osaka University; as well as Professors Hama and Okaichi of Doshisha University, Professor Imada of Kansai Gakuin University, Professor Tsujioka of Kansai University, Professors Hirano and Kinoshita of Kyoto University, and Professor Akita of Kyoto Semi University. On the Tokyo side, thanks are also due to Professor Motoaki, President of both the Kyoto IAAP Congress and the Preparatory Committee; Ms. Kazuko Asakura, Secretary-General of JPA; and Professors Oyama and Takizawa.

The fund-raising committee was composed of many psychologists from the Kansai, Kanto (Tokyo-Yokohama), and Nagoya areas. They did a great deal of legwork voluntarily and autonomously to arrange the financing for the Kyoto IAAP Congress. Serving as chairperson of the fund-raising committee was Professor Motoaki, with Professors Yamada, Uchiyama, and Nakanishi as vice-chairpersons.

The executive committee held "core" staff meetings once or twice every month in Kansai and Kanto throughout the four years or so, prior to the Kyoto IAAP congress. After those small group meetings came joint meetings of the executive committee, thereby making for step-by-step preparations. Formed within the executive committee were subcommittees to handle various aspects such as general affairs, scientific programs, workshops, fund-raising, finance, ceremonies, meeting places, exhibits, tours, and excursions. Altogether 14 committees engaged in their respective activities on an equal and horizontally coordinated, yet individually-oriented basis. All these activities were loosely monitored at the monthly joint executive committee meetings, with all the committee chairpersons attending. It may well be said that the executive committee was a "flat" organization and a kind of "project" organization. The committees which, in turn, centered on their chairpersons and vice-chairpersons, worked out creative and circumspect plans and made every effort to translate them into action. Most of the committees were made up of university professors, their research assistants, and graduate students all working as a group. Thus, cohesiveness among the various groups was quite strong. In that sense, they were well controlled groups. In other words, the Kyoto IAAP Congress was characterized by "temporary" organizational activities oriented toward goal-achievement and sustained group dynamics in small teams. As they worked, one problem after another arose, but most of them were usually solved within these small groups.

It is especially noteworthy that IAAP officers had so enthusiastically endeavoured to work out ways and means of organizing and executing the Kyoto Congress for the five years that preceded the Congress.

Professor Claude Lévy-Leboyer, IAAP President, Dr. E.A. Fleishman, IAAP Past President and Professor Charles de Wolff visited Japan in 1985, 1987 and 1989 respectively to personally check out the convention hall and its facilities and to intensively discuss such essentially important matters as participation fees, as well as the formulation of scientific programs together with the Japanese staff members.

The IAAP officers took pains to select the scientific program's keynote speakers and symposium members impartially and to make the contents of their discussions as substantive as possible.

If the program turned out substantive, it must be pointed out that it was largely thanks to the devotion with which the IAAP officers, travelling half-way around the world to Japan, made strenuous efforts to make the Congress a success. President Claude Lévy-Leboyer's powerful and flexible leadership and Dr. Fleishman's supportive, considerate, wide-ranging and pertinent information and advice were particularly impressive.

Scientific programs were worked out by the committee that revolved around its chairperson, Professor Oyama. Poster presentation was handled by Professor Nakajima, and the organization of the workshops was taken charge of by Professor Sugita.

The Hama-Imada committee prepared a detailed manual for use during the course of the congress. The committee also arranged bus transportation to and from the meeting hall and worked out excursions.

The program of the 1990 IAAP Congress comprised 29 keynote addresses, 117 symposia, 1 round-table discussion, 12 audiovisual presentations, 493 poster sessions, and 15 workshops. This compares to 9 keynote addresses, 49 symposia, 56 individual reports and 25 free discussions at the 1972 IUPsyS Tokyo Congress.

The addresses heard at the opening ceremony are printed in Volume 1 of these proceedings. Professors Hama and Imada, who are closely linked with Kyoto's cultural activities, deserve credit for arranging all the cultural events and entertainments offered to the participants of the Kyoto IAAP Congress. This program included a tea ceremony, demonstrations of ceremonial robes of court ladies of the Heian Period, a performance of Japanese *yokobue* flute music, glee-club singing, Suzuki-style children's violin playing, a demonstration of ritual dance with a lion's mask based on *noh* drama, and a pleasant reception.

Professor Nanba was responsible for the exhibition of machines displayed by corporations in the exhibition hall. He was also instrumental in providing free beverages to participants and in creating a relaxed, restful environment throughout the congress.

It was under Professor Akita's guidance and leadership that P.R. activities for the Kyoto IAAP Congress were conducted in Sydney and that the program and abstracts were edited, designed, and printed.

Prior to the 1990 IAAP Congress in Kyoto, it was important for us to draw our conclusions from a result of the 1972 conference in Tokyo. On that earlier occasion, we were told by an American psychologist that "the conference was beautifully organized and fun, but where is Japanese academic research?" That question kept haunting Japanese psychologists and led to the decision to publish a special issue entitled *Applied Psychology in Japan* (see *Applied Psychology: An International Review*, 38(4), 1989).The representative articles had been collected with incredible speed, as described by Professor B. Wilpert of the Technical University of Berlin. Under these circumstances, we were not able to cover all the research fields. This attempt to publish a special issue about a country seemed to have been the first of its kind in the IAAP journal. Free copies of the journal were distributed to all the participants in the Kyoto IAAP Congress.

Although we have not conducted a survey about the reactions to the Kyoto IAAP Congress, President Lévy-Leboyer of the IAAP wrote in a letter after the congress, "The Kyoto IAAP Congress was an exceptional success." As chairperson of the executive committee, I am very appreciative of the fact that more than 800 psychologists came to Kyoto from abroad to participate in the congress despite the unusually hot summer, that we received full support from so many psychologists, and that we were given whole-hearted financial support from Japanese industrial circles.

Last but not least, we must apologize to all the participants for our delay in publishing the congress proceedings. Despite the prior suggestions from President Lévy-Leboyer and Prof. E. Fleishman we were unable by the end of the congress to decide whether we should pursue the matter. At the executive committee meetings, we could not even take up the matter for discussion; no proceedings were ever known to have been published of IAAP congresses before. When we thought about the energy required to compile the proceedings, the skill needed to overcome the language barriers in editing the manuscripts, and the limitations of Japanese ability to deal with English publications, the process of publishing the proceedings seemed nearly impossible. Thanks to financial support from Japanese industrial circles in the last stage of the congress, however, the executive committee did decide to go ahead with the publication of the proceedings of the 22nd International Congress of Applied Psychology—a major project in its own right.

Fortunately, my long-time friend, Professor Bernhard Wilpert who is the IAAP's president-elect and, until recently, the editor of the IAAP's journal *Applied Psychology—An International Review*, came to our rescue, graciously agreeing to take this job in hand. To him and all his collaborators I express my deepest gratitude for a task successfully accomplished. The Proceedings have now been published by Lawrence Erlbaum, England.

At a time when the idea of a society without borders is in everybody's mind, let me close by articulating my hope that the Japanese psychologists who participated in the Kyoto IAAP Congress and came into personal contact with psychologists from abroad will think more globally than in the past and consider how to preserve the Earth.

Organizing Committee
Jyuji Misumi, Chairperson

Organizational
Psychology

THE UNDERUTILIZATION OF APPLIED PSYCHOLOGY

Frank Heller, Tavistock Institute, London

INTRODUCTION

The term 'applied' psychology conveys the message that whatever scientific work is covered under that name is practical and is therefore meant to be used. The title of this paper suggests that such an assumption is flawed, and my aim is to present some reasons for the frequent underutilization of our work.

We can start by asking two simple questions:

1. Who has the responsibility for application—do we, or does an imaginary client?
2. When we cannot ensure that research findings are translated into action, should we simply relax in the expectation that some day they will be picked up and put to use?

Agreement with the second question absolves us of all responsibility for application, and one suspects that this is what frequently happens. Such a delegation of responsibility does little to further the utilization of our research findings, and I will argue that a more active stance is necessary. The research community, however, is not the only group that needs to examine its role.

I want briefly to anticipate my conclusion so that, as the subject develops, the reader can judge whether the arguments and evidence are strong enough to support the underutilization case (Nowotny & Lambiri-Dimaki, 1985). The paper will conclude that there is indeed substantial scope for making better use of social science and of applied psychology in particular.

Three groups must assume reponsibility. First, there are the producers of applied psychology—ourselves. Second, there are the institutions that support our work—the funding bodies, the university structures, and the refereed journals. Third, there are the clients or potential users of our work. Some of the obstacles to utilization are unavoidable, but each of the three groups can and should do more to use scarce resources effectively.

It will also be suggested that although producers have no authority to influence directly the other two groups that make up the triangle of underutilization, we can do so indirectly.

A brief excursion into the recent past shows that university departments of social science have often been unware of, or indifferent to, the value of practical outcomes. In many cases the situation is unchanged today but, during the last decade, increasing pressure on research funding shifted attention away from initiatives based entirely on researchers' own academic preoccupations towards the needs of governments or other potential users. Even in the United States, which is still relatively well endowed with research support, and in old established disciplines, like economics, the consumer orientation trend has increased (Haveman, 1986).

Psychology is a younger, less well-established social discipline than economics and is therefore tempted to make great efforts to establish its scientific credentials by applying sophisticated methodologies to well-honed traditional fields, like laboratory experimentation, perception, individual differences, motor sensations, emotions, etc. Some of the work carried out under these headings has potential practical application, but this is not often seen as an important priority by the research community. Moreover, these traditional fields operate at the microlevel of life, leaving a great deal of psychological reality 'out there', uncovered in the social community.

This is not the place for reviewing the history of psychology and its gradual process of embracing wider topics like ecology (Barker, 1968) or Health and Unemployment (O'Brien, 1986; Warr, 1987). The definition of the scope for psychology has not changed much since Stout defined it in the 1930s (Stout, 1938/1945, p. 1) as: "the study of mental facts or the study of mental life." It was, and for many it still is, quintessentially the study of individuals.

Social psychology, of course, developed quite early in the first quarter of this century (Thouless, 1925), but on a lower level of prestige than psychology. Occasionally brave men and women, having achieved eminence in a more traditional area of psychology, branched out to study wider topics, like religious life, ethics and nationalism (McDougall, 1934). Very recently there has undoubtedly been some progress, and 'societal psychology' has been coined by Himmelweit and Gaskell (1990, p. 17) as: "the label given to a much-needed development within social psychology. It emphasizes the all-embracing force of the social, institutional and cultural environments and with it the study of the social phenomena in their own right as they affect, and are affected by, the members of the particular society." As we shall see later, this broadening has come about fairly recently and has yet to establish itself. In the meantime, other social science disciplines have fertilized the wider area and have benefited in terms of financial support and client interest.

It is significant that Himmelweit explains that the term 'societal psychology' was considered preferable to 'sociological psychology' because the latter name would have allied the concept to another existing discipline, which could equally have been anthropology, political science, or even economics. She is at pains to show that societal psychology is not the same as applied social psychology, which, she points out (Himmelweit & Gaskell, 1990, pp. 17-18), has also concentrated largely on: "the study of the individual's thoughts, feelings and actions, while paying little attention to the study of the environment, its culture and its institutions."

The analysis of underutilization could well apply to the whole field of psychology, but most of the examples in this article will come from a fairly narrow area of organizational psychology. This is due largely to the way a particular piece of research on utilization was commissioned and funded.

In theory at least, funding bodies are concerned with the utility of the research they support. In practice this rarely becomes a major preoccupation, unless external pressures are applied. In Great Britain the biggest financial support for social science research is channeled from the Department of Education and Science to the Economic and Social Research Council (ESRC).

In the 1970s, an ESRC committee with a brief to support industrial and management research set up a subcommittee to look at the relationship between producers and consumers of research in its area. It is significant that the report of this subcommittee never reached the policy-making arms of the ESRC and that it was only when government pressure for useful research increased, that the subcommittee's work was dug out, expanded, and given research support. The result was a book of eighteen chapters by social scientists from the United States,

France, Germany, the Netherlands, Sweden, and Britain (Heller, 1986). It then took the ESRC a further 18 months to convene a seminar to discuss the evidence assembled in this publication and to debate the pessimistic conclusions that emerged from the analysis. The present article updates and expands the evidence of the 1986 book and strengthens the theoretical model, which tries to capture the lessons to be drawn from such an assembly of multinational examples.

THE PRODUCER OF KNOWLEDGE

It is not true that producers of social science are reluctant to have their findings used. Psychologists do not refuse to discuss their results when journalists or government departments ask for information or show interest in applying their work. The problem is more subtle. Many social scientists believe that they have no *responsibility* for the application of their research. One prevalent view is that, if findings are well established, they will eventually be used. There is also the traditional argument that 'pure' science has nothing to do with application and 'pure' science is more important than applied science.

Our infrastructures and rewards support such beliefs. Experimental psychology has more prestige than social or organizational psychology, and promotion depends on publishing in certain highly regarded refereed journals, for which very condensed, specialized writing is necessary. This kind of communication remains incomprehensible to educated, nonsocial scientists and often even to social scientists in related fields.

Translations of our jargon into ordinary language carry no promotion prospects and are also discouraged because they take up precious time which should be used to produce more articles for refereed journals. The task of translation is therefore often left to nonscientists, journalists, or dedicated popularisers, who frequently misrepresent or misunderstand our work. Diffusion is only one small part of the problem. Equally important is the choice of research area and the choice of method.

Our Competitors:
There is a Market in Social Science

Over the last four decades, with few exceptions, applied psychology has continued to concentrate its attention on the individual and the small social group, but the problems facing us as individuals, and as families and institutions, have increasingly been conceptualized in much broader terms. We are faced with problems of:

1. Migration, race relations, and other forms of discrimination.
2. Women's issues.
3. Third World issues.
4. The growth of nationalism and fanaticism.
5. Poverty and the scourge of unemployment.
6. The arrival of constantly changing technologies.
7. The decline in ethical behaviour.
8. The growing fear of damage to the ecology of our planet.
9. The need to conserve nonrenewable energy.
10. The rise of lawlessness and hooliganism.
11. The constant, though statistically insignificant, danger from preventable disasters or near disasters to atomic power stations, aircraft, or oil tankers.
12. The problems of leadership in changing societies from one political-economic system to another, as in Eastern Europe.

These and similar issues have moved into the limelight. They are being debated at all levels of society, from the family to governments, and in even larger entities, like the European Community and the United Nations. They require analysis and research before improvements can be suggested. Is applied psychology capable of contributing ideas to any or all of these problems? At the moment other social sciences, like sociology, political science, social anthropology, and economics, are deeply involved with work in these fields of contemporary crisis. Hence they, rather than psychology, are receiving the lion's share of available research funds.

If it is true, as I believe it to be true, that psychology on its own (but preferably in partnership with other disciplines) could make a significant contribution to many or even most of the areas of social malaise mentioned above, then we have to ask ourselves why we allow these opportunities to pass us by.

On Methods

Some people say that the major reason for our reluctance to take on societal problems is the impossibility of applying our well-honed research methods to wider multidisciplinary problems.

One can have some preliminary sympathy with this argument, but it is not convincing. New problems require new methods, and it is only by entering these arenas that fresh approaches or adaptations of existing methods will be developed. Psychologists start from a position of strength compared with other social science disciplines (excepting economics) because methodological training is highly developed. The philosophy of science covers a vast and constantly expanding array of methodologies. Those who feel constrained are often those who have become wedded to specific techniques, which they use in line with what Kaplan (1964) has called 'the law of the instrument', which he attributes to a very human trait of scientists and describes (Kaplan, 1964, p. 28) as:

> Give a small boy a hammer and he will find that everything he encounters needs pounding. It comes as no surprise to discover that a scientist formulates problems in a way which requires for their solution just those techniques in which he himself is especially skilled.

Research based on the law of the instrument contributes to the underutilization of applied psychology, and there is evidence to support this contention. Evaluation of the impact of policy research from 120 projects by van de Vall (1986, p. 209) has shown "that the amount of the researchers' time devoted to methodological problems does not correlate positively with utilization, while the portion of time devoted to *ad hoc* meetings on policy formation shows a positive correlation with utilization . . .".

In other research on policy use, van de Vall was surprised to find that external researchers make significantly less impact on policy application than internal researchers. This finding opposes frequent claims about the better results achieved by external researchers. It seems that in-house workers have several advantages. They are less concerned than externals with high prestige experimental designs using before and after control group schemas. They are more inclined to use 'process methods' using quantitative as well as ethnographic techniques, and they make much more extensive use of feedback loops to engage with the client system. There is also the related finding that research utilization occurs more frequently and easily if the researcher continues involvement with the organization after the research report is submitted. This is more in the tradition of internal than external researchers.

The methods described by van de Vall bear a strong resemblance to Research-Action in the following description of a range of alternative ways of carrying out investigations in social science.

A Range of Research Approaches

The range of approaches to knowledge creation and its effect on utilization can be illustrated by describing five alternatives:

1. The Traditional Method: The 'scientific approach'. This is by far the most widely practised approach in all areas of psychology, including the area we call 'applied'. There is often no 'client'; the work is carried

out among students or in organizations that allow investigators to use their sites and take up the time of their personnel as a gesture towards academia. Large-scale surveys with distributed questionnaires or by interview also fall within this category, as do laboratory studies. The design and execution of the work is left entirely in the hands of the scientific staff. Occasionally, the subjects or organizations are given some information about the outcome of the research.

Diffusion: Specialized condensed language through academic channels.

2. Building Bridges Between Researcher and User. With this less frequently used approach, the researcher selects the area of work, decides the methodology, hypothesis, or theory (as in the traditional method, mentioned above) but is actively concerned with the application of results. The stimulus for application may come from different sources: the client, the funding body, or the investigator.

The client or potential user of the outcome (a special interest group, government department, business, hospital, church, etc.) is sometimes able to collaborate in the design or in the diffusion process. To prepare the way for application and thereby build a bridge between research and user, the dissemination process is given careful attention; it can be verbal as well as written and often takes the form of one or more feed-back meetings. To be effective, several diffusion channels are necessary.

Diffusion: Academic and more popular.

3. Researcher-Client Collaboration: Research-Action. The client can be any person, group, or organization with a problem requiring investigation. This method is much less frequently used than the two previously discussed. It is based on the belief that collaboration between client and researcher in the process of formulation, design, and execution has advantages for both. There is said to be greater depth and reality in the definition and mapping of the field, more extensive uninhibited access yielding data of greater validity, and less resistance to implementation of the results.

The method implies a social contract that sanctions the research so that both the process and the outcome are jointly owned and the action phase is part of the complete cycle. The initiative for this approach can come from the researcher or the client. It could, in theory, also come from funding bodies, although this is unusual.

This method is called 'Research-Action', to emphasize that the research phase has priority and receives adequate resources, as in the two aforementioned methods. The techniques of investigation chosen may be different, for instance less technology driven and more diverse.

The research results are jointly interpreted but can be separated from the action phase if that is thought necessary for publication.

Diffusion: To the client and other interested groups in simple language. Also through academic channels.

4. Client-initiated Projects. The client's brief to the researcher can be wide or narrow. In the latter, the client specifies a particular problem and expects the researcher to work on the basis of this diagnosis. However, extensive experience shows that what we call the 'presenting problem' may not be the real problem. An organization may feel that it has a problem of low morale or excessive labour turnover, but on investigation it may transpire that these are symptoms of inappropriate leadership methods, incentive schemes, or poor work design, etc. For this reason, researchers usually prefer a broad brief.

A broad brief may lead to Research-Action, as previously discussed, but there are occasions when the client is interested in buying into existing know-how and experience and will not support research. This is even more likely when the client believes that the nature of the problem has already been identified and brings in experts to deal with it. Under these conditions, a relatively short investigation leading to recommendations and implementation will be the chosen approach. The researcher may wish to negotiate a social contract in which there is joint responsibility for implementation of findings, or at least follow through to that phase. This can then be called Action-Research.

Action-Research is often criticized by the academic community because it is 'long on action and short on research' and because the two stages interpenetrate and the outcome is rarely written up or accepted by traditional journals. For this reason it is useful to differentiate between Research-Action and Action-Research, although the boundary is ill-defined.

Action-Research does not have to be confined to 'presenting problems', and a good case can be made out for an approach which builds on best current knowledge and experience derived from research and tests it in a practical setting. This is what happens in some projects in biology and medicine, where in-depth studies and small samples are also used for certain types of work.

However, there remains the problem identified by Cherns (1969) that Action-Research may be the most usable but also the least generalizable form of research.

Diffusion: Diffusion beyond the client may not occur with Action-Research. Occasionally, reports appear in popular and nonrefereed journals.

5. Client Consultancy. Client-initiated projects, as in Action-Research, discussed previously, and particularly those with a narrow brief, are a form of consultancy. However, under Action-Research it is assumed that the 'researchers' are specialists in the field, be they in teaching, consultancies, or other institutions.

Client consultancy describes more conventional consultant organizations, mainly staffed by management specialists with extensive experience in fields such as marketing, accounting, personnel, etc. The staff often have senior line or staff experience in business before becoming consultants. The company may or may not employ behavioural science advisers.

Under this form of consultancy (which has expanded rapidly during the last decade), research as described in the previous sections will not take place; instead, there is a short diagnostic phase leading to recommendations. If the problem falls within the area of applied psychology, the knowledge input may be at second or third hand. The books used for reference are sometimes decades out of date. Consultants tend to use carefully collated standard questionnaires or 'packages', which are applied to an extensive range of issues following the diagnostic. One very well known and widely used package is the Blake and Mouton Managerial Grid. It is based on leadership research that was state of the art in the 1950s (Blake & Mouton, 1964, 1968, 1978). There are many other more recent packages covering different problem areas.

Diffusion: Diffusion beyond the client is very rare. Occasionally, word-of-mouth reports leak out through the client or consultant.

The reader will appreciate that there is some artificiality in these five categories. Most real research does not fall neatly into any one of them, and there are omissions and in-between positions. They have been categorized in this way to draw attention to the wide variety within and between the methods and so to stress the existence of choices. Diffusion is an essential part of scientific work, and the methods of communicating results can be seen to differ very substantially in intensity and in the channels used. Furthermore, the first two methods are discipline-based, and the last three are field-based. Client consultancy contributes little to knowledge creation and is very inadequately diffused. The traditional method contributes little to application, at least in the short run, and is also inadequately diffused.

Even if we accept the limits of categorization, their relation to utilization and policy relevance is worth further analysis. An example from the traditional approach will illustrate the problem. A recent study of the U.K. National Health Service examined the way a large number of questionnaire studies were used. Their purpose was to discover ways of improving the quality of health service by discovering weaknesses in the existing system (McIver & Carr-Hill, 1989). It emerged that, in most cases, neither the design nor the execution of the survey had been shared with the staff who would be responsible for making changes. As a consequence, the surveys had almost no impact on policy or on the quality of the health service (Dixon & Carr-Hill, 1989).

The claim can be made that, in most circumstances, a degree of client involvement in the research process (as in the second, third, and fourth methods, discussed previously) will increase the probability that the results are used. Reviews of the literature (for instance, Karapin, 1986), justify the conclusion that what we have called Research-Action, as well as Action-Research, is particularly likely to bridge the knowledge-action gap. Van de Vall's work, mentioned earlier, and the long tradition of Scandinavian work at the Oslo and Stockholm work research institutes, give further support to this claim.

The term 'client consultancy' is controversial. It is meant to highlight the absence of research and lack of psychological specialization. This is certainly one end of a continuum, but some consultancies use specialists and there are academics who use part of their available time for consulting. The reason for emphasizing the absence of research specialization is to examine the proposition that utilization may to a large extent be independent of scientific work.

I believe that client consultancy, based on simple packages, is as likely or more likely to be translated into action than the results of work carried out under the other methods. If this is true, it requires our careful attention. Is the alleged higher propensity for utilization of consultancy packages due to their presentation, content, higher cost and prestige, or to some more subtle factors? Who or what is responsible for the use of standardized packages? One partial explanation will be discussed under the heading Gresham's Law, a proposition suggesting that the 'bad' drives out the 'good'.

Having looked at ourselves as researchers, we must turn to consider the position of the other main party, namely, the potential user of social science.

THE POTENTIAL USER OF SOCIAL SCIENCE

Let us assume, for the moment, that every reader of this paper has produced scientific work of adequate merit and utility but that nevertheless, disappointingly, it has not been taken up by those who could benefit from it. What obstacles can we identify to explain this underutilization? I will confine myself to three, although there are certainly more. One is power and sectional interests, a second is an adaptation of Gresham's law, and the third is Do-It-Yourself Social Science (DYSS).

Power, Ideology, and Sectional Interest

We should not be surprised that whenever a social science finding opposes existing strongly entrenched interests, power will prevail over science. There are innumerable examples. One that caused considerable irritation in Britain had its origin in the request from Sir Keith Joseph, the Secretary of State for Education and Science in the early 1970s, for the Social Science Research Council to engage in a programme of research into the 'cycle of deprivation'. Government ministers, including Sir Keith, were inclined to see this cycle as a function of the deprived families themselves, while most social scientists thought that a substantial part of the problem was due to socioeconomic factors located in the structure of British society. This difference in ideology was reflected in the way over seventy academics structured their 34 research projects. It also accounts for the unequivocal rejection of the final report by Sir Keith Joseph and the fact that none of the recommendations was accepted as an ingredient of government policy (Cherns, 1986). The government's displeasure had other repercussions. It is now widely accepted that this clash led to Sir Keith Joseph's instructing Lord Rothschild, an eminent biologist and close associate of the government, to carry out a critical review of the Social Science Research Council's work. To the surprise of the government, Lord Rothschild's analysis of the Council's work was favourable, thus saving it from extinction. Nevertheless, Sir Keith insisted that the word 'Science' be removed from the title of the Council, and it is now known as the Economic and Social Research Council.

Another example of a clash of values that led the more powerful stakeholder to refuse implementation comes from a project carried out by Lévy-Leboyer with the help of the French Post Office. Lévy-Leboyer was interested in an analysis of vandalism; post offices and telecommunications companies all over the world have their telephone booths vandalized. The French Post Office was no exception, and they agreed to the research, which was meticulously carried out. Lévy-Leboyer (1986, p. 28) came to the conclusion that the people who attack telephone boxes: "are ordinary angry customers, not the young unsocial delinquents." The reason for this behaviour was that telephones could not be used because the coin boxes were full. The research team suggested a simple and potentially effective action phase following on from the research findings. The method is close to

Research-Action (as discussed previously) but nevertheless, there was no implementation. Lévy-Leboyer (1986, p. 28) believes the principal reason was that the findings conflicted with the Post Office's ideology—based on no scientific evidence—that the vandalism was due to: "socially deviant behaviour and people guilty of malignant aggressiveness towards public property."

Gresham's Law

The second obstacle to research utilization is the application of a well-known economic idea to applied psychology.

Sir Thomas Gresham, a sixteenth-century financier, held the view that bad money always drives out good money. In economics in the twentieth century, this is no longer true (if you look at what happened between the poor Ostmark and the strong Deutschmark on July 1, 1990), but this tendency, for the bad to drive out the good, seems to hold over a wide area of social science.

One application of this idea is the use of graphology as a method of selection, a practice which is spreading rapidly. It has been used in Switzerland and some other continental countries for some time and is now moving further afield. There are several critical studies on the validity of graphology as an indicator of character. One very recent study also reviewed the literature and came to the conclusion that there is no empirically valid evidence to support the predictive claims of graphology. Most advocates of the method tend to rely on personal experience rather than on validated evidence (Cox & Tapsell, 1991). However, the critical literature on graphology does not seem to inhibit its popularity. On the other hand, successful group selection methods pioneered during the Second World War by the Tavistock Institute, and later taken up by the British Civil Service, have not spread very far (Murray, 1990).

Equally, or even more serious, is the recent proliferation of popular but misleading books on certain aspects of social science, particularly those aimed at business managers. One good example is the extraordinary success of a book called *In Search Of Excellence* (Peters & Waterman, 1982), which was followed by a number of imitators (for instance Goldsmith & Clutterbuck, 1984). *In Search Of Excellence* sold about 5 million copies and was translated into most languages. It is based on poor research and ends with a check-list of eight principles, which are put forward as recipes for success. Some 'excellence' books quote, with approval, extraordinarily naive statements by chief executives, who at the time they were interviewed were classified as highly successful. One memorable quotation (Goldsmith & Clutterbuck,

1984, p. 13) is as follows: "success is about leadership and leadership is about success." In spite of these failings, the books have penetrated boardrooms all over the world.

Another example comes from organizational psychology. Those who mix with managers, or teach them, will have heard of the 'Peter Principle'. Managers are very fond of this 'principle', which holds that managers are promoted beyond their level of competence. According to Peter (Peter & Hull, 1969), people are competent in some specialized activity and, as a reward, are promoted to higher levels, until they reach a level of incompetence. The little book by Peter and Hull is not based on any systematic evidence, but it appeals to thousands of managers. There is little reason to doubt that many people are promoted beyond their level of competence, but it is certainly not a 'principle' and, where this phenomenon occurs, it is likely to be due to inadequate training or the use of faulty selection or promotion methods. Those who raise this phenomenon to the level of a 'principle' tend to relate it to a particular senior manager whose work they do not respect. They do not see it in terms of an ongoing need for training and development or improved procedures of selection and promotion.

Furthermore, recent research has established fairly convincing support for an opposite trend. Heller and colleagues have found widespread evidence of underutilization of competence among senior managers in different countries (Heller, 1991; Heller, Drenth, Koopman, & Rus, 1988; Heller & Wilpert, 1981;). Although it is a research-established phenomenon, supported by a growing amount of evidence (Lawler, 1986), it is—like all such findings—contingent on certain situational factors. For instance, we find that the extent of underutilization varies from industry to industry; this has been supported by a recent research project in Australia (O'Brien, 1986). It is also particularly widespread among the more highly qualified (Heller & Wilpert, 1981). Is the untested Peter principle going to affect managerial thinking more than reasonably well established findings on unused competence?

Do-It-Yourself Social Science (DYSS)

A well-known European economist coined the phrase 'Do-It-Yourself Economics' to castigate people who made naive and unscientific pronouncements about economics (Henderson, 1986). The tendency among people who have no training to pontificate about this very technical subject is, he claims, widespread among politicians and senior civil servants, even in the Treasury. The habit of claiming that common sense is a substitute for specialized knowledge has also taken root in many social science fields outside economics, and I therefore feel justified in extending the concept to 'Do-It-Yourself Social Science', abbreviated DYSS.

In fact, it is obvious that psychology is particularly exposed to DYSS. Our subject has the appearance of being less technical than economics, and all the media describe and analyze human behaviour, often in great detail and using simplistic language and concepts, without reference to evidence. Television often conducts its own investigations by interviewing two or three people in the high street on some controversial subject and passing the resulting comments off as an adequate representation of public opinion. It is noteworthy that, while all newspapers have specialist correspondents in economics, politics, architecture, chess, all major sports, the arts, medicine, and many more fields, there are few examples of psychology correspondents. Every journalist is his or her own psychologist. It is likely that the effect of DYSS on research utilization is connected with Gresham's Law. If a simple common sense explanation can be given for a problem like football hooliganism, why bother to consult a psychologist?

Football hooliganism is quite a good example. It has given European governments, their police forces, and football clubs enormous problems; the British Government has even threatened to impose special legislation. Each newspaper and every sports correspondent has his/her own pet theory and remedy. A good and readable book on this subject, called *Football in its place: An environmental psychology of football grounds* by David Canter, Miriam Comber, and David Uzzell was published in 1989. It has received no attention from any of the parties that have to deal with this important social problem; Do-It-Yourself solutions are preferred.

CONCLUSIONS

The time has come to draw together the various strands of evidence and reach some conclusions, which will necessarily be tentative. I will use a Lewinian-type diagram to illustrate the main obstacles to the utilization of applied psychology as described in this article (Lewin, 1935). There is a great need to treat this subject more systematically by carrying out research into positive and negative infrastructures to social science research utilization. The present analysis is no more than a starting point.

Figure 1 leans on Kurt Lewin's method of mapping fields of social life space to indicate physical, social, and psychological movement. He defines barriers as boundaries which offer resistance to locomotion (Lewin, 1936).

Barriers can offer different kinds of resistance. Some are completely solid and impenetrable, others (like a garden fence) offer limited resistance and can be overcome if sufficient force or ingenuity is used. The resistance that a barrier offers is a function of the setting in which it is embedded and the complex dynamics of the locomotion from its source. In Figure 1 the source is the variety of research processes described previously, and locomotion is illustrated by arrows representing the motive or impulse for utilization.

Although, in reality, none of the five barriers is completely impenetrable, they can be regarded as important obstacles to application. Barrier 1 suggests that research areas derived entirely from the discipline of psychology itself, like analyses of interpersonal theory of love and hate formulated by different schools of research (Birtchnell, 1990), may serve useful academic objectives but are not likely to lead to

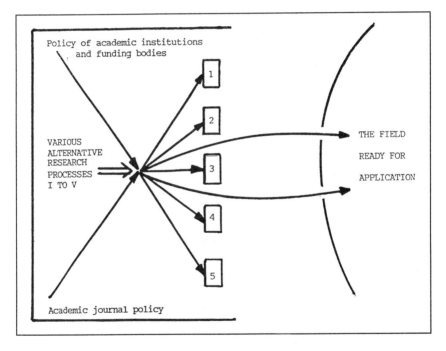

FIG. 1. Barriers and opportunities of research utilization.

Barrier 1   Discipline—rather than field oriented research
Barrier 2   Academic channels and abstract language
Barrier 3   Absence of client involvement and stress on sophistication rather than relevance
Barrier 4   Gresham's Law: the 'bad' drives out the 'good'
Barrier 5   Do-It-Yourself Social Science (DYSS): Common sense rather than evidence

early application in the field. At the same time, pressing societal issues do not receive the attention they deserve.

Barrier 2 reflects the well-known argument that publications confined to academic channels using abstract language and special jargon, for instance (Miner, Amburgey, & Stearns, 1990, p. 689): "buffering and transformational shields" will not easily be picked up by potential users, however important their findings.

Barrier 3 relates to the evidence, cited earlier, that the absence of any involvement with the client or potential policy user, in the formulation of the problem, the working through, or the feedback of results, is an inhibitor to application. The barrier is even stronger if the research concentrates on methodological refinements rather than relevance.

These three barriers are under the control of the scientific community, whereas others, like Gresham's Law and DYSS are not, at least not directly. However, it is plausible to argue that, if more projects in applied psychology circumvented Barriers 1 through 3, much less resistance would be offered by 4 and 5.

The two arrows that penetrate into the field of application in Figure 1 illustrate the superiority of some approaches over others. Although much more work needs to be done to reach firm conclusions, all the examples of successful research utilization described by the authors of Heller's (1986) book fall within the research-client collaboration approach called Research-Action, and they use a variety of field-relevant methods and different channels of diffusion.

The important roles of funding bodies and academic journals are shown in Figure 1. Although they have received little attention in the research evaluation literature, they are potentially the most powerful agents for change. In Britain, the Economic and Social Research Council has already adopted a policy of inviting applications for research priority areas identified by the Council in consultation with potential users. Furthermore, some journals, for instance the new European Work and Organization Psychologist and Human Relations, under its new policies, are taking steps to discourage the dry, mechanistic reporting typical of traditional scientific articles in favour of in-depth theory-oriented work which is likely to appeal to policy makers.

REFERENCES

Barker, R.G. (1968). *Ecological psychology: Concepts and methods for studying the environment of human behavior*. Stanford, CA: Stanford University Press.

Birtchnell, J. (1990). Interpersonal theory: Criticism, modification, and elaboration. *Human Relations, 43*, No. 12, 1183-1201.

Blake, R., & Mouton, J. (1964). *The managerial grid*. Houston, TX: Gulf Publishing Co.

Blake, R., & Mouton, J. (1968). *Corporate excellence through grid development*. Houston, TX: Gulf Publishing Co.

Blake, R., & Mouton, J. (1978). *The new managerial grid*. Houston, TX: Gulf Publishing Co.

Canter, D., Comber, M., & Uzzell, D. (1989). *Football in its place: An environmental psychology of football grounds*. London: Routledge.

Cherns, A. (1969). Social research and its diffusion. *Human Relations, 22*, 209-18.

Cherns, A. (1986). Policy research under scrutiny. In F. A. Heller (Ed.), *The use and abuse of social science*. London: Sage Publications.

Cox, J., & Tapsell, J. (1991). *Graphology and its validity in personnel assessment*. Paper to Occupational Psychology Conference, Cardiff, 5th January 1991.

Dixon, P., & Carr-Hill, R. (1989). *The NHS and its customers. Customer feed-back surveys: A review of current practice*. Centre for Health Economics, University of York.

Goldsmith, W., & Clutterbuck, D. (1984). *The winning streak*. Harmondsworth, Mddx: Penguin Books.

Haveman, R. (1986). Social science and social policy: Who uses whom? In F. Heller (Ed.), *The use and abuse of social science*. London: Sage Publications

Heller, F. A. (Ed.) (1986). *The use and abuse of social science*. London: Sage Publications.

Heller, F. A., Drenth, P., Koopman, P., & Rus, V. (1988). *Decisions in organizations: A longitudinal study of routine, tactical and strategic decisions*. London and Beverly Hills: Sage.

Heller, F. (1991). Participation and competence: A necessary relationship. In W. Lafferty and E. Rosenstein (Eds.), *International handbook of participation in organizations*. Vol. 2. Oxford: Oxford University Press.

Heller, F. A., & Wilpert, B. (1981). *Competence and power in managerial decision-making: A study of senior levels of organization in eight countries*. Chichester: John Wiley & Sons.

Henderson, D. (1986). *Innocence and design. The influence of economic ideas*. London: Basil Blackwell.

Himmelweit, H., & Gaskell, G. (1990). *Societal psychology*. London: Sage Publications.

Kaplan, A. (1964). *The conduct of enquiry: Methodology for behavioral science*. San Francisco: Chandler Publishing Co.

Karapin, R. S. (1986). A review of the literature. In F. A. Heller (Ed.), The use and abuse of social science. London: Sage.

Lawler, E. E. (1986). *High involvement management: Participative strategies for improving organizational performance*. San Francisco: Jossey-Bass.

Lévy-Leboyer, C. (1986) Applying psychology or applied psychology. In F. A. Heller (Ed.), *The use and abuse of social psychology*. London: Sage Publications.

Lewin, K. (1935). *A dynamic theory of personality*. New York: McGraw Hill.

Lewin, K. (1936). *Principles of topological psychology*. New York: McGraw Hill.

McDougall, W. (1934). *Religion and the sciences of life*. London: Methuen and Co.

McIver, S., & Carr-Hill, R. (1989). *The NHS and its customers: A survey of the current practice of customer relations*. Centre for Health Economics, University of York.

Miner, A., Amburgey, T., & Stearns, T. (1990). Interorganizational linkages and population dynamics: Buffering and transformational shields. *Administrative Science Quarterly, 35*, 689-713.

Murray, H. (1990). The transformation of selection procedures: The War Office Selection Boards. In E. Trist and H. Murray (Eds.), *The social engagement of social science*, Vol. I. London: Free Association Books.

Nowotny, H., & Lambiri-Dimaki (Eds.) (1985). *The difficult dialogue between producers and users of social science research*. Vienna: European Centre for Social Welfare Training and Research.

O'Brien, G. (1986). *Psychology of work and unemployment*. Chichester: John Wiley & Sons.

Peter, L. J., & Hull, R. (1969). *The Peter principle*. London: Pan Books.

Peters, T., & Waterman, R., Jr. (1982). *In search of excellence: Lessons from America's Best Run Companies*. New York: Harper & Row.

Stout, G. F. (1945.). *A manual of psychology*. London: London University Tutorial Press. (Original work published 1938).

Thouless, R. (1925). *General and social psychology*. London: London University Tutorial Press.

Vall, M. van de. (1986). Policy research: An analysis of function and structure. In F. A. Heller (Ed.), *The use and abuse of social science*. London: Sage Publications.

Warr, P. (1987). *Unemployment and mental health*. Oxford: Oxford Science Publications.

NOTES

This keynote address was published previously in *The European Work and Organizational Psychologist, 1*, 9-26.

---

*Keynote address: International Congress of Applied Psychology, Kyoto, 22 -27 July 1990. I am grateful for suggestions made by Peter Dachler and Dian Hosking, who helped me convert a speech into a paper, but any blemishes are my own.

EMPLOYMENT RESEARCH IN MULTI-ETHNIC SOCIETIES

Mary L. Tenopyr, AT&T, Morristown, NJ, U.S.A.

As political structures change in many countries around the world and democratization takes place, the division of economic as well as political power can be expected to take place along group lines. Even totalitarian governments have found it necessary to divide economic opportunities in line with group divisions in some cases. Some sense of economic equity among rival groups is necessary to support and legitimize a government. This is particularly true of newly formed governments, not yet of full strength and staffed with persons inexperienced in the particular form of government.

Thus, there are attempts at allocation of economic resources among various established groups. These often involve religious groups. Also, where a strong central government is replaced by a more decentralized one, old ethnic rivalries may arise, such as those between the Czechs and Slovaks. Some groups demanding economic considerations may be merely an underclass, such as peasants. Another case demanding the resolution of economic issues is that of transported populations, such as guest workers in Europe or the descendants of former slaves in the West. In many countries, the ingrained societal roles of the sexes is changing, and women are demanding a greater share of economic benefits.

All of the cases just cited defy resolution by free-market principles and eventually lead to governments' taking action to ensure some more equitable distribution of economic assets. The resolution depends upon the degree of conflict, the power positions, and relative potential for economic achievement of the groups. When two groups are of relatively the same size and both have approximately the same potential for achievement, as is the case with the sexes, only a minor modification of free-market functioning, such as antidiscrimination laws, may suffice. However, when the potential for conflict is great and some groups are deficient in education and job skills, more drastic measures may be necessary. The exact nature of the solution, of course, depends upon the nature of the political, religious, economic, and social systems involved.

When jobs are a focus of efforts toward economic equity for defined groups, various solutions are attempted. For example, jobs in government or in enterprises highly influenced by government may be assigned through a quota system. This type of solution is easy to effect by a strong central government. However, quotas are often frowned upon by the general public in many democracies. Those societies that envision themselves as meritocracies are likely to opt for government merit systems. Certainly, such systems appeared many centuries ago. In a country in which private enterprise is fostered, quotas for all employers are a possibility, but the notion of quotas for private employers appears to be in conflict with free-enterprise principles. Mandated merit systems for private employers are a possible solution, and not inconsistent in principle with the concept of free enterprise. However, having noted that most government merit systems involve so many complicated books of rules and restrictions on managerial freedom together with associated bureaucracy, many employers have been reluctant to adopt total merit systems. Moreover, organized labor has had much influence, in many cases, in opposing pure merit in private enterprise.

The solution to the problem of providing more economic equity in terms of jobs in the United States has taken yet another form. Out of the civil rights movement by African-Americans in the 1960s, came a comprehensive equal employment law, government agencies to enforce it, and a set of legal precedents that present a complicated system for transferring economic advantages to minorities and women. A pivotal person in this process is the industrial psychologist, whose research and development efforts are subject to continual legal challenge.

This whole process began with the importation of Africans as slaves in the formative days of the future United States in the seventeenth and eighteenth centuries. After the slaves were freed in the 1860s, there was purposeful discrimination. The African-Americans were denied access to high-quality education, jobs, housing, transportation, and even voting. A social upheaval, accompanied by violence, occurred in the 1960s and led to the national Civil Rights Act of 1964 and a host of state and local laws. As is usually the case, the simple statements of law led to governmental administrative guidelines and orders to implement the law. It is these latter pronouncements that formed the basis for the U.S. Supreme Court decisions and myriad other court pronouncements on psychological research and development, as was thought by the legal system to be required to put the transfer system into effect.

The basic 1964 law was straightforward. When a selection procedure excludes a protected group disproportionately, the employer concerned must prove the selection procedure to be job-related. This may seem like a sensible procedure to ensure test validation, which is, after all, a worthwhile business procedure. However, every aspect of test validation and test construction has come under legal scrutiny. Debates about the very nature of validity have ensued, and industrial psychologists have brought forth a plethora of research that has resulted in more progress in two decades in industrial psychology than in all recorded history.

The results of the U.S. Supreme Court decision that formed the basic law were many. As might be predicted, most employers fled from tests and other objective selection methods. The likelihood of costly litigation over the tests and educational standards was enough of a threat that employers took no chances. The unstructured employment interview that could be manipulated easily to obtain any result the employer desired became a selection procedure of choice. Most employers even stopped requiring high school graduation, and few even asked about the job applicants' grades and other achievements in high school. Psychologists, in the meantime, began accelerated research on possible unfair discrimination, validation, and utility. They have gone on to develop new procedures such as using meta-analysis to determine the degree of validity generalization from situation to situation.

As the legal situation has developed, psychologists have begun to face even further challenges. For some employers, the Civil Rights Act was extended in 1973 to cover unfair discrimination on account of physical and mental disabilities. In 1992, this law will be extended again to cover almost all employers relative to discrimination against persons with disabilities. Industrial psychologists in the United States are just starting to recognize the full implications of the proposed law. Particularly, with respect to so-called learning disabilities, there are really no accepted definitions and methods of diagnosis. In fact, diagnosis appears to be more dependent upon the diagnostician than upon the patient.

Various judicial decisions have drastically modified the basic civil rights laws in the United States. At present, the U.S. Congress is considering new civil rights legislation that will virtually rewrite the Civil Rights Act of 1964. This event has even more implications for psychologists.

Let us turn now to the results of the psychological research activity generated by the legal situation in the United States. First, after studying and debating many definitions of unfair discrimination, psychologists have essentially adopted one. Although U.S. law allows a group to make a tentative case of discrimination on the basis of average differences in group test scores, it is clear to anyone who has studied individual differences that such a difference is not evidence of unfairness of the selection procedure used. Instead, psychologists have essentially agreed that differences in intercept for groups relative to the regression of criterion performance on test performance can constitute a basis for inferring unfair discrimination (American Educational Research Association, American Psychological Association, & National Council on Measurement in Education, 1985). This model assumes that the slopes are the same for all groups, and in some accepted variants of the regression model, it is necessary to assume that standard errors of estimate are also equal for all groups.

The findings of research on possible unfair discrimination are not particularly complex. For almost all cognitive tests African-Americans and Hispanics score lower than Anglos (Linn, 1984; Schmidt, Pearlman, & Hunter, 1980). A common research finding is that African-Americans on the average score about one standard deviation lower than Anglos (Schmidt & Hunter, 1981). It is difficult to make any firm statements about the size of the Anglo-Hispanic difference since the United States has a number of distinct Hispanic populations: Cubans, Puerto Ricans, Mexicans, and South and Central Americans. No one statement pertaining to all of these groups can be made.

Women, on the average, score lower than men on tests of complex mathematics, space visualization, mechanical comprehension, and physical strength (Kimball, 1989; Reilly, Zedeck, & Tenopyr, 1979).

Relative to application of the regression model, it has generally been found that the same regression line fits all groups (Hunter, Schmidt, & Hunter, 1979; Schmidt & Hunter, 1981). When there are exceptions to this rule, they are seldom in the direction that would indicate that a protected group is subject to unfair discrimination. For example, in a small number of studies, the regression line for African-Americans has been found to be lower than that for Anglos, indicating that a common regression line would predict the African-American's criterion performance to be better than that actually achieved (Cleary, 1968; Wigdor & Garner, 1982).

Regarding recent research concerning criterion-related validity, it is clear that validities for cognitive ability tests are generally much higher than previously believed (Schmidt & Hunter, 1977). Adjustments for restriction in range and for validity attenuation resulting from unreliability of the criterion have become accepted (Linn, Harnisch, & Dunbar, 1981; Schmitt, Coyle, & Mellon, 1978). Also, as the validity of alternatives to cognitive ability tests has been assessed, it is clear that there are few alternatives as generally valid as these tests. However, work samples, job knowledge tests, and assessment centers also have relatively high validities (Hunter & Hunter, 1984).

The degree to which validities generalize from situation to situation is still a matter of debate in the United States. At one extreme are proponents of validity generalization who claim that all tests are valid for all jobs (Schmidt, Hunter, & Pearlman, 1982; Schmidt, Hunter, & Raju, 1988). At the other extreme are those who argue for a modicum of situational specificity (James, Demaree, & Muliak, 1989; Sackett, Schmitt, Tenopyr, Kehoe, & Zedeck, 1985). It is difficult to ascertain where the views of the majority of industrial psychologists lie, but it appears that at least for some types of job, e.g., clerical work, there is a consensus that validities generalize at least to some extent. I personally, however, do not believe that the debates about the mathematics of validity generalization are over.

Content validation has become a great matter of concern in the United States, merely because it has been the sole defense of tests used by various civil service jurisdictions. No city can develop a test for fire fighters or police officers without the near certainty of civil rights litigation. It has become clear that content validation refers primarily to test construction and the process of sampling from a content domain (Messick, 1989; Tenopyr, 1977). The difference between content and face validity has been clarified, so it is accepted that content validity is established by the operations of test construction and those leading up to it, not the appearance of the final test items (Messick, 1975; Society for Industrial and Organizational Psychology, 1987).

Construct validation had been depicted as a complicated, near-infinite process (Messick, 1989). However, more recent views suggest that a long process may not be necessary to justify the use of construct validity in selection (Cronbach, 1984, p. 150). However, I personally have not been entirely satisfied with the construct validation efforts I have seen to date. Although there probably never will be complete agreement among all psychologists on a taxonomy of constructs, there is still too much use of made-up-on-the-spot constructs in employee selection. As factor analytic studies of abilities and other personality characteristics progress, I foresee a coalescing of opinion on what some of the primary constructs represent. Even now, researchers are starting to realize that there are probably only five major personality factors (Digman, 1990). However, this view needs reconfirming before it obtains universal acceptance.

Relative to utility, the decision-theoretic approach of Brogden (1946) and Cronbach and Gleser (1965) is being widely studied and applied. Results of applications have provided overwhelming evidence that tests and other structured selection techniques are cost-effective. Most utility formulas require some measure of the standard deviation of job performance in dollar terms. In my opinion, the problem of estimating the required standard deviation of job performance in terms of dollars has not really been solved. Where actual data on the standard deviation are available, the estimates of the standard deviation have provided mixed results, and although results of application of the various methods tend to converge, even small differences in this value may result in grossly different over-all estimates of utility. There are four general classes of methods used to estimate the critical standard deviation. These are cost accounting, global estimation, individualized estimation, and proportional rules. Each method and variation thereof has strong and weak points. However, detailed discussion should be the focus of another presentation.

Raju, Burke, and Normand (1990) have recently published formulas for utility that do not involve an estimation of the standard deviation of dollar values but still involve estimation. This method should generate considerable research interest, but whether this technique will prove superior to the previous ones remains to be determined.

In view of the research in the 25 years that have passed since the effective date of the Civil Rights Act of 1964, most credible researchers do not believe that it is necessary to do differential prediction studies for African-Americans and Anglos. However, although some group differences, such as the difference in performance of complex mathematical tasks between the sexes, are declining markedly (Kimball, 1989), other ability differences among groups essentially remain the same.

Consequently, advocates of civil rights have shown renewed advocacy for the Darlington-Cole (Cole, 1973; Darlington, 1971) definition of discrimination that was essentially discredited earlier (Petersen & Novick, 1976). Psychologists are explaining again what is wrong with this definition. Civil rights advocates have also become concerned with the possibility of differential item functioning and are advocating different methods of test score use, such as selecting the highest scorers from each group first, regardless of group differences in test scores (Hartigan & Wigdor, 1989).

Although the major psychological organizations have endorsed the regression model for studying possible unfair discrimination, a model that deals with only half of a four-fold contingency model is being advocated by civil rights attorneys. The reason for this is obvious; given the usual racial group differences in test scores, the test will be found discriminatory unless the validity is 1.00 and the pass/fail dichotomy on the test and the succeed/fail dichotomy on the job coincide.

A second area in which there is renewed psychological activity is study of possible differential item functioning. Educational Testing Service (ETS), the producer of the most widely used college and university admissions instrument, the Scholastic Aptitude Test, also produces licensing examinations for various states. Among those produced was a licensing examination for insurance agents in the State of Illinois. One insurance company, Golden Rule, sued ETS and claimed that the examination was racially discriminatory. The case was settled out of court when ETS agreed to construct future examinations by preferring items for which the difficulty was 40% or better for African-Americans and the difficulty difference between Anglos and African-Americans did not exceed 15%. Almost all psychologists believe that ETS should not have settled the case on this basis, especially since the settlement terms have been proposed as law in several states. It can easily be shown that when items are studied according to item response theory (IRT), the Golden Rule provisions are likely to eliminate more psychologically desirable items than others (Linn & Drasgow, 1987).

The number of methods proposed and used to detect possible differential item functioning are myriad (Scheuneman & Bleistein, 1989). These techniques can be divided into two categories—those based upon the traditional test theory and those based upon IRT. I will discuss only two of them. The Mantel-Haenzel technique is a natural extension of the chi-square procedures that had previously been used to assess the possibility of differential item functioning for groups matched on a measure of ability. It provides a single degree-of-freedom chi-square that is powerful against alternatives to Ho. Most important, unlike the simple chi-square procedures involving the number in each matched group who responded correctly or incorrectly to an item, the Mantel-Haenzel technique provides a single summary measure of the magnitude of the departure from Ho exhibited by the item concerned. The main drawbacks of the procedure are that it requires large sample sizes and that the researcher must assume that the main group difference effect has no interaction with ability.

Three-parameter IRT methods of studying possible differential item functioning have been used extensively. The techniques have the advantages of providing a sound theoretical basis and using true ability estimates rather than observed scores. Differential item functioning is determined by likelihood ratio tests to assess the differences between item-characteristic curves for groups. These tests are considered statistically optimal when the postulated IRT model actually holds. However, item parameters are not always estimated well for groups differing in ability. Also, the number of subjects required is often out of the realm of possibility for the typical industrial-test developer. Computations are time-consuming and expensive. Furthermore, results can be difficult to explain to lay audiences.

It can be argued that differential item functioning techniques based on internal criteria are not only inadequate for the analysis of test fairness but also tend to hold a test developer to unattainable standards. If an item is found to be differentially functioning, the only advisable course is deletion of the item. There are no rules for revising items, as judges are notoriously inaccurate in detecting item bias, let alone correcting it. Furthermore, deletion of a few items rarely changes over-all test results.

Another area gaining prominence in employment psychology in the United States is advocacy of differential use of employment tests. Some have suggested uniformly lowered or different critical scores for separate groups. Others have opted for selecting from the top down, taking a proportional number from each ethnic or racial group despite group differences in test performance (Hartigan & Wigdor, 1989). Still others have advocated solutions like selecting from "sliding bands," a method by which most persons in the top band of test scores are chosen and the band is then moved downward to encompass another group of examinees (Cascio, Outtz, Zedeck, & Goldstein, in press; Schmidt, in press); others have suggested the "whole person" concept, in which a clinical employment decision is made.

In assessing these suggestions, there are several considerations. In the United States, persons of the majority group may sue employers for reverse discrimination; different test standards for different groups can not only lead to individual lawsuits but also result in illegal quota systems for employment. The "whole person" concept is inappropriate where labor unions and civil service rules demand objectivity. Also, the inferiority of clinical to actuarial prediction is well known.

Various researchers have pointed out that the loss of utility for some strategies of differential test use is not that great (Cronbach, 1980; Cronbach & Schaeffer, 1981). However, a number of matters have to be taken into consideration in deciding on the method of test use. There are certain well-known facts about utility, one being that utility usually is greatest when validity and critical scores, if any, are high and the selection ratio is low.

Other facts are less well known. For example, top-down selection separately for two groups results in a loss of utility, and this loss is greatest when the lower scoring minority group is large in size and the difference between means is large. In this respect, validity and selection ratios make little difference.

As the percentage of minorities in job applicant groups increases, average score differences between the groups have to decrease to maintain the same relative utility for separate group top-down selection as compared to top-down selection for the combined group.

Separate top-down selection does not always have an advantage in terms of utility over random selection of persons above a critical score. High validity and low selection ratio can contribute to making separate group top-down selection less advantageous.

The sliding-band method tends to yield results specific to the situation.

All in all, it is clear that less than optimal test use leads to less than optimal utility for the employer. In this area, as in the area of differential item functioning, there are continued attempts to mix science and social policy.

SUMMARY

It is clear that personnel selection in multi-ethnic societies can be very complicated. There are no clear paths to truth. Although many societies have successfully assimilated disadvantaged minorities economically, as well as socially and politically, there is always a period of time during which tensions arise and progress toward assimilation appears slower than might be desired. It is during these periods that the skills of the industrial psychologist must be put to full use. Psychologists must do more than fulfill their usual research and consulting roles; they must also reach out and find innovative ways to deal with the many inequities and resultant tensions that arise.

For example, in the United States, there is less than full partnership of the educational system and the employment system. I believe that both industrial and educational psychologists should take concerted action to merge these two systems into the interdependent whole they must be if economic progress for all groups is to be enhanced.

Other countries can expect the need to provide economic parity, not only for ethnic groups but also for other groups that wish to share in the rewards of society. In the United States, the racial and ethnic minority group movements were soon followed by pressures from women, the aged, persons with disabilities, and gays and lesbians. Although general research on ageing is well established in the United States, research on all these latter groups relative to the workplace needs to be expanded. Industrial psychologists certainly need to know more about mental disabilities, especially learning disabilities, which are a matter of some controversy even in the educational field.

Certainly, the breadth of the knowledge and skill bases of industrial psychologists has to be improved. It will be necessary to obtain more education not only in psychological areas in which industrial psychologists do not usually study but also in various other areas, such as economics and law.

Finally, all psychologists must learn to separate clearly what is science and what is social policy. Industrial psychologists in the United States have been thrust into the intersection between social policy and science, and many appear to be indecisive about which road to take. There need to be some clear sign posts at times so that one can tell which road is which, as science and social policy can lead in different directions. What some psychologists in the United States have been seen to do is take some action to promote a social policy and then call that action science. One can never separate value systems from science; however, one should be clear about what is science and what is not. Psychologists in other countries can well learn from our experiences.

REFERENCES

American Education Research Association, American Psychological Association, & National Council on Measurement in Education. (1985). *Standards for education and psychological testing.* Washington, DC: American Psychological Association.

Brogden, H. E. (1946). On the interpretation of the correlation coefficient as a measure of predictive efficiency. *Journal of Educational Psychology, 2,* 171-183.

Cascio, W. F., Outtz, J., Zedeck, S., & Goldstein, I. L., (in press). Statistical implications in personnel selection. *Human Performance.*

Cleary, T. A. (1968). Test bias: Prediction of grades for Negro and White students in integrated colleges. *Journal of Educational Measurement, 5,* 115-124.

Cole, N. S. (1973). Bias in selection. *Journal of Educational Measurement, 10,* 237-255.

Cronbach, L. J. (1980). Selection theory for a political world. *Public Personnel Management, 9,* 37-50.

Cronbach, L. J. (1984). *Essentials of psychological testing* (4th ed.). New York: Harper & Row.

Cronbach, L. J., & Gleser, G. C. (1965). *Psychological tests and personnel decisions* (2nd ed.). Urbana: University of Illinois Press.

Cronbach, L. J., & Schaeffer, G. A. (1981). *Extensions of personnel selection theory to aspects of minority hiring.* (Report 81-A2), Institute for Educational Finance and Governance, Stanford University, CA.

Darlington, R. B. (1971). Another look at "cultural fairness." *Journal of Educational Measurement, 8*, 71-82.

Digman, J. M. (1990). Personality structure: Emergence of the five-factor model. *Annual Review of Psychology, 41*, 417-440.

Hartigan, J. A., & Wigdor, A. K. (Eds.). (1989). *Fairness in employment testing*. Washington, DC: National Academy Press.

Hunter, J. E., & Hunter, R. F. (1984). Validity and utility of alternative predictor of job performance. *Psychological Bulletin, 98*, 72-98.

Hunter, J. E., Schmidt, F. L., & Hunter, R. (1979). Differential validity of employment tests by race: A comprehensive review and analysis. *Psychological Bulletin, 86*, 721-735.

James, L. R., Demaree, R. G., & Muliak, S. A. (1989). Validity generalization: Rejoinder to Schmidt, Hunter and Raju. *Journal of Applied Psychology, 73*, 673-678.

Kimball, M. M. (1989). A new perspective on women's math achievement. *Psychological Bulletin, 105*, 198-214.

Linn, R. L. (1984). Selection bias; multiple meanings. *Journal of Educational Measurement, 21*, 33-47.

Linn, R. L., & Drasgow, F. (1987, summer). Implications of the Golden Rule settlement for test construction. *Educational Measurement: Issues and Practice*, pp. 13-17.

Linn, R. L., Harnisch, D. L., & Dunbar, S. B. (1981). Corrections for range restriction: An empirical investigation of conditions resulting in conservative corrections. *Journal of Applied Psychology, 66*, 655-663.

Messick, S. J. (1975). The standard problem: Meaning and values in measurement and evaluation. *American Psychologist, 30*, 955-966.

Messick, S. J. (1989). Validity. In R. L. Linn (Ed.), *Educational Measurement* (3rd ed., pp. 13-103). New York: American Council on Education: Macmillan.

Petersen, N. S., & Novick, M. R. (1976). An evaluation of some models for culture-fair selection. *Journal of Educational Measurement, 13*, 3-29.

Raju, N. S., Burke, M. J., & Normand, J. (1990). A new model for utility analysis. *Journal of Applied Psychology, 75*, 3-12.

Reilly, R. R., Zedeck, S., & Tenopyr, M. L. (1979). Validity and fairness of physical ability tests for predicting performance in craft jobs. *Journal of Applied Psychology, 64*, 218-220.

Sackett, P. R., Schmitt, N. W., Tenopyr, M. L., Kehoe, J. F., & Zedeck, S. (1985). Commentary on forty questions about validity generalization and meta-analysis. *Personnel Psychology, 38*, 697-798.

Scheuneman, J. D., & Bleistein, C. A. (1989). A consumer's guide to statistics for identifying differential item functioning. *Applied Measurement in Education, 2*, 255-275.

Schmidt, F. L. (in press). Why all banding procedures in personnel selection are logically flawed. *Human Performance*.

Schmidt, F. L., & Hunter, J. (1977). Development of a general solution to the problem of validity generalization. *Journal of Applied Psychology, 62*, 529-540.

Schmidt, F.L., & Hunter, J. (1981). Employment testing: Old theories and new research findings. *American Psychologist, 36*, 1128-1137.

Schmidt, F. L., Hunter, J. E., & Pearlman, K. (1982). Progress in validity generalization: Comments on Callender and Osburn and further developments. *Journal of Applied Psychology, 67*, 835-845.

Schmidt, F.L., Hunter, J. E., & Raju, N. S. (1988). Validity generalization and situational specificity: A second look at the 75% rule and Fisher's Z transformation. *Journal of Applied Psychology, 23*, 665-672.

Schmidt, F. L., Pearlman, K., & Hunter, J. E. (1980). The validity and fairness of employment and educational tests for Hispanic Americans: A review and analysis. *Personnel Psychology, 33*, 705-724.

Schmitt, N., Coyle, B. W., & Mellon, P. M. (1978). Subgroup differences in predictor and criterion variances and differential validity. *Journal of Applied Psychology, 63*, 667-672.

Society for Industrial and Organizational Psychology, Inc. (1987). *Principles for the validation and use of personnel selection procedures* (3rd ed.). College Park, MD: author.

Tenopyr, M. L. (1977). Content-construct confusion. *Personnel Psychology, 30*, 47-54.

Wigdor, A. K., & Garner, W. R. (Eds.). (1982). *Ability testing: Uses, consequences and controversies*. Washington, DC: National Academy Press.

THE CHALLENGES OF MANAGING EMPLOYEE-ORGANISATION RELATIONSHIPS

Lyman W. Porter
Graduate School of Management
University of California, Irvine

This presentation addresses employee-organization relations (E-O-R's). I will discuss some of the characteristics of such relations and the ways in which these relations can be managed. I will specifically focus on the relations between organizations and their "knowledge workers" —that is, employees in professional, technical, and lower-level supervisory positions.

Unprecedented economic and structural changes in the world economy are creating new management challenges for contemporary organizations. In recent years, many firms have undergone sudden growth while others have experienced equally sudden decline. The frequency of large-scale mergers, divestitures, and other forms of restructuring has increased significantly. Many of these changes stem from intensified international competition.

These and other similar developments appear to have altered some basic features of traditional E-O-R's. For many employees, these changes have created new uncertainties and insecurities. For organizations, there is increased pressure to be able to make rapid changes and accommodations to new and often unforeseen sets of circumstances.

These changes have created challenges for employees, organizations, and researchers as well. A Price/Waterhouse executive (quoted in the New York Times) describes the dilemma for employees: "For generations

. . . it operated like this: 'I will always have a job. My benefits will increase. My salary probably will continue to go up faster than inflation.' [But now] all three of these ideas are basically at risk." (E.M. Fowler, 1990). For employing organizations, the new challenge is how to manage employee-organization relations under conditions of extreme turbulence and uncertainty. Finally, for organizational social scientists, the issue is one of how to research and study these new E-O-R's.

THE NATURE OF
EMPLOYEE-ORGANIZATION RELATIONS

The nature of E-O-R's can be explored by examining the psychological contracts between organizations and their employees. The term *psychological contract* refers to the set of mutual expectations between an individual and his or her organization. Each party holds expectations regarding particular inducements and contributions that should and should not be exchanged. Psychological contracts are largely implicit and cover a broad range of expectations.

Psychological Contracts Past and Present

An 1880 employee survey represents one of the earliest attempts to gather large-scale data on employee-organization relations from the perspective of employees. Who authored this survey? None other than Karl Marx. Marx drew up 101 lengthy, open-ended (and somewhat complicated) questions (Bottomore, 1964). To illustrate, one question read:

State the obligations of workers living under [so-called participation in profits] . . . Can they go on strike? Or are they only permitted to be the humble servants of their masters?

The characterization of the psychological contract between employees and organizations in more recent American history is exemplified in numerous articles in the popular business press. In issues of *Fortune* magazine from the 1950s, the employee-organization relation is consistently described as being characterized by mutual commitment, solid job security, and a strong employee work ethic. As stated in an article in March 1956 (Maurer, 1956), for example, "Most of the larger companies will make strenuous efforts to find some right place for the man whose work is not satisfactory or for the man not satisfied with his work."

A review of *Fortune* and the *Wall Street Journal* issues of 1989 and 1990 illustrates significant shifts in the nature of employee-organization psychological contracts—particularly in the areas of loyalty and job security. A *Fortune* article by T. P. Pare (June, 1989) states, "Restructuring has flattened organization charts, pared unprofitable businesses, and severed many of the ties that traditionally bound a company to its workers. Lifelong employment is now the exception; no deal is permanent." An article in the *Wall Street Journal* by A. Bennet (December, 1989) similarly comments, "Today, . . . managers . . . understand that companies are no longer in a position to make promises of lifetime security. But, they add, that also means that managers no longer have to swear fealty to those companies, either."

Review of past Research on Psychological Contracts

The notion that a psychological contract exists between an individual and an employing organization is implicit in the inducement-contribution models of several early organizational theorists (Barnard, 1938; March & Simon, 1958; Simon, 1945). Chris Argyris (1960) first introduced the term *psychological contract* into the organizational literature. The concept was developed further in ethnographic studies by Levinson et al. (1962) and Schein (1965).

Despite many rich conceptual discussions on the psychological contract, however, there has been little empirical research on the topic. In the latter two studies, both scholars concluded that mutually acceptable, satisfying psychological contracts are those that meet the expectations of both parties simultaneously. Kotter (1973) conducted a small-scale survey study of business school graduates. He asked these individuals to report on their expectations of what they should contribute to their organizations and what their organizations should provide them in terms of inducements. However, Kotter did not assess top management's expectations directly; only the employees' perceptions of the organization's expectations were obtained.

Current Research

At the University of California, Irvine, exploratory studies on the nature of employee-organization psychological contracts are in progress. The objective is to compare the mutual expectations of employees and their organizations. I report here on the work that has been conducted in the initial two organizations.

Instruments. In order to assess the expectations of both "knowledge workers" (i.e., employees) and organizations directly, two versions of a "Work-related Expectations Survey" were developed. In both the employee-version and the organization-version of the questionnaire, respondents were requested to report on prescriptive expectations, descriptive expectations, and perceived "actual" expectations. Brief definitions, along with example survey questions are provided below:

1. Prescriptive expectations—beliefs about what *should* be offered or received.

"To what extent *should* this organization provide employees with job security?"

"To what extent *should* employees take on the goals of the organization as their own?"

2. Descriptive expectations—*beliefs* about the expectations that the other party holds.

Asked of the organization: "To what extent do employees expect this organization to provide them with job security?"

Asked of employees: "To what extent does this organization expect employees to take on the goals of the organization as their own?"

3. Perceived "actual" expectations—*perceptions* regarding the "actual" contributions and inducements offered.

"To what extent does this organization provide job security to employees?"

"To what extent do employees in this organization take on the goals of the organization as their own?"

According to an inducements/contributions framework (Barnard, 1938; March & Simon, 1958), the exchange that binds the individual to the organization is the balance between expected organizational inducements and expected employee contributions. My colleagues and I focused on three categories of employee contributions and three categories of organizational inducements. The employee contribution categories include:

- Role behaviors—contributions specifically related to the assigned tasks of the employee.
- Extra-role/citizenship behaviors—contributions that go above and beyond assigned tasks but that contribute to the goals of the organization (including "prosocial" and "organizational citizenship" behaviors).
- Organizational precedence—contributions that require the employee to place the organization's interests before his or her own.

The organizational inducements categories include:

- Rewards for permanence—monetary and social rewards offered for good performance.

- Job/person growth opportunities—development opportunities in the form of job enrichment and education/training.
- Commitment to employees—concern for employees' interests and welfare.

Sample. The participants for the study were drawn from two organizations: (a) a division of a large aerospace firm, and (b) a subsidiary of a large electronics firm. In each organization, we administered both versions of the "Survey of Work-related Expectations." The organization-version was administered to the top-level executives (i.e., vice-presidents and senior managers)—16 executives in the aerospace organization and 10 in the electronics organization. Participants at this management level were chosen to act as representatives of the "organization" because they possess the primary responsibility for establishing the "organization's" expectations. The employee version of the survey was administered to "knowledge workers" in each organization. Each employee sample represented a cross-section of the organization's "knowledge workers" in terms of level, tenure, product-line responsibility, ethnicity, and age. These employees were asked to report on their own individual expectations.

Results. Our examination of data from the first two organizations we studied have yielded some interesting preliminary findings.

- Concerning employee contributions: In both firms, employees' reports of prescriptive, descriptive, and perceived "actual" expectations were relatively similar. This finding indicates that employees believed that they were giving an appropriate level of contribution. They were living up to what they believed was expected of them, and they were giving what they personally believed they should give. However, from the organization's perspective, employees were contributing less than they should.
- Concerning organizational inducements: In both organizations, each party reported that the organization was giving less than employees thought it should and less than the organization itself thought it should.

In sum, the results indicated some areas of strong disagreement between employees and their organizations. In general, from the organization's perspective, employees were not living up to their end of the "contract." However, the employees' viewpoint is that they were fulfilling their obligations. From both parties' perspective, the organization was not reciprocating at an appropriate level according to the "terms" of the psychological contract.

Approaches that Organizations Can Use in Managing E-O-R's

As noted earlier, the increase in competitive conditions has created challenges for organizations. Specifically, employers, more than ever, appear to have dual objectives: (a) to increase the degree of flexibility for the firm, in employment and disengagement of their workers; and (b) to generate a greater degree of employee flexibility (in accepting assignments) and commitment to the success of the organization. However, the challenge for the employer is that these two objectives are in direct conflict with each other. Pursuit of the first objective precludes the guarantee of job security for all employees; pursuit of the second objective implies that the organization wants commitment from employees. Can organizations simultaneously achieve both objectives? This dilemma is illustrated by a statement made by one of General Electric's corporate recruiters: " 'We're looking for people to make a commitment.' But [GE] has eliminated 100,000 jobs over the past eight years" (*Fortune*, June 5, 1989).

Strategies of Employee-Organization Relations

What strategies are available to organizations to deal with this dilemma? How can organizations obtain specific types of desired employee contributions under conditions of extreme turbulence? We propose two contrasting prototypical E-O-R strategies. They are distinguished by the forms of employee contribution on which each is focused (see Fig. 1).

Job-Focused Strategy.   The focus of this strategy is on generating a high level of employee job performance to the virtual exclusion of other types of employee contributions. This strategy involves a highly circumscribed and tightly defined arrangement or contract between the employer and the employee. The employee provides clearly defined "outputs" in exchange for equally clearly defined "payoffs." The job-focused strategy centers strictly on the job. It has the characteristics of a marketplace approach in which obligations do not go beyond the contracted transactions and there is no interest in building a long-term relation. An everyday example of this strategy is the agreement between the taxi driver and the passenger. In organizations, this strategy is exemplified by the traditional organization/consultant relation.

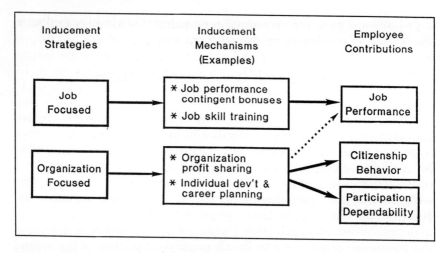

FIG. 1. Relation among inducement strategies, inducement mechanisms, and employee contributions (simplified model).

The job-focused strategy has distinct advantages for the organization. This strategy provides organizations with the flexibility to hire and fire particular employees at will in response to changing competitive demands. However, this strategy also has a distinct disadvantage to the employer in that employees will not willingly work on other tasks or cooperate with changes in job assignments without some equivalent guaranteed benefits in return.

Organization-Focused Strategy. The focus of this strategy is on inducing a broader set of behaviors and commitment from employees than those specified in narrow job performance. The organization adopting this strategy seeks to encourage employee activities intended to promote the welfare of the organization and cooperation with other employees working within it. Such activities include "citizenship behavior" and "participation dependability."

The organization-focused strategy emphasizes rewards for contributions that go beyond narrowly-defined job duties and take into account the goals, values, and objectives of the larger organization. An open-ended agreement between the employee and the employer is used. Each party has wide-ranging obligations to the other, and each has an expectation that the other party will be strongly concerned with its welfare and success. This strategy is exemplified by the traditional (1950s) organizational approach to managerial employees. An everyday example of this strategy is the relation between two friends.

The advantage to the organization pursuing this strategy is that it can rely on its employees for commitment and dedication to its larger and longer-range purposes as well as to shorter-term job performance. Furthermore, employees trust that the employer will not exploit them for a temporary advantage and so will more likely cooperate with changes in job duties and structures required by environmental pressures. The primary disadvantages of the organization-focused strategy to the employer are that options and flexibility in the termination of employment will be more restricted, and the organization's obligations to employees will be greatly increased.

The distinction between the two prototypical strategies of employee-organization relations can be summarized by the following elements:

- Focus: job only or job and organization
- Flexibility: employment or deployment
- Time: focus on relatively limited-term activities or focus on long-term relations

The elements listed above describe an extreme form of each of the two types of E-O-R. Most organizations are expected to adopt a strategy that falls somewhere in between these two extremes. The basic premise of the proposed E-O-R framework is that under conditions of intense pressure for increased flexibility in managing the employee-organization relation, firms will move toward adopting one or the other extreme form of E-O-R strategy. Also, we expect that most firms will not have a uniform organization-wide strategy across all job groups. Instead, organizations will differentiate their strategies across different job groups. For any specific employee or employee group, we assume one strategy will be more appropriate and more cost-effective (to the organization) than another.

Strategy Implementation

Organizations must translate their E-O-R strategies into actual, concrete "inducement mechanisms" in order to obtain desired employee contributions. Inducement mechanisms are patterns of action—structures, processes, and human resource policies—that can be designed to elicit or facilitate job performance, participation dependability, or citizenship behavior. The job-focused E-O-R strategy may be implemented through the use of such mechanisms as detailed job descriptions, finite-term employment contracts, job-focused socialization, and limited benefits. In contrast, the organization-focused strategy may be implemented by adopting more general job descriptions, open-ended employment agreements, organization-focused socialization, and extensive benefits. These represent just a sample of the possible inducement mechanisms associated with each E-O-R strategy.

SUMMARY OF E-O-R FRAMEWORK

Pressures have been increasing on organizations to utilize appropriate strategies to attract, motivate, and retain employees. These competitive circumstances have led organizations to desire flexibility in their relations with employees. We propose that this flexibility can be obtained by two fundamentally different E-O-R strategies, which we define as "job-focused" and "organization-focused." These two strategies are implemented through a variety of mechanisms for inducing particular types of desired employee contributions: job performance, participation dependability, and citizenship behavior. We have developed a conceptual framework to guide our research on the employee-organization relation. Figure 1 is a simplified schematic representation of the relation specified in the E-O-R framework.

CONCLUSION

In the context of contemporary economic challenges, organizations will need to increase the amount of attention they give to their strategic approaches to managing E-O-R's. This will be especially important in the case of knowledge workers. The "professionalization" of such workers makes them highly mobile. Their willingness to remain in a given organization and contribute to its welfare and success will depend on the manner in which the organization manages the employee-organization relation. The success of the organization's approach will therefore depend upon the attention given by the organization to effective implementation of the strategy it pursues with respect to these relations.

NOTE

I wish to acknowledge the valuable assistance of my research assistant, Angela Tripoli, in the preparation of this paper.

REFERENCES

Argyris, C. (1960). *Understanding organizational behavior*. Homewood, IL: The Dorsey Press.

Barnard, C. I. (1938). *The functions of the executive*. Cambridge, Mass.: Harvard University Press.

Bennett, A., (1989). "Broken bonds." *Wall Street Journal*, December, 8, p. R23.

Bottomore, T. B. (1964). *Karl Marx: Selected Writings in Sociology and Social Philosophy*. New York: McGraw Hill.

Fowler, E. M.,(1990). Job Turmoil Takes a Toll on Loyalty. *The New York Times,* March 20.

Kotter, J. P. (1973). The psychological contract: Managing the joining-up process. *California Management Review, Spring,* 91-99.

Levinson, H., Price, C. R., Munden, K. J., Mandl, H. J., & Solley, C. M. (1962). *Men, Management and Mental Health*. Cambridge, MA: Harvard University Press.

March, J., & Simon, H. (1958). *Organizations*. New York: Wiley.

Maurer, H., (1956). "Twenty minutes to a career." *Fortune,* p. 177, March.

Pare, T. P. (1989). "The uncommitted class of 1989." *Fortune,* June 5, p. 199, p. 206.

Schein, E. H. (1965). *Organizational Psychology*. Englewood Cliffs, NJ: Prentice Hall.

Simon, H. (1945). *Administrative behavior*. New York: The Free Press.

WORK MOTIVATION—WHAT'S NEW IN A COMPETITIVE GLOBAL MARKET?

Miriam Erez, Faculty of Industrial Engineering and Management, Technion, Haifa, Israel

The decade of the 1980s was characterized by rapid changes in the work environment: from manufacturing to service industry; from traditional technology to computers, automation, and sophisticated communication systems; from quantity to quality considerations; from local to global markets; and from national to multinational companies. These changes are accompanied by processes of organizational restructuring. Many single companies in the West have changed their identity through processes of mergers, acquisitions, downsizing, and restructuring, and their survival has become increasingly dependent on financial considerations of shareholders and self-interested management groups. The bottom line of all these changes is a highly competitive global market.

These environmental changes have a tremendous impact on employees' self-concept and self-identity, on work motivation and commitment to the work place, and on work behavior and its performance outcomes. In particular, the traditional mutuality between employees and organizations has been eroded, and commitment to work has become one of the central problems of organizations today (Beer & Walton, 1990; Lawler, 1986; Mowday, Porter, & Steers, 1982).

The need to adjust to changes in the complex environment brings into focus the cognitive mechanisms of information-processing that help explain how employees interpret and evaluate the situation and how their work motivation and work behavior is affected by these processes.

Such mediating processes are guided by the self, which interprets and evaluates information concerning the person.

The purpose of the present paper is to examine the relation between the changing work environment, the self as an interpreter of such changes, and the theory and practice of work motivation. The following model is proposed as a conceptual framework (see Figure 1).The model consists of four parts: (a) the work environment, which has two significant characteristics—globalization of the market and restructuring of organizations; (b) motivational techniques and the way they are interpreted by the self in relation to the environment; (c) the self, which functions as an information processor and interpreter, and (d) work motivation, as reflected in the commitment of employees and in their willingness to allocate cognitive resources to perform their tasks.

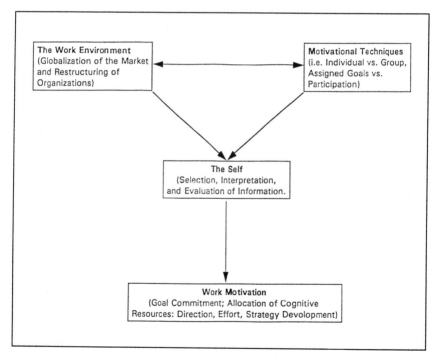

FIG. 1. An integrated model of work motivation.

THE CHANGING ENVIRONMENT

Most theories of work motivation focus mainly on the individual and represent an attempt to explain the motivated behavior by looking at individual goals, expectancies, self-efficacy, and need satisfaction. From a historical perspective, this approach is explained in light of the dominant stream in psychology, the liberal individualist, according to which the individual is viewed as self-contained and as one whose identity is defined apart from the world (Cushman, 1990; Sampson, 1989). However, very little research has been done on the impact of the environment and the way it interacts with different motivational techniques to affect employees' motivation. In real life situations, one often finds that a motivational technique that proved to be effective in one context is no longer effective in another. For example, attempts to implement Japanese quality circles in American companies have had only limited success.

Environmental effects can be ignored as long as models of work motivation are examined within one stable context. However, when the environment can no longer be held constant, its effect on behavior cannot be ignored. The work situation is changing in two respects. First, working organizations are unstable, and their goals and structures change rapidly. Second, the globalization of the market exposes employees from one culture to another. Therefore, the focus of attention should shift from the variance among individuals within the same situation to the variance in behavior among situations.

Eight significant changes in the work environment can be observed:

1. The scope of the work environment - from local to global and international markets. The United States, for example, is becoming part of an increasingly global economy. About 100,000 American companies do business overseas, including 3,500 multinational companies. It is estimated that one third of the profit of U.S. companies is derived from international business, along with one sixth of the nation's jobs (Cascio, 1989). The competitive global market sets new rules for survival, and employees have to become more competitive in order to help their organizations survive. They often have to compete outside their local environment and against less familiar players. The level of ambiguity and risk-taking increases, and there is a growing need to learn about the characteristics of new markets and to adjust to them.

The growing concern of the competition between Japan and the United States has been documented in a significant number of publications. In particular, the United States is concerned about its negative balance of payments compared to Japan's positive balance of payments.

2. The instability of the working environment. A substantial number of companies have gone through processes of mergers, acquisitions, and downsizing. In the three years from 1987 through 1989 in the United States, there were about 11,428 mergers, with a total value of 645,386 billion dollars ("M & A Demographics," 1990). Foreign acquisitions of U.S. companies accounted for 1,412 deals, and only 621 deals were of U.S. acquisitions overseas. Two of the famous cases, which may have a symbolic meaning, are the acquisition of the Rockefeller Center in New York and the acquisition of Columbia, the movie industry in Hollywood, both by Japanese companies.

These processes of mergers and acquisitions result in massive lay-offs. A survey of the American Management Association (Offermann & Gowing, 1990) showed that 39% of the 1,084 companies surveyed reduced their work force in 1989. From 1985 to 1988 approximately 15 million workers were affected by mergers and acquisitions, and nearly three quarters of the senior executives in acquired companies left within three years. These processes have a strong impact on the "survivors" as well as on those who were forced to leave (Offermann & Gowing, 1990). For the survivors, restructuring means a high level of uncertainty and dissatisfaction, stress, and increasing distrust. According to a survey conducted by *Fortune* (Farnham, 1989) more employees in 1989 than in 1983 were saying that their company did not treat them with respect, that they did not get enough information from top level management, and that the ability level of their management was low. Employees who were forced to leave have experienced economic problems, a high level of stress, and loss of personal worth, which has often resulted in physiological symptoms. This cost is paid not only by the individual but by society at large.

3. Organizational restructuring. In keeping with the processes of globalization, organizations no longer have distinct physical identities (Miles & Snow, 1984). Headquarters of organizations can be located in one country; manufacturing, in another location; sales and distribution, in a third country; and service, close to the customer in a nonlocal market. As a result, organizations change their structures to become flatter, with fewer layers of management and more diversification. Each distinct business is responsible for day-to-day operations, and the corporate office is responsible for overall financial control of the divisions and overall strategic development (Hill, Hitt, & Hoskisson, 1988). Globalization requires more joint ventures and results in a network of contracted relations and strategic alliances (Galbraith & Kazanjian, 1988).

Another aspect of organizational restructuring is the emergence of the virtual organization, whose members do not meet face-to-face, but are linked through computer technology instead. It has been estimated that about 16 million corporate employees in the United States now work at home (Offermann & Gowing, 1990).

4. Focus on teamwork. Organizations to date emphasize the formation of self-contained, close-to-the-customer work groups that learn customer preferences and forward the information to other divisions. As a result, there is a growing emphasis on teamwork and team-building (Sundstrom, Demeuse, & Futrell, 1990). This shift toward teamwork is of special interest to industrial and organizational (I/O) psychologists because it is implemented in a culture of individualistic values.

5. The growth of the service sector and the focus on the customer. The service sector now accounts for 71% of the workforce. It has created new jobs and redefined previous jobs. In addition, there is a growing emphasis on the sales and service functions. Even famous R&D labs have to take customers' needs into consideration more than ever before. A growing number of technicians and engineers have been required to shift their job focus from technical aspects to marketing and sales. Companies such as Procter & Gamble, which was known as the king of mass marketers, are now changing towards micromarketing, tailoring their marketing plans to the needs of individual retailers and consumers. Consumers in the 1990s are going to put emphasis on time-saving, product quality, and reliability. In the 1990s companies should increase their efforts to satisfy consumers' needs in order to compete in the market.

6. The emergence of high technology and telecommunication systems. The revolution in telecommunication systems is observed everywhere. There is an increasing number of users of electronic mail, fax, cellular phones, and teleconferences. The new technology facilitates communication across borders and geographical distances and significantly reduces the time needed to process information. In addition, software companies are now working on the development of simultaneous translations of written documents from one language to another.

In parallel, the revolution in office and factory automation is continuing. Yet, in many cases, automation has been implemented without taking the human operator into consideration. As a result, productivity improvement has not met expectations (Turnage, 1990). Office and factory automation have implications for skill requirements, job redesign, and the number of employees required to perform a given job. Thus, more attention should be given to the interplay between the human operator and the automated system to assure a high level of productivity and work satisfaction.

7. The financial forces in the market. The market is driven by financial considerations of the shareholders. As the value of the

company becomes lower than its stock, the shareholders prefer to sell the company and realize its assets. The dominant forces in the market are no longer product considerations, management considerations, the well-being of the employees, or even the survival of the company. Rather, the maximization of profit for shareholders is the main consideration (Hirsch, 1987).

8.   In the political arena, the processes of "mergers" take the form of unification among countries: the unification of Europe, the unification of East and West Germany, the end of the cold war, and the opening of talks between South Korea and the USSR, and South and North Korea. The exposure to different cultures and environments and the influx of immigration from one country to another increase the need to understand the relation between culture and behavior. The variance among situations has become as important for understanding work behavior as the variance among individuals. Thus, more attention should be given to the cognitive mediating processes of interpreting and evaluating the situational cues and transforming them into behavior.

THE SELF

The self is viewed as a dynamic interpretive structure that mediates most significant intrapersonal and interpersonal processes (Markus & Wurf, 1987). The self promotes differential sampling, processing, and evaluation of information from the environment, leading to differences in social and motivational behavior (Triandis, 1989). The self is anchored in the social system, and it is shaped by the shared understanding within a particular culture of what it is to be human (Cahoone, 1988; Cushman, 1990; Sandel, 1982). The self develops through direct experience and evaluation adopted from significant others (Bandura, 1986; Gecas, 1982). Reference groups' norms become the internalized standards against which individuals judge themselves (Gecas, 1982), and expectations of significant others directly influence individual behavior (Ajen & Fishbein, 1980; Triandis, 1972).

The evaluation process of the self is activated with respect to three different sets of standards that correspond to three facets of the self: (a) the public self—sensitive to the evaluations of significant others and seeks to win their approval through conformity, (b) the private self—directed by internal standards of achievement, and (c) the collective self—guided by criteria of collective achievement and the fulfillment of one's role as part of a reference group. It represents an internalization of the goals, norms, and expectations of important reference groups (Breckler & Greenwald, 1986). From a developmental approach, the public self is considered to be the least developed facet because it is driven by conformity to external standards and not by the internalization of such standards. In contrast, the collective self, which is guided by the internalization of external standards, is the most developed facet of the self.

The three selves are modified by the social culture. The private self is enhanced in individualistic cultures, which emphasize self-reliance, independence, and self-actualization (Triandis, 1989). On the other hand, the collective self is shaped by collectivistic and group-oriented cultures. These cultures emphasize the subordination of personal goals to the collective goals, and they value conformity, obedience, and reliability. The public self in collectivistic cultures is an extension of the collective self, whereas in individualistic cultures it is the extension of the private self. The public self is more likely to be central in tight cultures, which are known to be homogeneous and to place great emphasis on conformity with group norms. It is less central in loose cultures, which are often heterogenous and tolerant of deviations from group norms.

Research evidence demonstrates that cultures in East Asia sample their collective self more frequently than do Europeans or North Americans, whereas the private self dominates the Western societies (Triandis, 1989). However, a growing number of psychologists in the West recognize the importance of social identity and call for the development of a collective self in reaction to what they define as the individualistic, "empty" self (Cushman, 1990; Sampson, 1989).

Self-evaluation processes aim at developing and maintaining a positive representation of the self, whether it is the private or collective self. Three motives in the service of the self can be identified (Gecas, 1982; Markus & Wurf, 1987): (a) the need for self-enhancement, as reflected in seeking and maintaining a positive cognitive and affective state about the self, (b) the need for self-efficacy, which is the desire to improve and develop one's potential, and (c) the need for self-consistency, which is the desire to sense and experience coherence and continuity.

The experience of self-enhancement is affected by opportunities in the environment and by cognitive self-regulatory processes of sampling, assessing, and interpreting such opportunities. Research demonstrates a self-serving bias in information-processing (Kunda, 1987). Individuals are more sensitive to stimuli relevant to the self than to stimuli with a low relevance to the self. They process more efficiently self-congruent stimuli, and they resist incongruent information. Individuals prefer and seek out positive information about themselves, and they selectively sample, interpret, and remember events that support a positive self-concept.

The private and collective selves offer different criteria for evaluating the meaning of self-enhancement and self-efficacy. The private self positively evaluates and reinforces individual achievements, whereas the collective self positively evaluates and reinforces individual contributions to the success of the reference group. Thus, the two selves lead people to behave in different ways in different cultures. In the same vein, different motivational techniques that reinforce either individual or group behavior may be differently interpreted by individuals in different cultures and may have a differential effect on employees' behavior.

Self-enhancement is most strongly reflected in the notion of self-efficacy. Perceived self-efficacy is "a judgement of one's capability to accomplish a certain level of performance" (Bandura, 1986, p. 391). People tend to avoid tasks and situations they believe exceed their capabilities. Efficacy judgments promote the choice of situations and tasks with high likelihood of success and minimize the choice of tasks that exceed one's capabilities.

Self-efficacy has mainly been developed with respect to the individual (Bandura, 1986). However, a perceived collective efficacy is crucial for what people choose to do as a group, how much effort they put into it, and how persistent they are when facing failures. The strength of groups, organizations, and nations lies partly in people's sense of collective efficacy (Bandura, 1986). The relative salience of individual versus collective efficacy might be shaped by culture. Future research should examine the strength of collective efficacy in individualistic versus collectivistic cultures and its relationship to organizational success.

While the motives of self-enhancement and self-efficacy have been extensively studied, the motive of self-consistency has received little empirical attention. The sense of continuity and consistency helps individuals attach their current events of social life to past experiences and maintain a coherent view of themselves. Such a coherent view is necessary for operating effectively in the environment (Epstein, 1973). On the cognitive level, motivation for perceived self-consistency is manifested in the way individuals construct memories and selective perceptions in line with previous events. On the behavioral level, it is manifested in the individuals' choice to behave in accordance with the values and norms implied by their self-identity. In a changing environment this motive is less likely to be satisfied, and more concern should be given to the development of opportunities for self-consistency. All three self-driven motives constitute the link between the self and the dynamic processes of work motivation, which are examined in the next section.

WORK MOTIVATION

Work motivation is defined as a broad construct pertaining to the conditions and processes that account for the arousal, effort, direction, strategy development, and persistence of work-related behavior. All five factors reflect the motivation to allocate the cognitive resources necessary for task performance and long-term task accomplishment. Persistence conveys a long-term commitment to the course of action towards goal attainment.

Work motivation is mainly cognitively generated. Three different forms of cognitive motivators can be identified (Bandura, 1989): outcome expectancies, cognized goals, and causal attribution. Outcome expectancies and cognized goals operate through anticipation mechanisms for future behavior. Causal attributions are conceived of retrospectively for prior attainments, and they affect future behavior. In all three cases the underlying mechanisms are of self-enhancement. Thus, motivation can be conceived of in terms of achieving particular self-conceptions or desired selves (Schlenker, 1985).

Most theories of work motivation have not been concerned with the relation between motivation, the self, and the environment. The most effective theory of work motivation to date, the goal-setting theory, has focused mainly on the direct relation between goals and performance. Only recently have self-efficacy, valences, and strategies been introduced as mediating variables between goals and performance (Locke & Latham, 1990). The core findings of the goal-setting model demonstrated that specific and difficult goals lead to high performance levels *if* accepted by the individual and *if* feedback is provided (Locke & Latham, 1990). Some researchers argue that goal acceptance, or commitment, has a stronger motivational power than goals because it connotes a stake in the consequences and a willingness to persevere and sacrifice to realize the goal (Novacek & Lazarus, in press). Thus, an important motivational question is how to motivate employees to become committed to their goals.

It is reasonable to expect a high level of goal commitment when goal attainment contributes to self-enhancement. Such an evaluation is based on certain norms and standards, which may vary across situations and cultures. However, current theories of work motivation do not take the cultural factor into consideration. In a review of theories of work motivation, Katzell and Thompson (1990) admitted that cognitive theories of information-processing have not yet been the target of extensive research and application in work motivation. Furthermore, their review does not include any aspect of cross-cultural research on work motivation, although cross-cultural research provides explanations for the differential interpretations of motivational variables. Instead, Katzell and Thompson (1990) emphasize exogenous motivational factors that can be manipulated by the organization. Exogenous factors include incentives, reinforcement, goal-setting techniques, and job design. They contend that although endogenous theories, which deal with process or mediating variables, help explain what is going on in motivation, it is the exogenous theories that provide *action levers* that can be employed to change work motivation. They emphasize the need to improve the technology of work motivation and make several recommendations for such an improvement.

The approach proposed by Katzell and Thompson (1990) is probably useful within a given work environment, where all employees are likely to interpret the motivational stimuli in the same way. However, since the self is shaped by the environment, different interpretations might be given to the same motivational stimuli in different cultures. Thus, endogenous theories, or the mediating processes, seem to gain importance in understanding work motivation in the global market.

Three developments in psychology provide more insight on the evaluation process that leads to work motivation: research in cross-cultural psychology, models of social cognition, and theories of the self.

1. Research in cross-cultural psychology. Numerous cross-cultural studies have recently been conducted on work values and work motivation. The studies have clearly demonstrated that there are significant differences between cultures in collectivistic versus individualistic values, and in power distance, which is the psychological distance between different levels in the organizational hierarchy (Hofstede, 1980; Triandis, 1989; Triandis, Bontempo, Vilareal, Masaaki, & Lucca, 1988). Such differences correspond to the differential effectiveness of various motivational techniques. Motivational techniques that fit in with individualistic values, such as individual job enrichment, individual goal-setting, and individual incentives, were found to be effective in individualistic cultures. In contrast, motivational techniques that correspond to collectivistic, group-oriented values, such as quality circles, autonomous work groups, group goals, and participation in goal-setting and decision-making, were found to be more effective in collectivistic cultures such as Japan, China, and Israel (Earley, 1989; Erez, 1986; Erez & Earley, 1987; Matsui, Kakuyama, & Onglatco, 1987). Research in cross-cultural psychology contributes to the understanding of why certain motivational techniques are effective in some cultures but not in others.

2. Models of social cognition. Such models enable us to understand how information from the social environment, as well as from internal

cues is sampled, processed, interpreted, and stored in cognitive schemas. Information that fits in with the cognitive schema is more likely to be accepted than conflicting information (Wyer & Srull, 1989). Empirical evidence to support the above approach is provided by the classical study of French, Israel, and As (1960), who attempted to replicate Coch and French's (1948) study in Norway. They explained their failure to replicate the positive effect of direct participation by arguing that it was legitimate in Norway to have the union representatives participate in decision-making, but not the employees themselves. Since direct participation did not fit in with the cultural schema, it was not found to be effective. Similarly, Earley (1986) found that in British companies, unlike American companies, shop stewards are more highly trusted than supervisors and that their decisions are therefore more likely to be accepted by British than by American employees.

3. Models of the self that emphasize the function of the self as an information processor and interpreter. The self selects, processes, and evaluates information from the environment. Therefore, the evaluation of various motivational techniques as self-enhancing depends on the standards and norms used by the self for interpreting such information. The salience of criteria in the service of the private or collective self depends on cultural characteristics. Therefore, different criteria for evaluating the motivation potential of various motivational techniques are likely to be used in different cultures.

All the above developments open up a new stage in the study of the relation between culture, self, and work motivation. It is reasonable to argue that successful motivational techniques in one culture may lose their effectiveness in another culture. The differences in their effectiveness can only be understood if one takes into consideration the situational factors that lead individuals to interpret the same motivational techniques in different ways. As the market becomes increasingly global, more attention should be given to cultural characteristics because they set the norms and standards in the service of the self. Thus, endogenous theories seem to gain importance in the globally oriented work place.

An Integration of the Four Parts of the Model

Numerous examples can be used to demonstrate how the same motivational techniques are interpreted differently in different cultures and how they therefore have differential effects on employees' self-enhancement and consequent behavior. The first set of examples is taken from a line of research in which the moderating effect of culture on the relation between participation in goal-setting and performance was examined. The effectiveness of participation is influenced by norms prevalent in the culture. Group participation is congruent with collectivistic, group-oriented values and a low level of power distance rather than with individualistic values and a high level of power distance. Therefore, one expects to find that participation has a differential effect on goal commitment and performance in the two types of culture. This hypothesis was tested by Erez and Earley (1987) in a cross-cultural study that was conducted in Israel and the United States. The results supported the research hypothesis. The Israeli sample adversely reacted to assigned goals as compared to participatively set goals. Individuals who were assigned goals were less committed to them and performed less well than individuals who participated in goal-setting. Such differences were not observed in the American sample. Israel is known to be more collectivistic and egalitarian than the United States (Hofstede, 1980). In addition, the power distance between different organizational levels in Israel is one of the lowest in the world. Subordinates are not afraid to express their ideas even if they contradict their bosses. Therefore, goal commitment in Israel cannot be taken for granted, and participative approaches seem to be more effective than assigned goals.

A second study was conducted within Israel (Erez, 1986), but this time in three different industries known for their differences in collectivistic values. The most collectivistic sector is the Kibbutz, with emphasis on group rather than individual welfare and on egalitarian rather than utilitarian approaches to profit-sharing. Ultimate decision-making power in the governance of the Kibbutz resides with the general assembly of all the Kibbutz members (Leviatan & Rosner, 1980). Second, on the continuum of collectivistic values is the Histadrut sector, which is the Israeli Federation of Labor and the owner of 23% of Israeli industry. The ideological platform of the Histadrut is guided by collectivistic-participative values, and all of the Histadrut members are owners of the Histadrut industry called Hevrat Ovdim. There is constant pressure in the Histadrut sector to formalize employee participation in management and profit-sharing (Rosenstein, 1977). The third sector is the private sector, which is more individualistic than the other two. It represents privately owned firms, guided by utilitarian goals, with no explicit policy for employee participation. The study examined the effect of assigned goals, goals set by group participation, and goals set by group representatives. The highest effect of group participation was observed in the Kibbutz sector; the lowest, in the private sector. In contrast, assigned goals were more effective in the private sector than in the two other ones.

In another line of research, Latham, Erez, and Locke (1988) designed a joint series of experiments to identify the conditions that moderate the effect of participation on performance. In a brainstorming session preceding the study, they discovered that they conceptualized the episode of participation in different ways. For Erez, participation was conceived of as a process of group discussion, whereas for Latham participation took the form of a dyadic relationship between one superior and one subordinate. This example demonstrates how researchers from different cultures have different interpretations of the participation episode.

Another example can be cited in relation to group goals and group performance. Matsui et al., (1987) found that group goals were effective for Japanese people. However, in individualistic cultures group goals very often result in social loafing, free-riding, because group members in individualistic cultures do not share responsibility to the same extent as group members in collectivistic cultures (Earley, 1989). As a result, group performance tends to be less effective in individualistic than in collectivistic cultures unless employees are personally accountable for their performance. Perhaps one way to make group performance effective in individualistic cultures is to have the group members become personally accountable for their performance (Weldon & Gargano, 1988).

Differences in collectivistic vs. individualistic values may explain why models of job enrichment developed in the United States differed from those developed in Norway and Sweden or Japan. Hackman and Oldham's (1980) model of job enrichment, which was developed in the United States, focuses on the design of jobs for the individual employee. The critical psychological states that mediate the relation between job dimensions and work motivation reflect the private self. They consist of experienced meaningfulness of the work, experienced responsibility, and knowledge of results. However, the job-enrichment model does not include psychological dimensions that enhance the collective self, such as the formation of group identity and social support.

In contrast, North European countries have adopted models of autonomous work groups, and in Japan they have taken the form of quality-control circles. North European countries and Japan are known to have more collectivistic values than the United States (Hofstede, 1980). The implementation of different techniques of job enrichment in different countries is not a coincidence. Rather, it reflects the contingency between the cultural values and the motivational potential of different managerial techniques, as interpreted by the self.

An additional example is the case of Japanese management. It exemplifies how the four parts of the model—the work environment, motivational techniques, the self, and employee work motivation—are integrated to explain work motivation. The Japanese set of values is characterized by collectivism, group orientation, and respect for seniority (Hofstede, 1980; Odaka, 1986; Triandis et al., 1988). Group orientation conveys the priority given to the continuity and prosperity of the social system. Collectivism is reflected in self-definition as part of groups, subordination of personal goals to group goals, concern for the integrity of the in-group, and intense emotional attachment to the group (Triandis et al., 1988). This culture nourishes the collective self, which gains a central role in processing and interpreting information (Triandis, 1989). The core values of the Japanese culture were implemented at the corporate level and have shaped the Japanese management practices. Concern for the continuity of the organization and for the integrity of the group has led to the development of a system of life-time employment. The terms *management familism* (Kume, 1985), or *corporate collectivism* (Triandis, 1989) were used to describe Japanese Management, implying that both management and employees have a high level of life-long mutual commitment. In a study conducted by Erez (in press) in Japanese companies, Japanese managers explained that this system enabled them to develop mutual commitment between employees and employers, teamwork, and group cohesiveness. They attributed their companies' success to the system of life-time employment.

The focus on social identity and group orientation has led to the development of intensive communication systems in Japanese corporations. Top-down, bottom-up, and horizontal channels of communication are highly developed in Japanese companies. In particular, the bottom-up communication, conveyed by the Ringi system and the Small Group Activity, allows for employees' active participation in decision-making. The extensive flow of information enables employees to interpret their goals more accurately, gain knowledge on how to obtain the goals, and develop goal commitment. These cognitive and motivational processes lead to a high level of performance. As employees improve their knowledge, skills, and performance in the group context, their self-efficacy and collective efficacy are enhanced. Reciprocally, the enhancement of self-efficacy and collective efficacy leads Japanese employees to continue improving their performance not only on the individual level but on the group, organizational, and societal level. The interdependence between the individual, organizational, and societal levels is symbolically demonstrated by the company book of Hitachi, *Introduction to Hitachi and modern Japan* (1986). Namely, the success of Hitachi is viewed with respect to the success of Japan at large. The recognition of the reciprocal relation between the individual, the corporation, and society may partly account for the economic success of Japan at large.

What are the implications of the Japanese management techniques for the West? A simplistic approach may lead one to believe that some of these techniques should be implemented in the West. My argument is that a simplistic approach ends up with unsuccessful implementations of techniques that were found to be successful in other countries. Rather, the practice of work motivation should be based on the integrated model, which takes the link between the situation, the self, and work motivation into consideration. We should learn from the Japanese not how to use specific techniques but how to develop motivational techniques that provide opportunities for self-enhancement and self-identity as interpreted in our culture.

The Japanese example demonstrates that when the motivational techniques are congruent with cultural values, they contribute to self- enhancement and result in a high performance level. In Japan, the collective self was found to be more complex and more dominant than the private self. Self-enhancement is experienced when the individual makes a contribution to the group and receives recognition for his/her contribution. Therefore, motivational techniques that facilitate the contribution of the individual to group success are found to be effective. Reciprocally, effective group performance reinforces the collective efficacy, which further affects group and organizational performance.

THE PRACTICAL IMPLICATIONS OF THE MODEL

With the integrated model it is proposed that the motivational potential of various motivational techniques is evaluated by the self in terms of their contribution to self-enhancement and that the criteria for evaluation are determined by cultural norms and standards. The criteria and standards of evaluation in cultures that cultivate the collective self are different from the ones used in cultures that emphasize the private self. In the former case, enhancement is experienced through contribution to group success, whereas in the latter case it is experienced through personal achievements. Therefore, different motivational techniques are expected to be effective in different cultures.

In light of the integrated model, the following motivational approach is proposed for the selection and use of motivational techniques in Western culture:

Motivational Techniques for Self-enhancement

1. The setting of clear and specific goals becomes more important in a changing environment than in a stable one because past goals are no longer relevant in new situations. Furthermore, goal clarity can be enhanced by providing employees with detailed information on the nature of their jobs and how they are linked to the organizational mission. Specific difficult goals are more challenging than easy goals, and their attainment contributes to perceptions of self-enhancement more than the attainment of easy goals, provided that employees know how to attain the goals.

2. Training employees to use effective strategies for attaining challenging goals is gaining importance. Training improves the perceptions of self-efficacy and the chances to perform well and receive positive feedback and rewards.

3. In the absence of traditional local and organizational cues, feedback and information gain more value and become central to the development of employees' self-efficacy. Thus the new form of organizations requires that management develop the feedback loops that tie employees' self-efficacy into the mission of the company to make it successful.

4. The use of gain-sharing, or Employees Stock Ownership Plans, strengthen the relation between effort and outcomes, and enhance commitment to and identity with the organization. It is estimated that eight million workers, constituting 7% of the private-sector work force, are participating in employee-ownership plans in 7,500 companies (Blasi, 1988). For example, from 1988 through 1990 in the United States, Hospital Corporation of American sold 104 general hospitals to an employee-owned company; Avis Rent-a-Car sold the entire national system to its employees, and United Airlines is in a process of selling the company to its employees.

5. In a changing and unstable work environment there are limited opportunities to exercise control over one's behavior and career development. Therefore, the provision of such opportunities should be of utmost importance for self-enhancement. Perceptions of control may be enhanced by motivational techniques that allow for personal accountability and personal responsibility. Such motivational techniques may lead to a higher level of both organizational commitment and extra-role behavior as shown by aiding co-workers, volunteering for unpaid tasks, and putting forth effort beyond that required by a job (Staw & Boettger, 1990). However, it is important to note that if employees cannot perceive the relation between their personal performance and the macrolevel of organizational

competitiveness, it may discourage them from taking any personal responsibility.

Development and Maintenance of Self-identity

The need for self-consistency has hardly been examined in I/O psychology. This need is gaining more salience and centrality as rapid changes occur in the working environment. Self-consistency is affected by lay-offs, changes in the content and status of jobs, and changes in the managerial approach, the organizational culture, and the composition of the teamwork. These changes make it difficult to maintain and develop self-consistency. The lack of a consistent identity as an employee results in alienation, low commitment, and low levels of productivity. In times of organizational instability, other sources of identity, rather than identification with the company, could be emphasized to maintain self-consistency:

1. Professional identity may replace organizational commitment. Employees may become more committed to their profession and strengthen their ties with professional organizations.
2. Employees may strengthen their identity with their immediate project or teamwork and may maintain this identity as long as they work on the project or stay with the same team.
3. Work identity is one of multiple identities of the self. Perhaps more attention should be given to the development of family and community identities to counterbalance the identity crisis in the workplace (Zedeck & Mosier, 1990).

Maintenance of Self-consistency

1. Job continuity across organizations may be enhanced by enabling employees to transform benefit plans and tenure across organizations.
2. Companies may consider the possibility of developing one metafunctional unit of human resource management that serves several companies in the same industry. The formation of such a unit allows for more flexibility and mobility on the company level yet maintains continuity and consistency on the individual level.

Matching of Motivational Techniques with Cultural Characteristics

The process of globalization exposes employees to new cultures and new situations. From the individual perspective, the exposure to the global market activates cognitive information-processing in attempts to interpret and adjust to new environments. Members of one part of the global market encounter members of another part, who interpret and react to the situation differently. As a result, multinational companies and joint ventures may have to use different motivational techniques in different parts of the company and may have to delegate more responsibility to local managements. In the same vein, the approach that companies take to customers should be diversified and should be tailored to the characteristics of the local markets.

The values of collectivism versus individualism, together with the value of power distance, seem to be the most relevant factors for the development of effective motivational techniques. Group-based techniques should be implemented in collectivistic cultures. Such motivational techniques include the setting of group goals, the design of autonomous work groups, group participation in goal-setting and decision-making, group accountability, group incentives, and profit-sharing.

Analogously, attempts to enhance teamwork in individualistic cultures should be accompanied by a change in the organizational culture. A cultural change can be enhanced through the development of performance criteria at the group level, use of group incentives rather than individual incentives, and implementation of programs for employees' gain-sharing, and employees' stock ownership plans.

CONCLUDING REMARKS

1. When the motivational techniques are congruent with the cultural values, they contribute to self-enhancement and result in a high level of performance.

2. Theories of motivation, which draw on the interaction between the environment and the individual in enhancing the self, are more effective in explaining behavior than are theories that focus on the individual alone.

3. The exposure to foreign cultures increases individuals' awareness of their own selves as part of the comparisons they make. The ability to define the collective self through comparisons with others may be one of the great benefits of the process of globalization. American psychologists argue that the biggest challenge of psychology to date is to explore a new theory of the person, a theory that would be suitable for the global era into which society is rapidly heading (Sampson, 1989). Perhaps cross-cultural research can be used as a means to enhance the understanding of the differences and similarities among cultures. Reciprocally, identifying the differences and similarities among cultures will help to define one's own social identity.

AUTHOR'S NOTE

I would like to thank Sheldon Zedeck, Barry Staw, Hadassa Kubat, Kristi Whitney, Lynda Sagrestano, and Nilli Diengot for their comments and suggestions on earlier drafts of this paper.

REFERENCES

Ajen, I. & Fishbein, M. (1980). *Understanding attitudes and predicting social behavior*. Englewood Cliffs, NJ: Prentice-Hall.

Bandura, A. (1986). *Social foundations of thoughts and action: A social cognitive theory*. Englewood Cliffs, NJ: Prentice-Hall.

Bandura, A. (1989). Perceived self efficacy in the exercise of personal agency. *The Psychologist: Bulletin of the British Psychological Society, 10*, 411-424.

Beer, M., & Walton, E. (1990). Developing the competitive organization: Interventions and strategies. *American Psychologist, 5*, 154-161.

Blasi, R.J. (1988). *Employee ownership: A revolution or rip off?* Cambridge, MA: Harper & Row.

Breckler, S. J., & Greenwald, A. G. (1986). Motivational facets of the self. In R. M. Sorrentino & E. T. Higgins (Eds.), *Handbook of Motivation and Cognition: Foundations of Social Behavior* (pp. 145-164). New York: Guilford.

Cahoone, L.E. (1988). *The dilemma of modernity: Philosophy, culture and anti-culture*. Albany, NY: State University of New York Press.

Cascio, W.F. (1989). *Managing human resources: Productivity, quality of work life, profits*. New York: McGraw Hill.

Coch, L., & French, J. R. P. (1948). Overcoming resistance to change. *Human Relations, 1*, 512-532.

Cushman, P. (1990). Why the self is empty: Toward a historically situated psychology. *American Psychologist, 45*, 599-611.

Earley, P. C. (1986). Supervisors and shop stewards as sources of contextual information in goal-setting: A comparison of the U.S. with England. *Journal of Applied Psychology, 71*, 111-118.

Earley, P.C. (1989). Social loafing and collectivism: A comparison of United States and the People's Republic of China. *Administrative Science Quarterly, 34*, 565-581.

Epstein, S. (1973). The self-concept revisited, or a theory of a theory. *American Psychologist, 28*, 408-416.

Erez, M. (1986). The congruence of goal setting strategies with socio-cultural values, and its effect on performance. *Journal of Management, 12*, 588-592.

Erez, M. (in press). Interpersonal communication patterns in Japanese corporations: Their relationships to cultural values and to productivity and innovation. *Applied psychology: An international Review.*

Erez, M., & Earley, P. C. (1987). Comparative analysis of goal-setting strategies across cultures. *Journal of Applied Psychology, 72,* 658-665.

Farnham, A. (1989, December 4). The trust gap. *Fortune,* pp. 56-78.

French, J. R. P., Israel, J., & As, D. (1960). An experiment in a Norwegian factory: Interpersonal dimension in decision-making. *Human Relations, 19,* 3-19.

Galbraith, J. R., & Kazanjian, R. K. (1988). Strategy, technology, and emerging organizations. In J. Hage (Ed.), *Futures of Organizations* (pp. 29-41). Lexington, MA: Lexington Book.

Gecas, V. (1982). The self concept. *Annual Review of Psychology, 8,* 1-33.

Hackman, J. R., & Oldham, G. R. (1980). *Work Redesign.* Reading, MA: Addison-Wesley.

Hill, C. W. L., Hitt, M. A., & Hoskisson, R. E. (1988). Declining U.S. competitiveness: Reflection on a crisis. *Academy of Management Executive, 2,* 51-60.

Hirsch, P. (1987). *Pack Your Own Parachute: How to survive mergers, takeovers, and other corporate disasters.* Reading, MA: Addison-Wesley.

Hofstede, G. (1980). *Culture's consequences: International differences in work related values.* Beverly Hills, CA: Academic Press.

Introduction to Hitachi and Modern Japan (1986). Tokyo: Hitachi.

Katzell, R. A., & Thompson, D. E. (1990). Work motivation: Theory and practice. *American Psychologist, 45,* 144-153.

Kume, T. (1985). Managerial attitudes towards decision-making. In W. B. Gudykunst, L. P. Stewart, & S. Ting-Tooney (Eds.). *Communication, culture, and organizational processes,* (pp. 231-251). Beverly-Hills, CA: Sage.

Kunda, Z. (1987). Motivated inference: Self-serving generation and evaluation of causal theories. *Journal of Personality & Social Psychology, 53,* 636-647.

Latham, G. P., Erez, M., & Locke, E. A. (1988). Resolving scientific disputes by the joint design of crucial experiments by the antagonists: Application to the Erez-Latham dispute regarding participation in goal setting. *Journal of Applied Psychology, 73,* 753-772.

Lawler, E. E. III. (1986). *High Involvement Management.* New York: Jossey-Bass.

Leviatan, U., & Rosner, M. (1980). *Work and organization in Kibbutz Industry.* Norwood, PA: Norwood Editions.

Locke, E.A., & Latham, P.G. (1990). *A theory of goal setting and task performance*. Englewood Cliffs, NJ: Prentice-Hall.

M & A demographics of the decade: The top 100 deals of the decade. (1990). *Mergers & Acquisitions, 25*, pp. 107-112.

Markus, H., & Wurf, E. (1987). The dynamic self-concept: A social psychological perspective. *Annual Review of Psychology, 38*, 299-337.

Matsui, T., Kakuyama, T., & Onglatco, M. L. (1987). Effects of goals and feedback on performance in groups. *Journal of Applied Psychology, 72*, 407-415.

Miles, R. E., & Snow, C. C. (1984). Fit, failure, and the Hall of Fame. *California Management Review, 26*, 10-28.

Mowday, R. T., Porter, L. W., & Steers, R. M. (1982). *Employee-organization linkages: The psychology of commitment, absenteeism, and turnover*. New York: Academic Press.

Novacek, J., & Lazarus, R. S. (in press). The structure of personal commitments. *Journal of Personality*.

Odaka, K. (1986). *Japanese management: A forward looking analysis*. Tokyo: Japan Productivity Organization.

Offermann, L. R., & Gowing, M. K. (1990). Organizations of the future: Changes and challenges. *American Psychologist, 45*, 95-108.

Rosenstein, E. (1977). Workers' participation in management: Problematic issues in the Israeli Systems. *Industrial Relations Journal, 8*, 55-69.

Sampson, E. E. (1989). The challenge of social change for psychology: Globalization and psychology's theory of the person. *American Psychologist, 44*, 914-921.

Sandel, M. J. (1982). *Liberalism and the limits of justice*. Cambridge: Cambridge University Press.

Schlenker, B. R. (1985). *The self and social life*. New York: McGraw Hill.

Staw, B. M., & Boettger, R. D. (1990). Task revision as a form of work performance. *Academy of Management Journal, 33*, 534-559.

Sundstrom, E., Demeuse, K. P., & Futrell, D. (1990). Workteams: Applications and effectiveness. *American Psychologist, 45*, 120-133.

Triandis, H.C. (1972). *The Analysis of Subjective Culture*. New York: Wiley.

Triandis, H. C. (1989). The self and social behavior in differing cultural contexts. *Psychological Review, 96*, 506-520.

Triandis, H. C., Bontempo, R., Vilareal, M. J., Masaaki, A., & Lucca, N. (1988). Individualism and collectivism: Cross-cultural perspectives on self-ingroup relationships. *Journal of Personality and Social Psychology, 54*, 328-338.

Turnage, J. J. (1990). The challenge of new workplace technology for psychology. *American Psychologist, 45*, 171-178.

Weldon, E., & Gargano, G. M. (1988). Cognitive loafing: The effects of accountability and shared responsibility on cognitive effort. *Personality & Social Psychology Bulletin, 14,* 159-171.

Wyer, R. S., & Srull, T. K. (1989). *Memory and cognition in its social context.* Hillsdale, NJ: Lawrence Erlbaum Associates Inc.

Zedeck, S., & Mosier, K. L. (1990). Work in the family and employing organization. *American Psychologist, 45,* 240-251.

ORGANIZATION— ENVIRONMENT RELATIONS
Towards Overcoming Limited Perspectives in Organizational Psychology

Bernhard Wilpert
Berlin University of Technology

Business executives know it; politicians believe in it and do it; but psychologists seem to be too shy for it—namely, putting organization-environment relations squarely on the agenda. No viable corporate strategy could be conceived without an awareness of those environmental factors that have an impact on the organization's operations. No wonder, then, that it is mainly business schools that cultivate the art of dealing with organizational environments (Nystrom & Starbuck, 1981) and that it is management literature that "is increasingly interested in the organization/environment interface as well" (Beer & Walton, 1987:350). Similarly, politicians believe in it because otherwise they would not be so concerned with making rules and laws as a means to control the life of organizations.

Apart from the emotionally charged memories of East and West Berliners falling into each others' arms after the fall of The Wall, what remains as a striking example of the importance of this theme is the amazing dramatic change that occurred in the behavior of border guards. Virtually every traveller crossing the East German border after the November 1989 revolution reported that friendliness and casualness had over night replaced the stern and rough controlling behavior that had characterized the border guard system and its members. I firmly believe that this mutation was due to more than just a pleasant mood in the wake of a happy event: No, it was the outcome of a wholesale change of a complex system of behavioral controls, incentives, and threats.

Ever since systems-thinking began to consider organizations as living systems, the interdependence of organizations and of their environments should have been a natural given. After all, W. Köhler (1938/1959) spoke of living organisms as "parts of a larger functional context." In discussing the conditions of effective adaptation and regulatory processes operating in systems to achieve some kind of stability, Ashby (1956, 1960) speaks of the law of requisite variety, meaning that the regulatory unit (in this case, the organization, or a subsystem) must have at least the matching discriminatory potential, or "requisite variety," to cope with the complexity that characterizes given disturbing environmental factors. Only then is it possible for adaptation to take place, adaptation being "the ability of . . . a system to modify itself or its environment, when either has changed to the . . . system's disadvantage, so as to regain at least some of its lost efficiency" (Ackoff & Emery, 1972:125). In this light it is not too surprising that the practice of organizational development, as the one subdiscipline of work and organizational psychology concerned with adaptive organizational changes, has a relatively sizeable investment in organization-environment linkages (Beer & Walton, 1987). The same may certainly be said about some areas such as school, health, and community psychology, which analyze institutions in their context. But whence the relative self-restraint of mainstream organizational psychology in the past, especially given the experience-based and theoretically evident significance of environments for organizations?

I have puzzled over this question for some time and have come up with two possible explanations, which neither exclude each other nor serve as excuses for the noted neglect:

1. One reason may be linked to the "organismic" preoccupation of psychology in general (Graumann, 1974), which traditionally focuses on the individual person and his/her experiences and behaviors while largely losing sight of the contingent context: "the world of things." Thus, methodological individualism almost by necessity leads to a narrow perspective and an exclusion of collective phenomena and social processes.

2. A second reason may lie in the inherent epistemological complexities one raises with the attempt to describe "heteronomous" influences, that is, influences that are external to the individual, when they enter the psychological field from the nonpsychological environment (Heider, 1977). A fine illustration of this point at the individual level is the famous discussion between Brunswik and Lewin on the nature of psychological ecology, an exchange that did not reach its proper end because of Lewin's untimely death.

Kurt Lewin's concept of the *life space* refers to that segment of the "objective environment" that is of relevance to the individual, in other words, that part that has consequences for an individual's behavior. Life space in this conceptualization includes those parts of the objective environment that are reconstructed by the individual. In that sense one might speak of Lewin's position as one characterized by a "perspectivist holism" (Wilpert, 1990)—perspectivist because it is concerned with the environmental aspects relevant to the individual; holistic because the life space encompasses both the individual person and the psychological environment.

Brunswik (1934, 1939), on the other hand, attempted to conceptualize a psychology with the *Gegenstand*—the object—as the anchor and source of objective stimuli that are having an impact on the organism. He orders these stimuli along a continuum from distal to proximal, with proximal stimuli being considered to have stronger impacts on the organism's behavior than distal ones. Notwithstanding the criticism that the empirical work by Brunswik focused mainly on proximal stimuli and the organism's response to them (Kruse, 1978), his epistemological stance remains valid and might be labeled as one characterized by an "objective (metaphysical) dualism" (Wilpert, 1990); objective in the sense that he believes in the need to classify and describe environmental factors independent of an individual organism; dualist because he juxtaposes the objective environment with organismic reactions. Lewin's and Brunswik's positions will be shown below to be fundamentally different ways of looking at the world (von Saldern, 1987).

This early debate about organism-environment relations already highlights the epistemological complexities involved at the individual level. However, they do not even touch the complexities involved when one considers the relation between social systems and their often ambiguous environments.

More recently, psychologists have shown renewed interest in the environment as a focus of research. A rough, albeit not quite conclusive, indicator could be the number of entries on environmental issues in the *Annual Review of Psychology*, which contained 39 between 1968 and 1977 compared to 79 during the subsequent decade. Besides, the editors of the *Annual Review* now feel that the topic merits a special chapter every fourth year. Recent handbooks of work and organizational psychology also address the issue (Drenth, Thierry, Willems, & de Wolff, 1991; Roth, 1989). The reasons for this emergent interest may be manifold. However, two of them may be considered particularly important:

1. The ecological crises and major industrial disasters afflicting a wide range of complex technologies in recent years (e.g., the biological

death of the Rhine river as a consequence of fire-fighting in a chemical plant, or the more renowned instances of oil-tanker accidents, Bhopal, TMI, and Chernobyl) have made the public keenly aware of the role of the "human factor," as people put it in a self-distancing manner—the role of human error and of managerial or organizational "pathogens" (Reason, 1990).

2. In some instances the recent and often dramatic dynamics of changing socio-political environments clearly assume features of hyperturbulence and of vortical characteristics (Emery & Trist, 1977). The changes in the economic and sociopolitical landscape in eastern Europe may serve as a striking case in point. In short, there is little doubt that the environment is moving onto the agenda of psychology again.

The purpose of the subsequent three parts is:

1. to outline briefly and to probe the major theoretical approaches in organizational psychology to analyzing and understanding the relations between organization and the environment;

2. to illustrate both problems and the potential of some of my own and my colleagues' research approaches that seem relevant to organization-environment relations; and

3. to suggest some foci for further theory development and research on organizational environments.

THEORETICAL APPROACHES TO ORGANIZATIONAL ENVIRONMENTS

A review of the major attempts to study organizational environments and the link between organization and the environment suggests that one might usefully distinguish between two basic epistemological approaches and three different theoretical schools or traditions (see Figure 1).

Epistemological Vantage Points

The basic dichotomy between epistemological vantage points has already been encountered in the brief account of the dispute between Brunswik and Lewin, namely, the attempt to conceptualize environments in terms of their objective characteristics as opposed to the attempt to describe organizational environments in terms of phenomenological-perceptual characteristics.

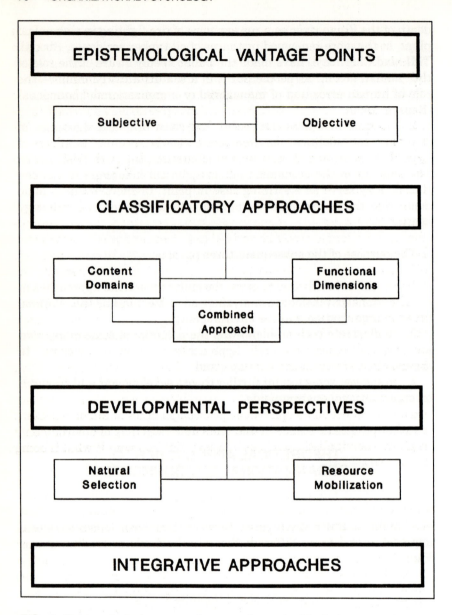

FIG. 1. Epistemological perspectives and methodological approaches to organizational environments.

Because there is no way to describe environmental aspects except by observing, that is, by perceiving them one way or other, one might try to simplify the issue by nominally positing that subjective characteristics of environments are those perceived by members of the organization and objective characteristics are those perceived by outside observers, such as social scientists (Yasai-Ardekani, 1986). However, as Starbuck (1976:1082) has pointed out: "The complexity of organization-environment relations and the ambiguity of organizational boundaries imply also that different perceivers will disagree about what constitutes dimensions of the organization and what constitutes dimensions of the environment." Why should, for instance, environmental turbulence as perceived by organization members (Lawrence & Lorsch, 1967) be an aspect of the environment rather than of the organization? On the other hand, of course, one can distinguish different environmental percepts: those individual perceptions that can reliably be verified only by a particular subject (e.g., experienced turbulence) and those variables that can intersubjectively be verified (e.g., frequencies of interactions). Both types imply different measurement strategies because they are different kinds of data—the former being an individual percept; the latter, a socially shared representation of environment.

The Cartesian differentiation between subject and object, between intra and extra, between organization and environment, evidently leads to a dilemma that seems irresolvable. When talking about organization-environment relations, one is usually talking about interactions, and interactions intrinsically imply that they are contingent upon interacting agents. This point will be pursued a bit later. Suffice it to say here that most approaches to the problem at hand either have not led one to reflect on its epistemological complexities at all, or represent a rather pragmatic stance in that one's understanding of environments is given a nominalistic touch, as if to say: "Environment is what is being measured as such."

Classificatory Approaches

Two types of attempts to classify environments can be distinguished: classifications according to domains of environmental content and classifications according to specific functional dimensions. Various authors have identified segments or different levels of organizational environments. Woodward (1965) and, similarly, Negandhi (1969) or Heller (1971) spoke of cultural, political, social, economic, technological, and task-related environments. Starbuck (1976), in an impressive attempt to classify studies on the effects of environments on organizations, chose a three-level approach of distinguishing physical, primarily microsocial, and primarily macrosocial environmental categories. Plausible as all such categorizations may be in their ordering function, they lack a theoretical framework that links these various categories to each other.

Rather different are those attempts that start from a theoretical assumption about the particular significance of certain environmental features or dimensions that may help to classify different organizational environments. In referring to Tolman and Brunswik (1935), Emery and Trist (1965) develop their now classical approach to the "causal texture of organizational environments." Their seminal contribution is well known to everyone in the field. Hence, it suffices here to recall the two dimensions they used to identify the four cells of types of organizational environments. One of their dimensions refers to low or high environmental concentration of factors that are considered beneficial/ detrimental to the organization; the other dimension refers to high or low environmental turbulence. The four types are seen to form a hierarchy of increasing environmental complexity and relevant uncertainty. The assertion or theoretical assumption of the polarity of environmental stability/predictability versus dynamics of change and unpredictability is shared by a great many organization scientists such as Bosetzky (1970); Burns and Stalker (1961); Hill, Fehlbaum, and Ulrich (1974/76) , and Ziegler (1970). More recently, Babüroglu (1988) and McCann and Selsky (1984) have expanded Emery and Trist's classification to a fifth type of organizational environment: the *vortical environment*, whose inhabiting organizations "collectively lack sufficient adaptive capacity relative to prevailing environmental conditions. These are the 'have nots' in terms of requisite resources and skills" (McCann & Selsky, 1984:466) for coping with hyperturbulence. Recent eastern European developments and the seemingly total disarray of organizational responses lend considerable credibility to such a notion. As theoretically plausible and practically useful as such classifications may appear to be, the reduction of environmental parameters to one or two dimensions appears to be too simplistic.

In that light Katz & Kahn's approach (1978:125) seems more palatable in combining both content domains (called *environmental sectors*) and a set of general dimensions, partly borrowed from Emery & Trist (1965) (see Figure 2). Their matrix provides opportunities to locate a great number of different environmental settings, so it appears to form a useful analytical tool even though its theoretical underpinnings may be wanting.

The x-axis of their matrix covers functional relationships: (a) Societal values: Cultural legitimation; (b) Political Legal norms and statutes; (c) Economic: Markets and inputs of labor and materials; (d) Informational and technological, and (e) Physical: Geography; natural resources.

The y-axis contains four environmental types categorized according to the dimensions: (a) Stability-Turbulence; (b) Uniformity-Diversity; (c) Clustered (Organized)-Random, and (d) Scarcity-Munificence. Thus different environments can be classified within the 20 cells of their matrix.

Developmental Perspectives

The question as to why certain organizations survive and thrive while others falter and die seems to be at the bottom of the two theoretical approaches that can be called "developmental": the natural selection model and the resource dependence model (Peiro, 1984).

Natural selection   According to the approach that is based on Darwinian notions of the evolution of species, organizations are conceived of as relatively inactive products of environmental influences exerting a selection of the fittest (Aldrich, 1979). If one takes a phylogenetic perspective with sufficiently large time horizons, the perspective may prove to deliver satisfying explanations for different subcategories of large organizational populations, but for the more pedestrian chores of organizational psychologists trying to analyze and comprehend behavior in and of *specific* organizations the prospects of the natural selection approach are definitely somewhat limited.

Resource mobilization   Contrasting the natural selection approach is the concept of environmental selection, that is, the notion that organizations develop strategies in order to mold their environment in their favor and image (Pfeffer & Salancik, 1978). Such strategies may cover a broad variety of options such as networking and coalition-building, product innovation or marketing differentiation, cost leadership, or niche selection in a circumscribed market segment (Porter, 1980). They are intended to produce higher levels of organization-environment fits and thus to obtain requisite resources for survival and growth. While the environmental selection process may work for a few (often the large and powerful) organizations, there is a variety of reasons why it more often does not work. One reason is the implicitness of the strategy development, another is the unsystematic and unorderly choice processes. As Starbuck (1976; 1980) points out: "The result is that organizations rarely achieve even the degree of environmental compatibility attainable with badly conducted selection processes, and the overwhelming majority of organizations inhabit environments characterized by extremely weak appropriateness."

By way of an interim summary: classificatory approaches have been seen to have certain deficiencies. But neither of the developmental approaches seems to provide satisfactory theoretical handles on the organization-environment   problem.   Both   seem   to   be   true:

Environments influence organizational viability, and organizations may have options to mobilize environmental resources proactively. "Probably, both causal directions interact in an interactive, dynamic process . . . Mutual causality is likely to be the rule" (Miller, 1988:282). In short, there is a need for a new paradigm that possibly encompasses the approaches so far presented and that might offer more solid theoretical bases. I believe organizational psychologists may profit from following the lead of integrative approaches.

Integrative Approaches

Probably the most radical formulation of an integrative, holistic approach to the problem of organism-environment relations can be found in Angyal's (1941) attempt to establish a "science of personality." In his biology-inspired perspective, all living systems are characterized by processes of self-transcendence and trends towards increased autonomy. "Life process does not take place *within* the organism, but *between the organism and the environment*. . . . Organism and environment are two indispensable poles of a single process—life" (pp. 31-32), "*organism and environment are not static structures separable in space, but are opposing directions in the biological total process*" (p. 92) (Angyal's emphases). Environment exists only if it interacts with the organism. Hence, he distinguishes the "external world" that is not interacting and thus not part of the life process, from the environment that interacts. That which envelops organism and environment is the biosphere in its "bipolar organization" (p. 124). It "includes both the individual and environment, not as interacting parts, not as constituents which have independent existence, but as aspects of a single reality which can be separated only by abstraction" (p. 100). Undoubtedly, one will note here the conceptual similarity to, or even identity with Lewin's "life space" and Angyal's "biosphere."

To Lewin's and Angyal's approach one might add Ashby's (1956). All three of them focus on system-environment relations as their unit of analysis. Referring to Lewin and Ashby, Emery (1972:18), acclaimed the "daring nature of their proposed solution and its essential correctness. To reduce the complexity of our systems models they proposed to add in the even greater complexity of the environment." However, it is impossible to describe adequately the totality of these complex relations. Once again, it appears that a dead end has been reached, unless one succeeds in identifying the genotypical factors that facilitate the survival and growth of systems.

Emery proposed three approaches to identify such genotypical conditions:

1. Values as indicators of system tendencies (presumably because values may trigger a large variety of phenotypes).

2. Starting conditions as indicators "that have arisen from the past adaptive responses and act as a constraining and guiding influence on subsequent preparative behavior" (Emery, 1972:21).

3. Analysis based on the leading part, in other words, an analysis that is guided by an assumption of a major factor of influence such as McClelland's achievement need in economic growth.

Inasmuch as organizations can be considered living systems, the rather abstract and theoretical notions developed above clearly have relevance to the problem of organization-environment relations. I do not claim to know a simple answer as to how an integrative theoretical framework such as Lewin's or Angyal's would have to be operationalized in organizational psychological research. Nor do I claim that I myself have always followed the lead of the giants on whose shoulders we dwarfs stand. But I am ever more convinced that this is the direction that ought now to be pursued. What is needed if organization-environment *relations* are taken as the focal problem is to come to terms with what is meant by relations, be it in terms of exchange, cause and effect, social contact and social processes, or whatever—in any case, in terms of socially shared representations. In short, more adequate conceptualizations are required.

What follows is a sketch of three lines of research that my colleagues and I have developed during the last two decades. More by accident than by purposeful planning, they seem to fall into Emery's proposed three research approaches. Therefore, they are used as devices with which to structure the subsequent parts. However, a warning may be in order here. These lines of research fall far short of the demands imposed by the kind of integrative conceptual model described above. At best, they represent a groping for relevant, but still limited, aspects thereof.

ILLUSTRATIVE RESEARCH EXAMPLES

Values as Indicators of Systems Changes - MOW

When G. W. England and I joined forces (England & Wilpert, 1978) with the intention of developing a multinational comparison of the Meaning of Working (MOW, 1987), we were moved by three propellants: (a) the then ongoing policy discourse, (b) theoretical considerations, and (c) practical considerations. First, we were somewhat disturbed by the policy debate about the decline of work-related values, a discussion that seemed to us to be precociously derived from simplistic opinion polls.

Furthermore, we wanted to develop and validate a coherent theoretical model that showed its robustness in different national settings. Finally, in doing so, we hoped to provide valid data for practitioners in politics and work organizations.

Since then, eight national teams[1] have continued to pursue the central research question: What is the meaning of working life for people in modern society? Through extensive stages of pretesting, pilot studies, and subsequent item analyses, we developed a set of instruments and indices based on a jointly developed heuristic model (see Figure 3). We used a two-pronged sampling approach: a target group sample in each country of ten different vocational/professional characteristics, and representative samples of the national work forces. Altogether the samples comprised close to 15,000 respondents. Field work was completed in 1982-1983. The teams from Japan, the United States, and Germany agreed to conduct a replication in the late 1980s, this time based only on representative samples of the work forces. This replication study is presently being conducted.

Apart from demonstrating the overall robustness of our general model, we were able to show convincingly in the original study the futility of sweeping generalizations about wholesale changes in work-related values and corresponding labeling of whole generations as a "new breed" having lost all traditional work ethics. Certainly, there are indications of change, but their measurement and interpretation requires much more complex models and methods than simple frequency statistics on a single item. Also, simplistic dichotomies of the "materialist-vs.-postmaterialist" kind seem insufficient.

For nine out of ten persons in both our combined target group and representative samples of the early 1980s, work still played an important-to-major role in one's life space. and every second young person under 20 expected work to play an even greater role in the future. Although the income-producing function of working remains of major importance as a basic rationale for working, new expectations seem to be emerging and growing with regard to work as an institution that owes something to the individual worker. It is the feeling of being entitled to meaningful and interesting work, receiving proper training, and being able to participate actively in decisions affecting one's work. If we can believe our preliminary results of the replication study, this trend seems to be accelerating, though at different rates in different countries.

How does all this relate to the problem of organization-environment relations? To be quite clear, our study of MOW was *not* designed as organization research. Its focus was the subjective meaning of working, a meaning that we conceived of as a concept of a complex, multidimensional ensemble of relatively stable, work-related, socially

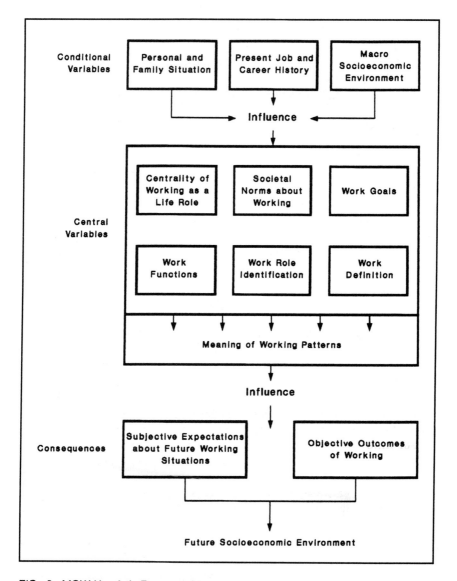

FIG. 2. MOW Heuristic Research Model

shared cognitions and evaluations. The unit of analysis is *not* organization-environment interaction. However, the preferences of a work force are a necessary input into work organizations: hence, they clearly form significant parts of the organizational environment. And indicators of changing work values are indicative of systems changes in

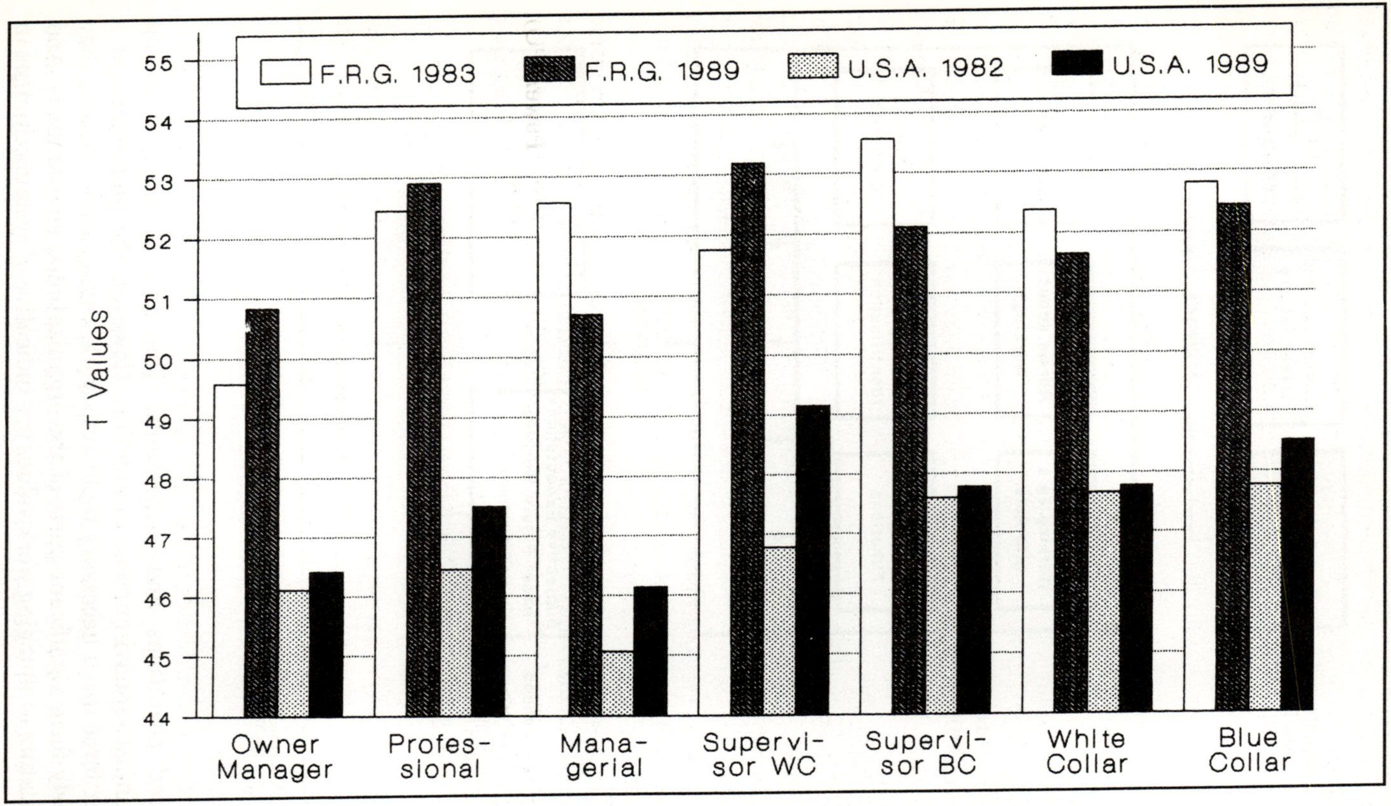
F.R.G. 1983
F.R.G. 1989
U.S.A. 1982
U.S.A. 1989
T Values
55
54
53
52
51
50
49
48
47
46
45
44
Owner Manager
Profes- sional
Mana- gerial
Supervi- sor WC
Supervi- sor BC
White Collar
Blue Collar

FIG. 3. Entitlement/Opportunity Norms and Employment Categories

the holistic sense of the life process of organizations. A major unresolved problem of the MOW study remains, namely, the question of how we can systematically relate our findings across various systems levels—from national aggregates to professional groups and specific work organizations.

Starting Conditions as Indicators - IDE

The research to be reported in this section is at least one step closer to the heart of the problem because the unit of analysis was largely the organization-environment relation. The origins of the research program entitled Industrial Democracy in Europe (IDE) date back to 1972 (IDE, 1981). Today, almost two decades later, the research is still continuing. In the early 1970s a group of some 25 social scientists from 12 countries agreed to conduct an international comparative, decentralized-collective research effort (Drenth & Wilpert, 1980) on industrial democracy in European countries and Israel. "Decentralized" means here the responsibility of each national team for funding, conducting, and interpreting national substudies. "Collective" refers to the whole international team's extensive sharing of joint theoretical and methodological developments, data ownership, and responsibility for the published international results. The central research question was: How are formal rules (e.g., laws/collective agreements—usually external to the organizational system) appropriated and enacted as lived practice of participation?

The essential theoretical model (see Figure 4) postulated a relation between formal rules for participation (Participative Structure, PS), the distribution of influence and participation in enterprises (Power, PO), organizational context factors (CON), and a set of social and attitudinal outcomes (O).

The field work was conducted in 1976-1977, and we employed a large variety of data collection techniques, including document analyses (laws, collective agreements, etc.), semistructured interviews of nearly 1,000 key informants, and a questionnaire survey among nearly 8,000 randomly selected employees of 134 enterprises that had been matched according to size and industrial sector.

Two of the main results are of particular interest in the present context:

1. Participation systems with relatively high degrees of formalization (e.g., Yugoslavia, Germany) were more positively evaluated by employees than were systems with lower levels of formalization.

2. The best predictors of *de facto* participation were indeed normative rules and regulations (PS) prescribing high levels of employee involvement and participation.

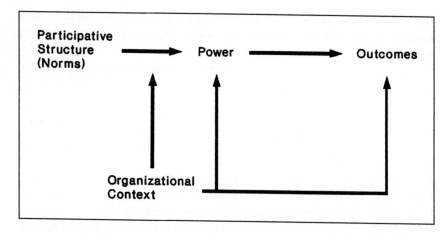

FIG. 4. Model IDE I

In other words, by systematically and (quasi-)objectively measuring certain features of the relevant environment *external* to the organization system and by relating these features to processes *internal* to the organization system, we believe we have taken an important methodological step forward in the analysis of organization-environment relations.

The environmental aspects we considered in this phase of the research could be called proximal because the rules and regulations we studied were more or less directly related to the types of organizations under study. But what about the more distal environmental aspects, such as the political climate in each of our countries, the economic situation, technological level of the economy? We were evidently not able to demonstrate their relation to organization systems. Furthermore, what about changes over time? Although the results of our study may be considered something like a base line influencing subsequent developments (Emery's "starting conditions"), it was still a cross-sectional study at one particular point in time.

This is where an idea emerged within the IDE team: Why not use the base line as a point of comparison to the situation ten years after and try once more to include systematically more distal environmental features? In 1983 it was decided to conduct a replication "ten years after" in the very same companies studied in the mid-1970s. Meanwhile drastic technological developments had affected organizations, unemployment figures had soared, and a number of countries had introduced new legislation relevant to participation. IDE phase II was on the road. What had started as cross-sectional research had turned into a longitudinal panel study of organizations, one that presented a unique opportunity to test the robustness of the findings ten years earlier and to introduce what could be important, more distal environmental facets not included in the first phase of the research. The model was slightly adjusted to serve our intentions (see Figure 5). Field work with a reduced set of instruments took place in 1986-1987. We had to cope with the usual set of problems encountered in any panel study, such as mortality. We had drop-outs in countries (only 10 of the original 12 national teams were able to join the effort); we had drop-outs in enterprises (some had gone bankrupt, others had been bought up by others); and the data documentation of IDE I was insufficient for a replication (genuine data archeology had to be practiced). Altogether, we were able to include replication data from 96 of the 134 original enterprises, and teams from Japan and Poland joined in as a bonus for the drop-out countries.

The international IDE team is presently preparing the final report of phases I and II on the basis of preliminary data analyses. Hence, again only preliminary results can be reported here.

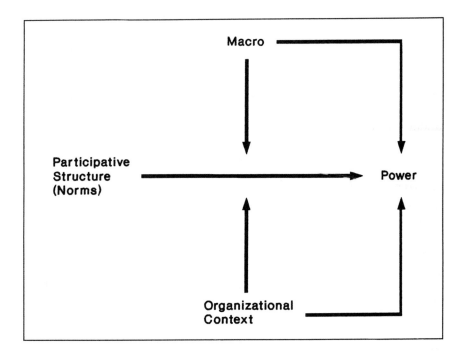

FIG. 5. Model IDE II

1. The best predictors of *de facto* participation at both measurement points (1977 and 1987-1988) were normative rules and regulations for high levels of participation. Thus, we were able to demonstrate that our essential model had a considerable degree of overall robustness.

2. In our comparison of IDE I/II, we used two macroenvironmental indices: growth in GNP over the ten-year period, and change in employment rates. Since both correlated highly, we continued our analyses on the basis of our labor-market indices. We were able to show that high unemployment rates (local labor-market conditions even more so than national indices) were strong predictors of significant reductions in the influence of workers and employee representatives as well as predictors of significant increases in the power of management.

In short, we were able to make use of base line data (starting conditions) based on a relatively robust research model and two measurement points in time. This data clarified an important aspect in the relation between environmental changes over time (labor market) and intraorganizational processes, in our case the relative influence that various groups within organizations have on decision outcomes.

Although far from offering a full-fledged and theoretically comprehensive integrative approach to environment-organization relations, we contend that the IDE research has gone quite far in that direction. However, we are also fully aware of our shortcomings in coping with the problems of measuring organization-environment relations under dynamically changing conditions.

Analysis Based on a Leading Part - Biblis A

Analysis based on the concept of a leading part reflects Emery's (1972) third approach to identifying genotypical conditions as being based on the analysis of a leading part, that is, an analysis based on the assumption that there is one major driving force or factor of influence. What is described here is a line of research less rigorous than that referred to in the previous two examples. It has to do more with the nature of conjectures and inferences developed from a specific case study. The case is an incident in the nuclear power plant Biblis A near Frankfurt on the Main. I am relying here exclusively on official government and company reports. The difficulty of obtaining precise information about what really went on inside the plant is part and parcel of the case. But the case illustrates, albeit speculatively and from a different methodological vantage point, problems of organization-environment relations similar to those identified in the larger studies reported above.

Briefly, what happened? After a routine shutdown of the Biblis A reactor for repair and maintenance, the reactor was restarted on the morning of December 16, 1987. A failure to close a valve separating the high pressurized (155 bars) primary loop from the residual heat removal system (32 bars) was signaled. The operator started the motor to close the valve, a maneuver that normally succeeds. The operator assumed the valve to be closed, although the signal remained, something that had occurred before. Neither the foreman on the shift nor the subsequent shift was informed. The third shift, working under heavy pressure to restart the reactor, neither noted the signal lamp nor followed prescribed routines to scrutinize the first shift's computer protocols. The third shift, by now more than 15 hours later, noted a curious increase in temperature in the primary loop, re-analyzed the situation, found the open valve, recognized the potential danger, and shut down the reactor again, which was by then operating at full power.

During this ongoing shutdown operation, the shift decided on a "last try" to close the valve by "tipping open" a second valve, the final one separating the inside and outside of the safety container separating the high pressure system from the lower pressure system. The rationale was that the opening of the second valve for a few seconds would produce a flow of steam that might close the critical valve. During seven seconds of this operation a jet of highly pressurized hot water entered the residual heat removal system, a 10- bar safety valve yielded, and radioactive steam reached the open air. Fortunately, the tipped-open valve closed again, but the first critical valve remained open. Shutdown operation continued. On December 21, 1987, the power company duly reported the incident to the control agency in charge, labeling the incident as "normal." Nine months later, in September 1988, governmental control agencies, after restudying the incident, reclassified it as "urgent." In December 1988 *Nucleonics Week* reported the incident, the German press picked it up, and a heated debate on the safety, reliability, and trustworthiness of nuclear energy production broke out in Germany, continuing for months. The company reacted by appointing additional reliability and safety officers and by introducing a reporting system on human error.

Why do I focus on this case, which seems to illustrate only problems of technical reliability and the error of an individual operator (who, incidentally, was publicly made culpable) or, at best, of an operator team? I do so precisely because the tendency is to reduce such incidents to technological shortcomings, individual slips, and negligence without considering their systemic imbeddedness. My own conjectures based on the case study (Wilpert & Klumb, 1991) suggest that systemic considerations would bring to the fore such factors as collective mental representations of workers that certain alarm signals are unimportant. Systemic considerations would highlight social dynamics such as group think; inadequate team compositions in terms of requisite competencies; the fact that peak work loads during restart operations make it difficult or impossible to follow prescribed procedures to the letter; economic pressures to get the reactor back to production; managerial reluctance to have to report yet another incident to interorganizational control agencies; and fear of public reaction. In other words, we would find much more than individual human error or technical failure within the system. We would find pathogens (Reason, 1990) much more upstream: in managerial perceptions and decisions, faulty design, and environmental pressures and constraints. And the leading part? In my mind it is technological development producing extremely complex sociotechnical high-risk systems, with their corresponding complex environmental links.

IMPLICATIONS FOR FUTURE RESEARCH

Recalling what was said in the two preceding sections, let me briefly pinpoint three directions that suggest themselves for future theorizing and research in the area of organization-environment relations. First, it seems desirable and necessary to develop a new paradigm for the study of organization-environment relations. Katz and Kahn (1978:122) have already lamented that the traditional conceptualization of organizational environments was an "arbitrary, organization-centered formulation, which involves a convenient and misleading implication. Everything in the universe, except for the organization under study, is treated under the single category of environment." In other words, environment becomes a residual category similar to culture in many comparative studies. And the list of characteristics outside the organization is virtually infinite. Rather, the focus, the unit of analysis, should become the interrelations of organizations and their relevant environments in a more holistic, inclusive perspective. What is called for is an attempt to address a task that is tantamount to the job taken on by the early Gestalt psychologists when, with a new paradigm, they began to analyze and understand psychological phenomena as intrinsically embedded in dynamic structures and characteristics of the psychological or social field. Organization-environment relations are still far from being understood in such terms. There is no ready-made recipe, and available studies are wanting in that respect. Conceptual ground work is needed. But the beginnings may be found in the works of such avant-garde researchers as Angyal, Emery, Lewin, and Trist.

A second desideratum is the further development and refinement of cross-level analysis. After all, how will it ever be possible to discover the genotypical factors and dynamics that have an impact on organization-environment relations if complex patterns of interrelations across various systems levels—from micro to macro and vice versa—are described only in dilettantish ways at best, if at all? Apart from the aforementioned theoretical groundwork, the development and refinement of cross-level analysis requires innovative methodological procedures and analytical tools hitherto largely absent.

Lastly, there is the time dimension. It is a matter of interactions; interactions are processes over time. The life process of organizations is an exchange relation with its environment over time. Hence, scientists will have a chance to make sense of the dynamically changing organization-environment relations only by systematically integrating the time dimension into their thinking and research. Why, then, is time consistently neglected?

This is, of course, a rhetorical question. For someone who has been involved in several studies in which the attempt was made to include the time dimension, the answer is clear: Longitudinal studies are costly in terms of energy, money, and motivation. My question is whether we researchers believe we have a better excuse than the proverbial drunkard who, having lost his watch in the dark alley, keeps looking for it under the street lamp because there that is where it is light?

NOTES

1. Members of the international research team are: P. Coetsier, R. Spoelders-Claes, and M. Holvost (Belgium); S. A. Ruiz Quintanilla, and B. Wilpert (Germany); I. Harpaz (Israel); J. Misumi (Japan); J. P. D. Drenth, E. Andriessen, and R. van der Kooij (Netherlands); F. A. Heller (Great Britain); G. W. England and W. T. Whitely (United States); and V. Antoncic (Yugoslavia).

I gratefully acknowledge the significant support of Ljeika Cuvaj in developing the paper and the constructive criticism of S. Antonio Ruiz Quintanilla and of H. Peter Dachler in improving it, without making any of them liable for its shortcomings.

REFERENCES

Ackoff, R. L., Emery, F. E. (1972). *On purposeful systems*. Chicago: Aldine-Atherton.

Aldrich, H. E. (1979). *Organizations and environments*. Englewood Cliffs, N.J.: Prentice Hall.

Angyal, A. (1941). *Foundations for a science of personality*. New York/London: Oxford University Press.

Ashby, W. R. (1956). *Introduction to cybernetics*. London: Chapman & Hall.

Ashby, W. R. (1960). *Design for a brain*. London: Chapman & Hall.

Babüroglu, O. N. (1988). The vertical environment: The fifth in the Emery-Trist levels of organizational environments. *Human Relations, 41*(3), 211-227.

Beer, M., & Walton A. E. (1987). Organization change and development. *Annual Review of Psychology, 38*, 339-367.

Bosetzky, H. (1970). *Grundzüge einer Soziologie der Industrieverwaltung*. Stuttgart: Enke.

Brunswik, E. (1934). *Wahrnehmung und Gegenstand. Grundlagen einer Psychologie vom Gegenstand her*. Leipzig: Deuticke.

Brunswik, E. (1939). The conceptual focus of some psychological systems. *Journal of Unified Science, 8*, 36-49.

Burns, T., & Stalker, G. M. (1961). *Management of innovation*. London: Tavistock.

Drenth, P. J. D., & Wilpert, B. (1980). The role of social contracts in cross-cultural research. *International Review of Applied Psychology, 29*(3), 293-305.

Drenth, P. J. D., Thierry, H., Willems, P. J., & de Wolff, C. J. (Eds.). (1991). *Handbook of work and organizational psychology*. Chichester: Wiley.

Emery, F. E. (1972). The next thirty years: Concepts, methods and anticipations. In F. E. Emery & E. L. Trist (Eds.), *Towards social ecology* (pp. 3-97). London: Plenum Press.

Emery, F. E., & Trist, E. L. (1965). The causal texture of organizational environments. *Human Relations, 18*(1), 21-32.

Emery, F. E., & Trist, E. L. (1977). *Towards a social ecology*. New York: Plenum Press.

England, G. W., & Wilpert, B. (1978). *The meaning of work, its nature and consequences—A comparative study in several European countries and the USA*. International Institute of Management, Wissenschaftszentrum Berlin. Discussion paper 78-9.

Graumann, C. F. (1974). Psychology and the world of things. *Journal of Phenomenological Psychology, 4*, 389-404.

Heider, F. (1977). *Psychologie der interpersonellen Beziehungen*. Stuttgart: Klett.

Heller, F. A. (1971). *Managerial decision making*. London: Tavistock.

Hill, W., Fehlbaum, R., & Ulrich, P. (1974/76). *Organisationslehre 1&2*. Bern: Haupt.

IDE (Industrial Democracy in Europe). (1981). *Industrial Democracy in Europe*. London: Oxford University Press.

Katz, D., & Kahn, R. L. (1978). *The social psychology of organizations* (2nd ed.). New York: John Wiley and Sons.

Köhler, W. (1938/1959). *The place of value in a world of facts*. New York: Meridian Books. (Original work published in 1938)

Kruse, L. (1978). Ökologische Perspektiven in der Allgemeinen Psychologie. In C. F. Graumann (Ed.), *Ökologische Perspektiven in der Psychologie* (pp. 98-104). Bern: Huber.

Lawrence, P., & Lorsch, J. (1967). *Organization and environment*. Cambridge, MA: Harvard University.

McCann, J. E., & Selsky, J. (1984). Hyperturbulence and the emergence of type 5 environments. Academy of Management Review, 9(3), 460-470.

Miller, D. (1988). Relating Porter's business strategies to environment and structure: Analysis and performance implications. *Academy of Management Journal, 31*(2), 280-308.

MOW (Meaning of Working International Research Team). (1987). *The meaning of working*. London: Academic Press.

Negandhi, A. R. (1969). A model for analyzing organizations in cross-cultural settings: A conceptual scheme and some research findings. In A. R. Negandhi (Ed.), Modern organization theory (pp. 285-312). Kent: Kent State University Press.

Nystrom, P. C., & Starbuck, W. H. (Eds.). (1981). *Handbook of organizational design* (Vols. 1 & 2). London: Oxford University Press.

Peiro, J. M. (1984). *Psicologia de la organizacion* (Vols. 1 & 2). Madrid: Universidad Nacional de Educacion a Distancia.

Pfeffer, J., & Salancik, G. R. (1978). *The external control of organizations: The resource dependence perspective*. New York: Harper and Row.

Porter, M. (1980). *Competitive strategy*. New York: Free Press.

Reason, J. (1990). *Human error*. London: Oxford University Press.

Roth, E. (Ed.) (1989). *Organisationspsychologie*. Göttingen: Hogrefe.

Saldern, M. (1987). *Sozialklima von Schulklassen*. Frankfurt on the Main: Peter Lang.

Starbuck, W. H. (1976). Organizations and their environments. In M. D. Dunette (Ed.), *Handbook of industrial and organizational psychology* (pp. 1069-1123). Chicago: Rand McNally.

Tolman, E. C., & Brunswik, E. (1935). The organism and the causal texture of the environment. *Psychological Review, 42*, 43-77.

Wilpert, G. (1990). *The "Aufhebung" (overcoming) of "A Philosophy of Doing Sociology"* (Unpublished Manuscript).

Wilpert, B., & Klumb, P. (1991). Störfall in Biblis A. Theoretische und pragmatische Überlegungen zu einer systemischen Betrachtung der Ereignisse. *Zeitschrift für Arbeitswissenschaft, 45*, 51-54.

Woodward, J. (1965). *Industrial organization: Theory and practice.* London: Oxford University Press.
Yasai-Ardekani, M. (1986). Structural adaptations to environments. *Academy of Management Review, 11*(1), 9-21.
Ziegler, H. (1970). *Strukturen und Prozesse der Autorität in der Unternehmung.* Stuttgart: Enke.

THE DIFFUSION OF ORGANIZATIONAL PSYCHOLOGY ACROSS CULTURAL BOUNDARIES: Issues and Problems

Organizer and Chair: S. Bochner, University of New South Wales, Australia

Contributors:

S. Bochner, University of New South Wales, Australia
The etics and the emics of work: An overview of the issues

S. Bochner, University of New South Wales, Australia
Summing up and implications for action

V. J. Callan, University of Queensland, Australia
Organisations and communication: Guidelines for other countries

K. Leung, Chinese University of Hong Kong, Hong Kong
A pan-cultural framework of conflict management

P. B. Smith, University of Sussex, U.K.
Cultural bias and theories of leadership: A suitable case for treatment

C. Taylor, W. Lonner, Western Washington University, U.S.A.
Methodological and conceptual problems in extending content of western industrial/organizational psychology to other cultures

The theme of this symposium was the cross-cultural transferability of the ideas, practices, and procedures of organizational psychology. It soon became obvious that diffusion rather than transfer would be a more appropriate term for the process. Transfer implies at least some two-way traffic, whereas, with perhaps a few exceptions, the flow has been predominantly one way, from west to east. More specifically, the models, theories, approaches, procedures, and solutions generated by American, British, and European organizational psychologists have found their way into the applied psychology of countries throughout the world (Blowers & Turtle, 1987; Melikian, 1984), with profound consequences for the development of the discipline in these places.

World-wide, research and practice in industrial/organizational (I/O) psychology tends to be conducted by western or western-trained psychologists, pursuing goals and guided, or at least influenced by, assumptions, procedures, and textbooks that embody the western cultural perspective of organizational behavior and the meaning of work (Azuma, 1984; Kiggundu, 1986). Taking this empirical fact as the point of departure, the contributors discussed the reasons for the diffusion, its consequences for theory and practice in the various areas of applied psychology both within and across cultures, and what future action might be taken to remedy some of the shortcomings that were identified in the discussion.

In his introduction to the symposium, Bochner pointed out that modern psychology in general and applied psychology in particular are a western invention, and a relatively recent one at that. To show how recent, he recalled speaking with and learning from senior, but still active, scholars such as Otto Klineberg and Solomon Asch, who themselves had been the students or the pioneers of modern psychology, by this count making the discipline a mere three or four generations old. It is thus even more remarkable that this predominantly western cultural manifestation has so captured the minds (Alatas, 1975) of non-western practitioners, together with the belief that this body of knowledge and its practices will readily transfer across cultural boundaries. For instance, it is not uncommon to find management systems that have been designed in the head offices of western multinational companies, installed with only minor modifications in their subsidiaries in other countries, presumably on the grounds that what was effective in Detroit would also work in Kuala Lumpur or Melbourne.

Against this background, the theme of the symposium was to explore which aspects of the current, western-based theories and their associated practices could be regarded as universal, that is, as being relevant to all or most organizational settings in the world, and to what extent there exist significant culturally determined variations of work systems, where the western models and their procedure would have to be modified and adapted to fit into local conditions. The issue of the two-way traffic of ideas also exercised the minds of all of the speakers.

There is considerable empirical evidence that work-related values and the meaning of work vary significantly across cultures (Hofstede, 1980; Triandis, Bontempo, Villareal, Asai, & Lucca, 1988). For instance, societies differ in the extent to which they value individualistic or collective effort and achievement, and the extent to which they distinguish and maintain social distance between superiors and subordinates. These values have implications for setting up individually or group-based incentives and decision-making systems, steep or flat supervision hierarchies, and all the other features of the psychological contracts that regulate behavior in organizations. This, in turn, implies that the cross-cultural transfer of I/O ideas will be a function of the similarity between the donor and receiving societies.

A useful method for examining cross-cultural similarities and differences is to invoke the emic-etic distinction (Lonner & Berry, 1986), which makes explicit that most human attributes have two characteristics; a universal, pancultural or etic component, and a culture-specific or emic component that differentially distinguishes particular cultures or groups. Another useful construct is to think of work as a socio-technical production system (Emery, 1969) that converts energy and materials into goods and services. The technical system consists of the machines, assembly lines, screwdrivers, fishing nets, blackboards—the hardware. The social system consists of the human beings in specialized roles with different skills, cooperatively interacting with each other and their machines to produce some intended output. All societies have such sociotechnical production systems, and, hence, work defined as the throughput in these systems is an etic—a universal process and a central human activity. But the way in which the work is structured and organized can be thought of as a cultural manifestation reflecting a society's core values. There exist many emic, that is culturally specific, variations of work patterns, particularly in societies' social systems. The problem of transferability can therefore be reduced to the potential mismatch between an etic, universal I/O psychology, and the many emic, culturally specific variations that characterize particular production systems.

However, translating these ideas into practice, defined as both research and application, has many pitfalls. In his contribution, Lonner provided what he called a survival kit for those engaged in cross-cultural I/O work, by which he meant the basic methodological and conceptual requirements that have to be satisfied. He identified two core issues; the problem of achieving equivalence between whatever group of phenomena were being compared, and the associated problem of sampling, of selecting appropriate groups or phenomena for comparison. Comparability depends on establishing functional, conceptual, and metric equivalence, and there is a fierce debate on how each of these can be achieved. For instance, is an automobile assembly line or a school in Kyoto functionally and conceptually equivalent to a car factory or school in Sydney? Metric equivalence refers to the measurement instruments used to collect and quantify the data. Do the items in a job-satisfaction questionnaire have the same connotations in Japanese as they do in English, even if they are linguistically equivalent? Sampling refers to who or what should be included in the study, why a particular group or activity has been selected for inclusion, and whether this process contributes to the various forms of equivalence required. An excellent discussion of these issues appears in Lonner and Berry (1986).

Taylor listed the traditional content areas of I/O Psychology, including personnel selection and training, job performance and evaluation, worker motivation and job satisfaction, leadership and group dynamics, and organizational development and change. He then deconstructed each of these areas into their constituent parts, and speculated about which aspects might and which might not transfer. For example, in the area of job satisfaction, Taylor suggested that strategies based on the principle of reinforcement, self-esteem, need achievement, and goal setting would transfer more readily than strategies based on the two-factor (Herzberg) or hierarchy of needs (Maslow) theories. The usefulness of such an approach is that it can lead to systematic theory-driven research as to which particular I/O features may or may not transfer and under what conditions of cultural similarity-dissimilarity.

In their papers, Bochner, Lonner, and Taylor dealt with general conceptual. methodological, and content matters. The next three speakers concentrated on more specific topics. Smith noted that traditional western theories of leadership are all to some extent based on the implicit behaviorist idea that leaders provide stimuli to which subordinates respond. Smith then reviewed the literature that showed that such a conceptual framework does not comfortably fit the case even in western studies of leadership. The reason, according to Smith, is that the western construction of leadership is based on an assumed individualist orientation to work, whereas even in the United States the work ethic is more collectivist than is generally acknowledged. Consequently, western leadership theory and practice could benefit from nonwestern ideas and concepts, which are more collectivist in their orientation. Finally, in terms of the conceptual framework proposed in the introduction to the symposium, a useful distinction can be drawn between the leadership *function* as an etic, and leadership *behavior* as an emic. An excellent recent summary of Smith's work appears in Smith, Misumi, Tayeb, Peterson, and Bond (1989).

Leung's topic was conflict management. The theories and data in this area originate in North America and Europe and transfer poorly because conflict and its resolution are closely linked to a society's core values, or in terms of the model used in this paper, have a high emic component. Furthermore, echoing earlier speakers, Leung noted that current western-based theories of conflict management do not work all that well even in their cultures of origin. He also drew a distinction between the American emphasis on achieving some intended outcome as the purpose of conflict management, as distinct from regarding the process of bargaining as a useful activity in its own right. Concentrating on process could have long-term consequences, such as the establishment of mutual trust and regard, unlike the emphasis on outcome, which may produce immediate results such as resolving a strike but have no impact on improving interpersonal relations and, hence, not resolve the underlying causes of the dispute. Finally, the point was made again that western constructions of conflict and its management might benefit from nonwestern inputs.

Callan's topic was communication in organizations, in particular between superiors and subordinates, an etic or universal aspect of all organizations, or as Callan put it, the water in which the fish swim. However, communication styles differ across cultures, and, more interestingly, the same style of communication may serve different functions in different cultures. For instance, in individualist societies open communication may give subordinates opportunities to contribute to the decision-making process, whereas in collectivist societies it may be used to reduce uncertainty. More generally, there exist cross-cultural differences in how people in organizations use communication to provide information, issue instructions, and establish working relations. As work settings become increasingly more diverse culturally, there will be a corresponding increase in on-the-job interactions between members of different cultures, and Callan drew attention to the usefulness of training such workers in culturally relevant social skills.

In summary, transferability was discussed within a theoretical framework explicitly recognizing that most organizational phenomena have two characteristics; a universal (etic) component that can be found in most societies, and a culturally distinctive (emic) component which reflects the core values of the society where the organization is located. Because these emic aspects of organizations are culture bound, they have to be taken into account in any consideration of transferability, which in practice means identifying and sorting out the emics from the etics and adapting the etic theories and procedures to make them more emically sensitive and appropriate. Another point that clearly emerged was that the traffic flow of ideas should become two-way because many western procedures and ideas would be enriched by nonwestern theoretical models of organizational behavior.

REFERENCES

Alatas, S. H. (1975). The captive mind and creative development. *International Social Science Journal, 27,* 631-700.

Azuma, H. (1984). Psychology in a non-Western country. *International Journal of Psychology, 19,* 45-55.

Blowers, G. H., & Turtle, A. M. (Eds.). (1987). *Psychology moving East: The status of western psychology in Asia and Oceania.* Sydney: Sydney University Press.

Emery, F. E. (Ed.). (1969). *Systems thinking.* Harmondsworth: Penguin.

Hofstede, G. (1980). *Culture's consequences: International differences in work-related values.* Beverly Hills. CA: Sage.

Kiggundu, M. N. (1986). Limitations to the application of sociotechnical systems in developing countries. *Journal of Applied Behavioral Science, 22,* 341-353.

Lonner, W. J., & Berry, J. W. (Eds.). (1986) *Field methods in cross-cultural research.* London: Sage.

Melikian, L. H. (1984). The transfer of psychological knowledge to the Third World countries and its impact on development: The case of five Arab Gulf oil-producing states. *International Journal of Psychology, 19,* 65-77.

Smith, P. B., Misumi. J., Tayeb, M., Peterson, M., & Bond, M. (1989). On the generality of leadership style measures across cultures. *Journal of Occupational Psychology, 54,* 97-109.

Triandis, H. C., Bontempo, R., Villareal, M. J., Asai, M., & Lucca, N. (1988). Individualism and collectivism: Cross-cultural perspectives on self-ingroup relationships. *Journal of Personality and Social Psychology, 54,* 323-338.

ESTABLISHING A GLOBAL VIEW OF LEADERSHIP:
East Meets West

Organizer & Chair:
R. Ayman, Illinois Institute of Technology, Chicago, U.S.A.

Contributors:

B. J. Avolio, State University of New York, U.S.A.
J. M. Howell, University of Western Ontario, Canada
Matching the leader-follower personality: The moderating effects on culture and performance

J. A. Conger, R. N. Kanungo, McGill University, Canada
The dawning of a new age of leadership theory: The charismatic leader

K. Korabik, University of Guelph, Canada
R. Ayman, Illinois Institute of Technology, U.S.A.
Gender and leadership: An acculturation model

J. Misumi, K. Maiya, Nara University, Japan
Y. Arima, Osaka University, Japan
M. Hafsi, Nara University, Japan
Recent developments in Leadership PM Theory

J. B. P. Sinha, A. N. S. Institute of Social Studies, India
The nurturant task style of leadership

F. J. Yammarino, D. A. Waldman, State University of New York, U.S.A.
A multiple levels perspective of leadership theory and research

Discussants: B. M. Bass, State University of New York, U.S.A.
M. M. Chemers, Claremont McKenna College, U.S.A.

Leadership has been of interest across the globe for centuries. In the East, in 5000 B.C. Confucius directed the village headmen in appropriate conduct of a leader. In the Middle East, in the 7th century Unsur Almaali wrote the *Qabus-nameh* advising the kings. In Europe, in the 16th century, Machiavelli wrote *The Prince*, advising the rulers of Europe. In modern times models and theories of leadership have evolved through scientific investigations using different methodologies and perspectives and being mostly restricted to certain geographical areas. However, there has not been major effort in integrating these findings over different cultural boundaries. In recent years, a model demonstrating the role of culture as an integral part of leadership process and patterns has emerged (Chemers, 1983). Also, Smith and Peterson (1988) have accumulated a volume of international efforts made in leadership research.

In the current symposium, researchers from North America provided the main concerns and perspectives that are dominant in leadership research as the twentieth century comes to a close. Bass reviewed the historical perspective of cross-cultural research. Papers by Yammarino and Waldman, and Avolio and Howell focused on methodological issues. Yammarino and Waldman presented a study utilizing the "varient approach," that is, variable and entities or level of analysis (Dansereau, Alutto, & Yammarino, 1984). Specifically, each view of leadership is reconceptualized in terms of its variables and multiple levels of analysis—individual difference, dyadic relations, and group processes. A statistical procedure that specifically tests for multiple-level effects, within and between analyses was introduced to assess the three alternatives mentioned above.

In Avolio and Howell's paper, a new approach to the study of leadership was introduced. They assessed the similarity of 76 leaders and their followers ($n = 237$) from a large Canadian financial institution on the locus of control (Rotter, 1966) trait. The result of the study showed that leader/follower level of congruence moderated the relation between the leader's perceived behavior and the subordinate's satisfaction and unit performance.

The two other North American papers represented new perspective and conceptual approaches. Conger and Kanungo presented their revised approach to charismatic leadership (Conger & Kanungo, 1988). They demonstrated historical evidence of its significance and provided empirical evidence using perception of the leader's charismatic behavior (Conger & Kanungo, 1988) in support of the effectiveness of it.

Korabik and Ayman presented a modified version of Berry's (1990) acculturation model (Ayman, 1989) to portray women's role both in positions of leadership (i.e., manager) and in leadership research. Through the review of the literature, they provided evidence that women leaders have been seen as being totally different from men—feminine leadership (Carroll, 1984). Yet reviewing the studies since the 1970s, they reported evidence that women leaders have been well assimilated into the male's style of leadership (Dobbins & Platz, 1986). However, there is evidence that this assimilation of women in leadership positions has had side effects of identity crisis (Buono & Kamm, 1983) and sense of marginality (Symons, 1986). Korabik and Ayman suggested a need to move towards an integrative approach where women and femininity are no longer on the periphery of leadership research. They also recommended that this process of integration in the inclusion of women in management will allow them to share the unique characteristics of their experiences.

From the east, two major research approaches were represented by Misumi, Kiyoshi, Arima, and Hafsi from Japan and by Sinha from India. Misumi and his colleagues provided an overview of a long line of research on the PM model of leadership, which was developed and validated initially in Japan and recently expanded to other countries (Smith & Peterson, 1988). The model brings a new perspective to the relationship between production (P), that is, task behaviors and maintenance (M), that is, considerate behaviors. Both the ratio of presence and absence of the two perceived behaviors and the specificity of the setting or line of work is an integral part of the model.

Sinha reviewed the research that has been based on a measure he developed in India. The measure not only represents leadership behavioral categories (i.e., considerate and structuring) present in other countries, it also represent the uniqueness of that country. His measure acknowledges a unique leadership style; task-nurturance. This style is represented in the measure by several contingency items that are valid in predicting effective leaders in India and in some other countries.

As the final discussant, Chemers of the United States presented a model of leadership processes that gives an important theoretical role to cultural and individual differences. Drawing on the diverse perspectives presented in the symposium, Chemers argued that culture influences leadership perceptions and prototypes, leader and follower expectations and needs, and behavioral actions and reactions. He also acknowledged the value of multilevel designs and methods of analysis. By juxtaposing theoretical approaches, methodological orientations, and cultural contexts, this globally oriented symposium may help to move the field of leadership towards more general and universal understanding.

REFERENCES

Ayman, R. (1989, August). *Women in management: A cultural integration approach*. Paper presented at the annual meeting of Academy of Management, Anaheim, CA.

Berry, J. W. (1990). Psychology of Acculturation: Understanding individuals moving between cultures. In R. W. Brislin (Ed.), *Applied Cross-cultural Psychology* (pp. 232-253). London: Sage.

Buono, A. F., & Kamm, J. B. (1983). Marginality and the organizational socialization of female managers. *Human Relation, 36*, 1125-1140.

Carroll, S. J. (1984). Feminist scholarship on political leadership. In B. Kellerman (Ed.), *Leadership: Multidisciplinary perspectives*. Englewood Cliffs, NJ: Prentice Hall.

Chemers, M. M. (1983). Leadership theory and research: A systems-process integration. In P. B. Paulus (Ed.), *Basic group processes*. New York: Springer.

Conger, J. A., Kanungo, R.N. (1988). *Charismatic leadership*. San Francisco, CA: Jossey Bass.

Dansereau, F., Alutto, J. A., & Yammarino, F. J. (1984). *Theory testing in organizational behavior: The varient approach*. Engelwood Cliffs, NJ: Prentice-Hall.

Dobbins, G. H., & Platz, 5. J. (1986). Sex differences in leadership: How real are they? *Academy of Management Review, 11*, 118-127.

Rotter, J. B. (1966). Generalized expectancies for internal versus external control of reinforcement. *Psychological Monographs, 80* (1, Whole No. 609).

Smith, P. B. & Peterson, M. F. (1988). *Leadership, organizations and culture*. London: Sage.

Symons, G. L. (1986). Coping with the corporate tribe: How women in different cultures experience the managerial role. *Journal of Management, 12*, 379-389.

THE MEANING OF WORKING: STATE OF THE ART AND FUTURE RESEARCH METHODS

Organizer & Chair: S. A. Ruiz Quintanilla, University of Technology Berlin, FRG

Contributors:

P. J. D. Drenth, Free University Amsterdam, Netherlands
Work meanings: The psychological view

G. W. England, University of Oklahoma, U.S.A.
J. Misumi, Nara University, Japan
The Meaning of Working II: Questions and answers from national restudies

F. Heller, Tavistock Institute of Human Relations, U.K.
The meaning of work and other activity

S. A. Ruiz Quintanilla, University of Technology Berlin, FRG
The meaning of working I: Results from a cross sectional study

W. T. Whitely, University of Oklahoma, U.S.A.
Antecedents and outcomes of meaning of working patterns

H. C. Triandis, University of Illinois, U.S.A.
Methodological issues in the study of the Meaning of Work

Panel discussion chair: B. Wilpert, University of Technology Berlin, FRG

This symposium aimed at integrating different strands of knowledge in order to improve understanding of how cultural, societal, group, and individual factors shape what work has meant, means, and is going to mean in future societies. Concepts and empirical data from the Meaning of Working-study (MOW, 1987, an eight country comparison of work values) and from complementary follow-up studies served as the "red thread" throughout the symposium. The speakers employed psychological, sociological, historical, and cross-cultural viewpoints to discuss the concepts utilized and empirical results derived.

For a more and elaborate treatment of the main ideas covered in the following summary, I recommend consulting a special issue (Ruiz Quintanilla, 1991), in which most of the speakers elaborate their views.

The first speaker, Pieter J. D. Drenth (Free University Amsterdam, Netherlands), distinguished three approaches to studying the meaning of work. First, the meaning of the word "work" itself is analyzed (conceptual approach). Second, the meaning that work has for individuals is analyzed (empirical semantic approach). Third, developments in work value throughout the individual's lifetime is focused on (developmental approach). When speaking about the conceptual approach, Drenth discussed the usefulness, completeness, and coherence of different definitions of "work," ranging from economic ones (paid activity) to Arendt's (1988) distinction between work and labor. He concluded by naming two crucial elements of work—that it produces something useful or valuable (instrumental side) and that work is a fundamental human function or activity (work makes humans human). A discussion of the changes in the meanings of work in different historical and cultural settings demonstrates the diversity of work contents (tasks) called work and evaluative feelings (good versus evil) related to work or used to legitimize its status quo.

What do people mean by the word "work"? Results from MOW (1987) showed that the most frequent response is "getting money for it." Grouping the meanings led to four clusters focused around concrete, social, duty, and burden aspects of work. In none of the countries studied were age, gender and the central concepts of the meaning of work (MOW, 1987) strongly related to these clusters of meaning. Related factors were education (higher education, higher duty, less social cluster) and country (with 50% of the Japanese and German respondents in the concrete cluster). Thus, Drenth concluded that what people mean by using the word "work" is mainly influenced by country-specific (cultural) and educational factors, and less a function of age, sex, work centrality, or societal norms. Finally, Drenth focused on the origin and development of work values during the lifespan of individuals. He discussed psychological (stability versus fluctuation of individual values) and sociological (values as part of the larger societal system) approaches. He suggested following what he terms an interactive approach, by which one tries to avoid the one-sidedness of stability or modification assumptions as well as the restrictiveness of sociological views.

Frank Heller (Tavistock Institute London, U.K.) suggested that one should widen the viewpoint and use "activity" as a unit of analysis instead of work. Work and its relations to the broader concept of *activity* should facilitate an understanding of attitudes and behavioral changes over time. A look at main differences in work centrality between countries and target groups as studied by MOW (1987) shows that the groups with the highest degree of self-determination are the ones with the highest work centrality. Heller concluded that people value activities that show a certain pattern of characteristics, regardless of whether they are called work or nonwork.

What was Heller's opinion about what the future might bring? According to him, paid activities (or work) will take up less time and decrease in importance. Also, the span between education and retirement will shorten, with longer educational times and earlier retirement, increasing holidays and fewer working hours. Finally, while life expectancy is growing, more time will be spent with nonwork activities.

S. Antonio Ruiz Quintanilla's (Technical University of Berlin, FRG, and Cornell University, New York, USA) preliminary point was the "end of a working society" in industrialized countries as claimed by a diversity of authors. After discussing the literature, he suggested a schema that allows one to categorize the hypotheses mentioned and the results presented. He distinguished the hypotheses and results according to degree of change, mode of change, and dimensions of change involved. Utilizing two representative labor-force samples that explored the Meaning of Working in 1982 and 1990 in the Federal Republic of Germany, he showed that changes in the work values held by the public, needed to be described in more than one dimension (work centrality, work goals, societal norms). Given the resulting multidimensional picture, they are better described as "moderate," not "dramatic."

Jyuyi Misumi (Nara University, Japan) explained how today's Japanese work attitudes can be explained in part by historical roots. Examples included the necessity of farming for survival combined with the understanding of nature as something humans should be submissive to and not try to conquer. Further, Misumi mentioned Japanese understanding of farming as a Buddhist practice and called attention to the scarcity of land, which led to an ideology of not "wasting" any. There is a variety of other work-emphasizing statements to be found among various Japanese religious philosophers. Still, these historical roots do not explain why work centrality among Japanese and Western young people just leaving school has a similary low value in all countries. Differences between Japan and the West are established after the respondents become members of a work organization. Thus, the meanings of work to young Japanese who have just graduated from high school and university increases after a relative short period of company training. This training, which most first-time employed Japanese undergo, might be as long as 9 months and includes motivational and skill-related components. Misumi conducted a study to explore his hypothesis that this company training for newly-recruited employees serves to reinforce and activate the work values. His study was a panel survey on young Japanese prior to and after completion of company training. It estimates the effect training has on work centrality. Comparison of pre-training values and post-training values showed an increase in the trainees' work centrality and importance of work. From this Misumi inferred that international differences in work values might in fact not be deeply culturally rooted in the societal value system but better explained as a result of social group norms active in Japanese work organizations; in that case, international differences in work values would be a sociopsychological phenomenon. Misumi names situational aspects as more important than cultural values. He mentioned the broader concept of work in Japan, which includes other social activities not included in Western countries, and the "Life Time Employment system," which takes charge of the employee for his or her whole working life.

George W. England (University of Oklahoma, Norman, USA) compared the data from a representative national survey of the labor force in the United States in 1982 (MOW, 1987) to the data from a survey conducted 7 years later in 1989. The main results can be summarized as follows: Because there have been no significant changes in the composition of the labor force, changes found in the meaning of work cannot be blamed on sampling errors. They do in fact, reflect "true" individual changes. Looking at the work goals, one finds that economic goals have become more important in the United States, and comfort goals have become less important. The level of importance attached to work has declined. People's definition of work has also changed significantly. Personal rationales for working (e.g. if it belongs to your tasks), as compared to collective ones (e.g., if you do it to contribute to society), have become more prominent. Terms for describing work put less emphasis on affective components and more on defining work in terms of constraints and controls. Finally, although there were some differences on the single-item level, overall the view of how the work force saw its working rights, as compared to how it saw its duties, showed no differences at the end of the seven-year period. England saw this result as indicating negative developments from both the perspective of individuals and the organizational viewpoint.

William Whitely (University of Oklahoma, Norman, USA) provided data from a case study utilizing cluster analysis as a methodological approach. The clusters were defined in terms of the MOW measures on work centrality, obligation norms, entitlement norms, expressive orientation, and economic orientation. Then he explored the relations between this MOW pattern and outcomes not included in the original MOW study, relations such as psychological well-being, commitment, and performance measures. The main results demonstrated the influence of factors like education and training, as well as gender, on MOW patterns. On the other hand, MOW pattern membership allowed the prediction of job satisfaction, emotional responses, psychological well-being, and commitment toward work, whereas no direct relation with job performance ratings was found.

Finally, Harry C. Triandis (University of Illinois, Champaign, USA) discussed methodological issues involved in the research approach present in this symposium. His remarks about how to improve our insight into the meaning of work in different cultural settings led to a final panel discussion that included questions from the floor. This discussion, which was led by Bernhard Wilpert (Technical University of Berlin, FRG) highlighted the importance of future research in this area. Among the mentioned tasks to be undertaken were the expansion of knowledge about the meaning of working in different cultures; the improvement in the understanding of relations between the meaning of work and historical, economic, and societal level data; and the establishment of a link between the meaning of work and psychological and behavioral outcomes.

REFERENCES

Arendt, H. (1988). *The Human Condition*. Chicago: University of Chicago Press.

MOW International Research Team (1987). *The Meaning of Working*. London: Academic Press.

Ruiz Quintanilla, S. A. (Ed.).(1991). Work Centrality and Related Work Meanings. *European Work and Organizational Psychologist, 1,* 2/3.

INFLUENCE PROCESSES, DECISION-MAKING, AND MANAGING EVENTS

Organizer and Chair: M. F. Peterson, Texas Tech University, U.S.A.

Contributors:

M. F. Peterson, T. K. Peng, Texas Tech University, U.S.A.
T. Kaji, International Christian University, Japan
Departmental decision-making as a contingency affecting the function of leadership in the U.S. and Japan

P. B. Smith, University of Sussex, U.K.
M. F. Peterson, Texas Tech University, U.S.A.
Z. M. Wang, Hangzhou University, China
Leadership as a management of a role conflict

T. Sugiman, Kyoto University, Japan
T. Atsumi, University of Michigan, U.S.A.
Effect of the amount of interpersonal influence during group work on the persistance of self-involvement in the task

The topic of the symposium was field research in which social influence and decision-making are analyzed. The symposium was designed to consider the areas of complementarity in a sampling of the varied theoretical perspectives and research approaches to the analysis of influence and decision making.

A field experiment on the effects of interpersonal influence in dyads on dyad members' task persistence was reported by Sugiman and Atsumi. The study draws attention to the importance of interpersonal influence not only on discrete, time-bounded choices and actions, but even more importantly on persistence over time outside the context of the direct face-to-face interaction where the influence process began. The study was conducted in the subway system of Osaka city in Japan. Subjects were asked to observe sightseeing spots from the windows of the subway train on the Osaka loop line and to reach a final choice about the sightseeing spot that best represents Osaka.

Measurements of interpersonal influence were based on changes in preference for each spot before, compared to after, interactions with partners. Persistence was measured by whether subjects continued to voluntarily send back three follow-up postcards requested, but not required, by the experimenter for up to two weeks after the paid experimental task was over. The results indicated that those subjects who either received or exerted more influence persisted more than did other subjects. Thus, even when people are not required to reach a consensus, the degree of influence they exert on one another's preferences affects the degree of task persistence. The results have implications for influence processes where task persistence is desirable such as those between doctor and patient, and between teacher and student.

The other papers presented some of the theoretical background and findings from two studies reflecting an "event management" perspective on decision-making and leadership. A paper by Peterson and Peng described a project concerning the sources that city managers use to handle various specific event situations. The sources used by senior local government managers have the potential to affect the relation between leadership from middle-level managers and the performance of supervisory and professional staff. Questionnaire data from senior managers, middle managers, and supervisory and professional staff in three U.S. local governments were analyzed. Sources that senior managers report having used for handling three event situations provided the basis for clustering departments into three sets of decision-making types. Performance evaluations provided by middle managers of the supervisory and professional staff who report to them were used to form four criterion measures. Measures of five aspects of middle manager leadership based on reports by these same subordinates were used as predictors.

Hierarchical regressions showed main effects of the leadership variables for three criteria, and a smaller number of decision type main effects and leadership X decision type interactions. The report illustrates ways in which patterns of influence at senior levels of organizations can affect the impact of leadership styles at lower levels.

A paper by Smith, Peterson, and Wang addressed some similar event management notions. The analyses reported were based on data obtained from managers and manager trainees regarding the relation of source used to decision performance in broader samples within the U.K., The United States, and China. In contrast to the analysis of leadership styles, the paper indicated some of the advantages of studying leadership processes in a wider cultural context. Leaders are viewed as encountering a steady stream of organizational events that present a recurring set of dilemmas. Leaders must implicitly or explicitly select which sources of information and support to rely on in interpreting and responding to events. The problem of reconciling the perspectives represented by different sources is simultaneously a problem of leadership, decision-making, and managing role conflict.

Although the Chinese data were limited, an analysis plan was described and examples comparing the relative emphasis on different sources in the three countries were provided. More importantly, instances were described where correlations between the extent to which each source is relied upon and reported role conflict, role ambiguity, and decision quality were found to vary by type of event and by country. From the standpoint of individualism and collectivism, a recurring theme in the conference, different types of events and different cultural contexts provide varying requirements for individual and collective action.

Jorge Jesuino commented on the utility of employing macro-level societal concepts, particularly global notions of individual-collectivism and power distance, to explain patterns of event management. He suggested that a careful examination of such global notions supports the need to examine details about the way particular events are handled. In the case of Portugal, Prof. Jesuino indicated that the feeling of the local social science community is that Portuguese collectivism does not imply the strong reciprocation of loyalty for protection of the in-group that seems to characterize Chinese and Japanese collectivism. Consequently, patterns in the way Portuguese handle work events may vary markedly from the patterns in other countries, which research to date suggests may be similar to Portugal on variables like collectivism. He argued for caution in trying to link the microlevel analysis of events with the macrolevel analysis of society, especially when simple dimensions like individualism-collectivism are used.

AUTONOMY AND CONTROL IN COMPLEX ORGANIZATIONS: The Dilemma of Centralization versus Delegation

Organizer & Chair: P. J. D. Drenth,
Vrije Universiteit Amsterdam, Netherlands

Contributors:

P. J. D. Drenth, Vrije Universiteit Amsterdam, Netherlands
Introduction

P. Coetsier, State University of Gent, Belgium
Professionals in large profit organizations: A case study

P. J. D. Drenth, Vrije Universiteit Amsterdam, Netherlands
Autonomy and control in universities

F. A. Heller, Tavistock Institute, U. K.
An airport as a decentralized bureaucracy

J. Pool, Vrije Universiteit Amsterdam, Netherlands
Hospital management: Intergrating the dual hierarchy?

Discussant: C. de Wolff, University Nijmegen, Netherlands

The organization and management structure developed some decades ago emphasized concentration of expertise, power, and decision-making and rather substantial homogeneous systems. It was felt that this was the best way to meet the requirements of growth and development in a prosperous and growing economy.

In recent years a number of important changes have challenged the management structure of the 1960s and 1970s. There is a rapidly changing market; increasing competition with a particular emphasis on the quality of the product or service; a rapidly developing information and communication technology, and revolutionary change and development in technology, automation, and robotization, replacing old tasks with new ones and requiring new job skills and abilities. Many of these changes will continue to be relevant in the coming decade as well.

A crossing point seems to have been reached right now. Some observers have stated that, in view of the increasing turbulence and complexity of the market, the social/legal environment, and changing expectations of both employees and customers, organizations should decentralize their responsibilities and competencies and follow the adage: "small is beautiful." Others have emphasized the increasing complexity of the economic and monetary environment and the need for a more comprehensive and integrated approach, requiring a stronger centralized system of decision-making and a more integrative monetary strategy. They follow the adage: "Big is powerful."

Here is the dilemma in a nutshell: Should organizations centralize or decentralize in order to meet the challenges of the more complex and turbulent environment of the future? This issue was discussed during the symposium using examples from various types of organization.

Coetsier described a case study in a large company where production had stagnated and communication between the center of decision-making and the various departments had become deficient. He has developed an action research program in which more autonomy was given to the different departments (e.g., finance, personnel, operations). The study showed that a reasonable delegation of decision-making power can be an effective means towards better communication and control of production processes, in industrial organizations.

In a study of the university, as an example of a professional organization, Drenth concluded that in university management the following principles should be followed:

1. Relative autonomy of the faculties and delegation of decisions to (groups of) teachers and researchers wherever possible. This pertains in particular to the content of teaching and research. This principle runs

counter to the simple structure model and to the bureaucratic model in which the central control of complex processes is realized through a high degree of standardization and formalization of procedures.

2. Integration and adherence to a common cause and the mission of the university. The definition of such a purpose should take place through democratic processes of consultations and rational discussions. Commitment to and identification with this common objective should be promoted by means appropriate to professional organizations: convincing, rational discussions, and intrinsic motivation. This principle runs counter to the classical model of the collegial organization and to the more modern version of a loosely coupled network.

This philosophy can be worked out with respect to the question of quality control and improvement of education within the faculties. As an illustration, the system of internal evaluation developed at the Vrije Universiteit in Amsterdam was discussed.

Following the university philosophy, in which the primary responsibility for control and improvement of education lies within the individual faculties, the system emphasizes that faculties are responsible for collecting information, drawing conclusions, and taking proper action. The executive board of the university stimulates, signals, and asks for explanations if necessary, but real improvement emanates from the faculties.

Another type of work organization was analyzed by Heller. A three-year research study of Stansted, London's third airport, was designed to study organizational decision-making procedures in semi-autonomous groups. The management at Stansted operated through 9 semi-autonomous organizations such as baggage-handling, aircraft-servicing, and security. Each of these mini-organizations had a separate contract with the airport lasting from 2 to 5 years, and most of them had their own management structures outside the airport.

Although airport decision-making is complex and must be ready to deal with the unpredictable, the semi-autonomous structures operated harmoniously and efficiently.

The findings (based on quantitative measures supplemented by ethnographic longitudinal data) showed that: 1. decentralized semi-autonomous structures can be effective and tend to be associated with high utilization of existing human skills; and 2. the limitations of autonomy, that is to say, the meaning of the term "semi" has to be carefully described, and this meaning has to be shared between the airport managers and the semi-autonomous group.

Based on measurements on 108 decision issues, the statistical findings of this longitudinal study show a causal link between participative decision practices and the utilization of existing experience and skill in semi-autonomous groups. During the monthly consultative meetings, employees had little influence at the start-up phase of decisions. Their major contribution came during the implementation phase. The successful decision collaboration between airport management and semi-autonomous groups was supported by a formal system of representative consultation at which all semi-autonomous groups were represented.

Pool made a study of the power structure and decision processes in hospitals. Traditionally, hospitals are seen as dual hierarchies. In addition to the formal administrative pyramid, the professional medical system forms a second line of authority. Equally traditional, this second line of authority poses substantial problems for hospital management. The present study took place as part of a larger research project on Industrial Democracy in Europe (IDE-2) aimed at studying changes in industrial relations and internal company influence relations in metal companies and insurance companies. In the Netherlands this project was enlarged to include hospitals.

A number of significant changes have taken place in the past decade in Dutch general hospitals. As a reaction to environmental changes, such as those in legislation, planning, and financing, organizational structures have shown interesting developments. Examples are increased hospital size due to mergers, the emergence of midlevel management, divisionalization (inpatient versus outpatient wards), and integration of medical specialists in the organization. As a result several changes in power positions have occurred, mainly on the strategic decision-making level: middle and top management have gained in influence. The medical professionals, on the other hand, have less influence than they had ten years ago. The works council, the obligatory council for employee representation in the Netherlands, in general established its power position. The councils made a significant gain, however, in influence in strategic decision-making.

On the basis of these data, it was concluded that the power balance in Dutch hospitals made a shift inwards. Whereas ten years ago the center of power was located at the triangle consisting of the board of trustees, executive management, and medical staff, nowadays this center can be located at the quadrangle of executive management, middle management, medical staff, and the works council. All in all, this implies a more integrated position of medical professionals in the hospital organization.

In his discussion, de Wolff recognized the subject of this symposium as a classical psychological dilemma: How to reconcile the need for control and the need for autonomy? The dilemma has a long history. The scientific management movement at the beginning of this century worked out various methods to control the behavior of workers. Particularly in the second part of this century, psychologists have advocated new approaches such as sociotechnical systems, participation, and coping with stress, which all intend to empower employees. Much of the discussions have ideological overtones often leading to government intervention through legislation.

It is interesting and useful to study the nature of control. In classical approaches, control through prescription has dominated. Supervisors used to "tell and sell." It is now known that such behavior elicits defensive and even hostile reactions and usually has negative effects on productivity.

Psychologists have recommended "problem-solving" behavior whereby supervisors concentrate on problem definition and ask employees to work out solutions themselves.

The papers presented in this symposium show the importance of the control process. Supervisors who use goal-setting and problem-solving approaches appear to be more effective. This is a long way from the scientific management approach but fits much better in the complex structure of present-day organizations.

TEAM EFFECTIVENESS:
Changing Views of Groups and Teams

Organizer & Chair: D. R. Ilgen, Michigan State University, U.S.A.

Contributors:

D. Eden, Tel Aviv University, Israel
True experiments on team development can be done

D. Hosking, Aston University, U.K.
Theorizing different kinds of groups: A political perspective

E. Salas, Naval Training Systems Center, U.S.A.
Toward a definition of teamwork: An analysis of critical team behaviors

H. Weiss, Purdue University, U.S.A.
Stress, automaticity and teamwork

Discussant: D. R. Ilgen, Michigan State University, U.S.A.

In his introduction to the symposium, Ilgen took a historical perspective on the scientific study of groups and teams. He argued that the early work grew out of compelling need for teams to function effectively in businesses, communities, flying aircraft, and other settings in which teams and groups were found. Lewin, Stouffer, and other psychologists and sociologists who were involved in the early research on teams to which much of the current work can be traced had a strong desire to show that behavioral science research could contribute knowledge that would improve the functioning of important groups and teams (McGrath, 1984).

Over time, in Ilgen's opinion, much of the research on teams and small groups shifted away from the concerns with the effectiveness of teams operating over time in real-life settings to a concern for the development of research and theories of team processes frequently studied with *ad hoc* groups in laboratory settings. In a sense, there was a figure-ground reversal from the focus on real-world problems, with the development of psychological and sociological theory playing the supporting role, to a primary focus on the theories, with real-world settings providing one of several contexts within which the theories were evaluated and, if necessary, modified. As a result, from the 1950s to the middle 1980s there was a decrease in time and effort devoted to the study of teams that were found in organizations involved in production of goods and services.

In the 1980s, there was a rebirth of interest in teams in organizations stimulated, in large part, by highly visible team failures that were, rightly or wrongly, attributed to teams. There was also an increased interest in organizing work around work teams. The most visible failures were crashes of civilian airlines that were later attributed to the deficiencies of the cockpit crews, and the misidentification of a civilian airline as a hostile military aircraft with the subsequent downing of the airline by a U.S. Navy vessel. Here, the error was attributed to the functioning of the command and control team responsible for monitoring aircraft and making decisions regarding engagement of the aircraft. A second factor that stimulated interest in teams during the 1980s was a general trend to increase in the use of small teams in many types of organizations. Structural changes in organizations were leading to the use of small teams as a basic organizational unit in a movement away from strict linearly organized hierarchical structures.

A primary thesis of the symposium was that much of the existing literature on teams and teamwork was not very useful for understanding and developing teams of the types that were demanding our attention in the last half of the 1980s. The focus of the symposium was on ways to avoid some of the perceived shortcomings of previous works on teams regarding their generalizability to ongoing teams in organizations.

The suggestions for avoiding past limitations could be classified on the basis of the content of the team constructs that are studied and the approaches taken to the study of teams. Papers by Weiss and Salas were most directly focused on content. Weiss used models and research on the effects of stress on automatic (habitual) behavior routines to suggest ways that these constructs might generalize to patterns of behaviors of teams under low and high levels of stress. Salas reported work by him and his colleagues (Glickman, et al., 1987; McIntyre, Morgan, Salas, & Glickman, 1988) on the construct of teamwork. He argued that the process of teamwork was considered critical for effective team functioning in almost all theories of teams, but attention was normally paid to the outcomes of team activity rather than the process of teamwork that was assumed to lead to the outcomes. He described some interesting work that they are doing on the measurement of teamwork and the demonstration of its effect on the performance of teams in long-term training programs.

Both Hosking and Eden also addressed content issues for teams. Hosking emphasized the dynamic interactive nature of teams where teams and team members create, and shape their own environment while they are, at the same time, part of that environment in a continuous stream of behavior. Eden discussed dynamic constructs as he reported his research on team development in which he was able to create field experiments that were better able to support inferences of causal effects than is the case with experiments typically described in the literature.

Although the papers by Eden and Hosking did address content issues, their primary focus was on approaches to the study of teams and, more basic, fundamental philosophy of science or paradigm issues. Eden's position was that a great deal more could be gained by tried and true experimental methods put into practice in field settings if the search for ways to design true experiments in the field were more creative. He argued that social scientists far too frequently accept the inability to control variables in the field and pay the price of confounded data sets and multiple alternative explanations for observed events that inevitably result from the lack of control. His own work provided an excellent example of both the value and the feasibility of controlled research in the field.

In direct opposition to Eden's position, Hosking argued that most organizational behavior research, including that on teams, assumes that persons and environments are independent, painting mechanical and lifeless pictures of people, social relationships, and social action. She suggested that persons, the environments in which they can be observed, and the relations among and between people and their environments are dynamic mutual creations that exist neither exclusively in people or settings. Her position was that, to attempt to understand teams and teamwork, it is necessary to take a dynamic perspective and view individuals as enacting their environment over time. Furthermore, more traditional research methods, such as those represented by the other symposium presentations, operated from the assumptions mentioned above and were incapable of understanding teams.

Ilgen, in his discussion of the presentations, agreed with the need to address dynamic constructs operating in teams found in naturalistic settings. He also agreed with Hosking that socially constructed realities with fuzzy boundaries between situations and persons are reasonable construals of teams and must be taken into account in our research on teams. At the same time, he did not accept the fact that many or most traditional paradigms necessarily operate from the limited static assumptions that Hosking attributed to them or that research imbedded in the more traditional views is necessarily deficient with regard to its ability to study important team constructs. He agreed with Eden that such methods were not only capable of dealing with important team constructs but also underutilized for the wrong reasons. The paradigm issues that were raised dominated much of the discussion and were not the types of issues that reach resolution in symposia or extended debates in the literature. They are, however, issues that should not be blindly ignored.

REFERENCES

Glickman, A. S., Zimmer, S., Montero, R. C., Guerette, P. J., Campbell, W. J., Morgan, B. B., & Salas, E. (1987). *The evolution of team skills: An empirical assessment with implications for training* (Tech. Rep. NTSC 87-016). Arlington, VA: Office of Naval Research.

McGrath, J. E. (1984). *Groups, interaction and performance.* Englewood Cliffs, NJ: Prentice-Hall.

McIntyre, R. M., Morgan, B. B., Salas, E., & Glickman, A. S. (1988). Teamwork from team training: New evidence for the development of teamwork skills during operational training. *Proceedings of the 10th Interservice/Industry training systems conference* (pp. 21-27).

TEAM EFFECTIVENESS IN ORGANIZATIONS: Recent Empirical and Theoretical Advances

Organizers and Chairpersons:
R. A. Guzzo, University of Maryland, U.S.A.
B. Schneider, University of Maryland, U.S.A.

Contributors:

H. P. Dachler, University of St. Gallen, Switzerland
Leadership as a forgotten relational phenomenon in team effectiveness

R. A. Guzzo, University of Maryland, U.S.A.
R. J. Campbell, New York University, U.S.A.
A diagnostic model of team effectiveness in organizations

B. Schneider, University of Maryland, U.S.A.
Where groups fit in a multi-level framework for conceptualizing organizational functioning

K. Takaishi, Japan Small Business Corporation, Japan
Quality circles in Japanese small business: Members' work values and organizational commitments

Discussant: A. P. Brief, Tulane University, U.S.A.

For many years team effectiveness has been a concern of social and organizational psychology. Traditionally, an input-process-output model has dominated the nature of theories of team effectiveness. According to this model, inputs such as team member characteristics (e.g., ability, expertise, status) determine the nature of the team interaction processes (e.g., communication patterns, influence attempts), which, in turn, determine the effectiveness of team outputs. A summary of literature underlying the input-process-output framework is found in Hackman and Morris (1975).

In recent years, however, a change has occurred in the nature of theories of team effectiveness. Specifically, theories have moved away from an input-process-output orientation and toward an emphasis on the context to understand teams. That is, group interaction process as traditionally studied in social-psychological terms is less emphasized. Instead, factors such as the relation of a team to its organization, the support and resources provided to teams by organizations, leadership of teams, and the culture in which teams exist are increasingly cited as important (Guzzo & Shea, in press). Also, a broader perspective has been adopted regarding the functions served by teams in organizations and their role in the experience of work.

The content of this symposium reflected these recent developments in research and theory. There is no singular school of thought currently dominant in contemporary views of teams in organizations. As is perhaps true of any emerging theoretical perspective, there is considerable diversity of viewpoints. Such diversity was evident in the symposium contributions.

Richard A. Guzzo (University of Maryland, U.S.A.) and Richard J. Campbell (New York University, U.S.A.) presented a paper titled *A diagnostic model of team effectiveness in organizations.* They define effectiveness in terms of outputs, adaptation, and sentiments. Outputs concern the timely delivery of high-quality products or services. Adaptation refers to a team's capacity to survive and change in variations in membership and circumstance. And sentiments refer to such things as team members' enjoyment of work. Effectiveness is regarded as a consequence of three critical aspects of the organizational systems in which teams exist. One is the extent to which the organizational systems are rich in resources for teams to use. A second is the extent to which organizations reward team accomplishments. The third is the extent to which team goals are aligned with broader unit or organizational goals. These aspects of the organizational context directly contribute to team effectiveness and to a sense of potency in teams. Potency refers to a belief shared among team members that their group can be effective. Organizational conditions that promote effectiveness also promote a sense of potency, according to Guzzo and Campbell, and that sense of potency acts to sustain and elevate team effectiveness.

Koichi Takaishi (Japan Small Business Corporation) reported a study of quality circles in two very different small business organizations (*Quality circles in Japanese small businesses: Members' work values and organizational commitments*). The cultures of the two organizations are very different, reflecting the degree of independence experienced by each firm. One company, a manufacturer of parts for office furniture, was a subcontractor highly dependent on another, larger firm for its business. The second company, a manufacturer of electrical parts, had no such dependence. Analyses indicated that quality circles were associated with productivity improvements in both firms. However, differences existed in the nature of the experience of workers in each of the two firms and how those experiences relate to quality-circle involvement. For example, the affective nature of organizational commitment related to quality-circle involvement among workers in the more autonomous company but not among workers in the subcontracting firm. Thus, the nature of the organizational context appears to shape the experience of working in teams such as quality circles.

H. Peter Dachler (University of St. Gallen, Switzerland) addressed the topic of leadership and team effectiveness in organizations (*Leadership as a forgotten relational phenomenon in team effectiveness*). Dachler challenged the adequacy of traditional methods of research on teams and leadership in organizations and offered as an alternative a relational perspective. That is, teams are viewed as embedded in multiple networks in organizations. In this view there are many points of contact based on complex, multilayered routes of exchange among teams and between teams and their environment. The information exchanged through such networks is the "stuff" from which leadership is constructed. That is, leadership is not some external factor that governs team effectiveness in organizations. Rather, leadership is a constructed reality, one which is defined through the process of working in teams. Team effectiveness and the role of leadership are thus matters of self-design by teams. Dachler illustrated his thesis with reports of how leaders define their own leadership reality within organizational networks, and addressed the role of the dominant culture in shaping definitions of reality in organizations.

Benjamin Schneider (University of Maryland, U.S.A.) presented the paper: *Where groups fit in a multi-level framework for conceptualizing organizational functioning*. Schneider's essential thesis is that teams in organizations can be understood as mediators between individuals and the management systems under which individuals work. Like Dachler, Schneider emphasized the interpretative role that teams can play in organizations. For example, teams are vehicles through which management objectives are translated into goals guiding individual behavior. Teams also serve as buffers between individuals and management. In this sense, teams provide mechanisms by which individual workers can cope with ambiguity, tension, and other potentially dysfunctional aspects of organizations. Organizational effectiveness and, thus, team effectiveness can be attained through clarifying and improving the team structures in organizations, according to Schneider.

The symposium discussant, Arthur P. Brief (Tulane University, USA), spoke of organizational psychology's contributions to the evolving view of teams. He raised the possibility that, while team-based management practices are now in vogue, they may prove to be but a fad, and wondered if recent advances in theory and research would survive when team-based management falls out of fashion.

Richard A. Guzzo and Benjamin Schneider were co-organizers and co-chairs of the symposium.

REFERENCES

Hackman, J. R., & Morris, C. G. (1975). Group tasks, group interaction process, and group performance effectiveness: A review and proposed integration. In L. Berkowitz (Ed.), *Advances in experimental social psychology* (Vol. 8). New York: Academic Press.

Guzzo, R. A., & Shea, G. P. (in press). Group performance and intergroup relations in organizations. In M. D. Dunnette & L. M. Hough (Eds.), *Handbook of industrial and organizational psychology* (2nd ed.). Palo Alto: Consulting Psychologists Press.

TRAINING ISSUES FACING WORK ORGANIZATIONS IN THE YEAR 2000

Organizer & Chair: I. L. Goldstein, University of Maryland, U.S.A.

Contributors:

H. Fujimura, Kyoto University, Japan
Implications of training issues for productivity of organisations in Japan

I. L. Goldstein, University of Maryland, U.S.A.
Impact of changes facing U.S. organisations on training research & practice in the year 2000

M. Killcross, The Training Agency, U.K.
Training issues in the European community

S. Ronen, Tel Aviv University, Israel
Transferability of managerial styles across cultures: Implications for the year 2000

N. Schmitt, Michigan State University, U.S.A.
Comments on training and selection in the 1990's

S. Zedeck, University of California at Berkeley, U.S.A.
Use of video technology in training and selection of employees

As the year 2000 approaches, there will be many changes facing work organizations in many places in the world. Each of the symposium participants considered the implications of these changes for the type of training that will be necessary and the way that training systems will be implemented. There were also discussions concerning the implications that changes in training systems have for other personnel systems, such as selection systems.

IMPACT OF CHANGES FACING U.S. ORGANIZATIONS ON TRAINING RESEARCH & PRACTICE ISSUES IN THE YEAR 2000

Irwin L Goldstein, University of Maryland at College Park U.S.A.

In this presentation the impact of changes facing U.S. organizations and their implications for training systems was discussed. Changes included a declining rate in the number of persons available for entry level jobs, and an increase in the number of undereducated youth. Also, jobs will both become more complex as a result of technological developments and yet will require more interpersonal contact between individuals who have different values. In addition, more jobs will involve working with persons from other countries in a more global environment. The changes will place more emphasis on the development of training systems to utilize the potential of each individual, including undereducated youth, women, minorities, and older workers. There will be a need to invest heavily in basic skill and support programs to develop the talents of undereducated youth. Managers will need training to work with a more diverse work force performing more complex jobs. Individuals in organizations will need training to help them learn to work with individuals who have not previously been traditional members of the workforce. Indeed, it may be that most training programs aimed at the entering worker are not of much value without equal effort targeting persons already in the organization.

TRAINING ISSUES IN THE EUROPEAN COMMUNITY (AND PARTICULARLY THE UNITED KINGDOM)

Dr. Malcolm C. Killcross, Department of Employment, United Kingdom

The paper gave some background on the European Community (EC), outlined EC training priorities, moved to the training issues and intentions in the United Kingdom, and presented speculations about next steps.

The Commission that serves the EC has training and education high in its priorities. Some £7 billion a year support training and development against guidelines aimed at the mobility of workers, (e.g., recognition of qualifications; new technology; and such special topics as retraining, women returners, and disadvantaged areas).

In the U.K. about £33 billion a year is spent on training, but this is seen as too little. A major public program is underway that is employer-led to identify the competence needed for successful job performance and to operationalize these requirements. Networks of local employer-led training and enterprise bodies have been set up.

Key psychological components in making progress towards a more skilled and flexible work force are a better understanding of non-job specific personal effectiveness; recognized means of accrediting prior learning that focus on the achieved competence and not the occupational track followed; recognizing the characteristics of the future learner that equip him or her to be a member of tomorrow's work force with the enabling skills to take advantage of the enabling settings that work organizations moving towards 2000 will try to create.

USE OF VIDEO TECHNOLOGY IN TRAINING AND SELECTION OF EMPLOYEES

Sheldon Zedeck, University of California at Berkeley, U.S.A.

Advances in video technology and computer-assisted graphics were discussed with a particular emphasis on how these advances can facilitate selection and training programs. Whereas much progress has been achieved with job simulations as a selection device, this presentation focused on how job simulations developed for presentation via videotapes can be adapted for training purposes. Of particular emphasis was how the tapes can be developed for situations when job behaviors cannot be modeled in an actual environment, for example, for fire-fighting positions.

The presentation focused on how the tapes are developed to accomplish several goals of selection, training, and performance feedback; the link between selection and training; and issues of content validity. The flexibility allowed by video presentation was stressed, such as being able to vary types of scenes, times when an event was supposed to occur, and the seriousness of the situation. A particular example pertaining to selecting and training officers in a fire department was used to illustrate the technology and issues.

TRANSFERABILITY OF MANAGERIAL STYLES ACROSS CULTURES

Simcha Ronen, Tel-Aviv University, Israel

The application of traditional leadership theories, popular in the field of management-organizational behavior, has been challenged recently by published data from cross-cultural and cross-national research. In particular, efforts to apply these theories to managerial training programs are often plagued by "dilemmas" resulting from cultural value differences. These dilemmas are expressed in conflicting messages appearing mainly in the area of cooperation versus competition, emphasis on teamwork versus recent emphasis on individual entrepreneurial and creative behavior, reinforcement of team responsibility through group rewards versus individual remuneration and promotional policies, and prediction of individual managerial potential versus promotional policies based on tenure.

In this presentation such dilemmas were related to cultural values, and the transferability of management style from one culture to another were critically evaluated.

COMMENTS ON TRAINING AND SELECTION IN THE 1990s

Neal Schmitt, Michigan State University, U.S.A.

Major trends will increase the need for training in the coming decades. Major demographic changes (fewer young workers who are less skilled, workers who stay on their jobs longer because of changes in retirement policy, and increased demographic and cultural diversity), increased technological change, and greater job security will all increase the need for training.

The increased emphasis on training will produce a number of trends in selection. There will be greater need to select people with the capacity to learn as opposed to those with existing skills. The demographic changes listed above will produce higher selection ratios, which, in turn, will require that organizations focus their attention on placement and counseling as opposed to selection. This increased need to counsel and place employees means that organizations will need information that allows them to catalog and profile their employees' strengths and weaknesses. Applicants' reactions to selection and recruitment will become more important. If organizations spend more time on training, it makes sense that they would also spend more time on career planning so as to retain and use their human resource talent optimally. As companies make longer term investments in human resources and as health-care costs increase, there is likely to be greater emphasis on selecting healthy workers and maintaining their health. Finally, if it is realized that employees must be continually retrained, there should be interest in how willing those employees will be to engage in retraining efforts.

There will also be increased pressure to develop and use performance systems that accurately document the need for retraining. Performance appraisal may become more of a problem-solving approach as both employer and employee seek to maximize human potential. As training requirements increase, there will be the usual pressure to compensate employees commensurate with their new skill levels.

IMPLICATIONS OF TRAINING ISSUES FOR PRODUCTIVITY OF ORGANIZATIONS IN JAPAN

Hiroyuki Fujimura, Shiga University, Hikone, Japan

The Importance of Production Workers' Skill

The skill of production workers consists of two parts: the skill for routine tasks and that for non-routine tasks dealing with unusual situations like defective products and machine malfunctions. The latter skill, "intellectual skill," becomes all the more important as the technological requirements of work become more advanced. It was commonly believed that skill would be less needed because of mechanization. But in practice just the reverse is true: the skill that is replaced by the machine is solely the dull and repetitive components of human work. As mechanization becomes more complicated, increased intellectual skill is consequently required of the workers who operate such machines.

On-the-job Training: The Best Way to Acquire Intellectual Skill

Japanese workers acquire intellectual skill mainly through on-the-job training (OJT). There are two reasons why OJT is superior to off-the-job training (Off-JT). The first is the character of skill itself; the knowledge-content of a skill is largely indefinable and only partially communicated through words. There exists no way to acquire these skills other than by following the teacher's pattern, which is precisely the content of OJT on the shop floor. The second reason is simply that OJT costs less than Off-JT.

OJT is not enough for production workers to acquire intellectual skill. OJT should be followed by Off-JT that helps them to organize knowledge obtained through everyday work.

ORGANIZATIONAL PSYCHOLOGY POSTER CONTRIBUTIONS

CROSS-CULTURAL APPLICATIONS OF THE MULTIFACTOR LEADERSHIP QUESTIONNAIRE AS A VALIDATED MEASURE OF TRANSFORMATIONAL AND TRANSACTIONAL LEADERSHIP

Bernard M. Bass, State University of New York at Binghamton, NY, USA, and Nobue Nokochi, NIKKO International, San Diego, California, USA

The four transformational factors (charisma [CH], inspirational leadership [IL], intellectual stimulation [IS], and individualized consideration [IC]); the two transactional factors (contingent reward [CR] and management-by-exception [MBE]; and the non leadership, laissez-faire factors (LF) are assessed by the Multifactor Leadership Questionnaire (MLQ), as completed by their subordinates or colleagues.

Internal consistency reliabilities range from .77 to .90 for subordinate ratings. The median correlations with subjective estimates of organizational effectiveness for each of the transformational factors in up to 17 business, military educational, and other studies were as follows: CH, .72; IL, .64; IS, .57; and IC, .59. The corresponding median correlations with the transactional and laissez-faire factors were: CR, .40; MBE, .15; and LF, −.34. Ordinarily, within every sample, transformational leadership correlates more highly with effectiveness than does transactional leadership, and laissez-faire leadership is contraindicated. Transformational leadership augments transactional leadership in multiple predictions of effectiveness.

Results tended to be similar in the fewer studies in which objective measures of effectiveness were available and have been replicated in Japan, Singapore, New Zealand, Italy, Spain, Israel, Belgium, Sweden, Canada, and elsewhere at hierarchical levels ranging from nonsupervisory project leaders to chief executive officers. An intensive interview of CEO's of 17 leading Japanese firms concluded that the CEO's were transformational but charisma revealed itself differently in Japan.

SELF-MONITORING AND LEADER EMERGENCE:
A TEST OF MODERATOR EFFECTS

Robert J. Ellis, Wilfried Laurier University, Waterloo, Ontario, and Steven F. Cronshaw, University of Guelph, Guelph, Ontario, Canada

The present research is intended to further understanding of the relation between self-monitoring and leader emergence in groups. It focuses on two proposed moderators of this relation: sex of the group members and nature of the task confronting the group. On the basis of previous research, it was hypothesized that high self-monitoring would be related to leader emergence for males, but not for females, in mixed-sex groups. Further, the relation between self-monitoring and leader emergence was hypothesized to be stronger for a task providing minimal feedback on the task competence of group members. These hypotheses were tested in a long-term study of natural mixed-sex groups. The sex moderator hypothesis was supported, but the task moderator hypothesis was not. *Post hoc* analyses suggested that high self-monitors emerge as group leaders because they are more adaptive in their behavior than low self-monitors.

ACADEMIC PERFORMANCE IN THE FIRST YEAR OF
UNIVERSITY ENGINEERING STUDIES AND ITS
RELATION TO ENTRANCE LEVEL

Rosa María Gonzalez Tirados, Polytechnic University of Madrid, Spain

Previous research conducted by the author of this paper has focused on academic success, various difficulties, academic backwardness, and the abandonment of studies, especially in the first year of university engineering studies. This paper presents results of recent work on the correlation between academic parameters used as a selection criterion for university admission and student progress by the end of the first year at the university. The sample used in this research consisted of 7,960 university students from 10 university study fields (6 academic years) including engineering, architecture, and computer science and from 9 shorter university study fields (3 academic years each).

The outcomes refer to the whole sample. The most valuable data related to:

1. the priorities in the choice of a university major,
2. the percentage of women studying engineering,

3. central values about the entrance level of the students at each engineering school and the average grades required by the university in order to be admitted to each school,

4. the overall and subject-by-subject performance of the whole sample and of subsamples by the end of the first academic year at the university, and

5. the correlation between the entrance level and the academic result at the end of the first academic year at the university and other interesting parameters identified, for example, through multiple regression analysis.

The results suggest that complex analytical studies be conducted with all relevant instructors and that a process of "instructional change" be started.

Other results are leading to a longitudinal study on all individuals during their university studies, the purpose being to identify a student's success or failure, abandonment of one's studies, the university majors that pose severe difficulties and those that provide adequate preparation and training. This paper intends to analyze a complete cohort step by step.

BASIC ASSUMPTION AS A DETERMINANT OF MANAGERIAL BEHAVIOR

B. N. Srivastava,
Indian Institute of Management, Calcutta, India

Following the logic that behaviors (explicit) are influenced by motivation or needs (implicit), which, in turn, are determined by basic assumptions (tacit), the author considers the latter as a crucial factor in explaining managerial behavior. The paper advances the concept of optimistic/pessimistic assumptions (Knowles & Saxberg, 1967) to encompass beliefs about people, tasks, and organisation. Basic assumptions are defined as generalized expectancies involving the individual's relation with the world of people, work, and organization. Drawing on accumulated experience with a diagnostic instrument and using an exercise for observing group processes in numerous management development programs, the author identifies nine dimensions of basic assumptions: (a) adaptability versus nonadaptability, (b) role-making versus role-taking, (c) system responsibility versus vulnerability, (d) resourcefulness versus resourcelessness, (e) employee optimism versus pessimism, (f) internal versus external attribution of success, (g) collaborating versus competing, (h) activism versus inactivism, and (i) interventionistic versus evolutionary change.

Considering optimistic/pessimistic assumptions and two important needs (orientations) of affiliation and power as high/low, the author presents a taxonomy of managerial/leadership styles: (a) counter normative-renormative (optimistic, high n-aff, high n-pow), (b) directive-problem solver (optimistic, high n-pow, low n-aff), (c) nurturant inspirational (optimistic, high n-aff, low n-pow), (d) normative rational (optimistic, low n-aff, low n-pow), (e) norms-compromiser (pessimistic, high n-aff, high n-pow), (f) autocrat (pessimistic, high n-pow, low n-aff), (g) democrat-abdicrat (pessimistic, high n-aff, low n-pow), and (h) norms-apathetic (pessimistic, low n-aff, low n-pow). The author also classifies sources and bases of power, methods of influence, and decision styles associated with each managerial/leadership style.

Reference

Knowles, M. P., & Saxberg, B. O. (1967). Human relations and the nature of Man. *Harvard Business Review*. March-April, pp. 22-40 and pp. 172-178.

PERCEPTIONS OF WORK AND WELL-BEING IN NEW ZEALAND MANAGERS

Judith A. Brook, Massey University, Palmerston North, New Zealand

This explanatory study investigated how a sample of New Zealand managers view their paid employment and other aspects of their lives. The term "work" is used as the equivalent of "paid employment," whereas nonwork refers to any other activities important to them. Previous research has found relations between subject's cognitive appraisal of work and feelings generated, for example, job satisfaction. In this study, the appraisal that managers give of both work and nonwork activities is related to their affective reactions, including work involvement, job satisfaction, job stress, life satisfaction, and general mental health.

The managers were a representative sample of middle managers from 56 large private section organizations throughout the country. The 77 women and 101 men came from finance (27%), marketing (22%), information technology (11%), and production (20%), with the remaining 20% from other management areas. Median age was 35 years, 52.2%

held university degrees, 79.8% had a spouse or partner, and 49.4% had dependent children.

Repertory Grid Technique (Kelly, 1955) was used to measure perceptions of work and nonwork activities. Subjects chose the eleven specific activities most relevant to their daily lives, for example, chairing meetings, cooking meals, and playing golf. They then rated them on a set of fifteen supplied constructs that had been selected on the basis of previous pilot studies. Factor analyses of construct ratings indicated that their most frequent activities, both work and nonwork, were evaluated according to similar criteria, for example, challenging, creative, involving self-development, and mental activity, whereas their most important nonwork activities were judged according to whether they were done alone, at their discretion, under their control, and for other people.

Specific (job-related) and general affect were measured with previously developed scales, including job satisfaction, life satisfaction, and work involvement (Warr, Cook, & Wall, 1979), job-related tension (Kahn, et al. 1964), and mental health (Hopkins Symptoms Checklist, see Derogatis, Lipman, Rickels, Uhlenhugh, & Covi, 1974). The pattern of correlations obtained between perceptions of work/nonwork activities and feelings of satisfaction and well-being suggested that viewing one's work and nonwork activities in a positive light (stimulating, enjoyable, etc.) is significantly related to job satisfaction, reduced job stress, and better mental health, whereas negative perceptions about one's activities (disliked, stressful, etc.) is related to poorer scores on these general and specific well-being variables.

References

Derogatis, L. R., Lipman, R. S., Rickels, K., Uhlenhugh, E. H., & Covi, L. (1974). Hopkins Symptom Checklist: A self-report symptom inventory. *Behavioral Science, 19*, 1-15.

Kahn, R. L., Wolfe, D. M., Quinn, R. P., Snoek, J. D., & Rosenthal, R. (1964). *Organizational stress: Studies in role conflict and ambiguity.* New York: Wiley.

Kelly, G. A. (1955). *The Psychology of Personal Constructs*, Vols. 1 & 2. New York: Norton.

Warr, P. B., Cook, J., & Wall, T. D. (1979). Scales for the measurement of some work attitudes and aspects of psychological well-being. *Journal of Occupational Psychology, 52*, 129-148.

EXCELLENCE IN MILITARY COMBAT LEADERSHIP IN THE ISRAELI ARMY

Uri M. Gluskinos,
PAN Institute for Organizational Development & Management Consultation
Ori Landau, Eliav Zakay, Esther Naveh and Micha Popper,
IDF School for Leadership Development

Two multiple case studies with Platoon ($N = 30$) and Battalion Commanders ($N = 9$) from infantry and the armored corps rated as outstanding by their superiors were conducted to discover characteristics of excellence. Each officer selected was studied for three days through interviews with subjects and subordinates, and through observation.

Seven characteristics contributing to excellence among platoon commanders were discovered:

1. Personal excellence; striving for high individual achievement, aura of professionalism, fanatic devotion to role and mission, high energy levels
2. Positive expectations for excellence by subordinates
3. Creation of very informal atmosphere
4. Individual consideration and development orientation
5. Communicated clear and consistent boundaries
6. Sophisticated use of punishment, used as an educational message, incrementally and tailored to the individual
7. Commitment to the welfare of the unit

In terms of the Bass (1985) model, excellent leaders used transformational leadership, except for intellectual stimulation, as well as transactional leadership. The transformation they accomplished was not that of the organization; they transformed adolescents into adults and provided them with a sense of identity and self-efficacy.

Generally, characteristics of battalion commanders rated as transforming (6 out of 9) were similar to those of platoon commanders. However, the following differences in emphasis were found:

1. Vision—values and education frequently emphasized, not just professional competence
2. Intellectual stimulation much more pronounced
3. Represented interest of the unit with superiors

Commanders rated as excellent by superiors, but not considered as transforming by subordinates exhibited one of the following behaviors :

1. Vision outside the scope of acceptance by subordinates
2. Lack of personal example with regard to behaviors demanded by commanders
3. Lack of individual consideration

The Bass model (1985) generally explains the behaviors of outstanding commanders but is not detailed enough to account for differences in context. The use of a contingency model such as the one by Conger and Kanugo (1988), which considers components such as follower characteristics, context, leader-follower relationship, and leader-context relationships may add to the refinement of the transformational leadership model.

References

Bass, B. M. (1985) *Leadership and performance beyond expectations*. New York: Free Press.
Conger, J. M., & Kanugo, R. N. (eds.),(1988). Charismatic leadership. London: Jossy - Bass.

PREDICTION FOR LEADERSHIP BEHAVIOR IN A JAPANESE ORGANIZATION

Mitsuru Shibata, Kansai University

The purpose of this study was to predict and assess leadership behavior using an intelligence test, personality variables, and behavior ratings.

The longitudinal data of two sessions half a year apart were obtained from 174 males in a public organization. In the first session, an intelligence test (Cattell's CF) and personality variables (YG Personality Inventory, DPI attitude Inventory) were obtained. In the second session, behavior ratings by teaching staff were obtained. Two factors were extracted by component analysis with oblique rotation using behavior ratings of leadership. Each factor was predicted by multiple regression analysis with an item selection method using an intelligence test and personality variables.

Performance and Maintenance factors were extracted (shown in Table 1). The statistically significant multiple correlations were found to predict leadership factors (see Tables 2 and 3).

These models are therefore useful to account for leadership behavior.

TABLE 1

Performance and Maintenance factor extracted by component analysis with oblique rotation using behaviour ratings of leadership obtained from 174 males in a public organization.

	Factor	
Behavior rating	Performance	Maintenance
1. Benevolent	0.136	0.492
2. Frank	0.459	0.075
3. Firm	0.718	−0.176
4. Ambitious	0.466	0.190
5. Composed	−0.302	0.344
6. Bold	0.625	−0.094
7. Discerning	0.265	0.418
8. Decisive	0.615	0.011
9. Progressive	0.036	0.480
10. Harmonious	−0.174	0.652
11. Good at talking	−0.076	0.599
12. Sociable	0.325	0.277

NOTE: Factor correlation: 0.450

TABLE 2

Performance factor predicted by multiple regression analysis with item selection method using personality variables and an intelligence test

Test	Variable	Structure
YG	Inferiority Feelings	−0.433
	Nervousness	−0.171
DPI	Attractive leadership	0.684
	Activity	0.839
	Endurance	−0.116

NOTE: Multiple correlation 0.414 ($P < 0.01$)

TABLE 3

Maintenance factor predicted by multiple regression analysis with item selection method using personality variables and an intelligence test

Test	Variable	Structure
CF	IQ	0.516
YG	Lack of Co-operativeness	−0.370
	Thinking extraversion	0.034
DPI	Attractive leadership	0.742
	Activity	0.701
	Endurance	0.104

NOTE: Multiple correlation 0.423 ($P < 0.01$).

ORGANIZATIONAL CLIMATE AND JOB SATISFACTION AMONG MANAGERS OF THE PUBLIC AND PRIVATE SECTOR

N. K. Chadha, University of Delhi, India

Every organization has a characteristic aura under which it functions and which is at times evident to a discriminating, but transient, visitor to the organization. The organizational climate can be manifested in diverse ways in the general behavior of the workers and state of discipline at the work place, the interest workers take in their work, the frequency of task-irrelevant activities among them, their relation with each other and with their supervisors, their sense of personal freedom, and so forth.

The public and private sectors coexist in the Indian economy, and both are equally important components of it. According to the World Bank, India's economy is one of the 10 largest among the industrialized nations. In recent years, the public sector has been consciously given a commanding place in the constitutional objectives and repeated policy pronouncements, and it has made India the 9th largest developed economy in the world.

Work plays a dominant role in one's life. It occupies more of one's time than any other activity. For most people, it is central to their self-concept, for people define themselves, in part, by their careers or professions. Further, while fantasies of a life of total leisure are intriguing, few persons can really imagine a full and satisfying life that does not involve some productive work. Any activity of such central importance must evoke strong positive and negative reactions.

This research was undertaken to understand the differences, if any, between managers of public-sector organizations and managers of private-sector organizations in terms of organizational climate and job satisfaction. The study involves a total of 120 managers, 60 from each kind of firm. Following similar conduction at both places, the subjects were given the questionnaires to be filled. The Job Description Index by Smith, Kendall, and Hulin (1969) and organizational climate scales by Pareek (1974) were used. Out of the eleven dimensions of organizational climate, the managers working in the private sector were found to be significantly different from public sector managers on orientation, interpersonal relations, supervision, communication, decision-making, managing problems, managing mistakes, managing conflicts, and risk-taking. Further, managers in the private sector were found to be more satisfied than public sector managers on promotion, satisfaction with co-workers, satisfaction with supervision, and satisfaction with work.

References

Pareek, U. (1974). Manual of Organizational Climate Questionnaires. In U. Pareek & T. V. Rao (Eds.), *Handbook of psychological and social instruments*. Baroda: Smasthi.

Smith, P. C., Kendall, L. M., & Hulin, C. L. (1969). *The measurement of satisfaction in work and retirement*. Chicago: Rand McNally.

MANAGEMENT-STYLE EXPECTATIONS IN BELGIAN AND BRAZILIAN UNDERGRADUATES

Maria Alice d'Amorim, University of Brasília, Brazil

According to Bordeleau (1985), management style must be seen as a macrosystem consisting of three microsystems of input — the superior, the subordinate, and the situation — a transformation system, and an output system, each marked by its own internal dynamism. Subordinates' expectations about management style are especially relevant, and to probe this area Bordeleau (1977) has developed the Personnel Management Style questionnaire. Two groups, 267 Belgian and 412 Brazilian undergraduates, used this instrument. Compared to Belgians, Brazilian subjects had higher management-style expectations for supervisor's flexibility, friendly relations with subordinates, and willingness to work in groups. Compared to women, men expected more independence in their work hoping for rather general supervision. Women's expectations were higher than men's on all scales except that of supervisor's flexibility, which showed no difference. Within the Belgian group, women expected more equity in management; Brazilian results for sex were similar to the general ones, with women having higher expectations of supervisor's flexibility. The Brazilian results showed no significant differences for ability to maintain supportive relations.

References

Bordeleau, Y. (1977). *Questionnaire sur le type de gestion du personnel / Personnel management style questionnaire*. Montreal: IRCO.

Bordeleau, Y. (1985). Les valeurs de travail et le style de gestion du personnel. *Canadian Journal of Behavioral Science, 17*(3), 246-262.

EFFECTS OF CULTURE ON RESOURCE ALLOCATION IN MIXED GROUPS: COMBINING OCCIDENTAL, ORIENTAL, AND LATIN DECISION-MAKERS IN CONSENSUS DISCUSSION

K. Galen Kroeck, Florida International University, Miami, Florida, U.S.A.

Reviews and integration of resource allocation (RA) literature (Deutch, 1975; Vemez, 1978) resulted in the identification of four general strategies used by individuals to base their RA decisions on need, power, proportionality, and merit. The model of RA strategies partially examined in this study is shown in Figure 1.

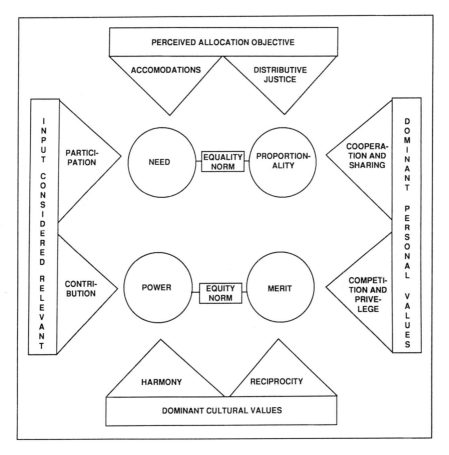

FIG. 1. A model of resources allocation preferences

In past studies (e.g., Kroeck, Avolio, Small, & Einstein, 1988) among corporate managers and hospital and military personnel, it was found that dominant cultural traits precipitate a shift from personal beliefs and values toward those of the discussion group and broader organizational / cultural objectives and values. In the present study, an attempt was made to test the effects of cultural values on RA. Past research has found cross-cultural differences in the allocation of effort and time towards work goals, the allocation of human resources for productive collaboration (Tjosvold & Tsao, 1989) and pay allocation policies (Beatty, McCune, & Beatty, 1988). In accordance with an open systems view of the RA situation, 4 hypotheses were formulated:

H1. There will be significant differences across ethnic/culture groups in preferences among four RA criteria.

H2. Panel discussion will have a significant effect on allocation preferences among four different criteria.

H3. Panel discussion will have a differential effect on the RA preferences of members of different cultures.

H4. There will be greater shifts from prediscussion preferences to panel allocation decisions when the panel has a heterocultural as compared to a monocultural composition.

Method

The sample consisted of 183 respondents representing several nations including Spain, Panama, Venezuela, India, China, and the United States. The sample consisted of 95 males and 88 females with a combined average age of 29 years. Most of the respondents were in the process of obtaining an advanced degree. The Allocation Dilemma Questionnaire (ADQ) comprises ten vignettes and assesses preferences for the four RA strategies. For each vignette respondents indicated their allocation choice on a scale ranging from most preferred (4) to least preferred (1). An individual's preference for allocating resources was summarized by a total score on each of the four allocation strategies, with higher scale scores indicating higher preference for a particular strategy. The exercise was repeated in panels who were instructed to obtain unanimous panel agreement on each vignette.

Results

The data were analyzed through variate and repeated measures MANOVA. Allocation on the basis of power was the least preferred strategy while need was the most preferred. H1 was partially supported, for significant cultural difference was found only on the POWER scale. Significant DISCUSSION effect was found on the POWER scale (F = 10.97, $p < 0.001$) and the NEED scale (F = 5.76,

$p < 0.05$). Hypothesis 3 was supported only for PROPORTIONALITY criterion (F = 2.54, $p < 0.05$). Hypothesis 4 was not supported even though there was a consistent indication that greater shifts are likely in heterocultural than in monocultural panel discussions.

Conclusion

It was shown that individuals from different ethnic backgrounds do exhibit different preferences in the allocation of resources. This difference could be expected to be manifested in a wide variety of real-world decisions and is a likely explanation for disagreement in allocation committees with mixed composition of members. The findings are in line with the model used, which assumes that an individual approaches the allocation process with a perception of the allocation objective, a belief in what the relevant inputs are, a set of personal values, and a set of cultural or contextual values within which the allocation is conducted.

References

Beatty, J. R., McCune J. T., & Beatty R. W. (1988). A Policy-capturing approach to the study of United States and Japanese managers compensation decisions. *Journal of Management, 14*(3) 465-474.

Deutch, M. (1975). Equity equality and need: What determines which value will be used as the basis of distributive justice? *Journal of Social Issues, 31*, 131-149.

Kroeck, K. G., Avolio B. J., Small R. L., & Einstein, W. O. (1987). Shifts in resource allocation preference following panel discussion. *Journal of Management, 13*(4), 713-724.

Tjosvold, D., & Tsao Y. (1989). Productive organizational collaboration: The roles of values and cooperation. *Journal of Organizational Behavior, 10*)2, 189-195.

Vemez, G. (1978). *Notes on alternative conceptions of equity* (Rand Paper P-6223). Santa Monica, CA: The Rand Corporation.

INTERNATIONAL PERSONNEL RESEARCH: A NEW APPROACH TO AN OLD PROBLEM

G. Jeffrey Worst, Bethesda MD, USA

As the conduct of U.S. business becomes more international, the need for quality information on how to manage a culturally diverse and geographically dispersed work force has probably never been more important. The academic and professional literature offers little guidance to international personnel managers for making decisions regarding the compensation, selection, and management of a firm's international work force.

One of the reasons for this lack of information is that very few empirical international personnel studies have ever been conducted. Some reasons for the lack of research activity in this area are (a) complicated logistics, (b) time, (c) experimental design problems, (d) publication standards, and (e) high cost. Hence, as the business activities of U.S. firms abroad have increased, understanding of how to manage an international work force has not kept pace.

During the 1990 conference of the U.S. Society for Industrial/Organizational Psychology (SIOP), a new group was formed of I/O psychologists interested in international personnel research. The group is attempting to form a consortium of U.S. firms to fund international personnel research projects.

There are many advantages and some disadvantages to consortium-funded social research. Major advantages are the sharing of project costs among many firms and increased sample sizes. The primary disadvantage is that the study's results may be considered proprietary and only distributed to firms participating in the study.

FACTORS RELATED TO OBSOLESCENCE IN ENGINEERING: AN INTERNATIONAL PERSPECTIVE

H. G. Kaufman,
Polytechnic University, Brooklyn, NY, U.S.A.

The rapid introduction of new products and processes is challenging the engineering work force in every country to keep up with technological advances. It is ironic that engineers, who are most responsible for technological change, are also highly vulnerable to its consequences — the obsolescence of knowledge and skills (Kaufman, 1974; 1975). In many countries, industry has responded to this global problem by providing continuing education for engineers. However, relying solely on this approach may be inadequate (Kaufman, 1974; 1986; 1989). Little is known about how cross-cultural differences affect the obsolescence of engineers and their motivation to stay up to date in different countries. By taking into account cross-cultural differences, one may better understand the etiology of obsolescence and more effectively address solutions to the problem. Some cross-cultural differences that may be worth exploring at different levels of analysis are:

1. Environmental factors, including type of economic system, level of technological development, and national policy regarding continuing education.

2. Organization/work practices, including organizational socialization, reward systems, career paths, knowledge and skill utilization, job rotation and training.

3. Individual differences, including abilities, local versus cosmopolitan orientation, risk-taking, and career versus family/personal values.

A research framework was presented that can take into account these cross-cultural differences and their impact on obsolescence.

References
Kaufman, H. G. (1974). *Obsolescence and professional career development*. New York: Amacom.

Kaufman, H. G. (1975). *Career Management: A guide to combating obsolescence*. New York: IEEE.

Kaufman, H. G. (1986). Continuing education of engineers: Motivation, participation and outcomes. *Proceedings of the World Conference on Continuing Engineering Education* (pp.1117-1130). New York: IEEE.

Kaufman, H. G. (1989). Obsolescence of technical professionals: A measure and a model. *Applied Psychology: An international Review*, *38*(1), 73-86.

REALLOCATION OF HUMAN RESOURCES

Robert F. Koning, Bavo, Centre for Psychiatry, The Netherlands

There is a growing interest in the contribution of human resource management to the quality of production processes and, in particular, to organizational innovation (Beer & Walton, 1987). This applies also for the nonprofit sector. I will describe the case of Bavo, a psychiatric hospital in a period of radical change.

Until recently Bavo was an old-fashioned hospital in a rural area. In conformance with the policy of the government to develop mental health care regions, Bavo decided to move the facility to an urban area 70 kilometers away. The personnel is forced to work elsewhere. They have to choose between staying or leaving the company, and moving or commuting.

Besides that, the hospital will be reorganized into a number of decentralized units in order to achieve more functional mental health care. The personnel is confronted with different categories of patients, will be working in smaller units, will have to carry more responsibility, and should be able to collaborate and establish functional relationships with other institutes.

For these reasons the organization had to prepare itself for change. The importance of employee participation in the change process was stressed right from the start (see Beer, 1976; French & Bell, 1984). Therefore, the management provided a participative reallocation project. The aim was to maximize the participation of workers in the reallocation of jobs to find a proper fit between workers preferences and job demands. A second aim was to reduce the resistance to change. The reallocation project contained seven stages: instruction, inventory, first proposal, consideration, second proposal, agreement, and final decision. Information was given in special meetings, visits of business units, bulletins, and a hot-line. During the inventory phase, over 700 workers were interviewed with a semistructured questionnaire. Use was made of a specially designed, partially structured decision aid (see Bass, 1983): the round table model, in which different components of the decision were represented by four participants, the manager (job demands), the social worker (social problems), the personnel worker (legal aspects), and a project member (the preferences of the employees). The participants were trained with instructions and role play.

The project took two years to carry out. The results were positive: the redistribution of jobs led to a high degree of agreement between managers and employees. The active role of workers in the reallocation led to a growing awareness of the situation; the workers learned to accept the new realities and were prepared to take an active part in the new organization. In the execution of the project we encountered several problems such as inefficient administration and lack of objective assessment instruments.

The project turned out to be a major contribution to the overall process of change. The active participation of employees and managers stimulated the generation of new ideas concerning the structuring of the new organization. This leads us to the conclusion that participation of employees helps in coping with change, that job reallocation is not a purely technical matter, and that there are no standard solutions for this kind of enterprise. The management of human resources calls for a tailor-made approach.

References

Bass, B. M. (1983). *Organizational decision making*. Homewood, IL: Irwin.

Beer, M. (1976). The technology of organization development. In M. Dunnette (Ed.), *Handbook of industrial and organizational psychology* (pp.937-994). Chicago: Rand McNally.

Beer, M., & Walton, A. E. (1987). Organization change and development. *Annual Review of Psychology, 38*, 339-367.

French, W., & Bell, C. (1984). *Organization Development: Behavioral science interventions for organization improvement.* Englewood Cliffs, NY: Prentice Hall.

INTERACTION EFFECTS OF PERSONALITY AND SITUATIONAL STRENGTH ON GOAL SETTING

Chaoming Liu, Fu-Jen Catholic University, Taipei, Taiwan, R.O.C.
Howard M. Weiss, Purdue University, West Lafayette, Indiana, U.S.A.

Two studies were designed to examine the interaction effects of personality and situational strength on goal-setting variables. Each study examined different dependent variables (i.e., self-set goal level in Study One and goal persistence in Study Two). Situational strength was manipulated by modeling films. Results were consistent with Mischel's (1973) theoretical proposition, which states that personality effects are stronger in weak situations, but weaker in strong situations. These findings also have two methodological implications: (a) situational strength can be successfully manipulated with fewer situational characteristics (or even one), and (b) inhibition of a particular response is also an effective way to manipulate a strong situation.

In organizational practice, at least two implications can be drawn. The first one is that individual differences can be eliminated with stronger situations or enhanced with weaker situations. Another one is that situational characteristics can be used to control employees' behaviors.

References

Mischel, W. (1973). Toward a cognitive social learning reconceptualization of personality. *Psychological Review, 80*, 252-283

TIME ORIENTATION AND WORK BEHAVIOR

Neelam Verma, Sundarvati Mahila College, Bhagalpur, India

For understanding the use of time, it is important to collect information on the several dimensions of each event. This will provide a complete event profile which will also render information on temporal location, (position, duration, and direction), spatial location, and social contacts. Another aspect of time to be examined is the proper characteristics of time, which can be regarded as having four dimensions: 1) sufficient-insufficient (amount of time), 2) self-related and other-related (internal vs. external control of time, i.e. how much time a person devotes to self-related or other-related activities), 3) structured-unstructured (planning). The planning will be about the most important activity, followed by preferable activities, desirable activities and avoidable activities. Three important strategies are to be considered while allocating time for events, namely a) sequencing or bunching the activities together such as pooling two or more events, b) scheduling activities throughout the day, and c) coordinating one's own time frame with those of others. The fourth dimension is 4) accurate-inaccurate, which is explained in terms of clockwise behavior. The main purpose of this study is to examine as to how Indian managers/academics manage time.

The study was conducted in two service organizations—a bank and a technical research institute. The sample was composed of 75 bank executives and 75 academics. A time-orientation scale consisting of 40 items (10 items for each dimension) was used. The data were gathered through personal interviews. The results suggest that the bank executives were more accurate, more structured, and more other-related than the academics and that the bank executives did not have sufficient time to do their work. The event profiles of academics showed that they get up late but take less time in subsequent activities and that they were engaged in overlapping activities or in studying on their own. The spatial location for both groups was the home and the work place and their social contacts were mostly family.

INTERNAL MODELS AND JOB SATISFACTION

Soili Keskinen,
Department of psychology, University of Turku, Finland

According to the theory of cognitive psychology, the individual's work performance is not directly regulated by objective, perceptible requirements and norms but by interpreted values, goals, concepts, and so forth, that is, by internal models. Internal models are hypothetical structures; their existence and development can ultimately be determined by work performance.

The purpose of the study was to find out how job satisfaction and work performance measured by the degree of development of internal models correlated and what kind of factors contributed to the highest correlation. The study material was obtained by questionnaires from day-care educators ($n = 136$) and children's nurses ($n = 125$) working at day-care centers. The validity of both the internal model measure and the working satisfaction measure has been tested by co-worker assessments.

In the material as a whole the degree of development of internal models did not correlate with job satisfaction. An attempt was made, by means of cluster analysis, to find groups where the degree of development of internal models would more clearly be connected with job satisfaction. Good internal models are connected with at least moderate job satisfaction, provided that the workers' mental health in general is good, and at they feel their work community encourages them and gives them a chance to influence matters.

ORGANIZATIONAL CULTURE, PATERNALISTIC LEADERSHIP, AND JOB SATISFACTION IN IRAN

Shahrenaz Mortazavi & Ahmad Saheli,
University of Shahid Beheshti, Teheran, Iran

It was proposed that job satisfaction could be predicted from organizational culture. In an effort to prove the above concept, three dimensions of organizational culture (perceived relations to co-workers, perceived efficiency of the organizational procedures and paternalistic leadership style) and four leadership-related aspects of organizational culture (supervisory span of control, autocracy, performance-related rewards, and supervisory support) were distinguished for analysis.

A 51-item questionnaire was administered to 520 Iranian employees. The items concerning leadership style were factor analyzed. It was found that the leadership behavior of consideration (composed of items on support and performance reward) and autocracy formed opposite poles of a single factor and therefore could not coexist as perceived dimensions. It was also found that consideration proved to be strongly linked to paternalistic organizational culture, whereas the effect of autocracy was significantly negative. Regression analyses showed that paternalistic leadership style was positively linked to high job satisfaction. Since control items were loaded on a separate factor, we could conclude from our results that the application of control associated with autocracy could be perceived as coercive, whereas its association with paternalistic behavior would be perceived as the use of the authority's legitimate power.

DOES PUNISHING "WHISTLEBLOWERS" INFLUENCE ATTITUDES OF EMPLOYEES? A PRELIMINARY EXPERIMENT

Sheldon S. Zalkind, Domniki J. Demetriadou, & Helene Schreier
Baruch College and the Graduate Center, City University of New York, U.S.A.

In the United States employees who report organizational wrongdoing are called whistleblowers. They can provide useful information and sometimes help avoid disasters but are often punished by managers. To explore experimentally if various simulated management actions influence employee responses, we used six scenarios (stories). Each subject (N = 319, all employed) was given a booklet that asked him or her to imagine working in a situation in which he/she learned about health and safety violations and reported these to the boss (i.e., blew the whistle). The scenario then continued with only one of six experimental conditions as the manager's response to the whistleblower. We varied the manager's response in two ways: (a) personal treatment of the reporter (punishment, neutral, reward) and (b) corrective action or inaction on the violations. The subject was then asked a series of questions. Hypotheses were clearly supported. With reward—as compared to neutral treatment or punishment—for whistleblowing, respondents showed greater job satisfaction, higher intentions to stay in the organization and improve work effort; and less likelihood to report violations to outside agencies. Similarly, when management took some corrective action—as compared to inaction—responses were more favorable. This suggests that corrective management action and favorable treatment of employees who speak up in a socially responsible direction may also benefit organizations internally. If these experimental explorations (which fit our prior survey findings) are supported in other settings, then punishing whistleblowers (which is a typical response in organizations) and not correcting wrongdoing seems dysfunctional. The complex issues of free speech, loyalty, and responsibility relate to traditional areas of psychology.

ANTICIPATION OF SELF-EMPLOYER WORK-VALUES HARMONY

Dale D. Simmons, Oregon State University, U.S.A.

Most research with human values has involved the measurement of the values of individuals and groups rather than the measuring of the congruence of individuals with community norms or with expectations of desired patterns of values. University students, in this study, were asked to rate 22 work values for themselves and for what they expected their future employers would desire of them. The mean correlation between personal ratings and anticipated future employer desires was only $r = .28$. Correlations between personal ratings and anticipated future employer desires on specific work values ranged from $r = -.18$ for creativity to $r = .37$ for physical activity. Only one work value (loyalty) was anticipated to be of more importance to future employers than to self, while 17 other work values were significantly ($p < .002$) more important to self. The greatest of these differences in work values emphasized more by self were on lifestyle, likeable associates, variety, and independence. Hence, these students anticipated little harmony between their current work values and those they believed would be desired of them by future employers. They also anticipated that future employers would give significantly less importance than they to most of their work values. Students above average in anticipated congruence gave higher future employer ratings to advancement, economic return, fair supervision, lifestyle, personal development, and working conditions, and lower self ratings to beauty and independence than those anticipating lower self-employer congruence.

JAPANESE WORKERS' WILL TO WORK AND THEIR ORGANIZATIONAL BEHAVIORS

Kazutoshi Nishikawa,
Momoyama Gakuin University, Osaka, Japan

The purpose of this study was to examine Japanese work motivation by using Japanese keywords such as *yarigai* and *yaruki*. Japanese frequently use the word *yaruki* (meaning something like the highly motivated will to work) when they talk about motivation in all matters. And they eagerly want the jobs from which they can derive *yarigai* (mainly, economically and psychologically rewarding jobs). The most important thing for them is to find the jobs worth having. Investigations were done at intervals of ten years in a general trading company (1980); a specialized trading company established by foreign capital, of which the president and all employees are Japanese (1981); a company making and selling home furnishings (1981); and a company dealing in and servicing automobiles (1990). Each employee was asked the following three questions: (a) On what occasions did you have a sense of *yarigai* at your workplace? (b) On what occasions was your *yaruki* exhausted at your workplace? (c) What is the most important condition that makes you work easily at your workplace?

The results of the surveys indicated that (a) it is necessary to make it possible to achieve the tasks set, to exhibit ability, and to make evaluation reasonable for workers in order to increase yarigai; (b) receiving a satisfactory evaluation and having the shop unified as one group are important in maintaining yaruki; and (c) conditions absolutely necessary to make employees work easily at the shop are good human relations, a sense of togetherness, harmony (wa in Japanese), and so on.

These results imply that few workers can attain the *yarigai* with *yaruki* without comfortable shops run according to the Japanese way of working even if the workers know what they can derive *yarigai* from and have a lot of *yaruki* to do so. These motivation structures result in the Japanese working styles, which lead people in other countries to suppose that Japanese work hard for many hours.

THE PSYCHOLOGICAL IMPACT OF UNEMPLOYMENT ON YOUNG PEOPLE

Anthony H. Winefield,
University of Adelaide, South Australia

Longitudinal data were presented from an Australian study of 742 young people. The following three target groups were compared on measures of personality and psychological well-being: satisfied employed, dissatisfied employed, and unemployed. The satisfied employed group displayed greater self-esteem (Rosenberg, 1965) and less externality (Nowicki & Duke, 1974), depressive affect (Rosenberg, 1965) and negative mood (Tiggemann & Winefield, 1984) than the dissatisfied employed and unemployed groups, which did not differ (see Table 1). Tests administered four years earlier, when the participants were at school, revealed that the dissatisfied employed displayed greater negative mood at that time than the other groups. Moreover, the satisfied employed showed a reduction in negative mood, the dissatisfied employed no change, and the unemployed an increase. Implications of the results for deprivation theories of work were discussed, and it was suggested that later job dissatisfaction may be predictable from personality characteristics identifiable before the individual joins the work force.

TABLE 1
Means on four psychological scales at Time 1 and Time 2 for three groups

| | Group | | | |
| | Satisfied | Dissatisfied | | |
Scale	employed	employed	Unemployed	Significance
Self-esteem T1	7.82	7.29	7.44	< .05
Self-esteem T2	8.92	8.08	8.08	< .0001
Locus of Control T1	13.48	13.76	13.43	n.s.
Locus of Control T2	9.76	10.78	11.56	< .05
Depressive affect T1	1.40	1.38	1.41	n.s.
Depressive affect T2	0.74	1.39	1.57	<.0001
Negative mood T1	13.00	14.16	12.99	< .001
Negative mood T2	11.88	13.85	13.68	< .001

Locus of Control T113.82

References
Nowicki, S., & Duke, M. P. (1974). A locus of control scale for noncollege as well as college adults. *Journal of Personality Assessment, 38,* 136-137.

Rosenberg, M. (1965). *Society and the adolescent self-image.* Princeton: Princeton University Press.

Tiggemann, M., & Winefield, A. H. (1984). The effects of unemployment on the mood, self-esteem, locus of control and depressive affect of school leavers. *Journal of Occupational Psychology, 57,* 33-42.

OCCUPATIONAL STRESS IN THE OFFSHORE OIL INDUSTRY

Karen Sutherland & Rhona Flin
Business School, R.G.I.T., Aberdeen, Scotland

The British sector of the North Sea oil and gas industry employs 25,000 individuals on drilling rigs, production platforms, and support vessels. Psychological research in this occupational area has been scant (see Sutherland & Flin, 1989). The present study examined the incidence of occupational stress, the levels of job satisfaction, and related phenomena in this unique work group. A questionnaire was designed to assess: (a) demographic details, (b) occupational stressors in offshore work, (c) job satisfaction, (d) Type A behavior, (e) physical health, and (f) mental health. It was distributed to 450 offshore employees, and the results are based on 212 responses (75% contractors, 25% operators).

The principal causes of stress relate to pay, job security, management style, organizational communication, and concern for family. Contractor staff members were significantly more dissatisfied with their jobs than those working for operating companies. The most frequently reported physical ailments were sleep-related problems and digestive system complaints. In terms of mental health, 28% of the respondents scored in the "high anxiety" range and 11% scored in the "high depression" range.

Preliminary results suggest that contractor staff members report higher levels of stress than their counterparts who are employed by the operating companies. This may be because contractors have traditionally had less job security, poorer wages, and, on some installations, a lower status in comparison to the operating personnel. There were also differences in levels of reported stress, job satisfaction, and anxiety associated with Type A behavior scores.

Reference

Sutherland, K., & Flin, R. (1989) Stress at sea. *Work & Stress, 3,* 1269-285.

DUAL-EARNER STRESS AND COPING

Jennifer Berdahl and Jack E. Rossmann
Macalester College, St. Paul, Minnesota, U.S.A.

During the past decade, there has been a dramatic increase in the share of college-educated married couples in the United States in which both husband and wife work full-time outside the home. This study collected questionnaire data from 88 women and 30 men who were a sample of graduates from an independent four-year liberal arts college in the years 1961-67 and 1970-75. All respondents had a spouse who worked full-time outside the home and at least one child under the age of 18 who was living at home.

Female respondents indicated that intellectual stimulation and personal fulfillment were their primary reasons for working outside their home, whereas the primary reason identified by men was financial. To cope with the stress of dual-income employment, both male and female respondents indicated that they leave some things undone around the house, believe there are more advantages than disadvantages to their lifestyle, and try to be flexible enough to fit in special needs and events.

Correlational analyses indicated that women who value working outside the home because of a commitment to the goal or purpose of their specific area of work are likely to perceive themselves as better parents, better spouses, and better role models for their children, to see working as good for their personal growth, and to see more advantages than disadvantages to their dual career lifestyle.

OCCUPATIONAL STRESS AND COPING OF JAPANESE WHITE COLLAR WORKERS

Naotaka Watanabe, Nanzan University, Nagoya, Japan

The present study was designed to investigate relations between occupational stress, coping strategies, and the resulting mental health of Japanese white-collar workers. The psychological instruments employed in the study were (a) a chronic stress scale, (b) an acute stress scale, (c) a coping questionnaire, and (d) the Hopkins Symptom Checklist. The data were obtained from a series of surveys of a total of 537 white-collar employees from three different Japanese companies.

The following findings were obtained as the results of multivariate analyses of the data:

1. Factor analyses showed that a trifactorial structure in stress coping strategies exists; they are problem-focused, emotion-focused, and fight/phantasizing.

2. Problem-focused coping was more conducive to good mental health than the others.

3. Significant relations were observed between chronic stress and mental health, but no significant relation was found between acute stress and mental health.

4. The hypothesized moderating effect of coping strategies on relations between occupational stress and mental health was not found.

STRESS, NEW TECHNOLOGY AND INTENSIVE CARE IN HOSPITALS

Eunice McCarthy, University College Dublin, Ireland

This research, which formed part of a larger study (McCarthy & Tiernan, 1987) focused on the psychosocial impact of new technology (medical technology) on the task and role of nurses in specialist hospital areas, in other words, in intensive care units (ICU's) and coronary care units (CCU's). A person-environment-fit model was developed to explore the interaction between nurses and their work environments (ICU-CCU work settings), with particular emphasis on (a) nurses' perceptions of the role of new technology in general and its specific impact on their jobs, on their skills, on the patient, and on overall job performance, and (b) identification of key stressors in ICU-CCU work settings, in particular stress arising from workload, machines, new technology, patient care, and factors relating to unit organisation.

Objective data was obtained by observational analysis of the tasks of the nurse in caring for patients utilizing the new technology (NT). Observations were guided and supplemented by in-depth interviews with 18 nurses and with suppliers of the equipment. Subjective perceptual and attitudinal data was obtained with quantitative, attitudinal scales, and statistical analysis. NT and stress/coping scales were specifically designed for this study. A sample of 52 female nurses in hospital units in five Dublin hospitals (four teaching hospitals) were selected.

The use of different questionnaire formats revealed that the majority of respondents viewed new technology in their units as helpful and as enabling them to do a good job. Given this overall view, with more specific questions relating to new technology, nurses demonstrated concern about handling the new technology and the extent to which it takes attention away from the patient. Accordingly, the impact of NT on nurses' skills was explored. It clearly emerged that nurses viewed NT as increasing the skill level requirements of their jobs. However, this perception is qualified with the concern expressed by the 77% who perceive their work as becoming more impersonal because of NT and by the 69% who agreed that they have become "a technician because of NT, rather than a carer." Thus, the pattern emerging suggests a dilemma for the nurses in relation to the impact of NT — it can have both positive effects (i.e., adding to their skills) and negative effects (i.e., intruding on their caring and personal role with the patient). This pattern suggests that the cognitive resources of the nurses were enhanced by NT, while social emotional resources of the nurses can be inhibited by NT. Sources of stress in ICU-CCU substantially involved unit-organizational variables, in particular, inadequate staffing, inexperienced staff and shift schedules, and lack of knowledge and skill in handling unfamiliar equipment and technology. More specific probing regarding nurses' perceptions of the impact of NT on the patient yielded the overall picture that NT is perceived as mediating the role between the nurse and the patient. Implications for training, work design, and hospital culture were mapped out.

Reference

McCarthy, E., & Tiernan, J. (1978). *The Impact of New Technology on Workers and Patients in the Health Services — New Technology, Nurses Roles, Stress and Coping*. Dublin: European Foundation for the Improvement of Living and Working Conditions.

VALUES OF THE THERAPIST:
THE HIDDEN DIMENSION

Nedra R. Lander and Danielle Nahon, Ottawa Civic Hospital, Canada

O. Hobart Mowrer offered the position that stresses in life most often reflect an infidelity to a personal value system and/or a lack of shared values with one's major group of affiliation. The identification of our values as individuals and the manner in which they interface with our values as therapists are increasingly vital concerns for the clinician. The concept of a cognitive dissonance in values offers a novel perspective for a reframing and beginning resolution of impasses in therapist-client and colleague-colleague interactions. Furthermore, the examination of a possible clash in value systems between the professional and his/her organizational structure provides a fresh perspective on the understanding of care-giver burn-out.

In both the clinical setting as well as through a series of value workshops offered to therapists of varying orientations, three major themes have arisen: the lack of emphasis on issues of valuing both in therapeutic training and in professional practice; the dilemma of allegiance to a given therapeutic framework versus the implementation of interventions based on the therapist's value system; and the concept of a clash in values between therapist and client as a viable means of reformulating a therapeutic impasse. Mowrer's Integrity Therapy model has emerged as a useful conceptual tool in facilitating a resolution of value conflicts both within and without the therapeutic encounter.

CROSS-VALIDATION OF CREATIVE
PROBLEM-SOLVING/CREATIVE STYLE INVENTORIES:
VALIDATING BASADUR'S CPSP WITH KIRTON'S KAI
INVENTORY

Min Basadur, McMaster University
Jiro Takai, Nagoya City University
Mitsuru Wakabayashi, Nagoya University

The Creative Problem Solving Profile (CPSP) was devised by Basadur, Green, & Wakabayashi (1988), based on the experience-thinking and ideation-evaluation dimensions of gaining and using knowledge, respectively. Four different styles of creative problem-solving — Generator, Conzeptualizer, Optimizer, and Implementor — were identified by cross-tabulating the above two dimensions. Blends of the four styles result in profiles unique to individuals. All four styles are

TABLE 1
Correlation between the Creative Problem Solving Profile (Basadur, 1988) and the scales of the Kirton Adaption-Innovation Inventory (Kirton, 1976)

Scale/Style	mean	SD	X	I	T	E	X-T	I-E	O	E	R	KAI	XxI	IxT	TxE	ExX
Experience(X)	30.2	5.2	-													
Ideation (I)	28.7	6.2	-0.18	-												
Thinking (T)	30.5	4.7	-0.69	-0.20	-											
Evaluation (E)	30.6	5.5	-0.16	-0.78	0.04	-										
(X-T)	-0.3	9.1	0.93	0.00	-0.09	-0.11	-									
(I-E)	-1.8	11.1	-0.02	0.95	-0.13	-0.94	0.06	-								
Originality	41.6	7.8	0.13	0.32	-0.25	-0.26	-0.20	0.31	-							
Efficiency	18.8	4.1	-0.03	0.18	-0.8	-0.12	0.02	-0.16	0.08	-						
Rule Conformity (R)	38.4	6.6	0.17	0.16	-0.20	-0.16	0.20	0.17	0.64	0.34	-					
KAI	98.7	14.5	0.14	0.29	-0.25	-0.24	0.21	0.29	0.85	0.48	0.90	-				
Generator (XxI)	861.9	219.1	0.55	0.72	-0.65	-0.77	0.65	0.79	0.34	0.14	0.24	0.33	-			
Conceptualizer (IxT)	870.1	208.9	-0.60	0.77	0.45	-0.68	-0.58	0.77	0.15	0.11	0.02	0.12	0.22	-		
Optimizer (TXE)	933.3	224.0	-0.55	0.71	0.66	0.77	-0.66	-0.78	0.36	-0.13	-0.25	-0.35	-0.98	-0.23	-	
Implementor (ExX)	918.9	211.0	0.60	-0.75	-0.48	0.68	0.59	-0.76	-0.09	-0.12	0.01	-0.08	-0.23	-0.97	0.20	-

NOTE: Coefficients over 0.31 are statistically significant at $P < 0.001$, 0.23 at $P < 0.1$ and 0.16 at $P < 0.05$.

required for the creative process to flourish in an organization. A sample of 101 engineers was taken to investigate the validity of Basadur's CPSP and Kirton's Adaption-Innovation Inventory (KAI; Kirton, 1976) in two different ways (see Table 1). First, subjects were divided into the four creative problem-solving style groups named above, and their KAI scores were compared. It was found that the Generator style scored higher on the KAI than did the Optimizer style as well as all the other groups combined. This result indicated, as expected, that Basadur's Generator-Optimizer distinction relates significantly with Kirton's Innovator-Adaptor distinction. Second, area scores were computed along the dimension axes for each of the CPSP styles to determine how each style correlated with the KAI scores. Results showed that Generator and Optimizer styles correlate significantly $(P < .01)$ at $r = -.33$ and $r = .35$, respectively. These results, along with the first analysis, suggested that, as predicted, the Generator style is consistent with the characteristics of the KAI innovative style of creativity, whereas the Optimizer style is consistent with the characteristics of the KAI adaptive style of creativity.

References

Basadur, M. S., Green, G. B., & Wakabayashi, M. (1988). *Identifying creative problem solving style*. McMaster University Research and Working Paper Series, No. 137.

Kirton, M. J. (1976). Adaptors and innovators: A description and measure. *Journal of Applied Pschology, 61*, 622-629.

APPLICATIONS OF A COMPUTERISED FUZZY GRAPHIC RATING SCALE

Beryl Hesketh, School of Psychology, UNSW, Sydney, Australia

The poster described various applications of a computerized fuzzy graphic rating scale documented in Hesketh, Pryor, and Hesketh (1988). The rating scale is a modified semantic differential that allows for asymmetrical latitudes of acceptance on either side of a preferred point to indicate flexibility or uncertainty about preferences. Fuzzy arithmetic operations can be used in the analysis of the data. Applications for the fuzzy ratings described included (a) measuring Occupational Social Space in order to test Gottfredson's (1981) theory of career circumscription and compromise (Hesketh, Elmslie, & Kaldor, 1990), (b) rating job demands in a cognitive work task analysis system, (c) testing Person-Environment fit models to see if incorporating flexibility improved predictions, and (d) as an aid to vocational and family counseling interventions. Potential applications in the area of knowledge engineering were also outlined.

Acknowledgements

Australian Research Council for funding.

References

Hesketh, T., Pryor, R., & Hesketh, B. (1988). An application of a computerised Fuzzy Graphic Rating Scale to the psychological measurement of individual differences. *International Journal of Man Machine Studies, 29*, 21-35.

Hesketh, B., Elmslie, S., & Kaldor, W. (1990). Career compromise: An alternative account to Gottfredson's (1981) theory. *Journal of Counseling Psychology, 37*, 49-56.

Gottfredson, L. S. (1981). Circumscription and compromise: A developmental theory of occupational aspirations [Monograph]. *Journal of Counseling Psychology, 28*, 545-579.

OCCUPATIONAL PRESTIGE: PERCEPTIONS OF AMERICAN, JAPANESE, AND THAI HIGH SCHOOL SENIORS

Roya Ayman and Fong Chang,
Illinois Institute of Technology, Chicago, USA
Kanetoshi Hattori,
National Rehabilitation Center for the Disabled, Tokorozawa City, Japan
Sunturee Komin,
National Institute of Development Administration, Bangkok, Thailand

The authors report the result of a study of 400 high school seniors from Japan, Thailand, and the United States. The participants were asked to rate the prestige of 100 traditional and contemporary occupations and to determine factors influencing the attainability of these occupations and meaning of prestige in different countries, using the *Occupational Standing Scale* (Parker, Chan, & Saper, 1989) and the *Meaning of Prestige Scale* (Ayman & Chan, 1990). There are four main points that resulted from this study: (a) The Spearman Rho coefficients demonstrated more similarity between the American and Japanese (rho = .76) and between Americans and Thais (.71) than between Thai responses and Japanese (.42). These findings demonstrated country differences that are contrary to previous findings (Trieman, 1977). (b) Rating of the traditional occupations (e.g., lawyer, accountant, and physician) concurred with the National Opinion Research Center studies (Reiss, 1961) for both the American and Thai samples. However, on the more contemporary occupations (e.g., computer operator and computer program analyst), the American and Thai respondents showed more difficulty assigning scores than the Japanese respondents. (c) The possibility of contribution of cultural values was evident on some occupations such as police officer, which Japanese and Thais rated much higher than their American counterparts did. (d) The result of a MANOVA on meanings of prestige yielded two main effects: gender and country. Women put more emphasis on education than men did. Japanese emphasized hard work more than their counterparts from the other two sampled countries did, and American and Thais emphasized wealth more than Japanese did.

References

Ayman, R., & Chan, F. (1990). *Occupational prestige: Perceptions of American, Japanese, and Thai students*. Unpublished manuscript, Illinois Institute of Technology, Chicago.

Parker, H. J., Chan, F., & Saper, B. (1989). Occupational representativeness and prestige rating: Some observations. *Journal of Employment Counseling, 26*, 117-131.

Reiss, A. (Ed.) (1961). *Occupations and social status*. New York: Free Press.

Trieman, D. J. (1977). *Prestige in comparative perspective*. New York: Academic Press.

OPERANT CONDITIONING THEORY AND SUPERVISION

Marita Hyttinen,
The University of Tampere, Finland

According to operant conditioning theory, it is important that a supervisor actively provides instructions for the performance of a subordinate (antecedent), collects information (monitor), and indicates knowledge of that performance (consequence). Positive consequences are viewed as strengthening the behavior after it has occurred.

In the present study, the behavior of the supervisor was analyzed through the Operant Supervisory Taxonomy and Index. How much does the behavior of the supervisor contain antecedents, monitors, and consequences. Do any of these categories based on operant theory relate to successful supervision? The subjects were 31 supervisors at construction sites. Subordinates evaluated the successfulness of leadership behavior according to the above criteria.

As a group, supervisors spent about one fourth of their time dealing with the performance of their subordinates: 10.5%   providing antecedents, 11.7% monitoring, and 4.2% providing consequences. On the basis of our study successful leaders provided more consequences but fewer antecedents than unsuccessful ones. The category of monitors did not distinguish between the two groups.

The theory of operant conditioning was verified only in part. The results showed that the worker does not fit the operant model of the human being: He or she is not the passive object of the acts of the supervisor. On the contrary a worker is an actively oriented subject who is capable of planning and monitoring his or her own performance. The role of the leader is to support these active acts and to show knowledge of the final performance.

AN EXPERIENTIAL LEARNING MODEL AND THE TRAINING OF MANAGEMENT TEAMS: EXPERIENCES AND RESULTS

Rosa María Gonzalez Tirados, Polytechnic University of Madrid, Spain

The experiential learning model that I have developed and applied in various research works makes it possible to find out "how" to learn, what the "process" of learning is, and what its relation is with both decision-making and problem-solving. Likewise, knowledge of this model makes it possible to analyze the influence that each mode of learning has on the organization of management and its development.

Research thus far (Gonzalez Tirados, 1983, 1986, 1989) has led to:

1.   Proof of the reliability of an instrument able to define the "individual mode of learning" and the development of its "capacities" in Spain.

2.   Results and opinions that contrast with those obtained by researchers at the Massachusetts Institute of Technology (MIT) in the United States.

3.   Testing of whether the mode of learning and, hence, subsequent problem solving among Spanish graduates has changed in the course of their studies.

4.   Inquiry about whether there is a definitive mode of learning in certain studies and whether that mode of learning is a parameter that has an influence on the degree of graduate's academic failure or success.

Many results of the research have contributed to the discovery of certain hidden motives. Knowledge of the model also contributes to a very useful methodology for training management teams, eventually for improving their own personal development.

References

Gonzalez Tirados, R. M. (1983). *Influencia de la naturaleza de los estudios universitarios en los estilos de aprendizaje de los sujetos*. Doctoral dissertation, Facultad de Psicología. Universidad Complutense de Madrid. (Published November 1985, Servicio de publicaciones de la Universidad Complutense.)

Gonzalez Tirados, R. M. (1986). Estudio de la fiabilidad y validez del Inventario de Estilos de Aprendizaje. *Bordón*, No. 262, 8-12.

Gonzalez Tirados, R. M. (1989). *Análisis de las causas de fracaso escolar en la Universidad Politécnica de Madrid*. Ed. Ministerio de Educación (C.I.D.E.).

A MODEL OF BEHAVIORAL CHANGE IN MANAGERIAL TRAINING

Takao Satow, Kagoshima University of Economics, Shimofukumoto, Kagoshima, 891-01, Japan

The mechanism of behavioral change in managerial training can be understood as four steps of questioning and answering. The steps of inquiry may be shown as follows:

1. Clarification of the status quo.
2. Interpretation of meanings.
3. Insight into the inward cause.
4. Find solution to cope with.

The output of each step of inquiry may be shown as follows:

1. Dominant characteristics of one's behavior observed.
2. Espoused theory of one's behavior explained.
3. Theory-in-use of one's behavior understood.
4. Oriented emphasis of one's behavior expressed.

The approach used was phenomenological, descriptive, and clinical including the observation of behaviors, interpretation of meanings and understanding of inward causes with mutual discussion among members to confirm validity.

Although the approach can be done without step 2 in the process, one's behavior would remain unchanged if step 3 were to be neglected, for one's theory-in-use functions as the motive and dominates one's behavior unconciously. Therefore, one must test oneself and gain insight into one's own theory-in-use. One should be provided feedback of one's reality from others to test oneself. If one is open to such cues, then double-loop learning will take place: open to reality; testable self; gain insight into one's theory-in-use; choose more valid behavior; self-innovation.

TABLE 1
Symptoms and consequences of single-loop learning

Features of dissociation from reality (its model)	Anxiety caused by uncertainties	Defensive behavior
Indifference to reality (red tapism)	Is the institution safe?	Avoid risks
Distortion of reality (Groupthink)	Is the position righteous	Exclude objections
Discarding reality (scientism)	Is the procedure strict enough	Avoid ambiguity

If one is closed to feedback from reality, then single-loop learning begins: closed to reality; untestable self; keep one's espoused-theory; behave as before; dissociate from reality. These processes do not remain personal. Organizations sometimes show the same symptoms of dissociation from reality as individuals do. Each of these symptoms can lead organizations to fail in achieving their own relearning-innovation.

EVALUATION OF TRAINING:
NEW METHODS AND APPLICATIONS TO INDUSTRY

Mitchell E. Kusy, Jr., College of St. Thomas, St. Paul, MN, USA

In the 1990s, organizations are becoming more cost conscious than they have been historically. This situation suggests that training professionals demonstrate their contributions to organizations by becoming more concerned with bottom-line productivity. Since top management often views training as an investment, training evaluation is critical. It can demonstrate training's impact on the organization's bottom line (Bakken & Bernstein, 1982).

The purpose of this study was to determine which type of training evaluation method (reaction, learning, behavior, or results), borrowed from Kirkpatrick (1983), elicited the most management support of the training function among corporate managers. A case study survey instrument (TEMS) was designed to assess the extent of this support. Two samples of respondents to the TEMS were 63 part-time MBA students who were full-time managers and 42 managers in a large health-care organization.

The TEMS described four scenarios that illustrated one of the four evaluation methods. To be certain that each scenario was an accurate illustration of each evaluation method, a validity study was conducted; to assess reliability, a test-retest reliability procedure was used. The data indicated that the results evaluation method received the most support; progressively less support was received for behavior, learning, and reaction evaluation methods, respectively. This study provides training practitioners with a perspective for demonstrating training results to management and an accountability system for gaining management support of training. It also describes an effective training evaluation strategy — the multiple baseline design.

References
Bakken, D., & Bernstein, A. L. (1982). A systematic approach to evaluation. *Training and Development Journal, 36*(8), 44-51.

Kirkpatrick, D. (1983). Four steps to measuring training effectiveness. *Personnel Administration, 28*(11), 19-25.

CREATIVE GROUP THINKING (C.G.T)

Toshiyuki Otsubo, Japan Airlines

Thinking, decision-making and taking action in a group are usually difficult and make a group foolish in some cases. The author has recently developed a tool named the Creative Group Thinking (CGT) method to make thinking, decision-making and taking action in a group effective.

CGT consists of the *Key statement Integration Method* (KIM), the *Definitive Action Program* (DAP), and 10 rules that are closely related to psychology. KIM is the method to establish the order of the actions proposed for the theme (or target). The key statement is allowed to be written only in the format "to + verb + the subject." Because of this restriction, it is possible to express the action simply, clearly, and step by step. DAP is the schedule established through the process of KIM and is completely achieved except for the case of the *force majeure*. This matter can be explained by the psychological hypothesis that the person who wrote the key statement already had the corresponding image. In other words, the realizability of the DAP is very high.

At a glance, KIM and DAP seem simple. However, it is possible to carry out group thinking effectively and speedily if the rules are applied. The success of the CGT is based on the *Artificial brain configuration model theory*, which is being formulated by the author on the basis of cerebral psychological research. The origin of CGT is "Design to Cost," which was established by Mr. Michihiko Ezaki in Japan. Some of the cases in which CGT is applicable are:

1. Planning of the management by several members;
2. Systems-engineering such as factory or airplane design;
3. Strategy-making;
4. Creation of a "new project" schedule; and
5. Project management of the joint venture of several companies.

MAILBOX '90:
A COMPUTER-ASSISTED IN-BASKET TEST

Norbert K. Tanzer and Frits H. J. Roest, University of Graz

MAILBOX'90 (Roest, Scherzer, Urban, Gangl, & Brandstätter, 1989; Roest & Tanzer, 1990) is a computer-assisted In-Basket Test. The main task of the classical paper-pencil version, which is to deal with a number of letters and notes, was maintained. However, in the computer-assisted form, tasks can be delegated to fictive divisions and new tasks may appear in the course of the test. All actions and decisions of the testee are recorded and seven scales are computed: Four scales (Working Time, Planning, Target Orientation, and Performance) assess task-oriented behavior, and three scales (Activity, Delegating, and Structuring) assess course-oriented behavior. The validity of the test was studied in a sample of 105 undergraduate psychology students and in a sample of 196 applicants to a management consulting office. The task-oriented scales have a satisfactory reliability (e.g., = .79 for Work Performance). As expected (see Sackett & Dreher, 1982), the correlations with various intelligence tests and personality scales were rather low. First proof of test validity was given by significant differences in both performance and course-oriented behavior between the two samples. In general, the results show that MAILBOX'90 measures a consistent behavior that cannot be assessed by traditional paper-and-pencil-tests. Hence, the test can contribute significantly to the selection and training of executive officers.

References

Roest, F., Scherzer, A., Urban, E., Gangl, H., & Brandstätter, C. (1989). *MAILBOX '90: Ein computergestütztes Test- und Trainingsverfahren zur Personalentwicklung* [MAILBOX'90: A computer-assisted instrument for the assessment and training of organizational behavior]. Vienna:SciCon & Weinheim, FRG: Beltz Test.

Roest, F., & Tanzer, N. K. (1990). Mailbox'90: A computer-assisted instrument for the assessment and training of organizational behavior. In K. Noro & 0. Brown, Jr. (Eds.), *Human Factors in Organizational Design and Management III* (pp. 313-316). Amsterdam: North Holland

Sackett, P. R., & Dreher, G. F. (1982). Constructs and assessment-center dimensions: Some troubling findings. *Journal of Applied Psychology*, *67*, 401-410.

USE OF ASSESSEMENT CENTER TECHNOLOGY IN MANAGEMENT DEVELOPMENT

Allan Williams and Paul Dobson,
City University Business School, London, England

In our Center for Personnel Research and Enterprise Development, we are designing and evaluating a two-and-a-half-day management development workshop (MDW) based on assessment center technology. Its main aims are (a) to help participants to become more aware of their strengths and weaknesses as managers and to identify development activities that will enable them to become more efffective managers; (b) to help participants develop skills in assessing the behavior of others and in helping them become more effective managers.

The main changes taking place over a series of 5 workshops (involving 149 individuals) reflect an underlying shift from an implicit "selection" to an explicit "development" frame of reference. Thus, one of the features that distinguishes this MDW from traditional development assessment centers (i.e., those that also have a selection objective) is its reliance on self-assessment and peer assessment. This change has, in turn, led to other appropriate changes so as to ensure the efficient achievement of the MDW's objectives. The action research approach applied has resulted in useful learning taking place in the design of such workshops, and these lessons will be shared with others.

Research in progress aims to accumulate quantitative data on the effectiveness of the MDW, including follow-up data relating to the personal action plans of participants.

ACCEPTANCE OF THE INTRODUCTION OF NEW TECHNOLOGY IN ORGANISATIONS: A PROPOSED MODEL

John Hurley, Dublin City University, Ireland

This article proposes a model of the acceptance of New Technology in Organizations. This model is based on the psychology of work and organizations. The New Technologies are defined to include both Information Technologies and Advanced Manufacturing Technology.

The relation between New Technology and Job Redesign is described. The model proposed in this presentation is intended as a framework for the exploration of acceptance by employees of technological innovation. It should form the basis for research on the introduction of the New Technologies in relation to manufacturing and problem areas associated with it. A research procedure is described for testing this model in an organizational setting.

The model is based on the Theory of Reasoned Action (Ajzen & Fishbein, 1980) and is critical of a model described as the Technology Acceptance Model of Davis, Bagozzi, and Warshaw (1989). This latter model does not admit of any organizational variable whereas the model proposed in this paper incorporates a comprehensive coverage of organizational variables.

References

Ajzen, I., & Fishbein, M. (1980). *Understanding attitudes, and predicting social behavior*. New Jersey: Prentice Hall.

Davis, F., & Bagozzi, R. (1989). User acceptance of computer technology: A comparison of two theoretical models. *Management Science, 35*, (8), 983-1003.

FITTING THE INTERVENTION TO THE CLIENT'S NEEDS: A THREE YEAR FLEXIBLE OD EFFORT

Renate R. Mai-Dalton, University of Kansas, USA

The approach to OD that is described in this paper is offered as an alternative to a more traditional scientific methodology that has been viewed critically by Beer and Walton (1987) and Burke (1985). According to these researchers, OD projects should place emphasis on long-term involvements with organizations and include contextual variables and system dynamics into the research design. Intuitive skills should be used to sense and observe ongoing changes in the organization that influence the OD work. Flexibility of planned interventions must be a vital part of this process (Schein, 1989).

The paper describes the ongoing work of an OD consultant in a rapidly growing service organization ($N = 130$) during the past three years. Bullock and Batten's (1985) theoretical framework was used to conduct OD interventions. The paper follows the client-consultant relationship from entry to the first diagnosis, first interventions, evaluations of these interventions and the continuation of this cycle to the current status of the work.

Issues addressed in the paper include (a) client and consultant goal compatibility, (b) power issues in top management, (c) the need to recognize the client's constraints from its constituents, (d) the readiness of these constituents to accept a new work philosophy, and (e) the need to sense the organization's culture carefully in order to synchronize intraorganizational events, external events, and specific OD interventions.

References

Beer, M., & Walton, A. E. (1987). Organization and development. *Annual Review of Psychology, 38*, 339-67.

Burke, W. (1985, March). Organization development, You and the future. *OD Practitioner*, 107.

Schein, E. H. (1989, August). *Organizational development: Science, philosophy, or technology?* Presentation at the 49th Annual Meeting of the Academy of Management, Washington, DC.

ORGANIZATIONAL PSYCHOLOGY WORKSHOP AND AUDIOVISUAL PRESENTATIONS

MEASUREMENT AND ANALYSIS OF LEADERSHIP BEHAVIOR IN THE EAST AND WEST FROM SENIOR EXECUTIVE TO FIRST-LINE SUPERVISOR IN ORGANIZATIONAL SETTINGS

J. Misumi & M. Hafsi, Nara University, Japan

Based on the general hypothesis that states that leadership fulfills two basic functions (performance and maintenance), the PM theory suggests a quadritypology of leadership: PM-type, M-type, P-type, and pm-type (Misumi, 1985). The leader's leadership style is determined on the basis of the score attributed to him/her (by the subordinates) on these two functions. The PM-type was found to be the most effective and the pm-type the least effective leadership style, with, respectively, the M-type and P-type in between. This typology is one of the main characteristics distinguishing the PM Theory from the dichotomic approach that characterizes many previous leadership studies.

Beginning from a replication of an American study on leadership style and social climate, the PM leadership theory has developed as an extensive interdisciplinary and cross-cultural approach to leadership (Smith, Peterson, Misumi, & Sugiman, 1990). The PM leadership theory not only proposes a new paradigm for leadership research, but also an intensive leadership training program that is based on the general assumption that effective leadership is a learnable behavior.

References
Misumi, J. (1985). *The behavioral science of leadership* (2nd ed.). Ann Arbor: Michigan University Press.
Smith, P. B., Peterson M. F., Misumi, J., & Sugiman, T. (1990). Cross-cultural tests of PM leadership theory: East meets West. *The Japanese Journal of Experimental Social Psychology, 29* (3), 53-63.

AFFIRMATIVE ACTION FOR WOMEN IN THE UNIVERSITY

Leader: Esther R. Greenglass,
Department of Psychology, York University, Toronto, Canada

The purpose of this workshop was to examine the role of the psychologist in affirmative-action programs designed to increase opportunities in the university for qualified women PhDs. Various theories of social psychology were applied to examine how systemic discrimination functions as a barrier to women's academic achievements. Four guiding principles were used: The need for the development of a policy to implement affirmative action; the role of structural elements in sustaining affirmative action; organizational requirements necessary for implementing affirmative action; and the role of equity assessors in monitoring the hiring process. The workshop also focused on steps to be incorporated into a university affirmative action plan, including collection of background information, specifying subfields in which they are found, and their academic status. Departmental planning should integrate affirmative-action plans such that narrowly-defined departmental "needs" do not exclude women not in these narrow specialties. A more general definition of departmental priorities may facilitate the location of qualified women faculty. The hiring unit should use all means to enlarge the pool of qualified women applications by targeting ads to women's caucuses, networks, and nonacademic settings (where many qualified women may be found). Short lists should consist of women candidates. A goal should be specified in terms of the proportion of academic female appointments that could be achieved in reasonable time. The perception, evaluation, and hiring of women as faculty are integral processes, each of which must be dealt with if equality for women in the university is to be achieved.

ADAPTING A VIDEO SELECTION TEST FOR USE IN ANOTHER CULTURE

Sandra A. McIntire and James N. Thomas
Assessment Designs, International, Longwood, Florida

A large Australian financial institution wished to use the Teller Assessment Program (TAP) and the Financial Salesperson Assessment Program (FSAP), videotests developed for banks in the United States, to assess applicants for the jobs of teller and service advisor. Subject matter experts verified the content validity of the tests using a job-match procedure. In addition, 384 Australian bank personnel were administered the tests in a four-day pilot. Mean scores for the Australian sample were significantly higher for TAP and significantly lower for FSAP. Since data gathered from subject matter experts in Australia showed the jobs to be similar in Australia and the United States, differences in mean test scores were attributed to cultural differences. Overall, the tasks, environment, and bank products were believed by subject matter experts in Australia to be similar enough to warrant using the same test after adapting the script and reshooting the video. Changes were made in the video to accommodate differences between U.S. and Australian currency, appearance of checks, interest rates, spelling and language, and product offerings.

Ergonomics

FUTURE DEVELOPMENT OF ERGONOMICS IN JAPAN

Masamitsu Oshima,
Medical Information System Development Center,
Tokyo, Japan

The development of ergonomics in Japan has been closely linked with the country's rapid industrial growth over the past two decades. The field started out with studies on the arrangement of machines and the human being's environment to ensure their compatibility with human capabilities. Recently, another step forward was taken in the field when researchers began studying comfort. The fact that one can hear or see something about comfort every day through mass communication and mass media reflects the great awareness and concern people have about comfort nowadays. Not surprisingly, then, it is precisely this attention to comfort that has become the trend in ergonomics in Japan. When talking about the future of ergonomics, one cannot help but focus on ways to make people as comfortable as possible. With this point in mind, I focus this contribution on the present and future pursuit of comfort in Japan.

Figure 1 depicts at least one way of considering the many conditions that contribute to comfort, which is addressed to the area of mental hygiene represented at the top of the triangle. Ergonomics in Japan was initially centered on the conditions relating to materials and devices and gradually came to deal with conditions in the mental sphere.

There are many conditions that produce comfort. According to Yagi, the first factor to afford comfort is a sensory factor that stimulates specific sensory organs reacting to colors, odor, sound, and still more complicated patterns such as melody, tone, picture, and scenery. The

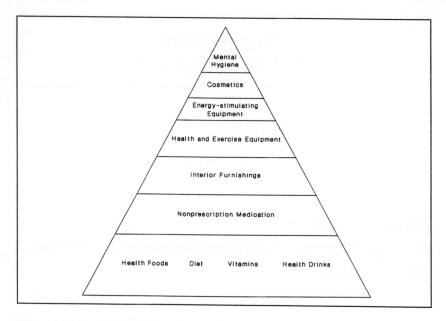

FIG. 1. Hierarchy for health improvement as seen in Japan

second factor is ready access to physical exercise such as dancing, running, jumping, skiing, or skating. The third is facile imagination, quick understanding, and the capacity to react through insights. The fourth factor is observed when digestion and circulation are functioning well and when muscle tone is at its best, which is one of the conditions linked to relaxation. Under the same condition the following are obstructed: appetite, affection, and friendship (which are received if sought) and anger (which is allowed to be expressed freely).

Everything that produced the opposite effect is a "discomfort-causing factor." It would be difficult to list every factor of this sort that has been studied in ergonomics, but I would like to point out the major factors and talk about them in terms of their psychological function. Initially, the main thrust of ergonomics has been to combat such factors, beginning with the elimination of unwieldiness in tools. Today, the main effort is to increase comfort by eliminating that which is poor in texture, hard on the skin, too high, too low, hard to see, hard to hear, excessively noisy, and so forth.

For example, in 1983 the office of the prime minister conducted a public opinion poll on the Japanese life style. This survey contained an item on the "time when one feels satisfaction." The response with the highest frequency was "when with the family," followed by "when

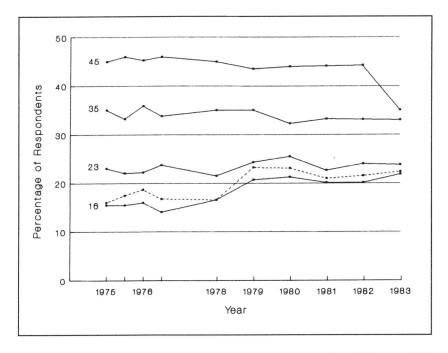

FIG. 2. Responses of Japanese and non-Japanese to the question of when one feels satisfaction (Prime Minister's Office, 1983)

working," "when resting," "when meeting friends," and "when pursuing my hobby," in that order (see Figure 2). These responses are certainly closely related to ergonomics. Experiencing genuine satisfaction during and after work is very important. To be sure, the optimal life style would include the pursuit of comfort both at and outside the workplace.

An analysis of the results of this public opinion poll showed that, deep inside, Japanese respondents were in general more dissatisfied than non-Japanese respondents, at least with the social aspect of their comfort (see Figure 3). This finding must be borne in mind in international comparative studies on the pursuit of comfort.

As illustrated in Figure 4, the percentage of respondents who emphasize mostly material richness is gradually decreasing, whereas the percentage of those who find more value in emotional richness is increasing according to the 1986 results of the national opinion poll. This finding shows that value judgment in Japanese society is shifting from material richness to emotional richness, which is one of the prerequisites for comfort. The study of ergonomics should, therefore, also include the changes in people's value judgments as well.

As concerns the conditions necessary for comfort, the shape of the

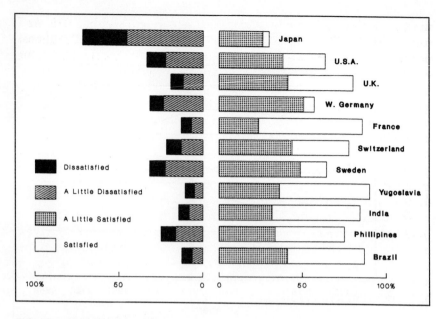

FIG. 3. International comparison of the degree of satisfaction in social life (Prime Minister's Office, 1972)

rectangle has been an issue for many years. The Golden Ratio, for instance, is said to provide what for human beings is thought to be the

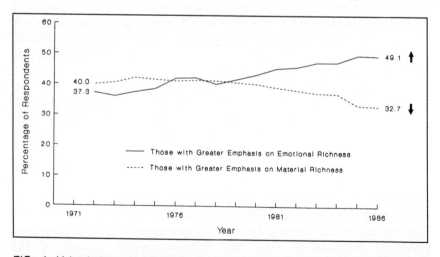

FIG. 4. Value judgment changes in Japanese society as shown in the respondents' shifts of emphasis from material to emotional richness (from the Public Opinion Poll conducted by the Prime Minister's Office, 1986)

most agreeable optical relation between length and width, 1.618. As I understand it, this relation conforms, perhaps coincidentally, almost perfectly to the physiology of the human eye (see Figure 5). Let us examine the length/width ratio of a variety of objects on this earth: files, 1.34; typing paper, 1.41; small television, 1.47; passports, 1.63; business cards, 1.67; calculators, 1.71; and a ten thousand yen bill, 2.06. The numbers lead to the conclusion that these objects all have dimensions approximating the Golden Ratio regardless of the different shapes they have for fulfilling their purposes. It is also interesting to note that people, when asked to pick out the best rectangle among rectangles of many different shapes, are most likely to choose the one whose dimensions most closely approximate the Golden Ratio.

Adequate illumination has been an issue in comfort as well. If the lighting is too bright, one feels dizzy, and the pupil, which is the organ adjusting the amount of light intake, will be at the minimum dilation, which is 2 mm to 3 mm in diameter. If the lighting is too dim, one cannot see things clearly, and the pupil will be at maximum dilation, a diameter of 7 mm to 8 mm. Physiologically, the diameter of the pupil that is "just

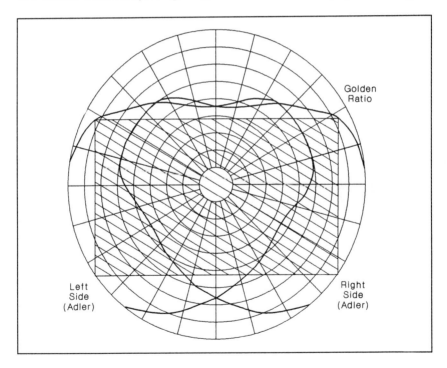

FIG. 5. Relation between the visual field and the Golden Ratio

right" lies between its "closed minimum" and "open maximum," that is, around 5 mm, which corresponds to illumination ranging between 400 lux and 500 lux. In my opinion, these optimal conditions provide the human pupil with maximum freedom and therefore have physiological bearing on what constitutes comfort for the individual.

Temperature, too, is a factor in comfort. People say that they are comfortable when the air temperature is 21° and 22° centigrade. Interestingly enough, the state of excitement (which is demonstrated by Flicker values), then the body's metabolism and tensity, rises with the air temperature—until somewhere between 21° and 22° centigrade. Within that range, Flicker values begin declining. The atmospheric temperature of the highest tensity level which allows for sufficient brain activity is likewise between 21° and 22° centigrade. It can therefore be concluded that people feel the greatest comfort when they can work with the highest level of tensity. For manual labor, the most comfortable air temperature is around 17° and 18°, at which point body temperature ranges between 21° and 22° C with the movement of the body. Therefore, the most comfortable temperatures for both intellectual and manual labor are substantially the same.

Color is also a factor contributing to comfort. There is a vertical "value" (black and white) and a horizontal "chroma" (see Figure 6). A low value causes gloominess; a high value, cheerfulness. If the value is excessively high or low, a zone not conducive to comfort is entered. The lower band of chroma also falls into such an unfavorable zone. The comfortable zone is determined by chroma and value indices. The favorable zone is at the center of chroma. Because the vertical (black-white) value may be either high or low in the favorable zone, it is the color itself that contains the factor that contributes to the human sense of comfort. Moon Spencer is a matter of color harmony.

The color circle, represented by 360°, if represented as a horizontal line, is called the "angle of distance in color relations." This angle ranges from 0° to 360°. The concept is based on the apparent shift of hue that occurs when a given color is placed in proximity to other colors. The shift follows the curved line in Figure 7. If neighboring colors are identical, no difference, or gap, between the two perceived colors is observed. If no gap is observed at 360°, it means that the gap does not exist at 180°, either. The gap perceived between two colors will exist regardless of the direction in which one moves around the color circle. The harmonious and unharmonious zones of Moon Spencer, when put together, produce a major gap between the colors that a viewer perceives. Zones in which the gap between the perceived colors is large are unharmonious, as are zones in which minimal gap is perceived. Harmonious zones are considered to lie between 100° and 260°, where small color gaps are

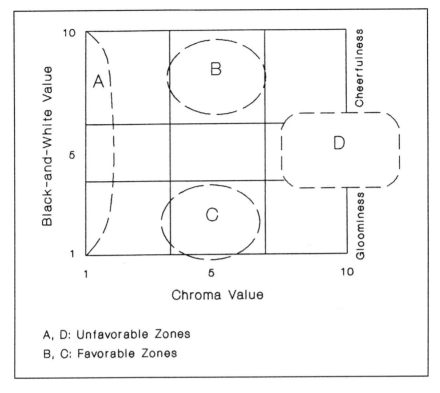

FIG. 6. Comfort zones within the value chroma zone

observed. There are two other zones (between 25° and 43° and between 317° and 336°) where colors can be seen as they appeared originally, that is, with no observed gap—one of the conditions for harmony. The harmonious zone is where no color sense gap is recognized by the human eye. If color initially recognized becomes distorted, a feeling of discomfort results.

Ergonomics has also implications for advertising, where placement, size, and juxtaposition of salient information is crucial to effective communication. For example, if a picture featuring a person is 9cm wide, the head of the person should be 0.5cm from the left, that is, 5.6% of the total width (see Figure 8). In Figure 9, the width of the picture is 13.6%, and the head is placed at 2.7cm from the left, that is 19.9% of the total width from the left. The human positions are set between 30% and 39% of the total width from the left in most cases. Some are 70% to 79.9% from the right, which is another peak area, though the peak ratio for the positioning on the left is of higher frequency. I think it can be

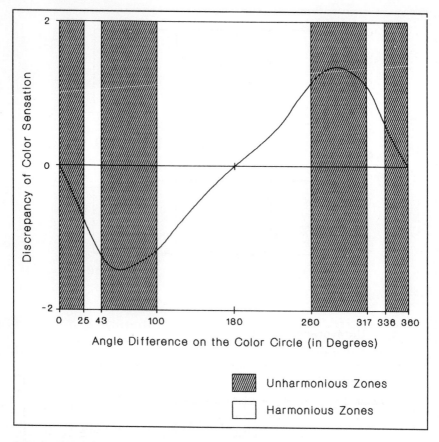

FIG. 7. Relation between discrepancy of color perception and harmonious zones (Moon Spencer)

concluded that the best ratio for locating the human figure in a picture—called the positional comfort ratio—is between 30% and 39.9% from the left.

When shown a magazine band in four different sizes—($\frac{1}{10}$,$\frac{1}{5}$,$\frac{6}{20}$, and $\frac{1}{2}$ of the magazine's own size) and in several different positions on the cover, only certain combinations of size and position are rated as favorable (see Figure 10). For example, the middle position is rated as favorable regardless of the width of the band. If the band is $\frac{1}{2}$ the size of the magazine, the position at the top and at the bottom will also be satisfactory. If the band width is $\frac{3}{4}$ the size of the magazine, neither the upward nor downward position is approved as favorable.

As to human vision, Figure 11 shows nine different patterns of crosses, ranging from a very narrow one to a very broad one. Which of

FIGS. 8. & 9. Optimal position of a human figure in an advertisement

these nine patterns is the easiest to see? The fourth cross, the width and
length of which are the same, is the one many people would choose as

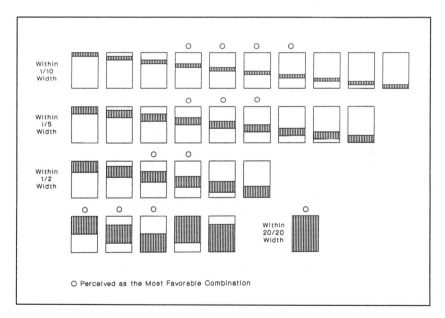

FIG. 10. Appraisal of the size of a magazine band and its positioning

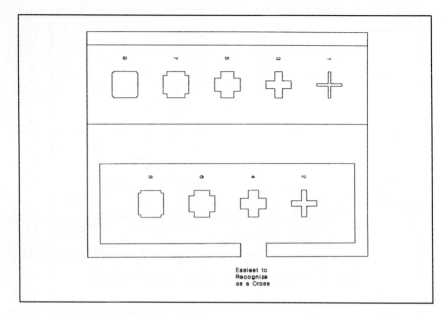

FIG. 11. The ease of recognition of a cross

the most comfortable. In testing people's selection, one can either have them choose from among the many different patterns or between just two different patterns. I would advise letting them choose from many different patterns.

What about the shape of a star? Figure 12 shows 10 different patterns of star shapes. The second pattern, which has an inner/outer circle ratio of 4 to 10, is one most people find to be most comfortable. The most comfortable star shape thus has an inner-circle diameter of 4 and an outer-circle diameter of 10.

What about the shape of a diamond? Figure 13 shows nine different patterns. The seventh pattern is found by most people to be the most comfortable one. The ratio of length of the diagonal lines is 1 to 1.6. The diamond shape is found to be the most comfortable when the horizontal line is 1 and the vertical line is 1.6.

There are various patterns as to the distances between lines, columns, and letters. In the case of Japanese letters, the distance between letters and the distance between lines are of concern. With regard to the vertical length of letter A, the distance is A length in one case and two times A in another. Both these letters are found to be the comfortable ones. A letter any longer or shorter than this would no longer be comfortable. It would be either too narrow or too wide. As for the

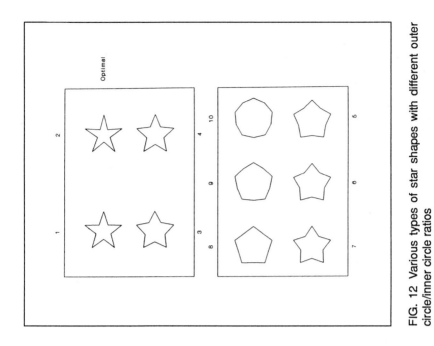

FIG. 12 Various types of star shapes with different outer circle/inner circle ratios

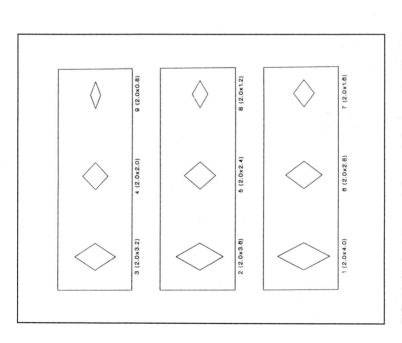

FIG. 13 Various types of diamond shapes with different ratios between the diagonals (in cm)

183

distance between letters, half the width of the letter is appraised as being too little. One should not forget that reading speed and other factors are also related.

In another test concerning comfort, black and yellow stripes are used (see Figure 14). Most people find it comfortable when the width of both yellow and black stripes is the same. Also, the most comfortable angle of slant is 45°.

In assessing how comfortable a chair was, Slechta et al. divided the comfort/discomfort scale into nine different degrees. The three major levels included comfortable, neutral, and uncomfortable. The appraisal of *comfortable* was divided into four different degrees: ideal, very, average, and slightly. The appraisal of *uncomfortable* was likewise divided into four different levels: slightly, average, very, and impossible. Other factors included in the evaluation included sitting time, hourly evaluation of comfort, total comfort scores, onset of discomfort, physical discomfort, and summaries of seat evaluation. Ratings by this instrument usually refer to objective meanings, and the degrees are based on the comfort/discomfort appraisal.

The number of self-reported symptoms rose little by little. Starting with small numbers, they increased dramatically at midway, and after 25 minutes the numbers leveled off, describing the shape of a *S*, so to speak. When evaluating comfort, one must take the passage of time into consideration. In reality, the evaluation of how comfortable a chair is should be made after a short sitting as well as after a long sitting. Indeed, the factors of time should be included in any question of comfort/discomfort. The human being lives the passage of time. Comfort and discomfort while working, taking a break, or changing one's work content, for instance, should be observed with due consideration to time

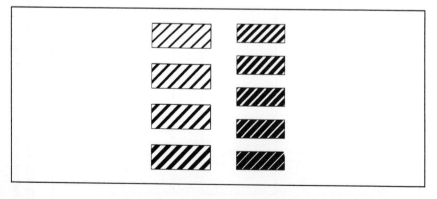

FIG. 14. The visual difference of yellow and black stripes with different ratios

compositions. Time cannot be ignored when it comes to issues of comfort and discomfort.

These results suggest that there exist not only comfortable shapes but also comfortable postures, although it is impossible to give simple explanations about how they relate to human intuition, by which the middle is recognized to be the most agreeable.

When talking about sleeping hours, there are expressions in Japan like "sleeping soundly" or "having enough sleep." However, is it really good to sleep long? The feeling one has upon waking up indicates how well one has slept. When 248 subjects were asked to report how they felt upon waking after a certain period of sleep, it was found that discomfort upon waking was reported by fewer people who had slept 8 to 9 hours. Hence, when it comes to sleeping hours, having the proper amount of sleep rather than having more than enough sleep is necessary if one is to be comfortable upon waking up.

With temperature, illumination, shape, color, relative position, and sleep, superlatives such as "the highest" (or "lowest") and "the most" (or "the least") do not apply. Either extreme produces discomfort. It is not the rule of linearity—"the more you do, the better you feel"—but rather the proper degrees that agree with human physiology, intuition, and the human sense of comfort. In the continual search for that Golden Mean and the comfort it can afford in whatever human beings undertake, ergonomics can be a vital tool.

MENTAL WORKLOAD IN MULTIPLE-TASK PERFORMANCE: Conceptual and Methodological Perspectives

Organizers: R. Wieland-Eckelmann,
University of Wuppertal, FRG
U. Kleinbeck, University of Wuppertal, FRG
Chair: R. J. Hockey, University of Sheffield, U.K.

Contributors:

M. Frese, University of Gießen, FRG
Action-related errors in human-computer interaction

P. A. Hancock, University of Minnesota, U.S.A.
A theory of mental workload

R. Wieland-Eckelmann, U. Kleinbeck, University of Wuppertal, FRG
Workload research: Current theoretical and methodological developments

Rapid advances in technical information-processing systems and display technology have increased both the capability of presenting multi-element, complex information on a single screen display and the freedom of the operator to select the aspect and mode of presentation. This state of affairs raises the question of limitations of the human ability to attend to diversified sources of information, to process, transform, decide on, and carry out the necessary responses. Consequently, the need to assess the mental workload imposed on operator processing capacities is particularly critical in high technology systems.

A systematic attempt to assess mental workload, however, requires that the designers have access to both adequate theoretical models that are able to predict the future in practical work (e.g., Gopher & Kimchi, 1989) and techniques and criteria for measuring workload (e.g., Eggemeier, 1988). The main concern of this symposium was to evaluate current theoretical and methodological developments in mental workload research with regard to the requirements mentioned above.

To meet these requirements, Hancock argued in his paper that, in light of the present difficulties in assessment, there is a pressing need for a general theory of mental workload (MWL). In order to avoid the difficulties of approaches defining MWL as a multifaceted construct that embodies the interaction between task demands and the capabilities of the operator to meet them, he made a distinction between task demands as an independent variable and MWL (as an organismic response) as a dependent variable. Task demands constitute a stress, and human operators adapt to these demands much as they would to any other form of stress.

Considering the task itself as a primary influence in the generation of stress (task as input stress), Hancock suggested that MWL in human-machine systems be assessed from the *pattern* of operator performance (output stress). Mental overload or output stress occurs if the physiological and/or psychological adaptive capabilities (the latter is equated with the operator's attentional resource capacity) is taxed or exceeded, and the regulatory system changes modes of operation from steady-state negative feedback to positive feedback operation. Examples of indices for such maladaptive functioning, and thus MWL, are attentional narrowing, functional fixedness in problem-solving, and generally reduced flexibility in responding (e.g., Hancock, 1989).

The major concern of Wieland-Eckelmann's and Kleinbeck's paper was to summarize contemporary efforts in the field and to give at least some future directions that mental workload research might take. Their review of the current status concentrated on three problem areas. The first concerns the multifaceted nature of MWL and theoretical models that can be summarized under the general label of resource volume and resource strategy theories. The second involves critical properties of MWL assessment techniques, e.g., sensitivity, intrusiveness, and diagnosticity of a technique (e.g., Eggemeier, 1988). The third refers to critical issues concerning moderating factors; that is, dissociations between categories of measures (subjective, performance-based, and physiological) and individual differences (personality traits, coping styles).

The composite model (Wieland-Eckelmann, 1991) outlined in the second part of the presentation tried to offer a systematic view to untangle the complex interrelationships between such elements as task and system demands, their discernible (additive and/or interactive) influences on the human processing system (e.g., allocation of attentional resources), and the observable effects (changes of organismic state) and consequences (performance outcome). The model differentiated three distinguishable levels of analysis: demand component analysis, action and load analysis, and analysis of effects and consequences. On the second level, there are two basic issues to consider in analyzing the processes in multiple-task performance. One is related to the interrelationship between mental, emotional, and motivational demands and the operators ability to cope with them. The other is related to the locus of currrent control activity that may be passed between levels of operation from the "top" to the "bottom" of the human processing system as emotional, motivational, or task demands require.

Selected data from dual-task studies presented in the last part provided evidence for the possibility of the empirical corroboration of the model. The goal of Frese's paper on *Action-related errors in human-computer interaction*, was to look at the MWL problem from an action-oriented perspective. Frese argued that the user's conceptual model developed during learning and adaptation to the requirements of human-machine systems constitutes the critical feature of erroneous performance. In particular, he stated that different modes of cognitive control and action regulation (as reflected in different modes of error-handling) had to take into consideration the different pathways made up by the functional relations between computer system parameters, task characteristics, and user-outcomes in man-machine systems. Since errors are related to cognitive and emotional disturbances, modes of error-handling are considered to have an important influence on the amount of mental load. However, as Frese convincingly demonstrated on the basis of empirical data, a useful approach to assisting users in operating a computer based system, is *not* to teach him or her to avoid errors. What is needed instead, are instructional aids enhancing the user's ability in error management, which should be based on the feedback-directed control of actions necessary to meet task demands. Frese concluded his talk with the notion that the three-part causal linkage mentioned above and its specific functional pathways should be used as a theoretical frame of reference for research on error management (for detailed information. see Frese & Brodbeck, 1989).

The discussion revealed that MWL research should concentrate in the future on the following aspects:

1. Because of the rapid advances in computer technology, there was consensus among most of the discussants that the best strategy mental workload research should adopt is *not* to focus on specific elements of technology but to elaborate its linkage with basic theoretical research.

2. Basic theoretical and empirical research should integrate both the experimental approach (e.g., the dual-task paradigm) and action-oriented approaches. The former could provide information about relevant properties of measurement tools; the latter could reflect more comprehensively the reallocation of tasks between humans and machines that results in a new set of tasks for both operator and machine.

3. The need for the incorporation of individual differences in MWL assessment models was strongly recommended by most of the discussants.

4. Finally, it was pointed out that MWL research should concentrate its efforts more intensively on the problem of "how to bridge the gap between designers, users, and work psychologists."

REFERENCES

Eggemeier, F. T. (1988). Properties of workload assessment techniques. In P. A. Hancock & N. Meshkati (Eds.), *Human mental workload* (pp. 41-61). Amsterdam: North-Holland.

Frese, M. & Brodbeck, F. C. (1989). *Computer in Büro und Verwaltung. Psychologisches Wissen für die Praxis*. Berlin: Springer.

Gopher, D. & Kimchi, R. (1989). *Engineering psychology. Annual review of psychology, 40,* 431-455.

Hancock, P. (1989). A dynamic model of stress and sustained attention. *Human Factors, 31,* 519-537.

Wieland-Eckelmann, R. (1991). *Kognition. Emotion und psychische Beanspruchung. Zur Theorie und Empirie informations-verarbeitender Tätigkeiten*. Göttingen: Hogrefe.

ERGONOMICS
POSTER CONTRIBUTIONS

DEVELOPMENT OF A SECONDARY TASK TECHNIQUE FOR MEASURING OPERATOR WORKLOAD

Y. Nagasawa, N. Utsuki and S. Aramaki
Aeromedical Laboratory and Air-Safety Service Group, JASDF

An auditory discriminative task (ADT) was devised and tested as a secondary task for measuring operator workload in both laboratory and field situations.

The 12 subjects, who participated in a series of experiments, were requested to discriminate a target signal of either a high-tone (1200Hz) or low-tone (800Hz) burst from another signal while performing a primary tracking task. Interstimulus intervals of the tone bursts and difficulties of the primary task were systematically manipulated. Subjective workload ratings and evoked responses to the auditory signals were measured.

The results showed that error rates and response time on the ADT as well as subjective workload rating scales increased in accordance with enhancement of difficulty of the primary task. By contrast, auditory evoked potentials decreased. We also applied the ADT to a simulated flight situation by using a LINK trainer and to an actual flight of a C-1 jet transport. The results were similar to those described above.

In conclusion the ADT has been recognized as a convenient tool for measuring operator workload or mental space capacity in both the field and laboratory conditions.

PHYSIOLOGICAL RESPONSES AS MEASURES OF MENTAL WORKLOAD

Mieko Ohsuga, Hiromi Terashita, Futomi Shimono, Chie Akashi,
Mitsubishi Electric Corp., Hyogo, Japan
Akihiro Yagi, and Yo Miyata, Kwansei Gakuin University, Hyogo, Japan

The purpose of the present study was to develop a method for objective evaluation of mental workload (MWL) during computer work. The quantitative evaluation of MWL is helpful for the improvement of the usability of computer S/W, the working environment, and schedule management. Methodological requirements included being able to compare MWL between various kinds of tasks, capturing the time course of MWL, evaluating MWL in relation to individual differences and evaluating MWL without giving subjects extra load. Some physiological responses met the first two requirements. They may be promising measures if a proper methodology is applied in order to satisfy the 3rd and 4th requirements. The present paper concerns the similarities and differences in physiological response patterns among subjects as a function of MWL caused by various tasks.

The subjects, 20 normal males aged 23 to 27 years, were selected to show various response patterns by referring to the results obtained from 48 normal subjects who participated in a previous experiment.

The experiments were conducted in a half soundproofed room. Subjects were seated except in the standing condition. The conditions were 3-min adaptation, 3-min baseline with open eyes, 1-min deep respiration (DR), 1-min baseline with eyes open followed by 2-min standing (ST), 3-min baseline with eyes closed, 1-min mental arithmetic (MA1), 3-min baseline with eyes open, 3-min mental arithmetic by watching CRT (MA2), 3-min baseline with eyes open, 3-min color matching (CM), 3-min baseline with eyes open, 3-min programmer's aptitude test (PA), 3-min baseline with eyes open, and 1-min cold pressor test (CP).

The measured responses were ECG (chest lead, lead III), respiration (abdominal lead), photo plethysmogram (index finger, ear lobe), EOG (horizontal, vertical), and EEG (12 leads). The present paper refers only to ECG chest lead and respiration results.

The measures were heart rate (HR), heart rate variability (HRV, 0.1 Hz high passed component normalized by mean HR), T-wave amplitude (TWA), and respiration rate (RR). Means were obtained for each measure using 40 s of data from each condition (10-50 s for 1-min conditions, 50 - 90 s for 3-min ones). Concerning HR, HRV, and RR; means during prebaseline periods and differences in means between task conditions and prebaseline were included in the analysis. For TWA only percentage changes in means were adopted.

A factor analysis was applied to each task condition. The above-mentioned seven scores were used. The eigenvalues above 1.0 were adopted and Varimax rotation was executed. Three factors were derived from each condition, with the cumulative percentage of eigenvalues ranging from 73 to 85. Two common factors were identified. Factor 1 was common for six conditions except CP, reflecting parasympathetic withdrawal (activation during DR), that is reduction in HRV with elevation in RR. Factor 2 was common for four conditions (ST, MA1, CM, PA), reflecting sympathetic activation, that is, acceleration in HR and reduction in TWA.

Pearson coefficients based on the artefact-free subjects (N = 17) were obtained for the two common-factor scores between every pair out of six task conditions. Moderate, but significant, correlations were obtained between three pairs (DR:ST, MA2:PA, and CM:PA) for factor 1, and between two pairs (MA1:CM, MA1:PA) for factor 2.

The factor structures for three out of four cognitive tasks (MA1, CM, PA) showed similarity; however, individuals differed greatly in response patterns. Through cluster analysis, the subjects were classified into 8 groups with respect to the two major factor scores for these three tasks.

The present findings suggest the importance of the multidimensional use of physiological indices in the evaluation of MWL.

EVALUATION OF MENTAL WORKLOAD DURING DOCUMENT-PROCESSING WITH COMPUTER SYSTEMS

Chie Akashi, Mieko Ohsuga, Futomi Shimono, and Masaaki Sadahiro, Mitsubishi Electric Corp., Hyogo, Japan

To develop a more comfortable and user-friendly interface, it is very important to assess mental workload (MWL) objectively and quantitatively. The present paper concerns the results of a preliminary field experiment conducted to compare MWL evoked by document processing between two computer S/W tools and among various functions of each tool. Three physiological indices derived from ECG were used to evaluate MWL multidimensionally during document-processing. The indices were the RR interval, which is influenced by the sympathetic nervous system (SNS) as well as the parasympathetic nervous system (PNS); T-wave amplitude, which is mainly controlled by SNS; and the respiratory component of RR interval variance, which is predominantly affected by PNS.

The subjects were four normal males aged 22 to 26 years. Two of them had once been assigned to a similar experiment, whereas the others had not. Before the experiment, each subject was required to practice document-processing using each tool to complete the examples in a given time.

All experiments took place over 5 days. Adaptation and two experiments were assigned to each subject. Subjects were rotated in using tools. Experiment 1 (EXP1) consisted of adaptation, 2-min controlled respiration, self-report 1, 3-min rest with eyes closed (RT-1A), 1-min mental arithmetic (MA-1A), 30-min or 40-min document-processing for task 1 using tool A (TK-1A), self-report 2, 2-min controlled respiration, self-report 3, 3-min rest with eyes closed (RT-2A),

1-min mental arithmetic (MA-2A), 30-min or 40-min document-processing for task 2 using tool A (TK-2A), and self-report 4. The experimental design of experiment 2 (EXP2) was the same as that of EXP1, except that tool B was used instead of tool A.

The measured physiological responses were ECG (chest lead, lead III), respiration (abdominal lead), photo plethysmogram (ear lobe), and skin temperature (top of nose, forehead). The present paper refers only to ECG chest lead results. In addition, video recording of the CRT display was made during document-processing to determine what function of the tool (such as copying, moving, and character input) was used at each point in time.

The physiological indices derived from ECG were RR interval time (RRT), T-wave amplitude (TWT), and the respiratory component of RR interval variance (RHT). RRT and TWT were obtained for every second by averaging 15 seconds of data around that time. RHT was estimated by averaging amplitude spectra in the respiratory frequency band obtained from 31 seconds of RR interval time series by FFT. Moreover, the data of VTR were classified into 7 BHT codes (form code A to code G) second by second according to the function of the tool that the subjects were using.

The following analysis was applied to the data during the RT, MA, and TK conditions. Concerning RRT and RHT, means and SDs during the above-mentioned conditions were calculated. For TWT, relative values to the previous RT condition were obtained.

The differences during TK suggest that MWL was higher when the subjects were using tool B than when they were using tool A in accordance with self-reports. The differences during control conditions (RT and MA) might have been caused by anticipation, however. The cause remains uncertain because of the small number of subjects.

We obtained the means of each physiological index for 7 BHT codes by averaging the value every time the Ss used the code within a task within a tool (namely, within each TK), and they were transformed to Z scores within each TK. By comparing these scores, we evaluated MWL evoked by the use of each BHT code. There were significant individual differences in evaluated MWL patterns. However, there were findings common to all Ss, to both tasks, and to both tools. For example, MWL was high when code A (input character) was used and low when code F (draw curve) was used. In addition, the three indices did not change in parallel and showed different aspects of MWL.

In conclusion MWL evoked by the use of tool B was higher than that evoked by the use of tool A. The present findings suggest the importance of the multidimensional use of physiological indices in the evaluation of MWL.

A STUDY OF AIRCREW WORKLOAD ON THE BASIS OF SUBJECTIVE AND PHYSIOLOGICAL RESPONSES

Yukiko Kakimoto, Yuko Nagasawa, Hideo Tarui, Fumiko Tajima,
Fukumi Nozawa, Akio Nakamura
Aeromedical Laboratory, JASDF, Tokyo, Japan

This study was designed to determine whether different physiological demands in flight missions differently affect stress responses in flying activities. Subjective and physiological measures were used in a series of mental work load studies. Relations between psychological and hormonal responses were also discussed.

Subjective self-reports (questionnaire), heart rate (measured in beats/min.), CFF, the saliva cortisol level, and urinary catecholamine were used as measures of psychological stress under three sets of conditions: except for the heart rate, which was recorded throughout the flights, all data were collected *before* flight, *after every* flight, and *before* the members of the crew *returned home*.

Significant differences depending on the flight missions appeared before taxi and after landing. The HR, urinary chatecholamine excretion, NE/E ratio, and saliva cortisol was higher in mission A (highest task demands, high time stress and heavier cognitive demands as compared to mission B (medium task demands with high time stress) and to mission C (passenger transport). Elevated HR and catecholamine excretion before taxi in mission A was interpreted as strong mental involvement with anticipatory stress. The self-reported effort seemed to be related to the demands in the missions. Measurement indices, especially HR, changed in connection with different psychological demands during flights, but not so much the saliva cortisol level. Further studies concerning mental and hormonal responses are required.

BRAIN POTENTIALS ASSOCIATED WITH EYE-FIXATION PAUSES DURING SIGNAL DETECTION TASK

Akihiro Yagi, Tohru Okuno, and Jun'ichi Katayama
Department of Psychology, Kwansei Gakuin University, Japan

Since the movements of eyes are usually restricted in studies of event related potentials (ERP) ERP technique is very hard to apply to ergonomic studies. The brain potentials associated with fixation pauses (FP) following saccadic eye movements may be applicable as an index of information-processing during eye movement situations. This study examined whether the brain potentials associated with FP show the variations similar to ERP during a signal detection task.

A random number was presented at one of the three horizontal positions separated 8 deg. on a CRT every 780ms. Eight subjects were asked to move eyes to each stimulus and detect a target number (10%). EEGs and EOGs were recorded. EEGs time-locked to the onset of FP were averaged to obtain potentials associated with the offset of saccades, that is, the onset of FP.

The potentials with latency of about 100ms appeared predominantly at the occiput and showed no definite difference between targets and nontargets. When targets were detected, the large positive potentials with latency of about 400ms coincided with the fixations on the targets. The positive component would be considered as P3 in studies on ERP. Endogenous potentials like P3 were obtained in the natural eye movement situation. Thus, the potentials associated with FP are applicable as an index of information-processing in practical ergonomic situations.

PERCEPTUAL CHARACTERISTICS OF CHRONIC AND INDUCED PAINS ASSESSED WITH A 30-WORD LIST

Aiko Satow, Hamamatsu University School of Medicine
Shunji Taniguchi, Sugiyama Jogakuen Junior College

Fourteen chronic-pain patients, being cared for in a hospital categorized their pains with a 30-word list compiled to assess perceptual characteristics of pain. In Table 1, words reported by the patients were arranged in rank order of intolerability (Satow, Nakatani, Tanigushi, & Higashiyama, 1990).

Chronic pains were complex and intolerable more than electrocutaneous pain that was induced in 29 pain-free subjects. Eight pains—darting, throbbing, dull vibrating, tingling, tugging, and pricking—were evoked by both high and low currents.

Reference

Satow, A., Nakatani, K., Taniguchi, S., & Higashiyama, A. (1990). Perceptual characteristics of electro-cutaneous pain estimated with a 30-word list and visual analog scale. *Japanese Psychological Research, 32*, 155-164.

TABLE 1
Nature of chronic pains reported by patients

Syndrome	Number of patients	Pain described in words
Postherpetic neuralgia	(11)	throbbing, wrenching, pulsing, cramping, it hurts me upon touch, tugging, pricking, heavy, scorching, tingling, numb, smarting, and 11*
Trigeminal neuralgia	(9)	dull, numb, it hurts me upon touch, tugging, drilling, pricking, and 6*
Herpes	(6)	throbbing, pulsing, and 5*
Rheumatoid arthritis	(3)	9* only
Headache (including migraine)	(2)	pounding, pulsing, and 4*
Intercostal neuralgia	(2)	tugging, and 5*
Neck, shoulder, elbow,, wrist diseases	(2)	heavy, pulsing, and 2*
Back pain	(1)	6* only
Cancer pain	(3)	pulsing, [3*]
Duplay disease	(1)	2* only

*Number of words used only once.

READABILITY OF COLORED TELE-TEXTS OF LOW LUMINANCE CONTRAST BY SUBJECTS HAVING DIFFERENT TYPES OF COLOR VISION

Takashi Hasegawa
University of the Sacred Heart, Tokyo, Japan

CRT displays have been popular for showing various types of information that are often presented in characters. In order to catch the public eye, various colors are adopted without any consideration as to luminance contrast and for the aged and people with anomalous color vision. It thus seems necessary to provide a guideline on sets of colors (character and background) in such texts.

Two normal, two protanomaly and four deuteranomaly subjects assessed the readability of the teletexts of 8 x 15 Japanese characters (kanji and two types of kana) differing in colorsets whose luminance contrast ratios were around 1:1. A CRT screen of 20 inches was watched from a viewing distance of 1.8m. Readability was ranked on a five-point scale.

The results showed that (a) each set of colors had an inappropriate contrast ratio; (b) upper and lower limens of undesirable ratio depicted wave-form envelopes as the function of the colors of the characters regardless of the background color and, similarly in each subject; (c) these envelopes were very similar for the normal and the deuteranomaly subjects, but they were counterphasic for the protanomaly subjects; (d) similarity and discrepancy were considered to depend on the characteristics of the luminous efficiency functions; (e) the inclusive ratio of all the sets of colors was 0.7-1.8 for the normal and 0.2-3.0 for the anomalous; and (f) white and warm-color letters on greenish and cianish background were valid.

SUBJECTIVE SPATIAL FREQUENCY AND ITS APPLICATION TO PICTURE QUALITY ESTIMATION

Akira Watanabe, Nippon Institute of Technology

In the field of picture engineering, various types of formulae as functions of spatial frequency have been proposed for objectively estimating subjective picture quality. Except the sharpness of the picture, however, these formulae are not valid for the estimation of subjective factors.

In this paper the author proposed a widely applicable new formula defined as a function of subjective spatial (SS) frequency.

First, grating patterns were used to measure SS frequencies as a function of viewing distance. Results showed that the SS frequency was kept almost constant regardless of variation of viewing distance while the physical spatial frequency changed. Second, the following picture-quality estimating function was proposed:

$$P = A \int_{v_e}^{v_h} \{G(v)R(v)\}^2 dv$$

where P is a subjective impression, G(v) is the modulation transfer function (MTF) of a physical image system and R(v) is MTF of the visual system as a function of subjective spatial frequency v. It has been confirmed that this function successfully estimates the impression of presence in the real environment perceived from a picture.

DIRECTION OF MOTION STEREOTYPES FOR CONTROL FUNCTION CONCEPTS OF APPLIANCES AND EQUIPMENT IN LIVING SPACE

M. Yoshioka, A. Hotta,
Industrial Products Research Institute, Tsukuba, Ibaraki, Japan

The aim of this experiment was to investigate the relation between direction-of-motion stereotypes for turning and sliding controls, and control function concepts as basic data for designing control systems for appliances and equipment used in the living space.

The subjects, 14 persons over 60 years of age and 13 persons younger than 60 years, were asked to turn or slide controls in either direction in response to the stimuli, which were 50 written control-function concepts about appliances and equipments such as heaters, TVs, lights, water units, and gas units. There were 12 types of control conditions, decided by controlled plane and controlled direction. Stronger stereotypes were found for sliding controls than for turning controls. Strong sliding control stereotypes were found in up-down controls. Strong stereotypes were found in concepts of control functions for operating heaters, TVs, doors, lighting, and air conditioners. Weak stereotypes were found for control functions regulating water and gas flow.

In the ON concept ("on," "start") and the INCREASE concept ("increase," "up," "raise") of control functions, strong stereotypes were found for motion that was clockwise, to the right, forward, and upward. In the OFF concept ("off," "stop") and in the DECREASE concept ("decrease," "down") of control function, strong stereotypes were found for motion that was counter clockwise, to the left, backward, and downward.

OBJECTIVE MEASUREMENT OF PAIN IN THE WRIST BY PLATE-PUSHING WITH VARIOUS PRESSURE LEVELS

Shunji Taniguchi, Sugiyama Jogakuen Junior College
Aiko Satow, Hamamatsu University School of Medicine

The objective method for measuring endogenous pain in the wrist that originates in cervicobrachial disorders was improved. The method employed the plate-pushing task, which was reported by Taniguchi and Satow (1988a, b). The first point of improvement was the introduction of a way to cause a great load to be placed on the wrist while subjects were pushing the plate. This made it easier to induce pain due to disorders in the wrist. Another improvement was a new procedure in which a subject was told to change her pressure against a balance as instructed (shifting from 1-2-4 (or 3)-2-1-2-4 (or 3)-2-1 kg). This made it possible to identify the degree of pressure that produced pain. Effects of left-hand or right-hand dominance and of sequences of trials that began with the dominant hand and switched to nondominant or vice versa were also examined. However, they were not found to be significant. The variation of the client's pressure was largest at 4 kg in the hand with pain. The client reported after the measurement that she felt the strongest pain in her wrist at 4 kg. Finally, the new method proved to be highly useful as an objective method for measuring this sort of pain because the method could produce conditions very similar to those associated with the ordinary motion that causes pain.

References

Taniguchi, S., & Satow, A. (1988a). Pilot study for objective measurement of pain: Method and analyses of basic factors for normative data. *Perceptual and Motor Skills, 66,* 147-157.

Taniguchi, S., & Satow, A. (1988b), Objective measurement of pain in the wrist: Analyses of basic factors for normative data and a case study. *Perceptual and Motor Skills, 67,* 37-38.

AN EPISODIC APPROACH TO ENGINEERING-DESIGN SUPPORT

Yoshio Nakatani, Makoto Tsukiyama, and Toyoo Fukuda
Industrial & Electronics Systems Lab., Mitsubishi Electric Corp.

We propose a new approach to engineering design support by adopting case-based reasoning (CBR) and an analogical case-retrieval method. Based on the episodic-memory theory, CBR enables one to reuse similar cases in the past to solve a new problem (see Hammond 1989). We focus on the conceptual design process, which is the essence of the whole design. Our approach is implemented as a computer S/W, named SUPPORT, on an Engineering Work Station (EWS).

Design-support process

The design-support process has four steps: specification analysis, functional design, parts selection, and parts layout (Nakatani, Tsukiyama, & Fukuda, 1989). The designer analyzes a customer's requirement into specification items. The ready-made items are developed into parts automatically, and special items are interactively developed into hierarchical function trees. The lowest-level functions are related to parts. The parts are laid out. These steps can be repeated until the design has been completed.

Case reusable phase

Our approach is based on the observation that experienced designers make new designs by using their episodic memory. The designer can therefore reuse the past cases (see Figure 1). First, special specification items utilized in the past can be reused to meet a customer's demand. Second, an entire function tree having those items that are the most similar to a current case can be reused. Third, not only entire function trees but also pieces of them can be reused at any level to develop and modify the function tree of the current case. Fourth, parts used in past cases can be reused if standard parts cannot satisfy the demands.

Case retrieval

Case retrieval is a central issue of CBR. Our system has a semantic memory unit, which organizes concepts used in the product domain in the form: (CONCEPT A, RELATION TYPE, VIEWPOINT, CONCEPT B). The relation types classify relations of the concepts involving instance-of,

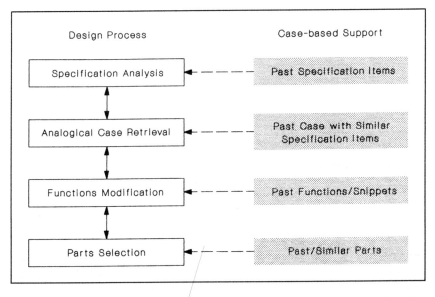

FIG. 1. Case reusable phase in an episodic approach to supporting engineering design

kind-of, part-of, value-of, and equivalent. The viewpoints represent the conditions under which the two concepts are related. For example, an apple as a fruit is represented as (fruit, kind-of, food, apple) while a botanical apple is represented as (bramble, kind-of, botanity, apple).

Two concepts are thought of as similar when they are related to a concept with (a) the same relation type and viewpoint, (b) the same relation type, (c) another relation type, in the order of similarity.

When searching for past cases, the designer uses the case names (specification items, functions, or parts) as keywords. If no past cases with the same name as the keyword can be found, the system replaces the keyword by a similar concept and tries again.

References

Hammond, K. J. (1989). *Case-based planning.* San Diego, CA: Academic Press.

Nakatani, Y, Tsukiyuma, M, & Fukuda, T. (1989). A Design Support System with Case-based Problem Solving Methodology, in: *Proceedings of 1989 IEEE International Conference on SMC,* 259-260.

INADEQUACY IN THE EVERYDAY LIVES OF STUDENTS:
FROM THE VIEWPOINT OF ENVIRONMENTAL COMFORT AND SAFETY

Takako Mochizuki, Tokai University, Kanagawa, Japan
Yukiko Kakimoto, Aeromedical Laboratory, JASDF, Tokyo, Japan

Recent progress in technology has resulted in many new machines and devices in daily life. Some are convenient and prevent accidents, but others are often bewildering. Especially in the metropolitan area of Japan, remarkably developed for the last decade, unfamiliar and unimproved technology has been a problem.

The aim of this research was (a) to notice things in everyday life that do not enhance living and the prevention of accidents, and (b) to discover problems in daily life rather than in the laboratory.

The subjects, 301 undergraduate students answered our questionnaire about inconvenient and unsafe machines and equipment around them. The items of the questionnaire were selected from the answers to open-ended questions that had been posed as a pretest. Most of the students pointed out (a) incompatibilities between new systems and traditional ones (e.g., public phones not operable with both prepaid cards and coins), (b) opposite or ambiguous meaning of designations (e.g., open or shut indications on door knobs and the on or off indications on water taps), (c) awkwardness (e.g., pocket-size calculators), (d) lack of fail-safe design (e.g., geysers without timers), and (e) excessive and competitive information simultaneously presented (e.g., traffic signs). These results suggest (a) lack of prudence by engineers, (b) lack of responsibility by authorities, and (c) laziness, faulty operation, and insensitivity to danger on the part of users. Students' observations in daily life provide many fresh perspectives and serve the aim of this research.

HOW DO COMPUTER USERS RESPOND TO IMPOLITE FEEDBACK FROM THE COMPUTER?

Yasuhisha Hama, Hokusei Gakuen University

The purpose of this study was to clarify the effects of computer messages of varying degrees of politeness on subjects' task performance, mental state, and attitude towards computers. In particular, I wanted to clarify the effects of impolite feedback from the computer.

The subjects, 72 male university students, were requested to type characters and symbols for 30 minutes. When the subjects made an input mistake, or exceeded the time limit, or required aid (used the HELP key), a message was given by the computer. If they made the same kind of mistake repeatedly during the same period (50 characters), the messages were changed. Ss were divided into following three conditions. In the impolite message (IM) condition they were given an impolite message from the computer when they made a mistake. In the polite message (PM) condition the subjects were given a polite message. In the no message (control) condition they were given no verbal messages, but a buzzer was sounded. When the message was given by the computer, the subjects had to reply by pressing either the "Shut up!" button or the "I am sorry" button.

Before and after the experiment, the subjects were required to answer a questionnaire concerning their image of and attitude towards computers and the unpleasantness of typing.

It was found that the subjects who received impolite messages felt the message was unfriendly but felt less unpleasantness in typing than the subjects who received no message. It was also found that the subjects became aggressive when impolite messages were given repeatedly. The subjects who received impolite messages showed positive attitude toward computers despite the impolite messages.

NEGATIVE EFFECTS OF LONG-TERM KEYBOARD TRAINING ON REACTIONS TO COMPUTERS

Kioyshi Maiya, Nara University, Nara, Japan

Recent contributions to user-centered computer design, which have been made mainly in cognitive psychology (e.g., Norman, 1988) seem to be exclusively task-oriented. However, problems of mental health, such as *techno stress*, also exist in the interaction of humans and computers. Many instructors of computer courses know that people who have trouble in learning how to deal with computers have negative feelings toward computers similar to "techno fear" (Pask & Curran, 1982). In this study, the features and developmental course of such negative computer images were investigated.

College students were surveyed by the semantic differential method for their feelings towards computers. The results of factor analysis indicated three main factors of these feelings: familiarity, simplicity, and prettiness. The first two factors are equivalent to those found in a previous study (see Okamoto, Kakimoto, & Maiya, contribution to Kyoto Congress). Familiarity is suggested to be a determinant of the mental image of computers.

The subjects, 82 college students, participated in keyboard training. They were asked to complete a questionnaire before the training began (Phase I), in the second week of training (Phase II), in the third week (Phase III), and two months later, (Phase IV). The students learned how to type by using the programmed self-learning computer system developed by the author. The dates and times of the learning sessions were not fixed, frequency and duration of the sessions depended upon each student. The number of respondents for Phases I, II, III, and IV were 82, 58, 29, and 14, respectively. All of the last-named fourteen participants learned the skill of "blind touch typing" in Phase IV.

The negative image that the subjects had of computers increased in Phase II and gradually decreased until Phase IV, whereas the positive image did not change until Phase III and decreased drastically in Phase IV. Moreover, the subjects' attribution of the uncomfortable feelings to the software setting temporarily increased in Phase II. It was found that the negative image of computers did not change in accordance with the positive image, and that the primary and temporal negative images tended to be attributed to the system. It is suggested that the negative computer image is not always caused by the long-term monotonous job but rather by other factors that may be called affective interface.

References

Norman, D. (1988). The psychology of everyday things. New York: Basic Books.

Pask, G.. & Curran, S. (1982). *Micro Man*. London: Century.

EFFECTS OF COMPUTER GENERATED LEADERSHIP INSTRUCTIONS ON IMAGE FORMATION

Yusuke Okamoto, Toshikatsu Kakimoto and Kiyoshi Maiya
Osaka University, and Nara University

The purpose of the present study was to investigate how subjects' attitudes towards the computer changed according to the different types of instructions given by the computer. The subjects (male and female university students) were required to learn typing skills, using the keyboard of the computer. The experimental instructions were displayed automatically on the computer screen. Three types of instructions were given: (a) P or Performance type (task oriented), (b) M or Maintenance type (tension reduction and consideration), and (c) PM type (combination of P and M). The subjects' attitudes toward the computer were measured by the Semantic Differential scale (7 points; 14 items) and analyzed by factor analysis. Among the scores of three factors found by factor analysis, a significant change was found only in the score of the first factor, *distance* (unfamiliar-familiar, harsh-mild, cool-warm, etc.), which was decreased by the M-type instructions.

EFFECTS OF COMPUTER-GENERATED PM LEADERSHIP IN LEARNING HOW TO TYPE

T. Kakimoto, Osaka University
K. Maiya, Nara University

The purpose of the study was to examine whether the effect of leadership behavior would be the same in a computer instructed learning situation.

In leadership studies, it has been pointed out that the effectiveness of leadership is determined by two factors. One is initiation factor; the other, consideration factor. Among these studies, it has been found in research on PM leadership that the combination of these two factors leads to the highest performance of the followers. This finding has been explained by the hypothetical "catalysis" function of the consideration factor behavior. Although the process of the catalysis has not been clear so far, no doubt it has something to do with interpersonal relations between the leader and the follower. The present study examined whether the effect of leadership type would be the same when a computer is substituted for a human leader.

Sixty-three university students participated in an experiment in which they learned how to type. Each subject learned typing on his or her own after instructions were presented on a video screen. Types of leadership were manipulated through the content of the instructions presented. The other independent variable was task difficulty, which was manipulated through changes in the response tempo required.

As for dependent variables, three indices were analyzed. The first was the subject's achievement during the learning sessions. The second index was recall, which meant, in this case, the difference between two test scores across a break. The third index was blocking, which was defined as more than three successive nonresponses to a prompt.

The pattern of results did not contradict those found in the experimental studies on human PM leadership. The right two bars in Figure 1 (PM type) correspond to the combination leadership condition. The fact that the subject's achievement in the combination leadership condition was not as great as that found in previous research may be attributed to the brevity of the exercise period, which was 25 minutes.

In Table 1, the PM type corresponds to the combination leadership condition. The relatively small number of nonresponses by the subjects

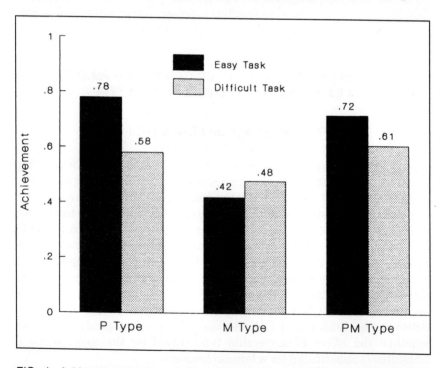

FIG. 1. Achievement for three types of instruction in typewriting. Achievement is indicated in terms of a ratio of the number of the steps completed in trial-sequence 1 to that in trial-sequence 2.

TABLE 1
Blocking[a] and Types of Instruction

	p-type	M-type	PM-type
With Blocking	16 [b]	12	7
Without Blocking	5	9	13

$x2 = p < .03$
[a] Blocking is defined as more than three successive nonresponses to a prompt on a typewriting task
[b] Figures signify the number of the subjects

in the combination leadership condition suggests that their achievement should improve greatly after a longer practice period because lack of blocking could mean that the subject is motivated to perform the task. The results on recall supported this inference.

To sum up, although computer-generated leadership showed a pattern of results slightly different from that of human leadership, the pattern can be interpreted in conventional terms.

DIFFERENT TYPES OF EXPERTISE IN A POPULATION OF FARMERS USING A COMPUTERIZED ADMINISTRATIVE SYSTEM

Christian Guillevic and Thierry Beliere,
National Institute of Applied Sciences (INSA) and
Toulouse le Mirail University, France*

Numerous studies on the use of computers are based on the dichotomy between experts and novices. Recent research shows, however, that this distinction is irrelevant (Chi, Glaser & Farr, 1988; Falzon, 1989). Based on a study of farmers using a computerized system of administration our hypothesis is that the construction of the operator's skill results from a process of cognitive appropriation of the instrument, leading to different types of expertise.

References
Chi, M. T. H., Glaser, R., & Farr, M. J. (1988). *The nature of expertise.* Hillsdale, NJ: Lawrence Erlbaum Associates Inc.
Falzon, P. (1989). *Ergonomie du dialogue.* Grenoble: P.U.G.

NOTE: *This study was partly supported by a grant from the local government of the Département du Tarn et Garonne.

RELATION BETWEEN WORKING HOURS AND FATIGUE OF SUPERMARKET MANAGERS

Koya Kishida, Takasaki City University of Economics, Japan

In recent years, working conditions in supermarkets have gradually changed. A work schedule with two days off per week has been implemented by several large supermarket chains. After the introduction of this schedule, many part-timers were hired by supermarkets. Most of these employees have been middle-aged females in their 40s and 50s, a circumstance that has resulted in new problems in supermarket management.

In the present study the workloads of employees in a supermarket chain were investigated during the busiest week in December 1988. The subjects were 172 employees (50 males, 122 females) at two stores, one with 103 employees and the other with 69. Of these, 106 were part-timers, all of them female. The duty time for full-timers was nine hours, including a one-hour break. The duty hours for part-timers varied, but half worked six hours or more. The two stores were normally open from 10:00 a.m. to 7:00 p.m. However, one store was open until 7:30 p.m. during December. Many full-timers were on duty from 9:00 a.m. to 8:00 p.m. Several managers were on duty from 8:00 a.m. to 9:00 p.m.

Several surveys were conducted: time study, job structures, subjective feelings of fatigue, local fatigue symptoms, and daily-life time-structure. The results pertaining to subjective feelings of fatigue showed that complaints of drowsiness among sections chiefs increased from 18.9% before work to 30.2% after work. Total complaints of subjective feelings of fatigue among section chiefs increased from 11.8% before work to 19.2% after work. The complaints of subjective feelings of fatigue among part-timers were fewer than those of managers. These results show that the higher an employee's job status, the greater the workload. Among part-timers, those working for six hours or more had more complaints about subjective feelings of fatigue than had part-timers working fewer than six hours. This result shows that subjective fatigue feelings are based on working hours.

The results of the daily-life time-structure survey showed that off-duty time for section chiefs was less than 11 hours. In these cases, it was difficult for section chiefs to obtain 6 hours of sleep. In fact, 30% of the section chiefs slept fewer than 6 hours.

These results suggest that managers continue to feel more tired than other employees. Moreover, they suffered from cumulative fatigue caused by long working hours. In addition, I believe that increased reliance on part-timers places greater responsibility on managers and contributes to overall fatigue.

BEHAVIORAL INTERVENTIONS FOR HAZARD CONTROL AT THE WORKPLACE

Alexander Cohen,
National Institute for Occupational Safety & Health, Cincinnati, OH, U.S.A.

Three cases involving worksite trials illustrated the merits of behavioral techniques to control workplace hazards.

Case 1: A worker participation approach was adopted to promote hazard recognition and control at a hospital site. Procedures involved a special committee to encourage worker reporting of unsafe conditions and suggestions for corrective measures, and prompt feedback to reports on actions taken. Pre-post trial monitoring found worker hazard reports to increase and control actions and injury incidents to decrease. Worker reports versus usual inspection data showed the workers detecting more physical hazards (e.g., slip/trip risks re working/walking surfaces, struck by/against objects) but overlooking procedural ones (e. g., overexertion from patient handling, needle punctures). Worker training focused on these problems was suggested.

Case 2: Material safety data sheets (MSDSs) at two worksites were revised through use of simpler language, pictorial representations, and highlighted text to aid worker appreciation of toxic chemicals used in their jobs. Quizzes at both sites showed these changes had little effect on chemical knowledge scores. Debriefings revealed worker preferences for audio/video presentations of MSDS information.

Case 3: Lumbermen were counseled in use of protective clothing, barrier creams, and personal hygiene to limit skin contact to a toxic preservative agent, chlorophenol. Tagging this toxin with a chemical that fluoresces in ultraviolet light enabled the workers to visualize how these practices could reduce their exposure to the phenol. Before/after questionnaire surveys and urine sampling for chlorophenol metabolites found this feedback to enhance worker consciousness about the hazardous exposures and to reduce their contact with the toxic material.

HUMAN ERRORS IN EVERYDAY LIFE:
STUDY ON THE PROBLEM OF LOCKING ONE'S KEYS
IN THE CAR

Shinnosuke Usui,
Research Institute of Industrial Safety of Labor Ministry, Kiyose-shi,
Tokyo, Japan

The aim of this study was to detect the factors of human error that cause drivers to lock their keys in their cars unintentionally (key lock-in trouble). A questionnaire was administered to drivers who had experienced lock-in trouble in Osaka, Japan. The questionnaire was composed of general information about parking, psychological and environmental situations, and general characteristics. In the present study the drivers' sequential behavior and the trouble-generating processes were analyzed.

The main results are as follows: (a) There were four typical patterns regarding parking place, parking purpose, and parking time when the errors occurred: long-time parking in the parking area, short-time stopping on the road, long-time parking on the road, and parting after having returned home. (b) The most frequently marked items under the heading "environmental and psychological situations" were hurry, doing other things before getting out of the car, and thinking about other things. (c) In factor analysis the above result was clarified, and six additional factors contributing to key lock-in trouble were extracted: interruption of chain behavior, thinking about upcoming matters, thinking about other things, hurrying to get out, hurrying on business, and having to deal with a crowded situation. More detailed studies of the human error processes are being carried out.

PSYCHOLOGICAL ASPECTS OF ADVANCED
AUDITORY WARNING DESIGN

J. Edworthy, S. Loxley & E. Hellier
Polytechnic South West, Plymouth, Devon, England

Auditory warnings such as bells, buzzers, and sirens are often startling and tend to disrupt thought, performance and communication instead of alerting and warning the hearer.

Patterson (1982) has proposed a method of warning construction that reduces many of the traditional problems associated with the use of auditory warnings in high-workload environments.

Designing warnings within these guidelines allows a much greater degree of matching between the psychoacoustic qualities of the warning and the situation or condition that it is designed to signal than could normally be achieved using traditional warning sounds. In particular, the urgency of the warning can be matched to the urgency of the situation so that high priority situations are signaled by warnings that possess a high degree of psychoacoustic urgency, and low priority situations by warnings with low psychoacoustic urgency. To this end, a data base charting the effects of a range of sound parameters on perceived urgency has been collated, and the relative urgencies of sets of auditory warnings successfully predicted (Edworthy, Loxley, & Dennis, 1991).

References

Edworthy, J., Loxley, S. L., & Dennis, I. D. (1991). Improving Auditory Warning Design: Relationship Between Warning Sound Parameters and Perceived Urgency. *Human Factors, 33,* 205-232

Patterson, R. D. (1982). Guidelines for Auditory Warnings Systems on Civil Aircraft (Civil Aviation paper 82017). To be obtained from CAA House, Kingsway, London.

THE DESIGN AND EVALUATION OF HELICOPTER TREND MONITORING SOUNDS

S. Loxley and J. Edworthy

Polytechnic Southwest, Plymouth, Devon, England

The safety of helicopter flying can be enhanced by ensuring that the pilot is able to monitor important flying parameters when they are exceeded beyond their normal limits. Five prototype trend-monitoring sounds (trendsons) were designed at the request of the Royal Aircraft Establishment, Farnborough, to monitor rotor speed (both over and underspeeding), torque (power), and "g" forces. Each trendson comprised five levels, representing increasing deviations from normal flying limits. They were complex sounds, to guard against masking, and the levels were differentiated by changes in more than one parameter. In a set of experiments, confusions and similarities between different trendsons were looked at, as were the levels within each trendson, to see whether they were acoustically similar enough to be recognized as signaling the same flying parameter. They were systematically varied to convey trend information. They differed from each other sufficiently to allow pilots to identify the level being signaled. On the whole, the data suggested that the basic design principles used were sound. However, consistent confusions did arise. The similarity data helped to interpret them. Changes in harmonic structure introduced between levels within a trendson sometimes made a level so dissimilar that its group identity was lost, so these changes should be used with care. Changes in speed and pitch did not alone convey enough information for consistent absolute identification of levels but preserved relative relations. Changes in rhythm and pitch contour can be used to enable pilots to make absolute level identifications where they are most important, namely, level 1 (the first deviation from normal) and level 5 (where critical levels are imminent).

Economic Psychology

THE STUDY OF ECONOMIC BEHAVIOR: A New Role for Psychology?

Karl-Erik Wärneryd
The Stockholm School of Economics

APPLIED PSYCHOLOGY AND PROBLEMS IN SOCIETY

The applied fields in psychology deal with psychological problems of many kinds. Still, there are important sectors in human life and in society where psychological research is scanty, sometimes even nonexistent. The main alternative to research-based psychological knowledge is everyday psychology based on life experience and speculation and more or less derived from casual observation.

In fact, psychological research constantly faces the onus of proving its superiority over everyday psychology. If research results fail to convince people of their usefulness in a field, the research will not survive in the long run as something worth spending research money on. At the same time, there is undeniably an upper limit to the progress that most people allow psychological science, since it may be perceived as providing increasingly improved means of manipulating people.

In the early history of psychological science, most psychologists were somewhat hesitant about using psychological theory on practical problems outside the laboratory. A few of the early, famous psychologists worked as consultants to schools, the armed forces, and business, especially the advertising business. Kenneth Spence (1964), who long served as a paragon for experimental psychologists, stressed that psychology was a laboratory science. In his view, too many psychologists did not have the true scientific attitude. They were too eager to apply psychological research to practical problems or they gave in too easily to pressures from their environment to do so.

New applications can serve as a testing ground for basic theories. The boundaries between basic research and applied research are far from fixed. Many researchers move freely across the boundary lines. Faced with a practical psychological problem that has baffled theorists, the applied researcher may do some basic research to further improve the relevant theory.

Whereas, in recent years, economic behavior in some fields like the workplace and the marketplace has received a lot of research attention by psychological researchers; economic behavior that is related to macroeconomic problems such as saving, taxation, and unemployment has usually not met with the same interest. When economic behavior is studied in basic psychological research, the purpose is typically to contribute to the development of psychological theory, not to solve or elucidate economic problems.

Economic behavior at some level of aggregation, usually the macroeconomic level of an entire national economy, is the primary concern of economists. Psychologists tend to work at the level of the individual or small group and thus find it irksome to communicate with economists. More macropsychological thinking among psychologists would, in my opinion, not only improve relations, but also enrich psychological theory.

The Purpose and Contents of the Paper

In this paper, it is suggested that the psychological study of economic behavior move towards better understanding of the contexts into which research results have to be fitted to have practical consequences for economic and social development. The aim of the paper is to assess the role of psychological research on economic behavior and relate it to economic research. I do this by exemplifying problems in the domain of economic behavior and by giving some examples of rough-and-ready psychological models that can be used in discussions of economic problems.

Attention in this paper is directed particulary to macroeconomic problems because it is felt that psychologists should become qualified to participate in discussions of economic and social development more than is presently the case. With the economic and social development that is expected in the Eastern European countries, in the EEC, and in the developing countries over the next decade, it should be ineluctable to include psychological factors and reactions in policy discussions and thinking at the policy level.

The general theme of the paper is that psychological knowledge deriving from research has an underestimated, too-modest role in the discussion of economic problems in society. The proper psychological study of economic behavior can improve this situation.

WHY STUDY ECONOMIC BEHAVIOUR?

Psychology and Economics through the Ages

A few names appear both in the history of psychology and the history of economics. Murphy (1951) cites Adam Smith, who was the father of classical economic theory. Before Smith published *The wealth of nations* in 1776, he had authored a book that was essentially psychological in its orientation: *The theory of moral sentiments* (1982/1759).

Tarde (1902) who, in 1881, launched the concept *Economic Psychology*, complained that Adam Smith unfortunately did not use his knowledge of psychology when writing his economics text. Adam Smith seems to have adopted the idea of pursuit of self-interest as a dominant human characteristic from the Dutch physician Bernard Mandeville, who, in *The Fable of the Bees* (1924/1732) brought forward the importance for society of individuals pursuing their self-interest. Mandeville was a precursor both of modern economics and modern psychology. He made many astute observations on the development of society.

The political economists, beginning with Adam Smith, opposed the French physiocrats and their fixation with the role of property. The political economists turned their interest toward the human being as an economic actor. In the 19th century hedonism was a common concern to psychologists and economists. In their history of psychology books, both Murphy (1951) and Boring (1950) cite Bentham, James, and John Stuart Mill, all three of whom are part of the history of economics. Utilitarians like James Mill and Bentham stressed pleasure and pain as the main or only motives for human behavior (Murphy, 1951). This idea was taken up by Jevons (1911/1871), who formulated the mathematical theory of marginal utility, and by Menger (1923/1871) who performed something similar without mathematics.

Psychology and economics thus have some common philosophical roots and, over the ages, have sometimes complemented one another in their treatment of human behavior, including economic behavior. In the 19th century they increasingly specialized, with psychology going in the direction of concentrating on mind-body problems and economics, that is, political economy, focusing on societal problems. Psychology became an experimental science and more of a rival to philosophy than to economics. On the basic postulate of utility maximization or economic rationality, the economists constructed an impressive framework for analyzing and dealing normatively with economic problems at the level of society. In so doing, they employed more and more mathematics. With the increased formalization of economic theory in the 1930s, the psychological foundations were uprooted. A final blow was delivered by Robbins (1979/1935,p.40), who defined economics as dealing with the logic of choice between scarce resources. Rationality essentially became equal to consistency of choice.

Recently, many economists have turned to scientific psychology for help in developing economic theory. A most promising sign is the interest bestowed on prospect theory (see, e.g., Arrow, 1982). Prospect theory (Kahneman & Tversky, 1979) is abstract and general, which is a prerequisite for acceptance in economic theory development. It is not one of the limited domain, low-level empirical theories that dominate in psychological research.

Apart from rather speculative attempts to use early results from psychological research and thinking, notably as described by William James (1890), the first real applications of scientific psychological knowledge appear to have been in the advertising field. Some of the early experimental psychologists used their skills in developing methods for pretesting advertisements.

Arrow (1963, p.726) points to a similarity between Freud's writings and economic theory:

> I cannot help being struck by the parallelism between the economists' concepts of tastes and obstacles and Freud's pleasure principle and reality principle. ... Freud's use of the term "economic" in his discussions of metapsychology is remarkably precise. He is referring to the allocation of the scarce resources of the libido among competing uses, just as the individual allocates his scarce income among competing commodities. It might be interesting for the historian of thought to see what, if any, influence the thought of economists had in Freud's development. Vienna in the 1870's and 1880's was the center of a great school of economists who were very much interested in the utility theory—indeed this group was one of its originators.

The early classical and neoclassical economic thinkers developed psychologies of their own (see, e.g., Böhm-Bawerk, 1912/1888; Marshall, 1947/1890). Unfortunately, their ideas were usually not empirically testable in their own days. Today, psychologists have developed arsenals of methods that make it possible to test many of those ideas. Again there are economists working on developing psychological theories that will fit economic thinking (see, e.g., Akerlof & Dickens, 1982; Scitovsky, 1976; Shefrin & Thaler, 1988; Thaler & Shefrin, 1981).

Reasons for the Psychological Study of Economic Behavior

There are some simple reasons why economic behavior should be an important area for study in psychology. In everyday life economic problems with psychological dimensions are plentiful. For national economies, problems associated with the economic behavior of investors and consumers are constantly objects of discussion and speculation. Economic problems give substance for frequent public debates. In fact, the mass media obtain an important part of their news from the field of economic problems.

In public debates about current economic issues, recourse is often taken to psychological explanations, also by economists. These explanations derive mostly from everyday observation and speculation, not from scientific psychology. Treatments of economic problems in the mass media are replete with psychological assumptions and show little recognition of the fact that there may exist scientific psychological knowledge from research that can be applied to improve the solutions of the problems.

It should then be intriguing and fascinating for psychologists to study even further how people deal with economic problems, how they react to economic conditions and economic stimuli, how they earn and spend money, what they get out of their spending and the feelings and emotions that accompany economic behavior. When psychological researchers look for problems to study in the laboratory or in correlational research, they could turn more often than at present to economic behavior for proper problems. Attitudes towards saving and towards paying taxes may be as interesting as political or religious attitudes. The study of the use of rewards to reinforce behavior may in some cases need only slight changes to uncover essential aspects of economic behavior.

There are some more complex and elaborate reasons for augmenting and intensifying the study of how people deal with economic problems. Economics is based on fundamentally very simple assumptions about human characteristics. Despite the fact that economic reasoning often proceeds from a model of individual behavior, the main aim is to explain the behavior of large aggregates of individuals over time, not the behavior of single individuals. The analysis of individual behavior is carried through "as if" the individual acts rationally. Economic theory has major advantages as a normative theory, but is deficient as a descriptive theory of individual behavior (cf. Herrnstein, 1990).

Many attempts have been made to modify the assumptions underlying the rationality postulate. The sociologist Parsons (1954:51) had the following to say about the business leader in economic theory:

> In a certain empirical sense it has seemed a wholly justifiable procedure to assume that he acted to maximize his "self-interest," interpreted as the financial returns of the enterprise, or more broadly, he could be trusted to prefer a higher financial return to a lower, a smaller financial loss to a greater.

As a true sociologist, Parsons (1954, p.53) points to the impact of the social system on economic motivation:

> Its [economic motivation] remarkable constancy and generality is not a result of a corresponding uniformity in "human nature" such as egoism or hedonism, but of certain features of the structure of social systems of action, which, however, are not entirely constant but subject to institutional variation.

Despite this emphasis on structural factors, Parsons (1954) suggested that self-respect and recognition are important motives and that profit and money had their main motivating effect as a sign of recognition and success. This has also been maintained by others, such as McClelland (1961). These authors tend to see rationality as the pursuit of goals that are not exclusively financial.

If more of something favorable and less of something unfavorable is allowed to include feelings and emotions and other phenomena in addition to financial return, economic rationality can handle all sorts of choices. A major objection is that economic theory becomes too inclusive if the criterion of financial return is relaxed. Feelings and emotions are hard to express in financial terms.

As distinct from economic rationality, rationality in a psychological sense could be defined to include both financial returns *and* consequences for recognition and self-respect. The consideration of fairness (Kahneman, Knetsch, & Thaler, 1986) and the moral dimension (Etzioni, 1988) are noteworthy extensions of this idea. Here is room for more psychological research relating to economic contexts. Kahneman et al. (1986) raise the important question of what happens to markets if people reduce their pursuit of self-interest in favor of consideration of fairness norms.

Another attempt to modify the concept of rationality as used in economics focuses on the cognitive limitations of the individual. They make it necessary to use bounded rationality, which essentially involves the application of simplifying rules to make decisions. Simon (1990), who introduced the concept of bounded rationality some 35 years ago, concedes that the rationality concept as used by economists to describe and prescribe human adaptiveness has some advantages. "Accepting this assumption enables economists to predict a great deal of behavior (correctly or incorrectly) without ever making empirical studies of human actors" (Simon, 1990, p.6).

Simon (1990) suggests that a few cognitive principles such as recognition processes, heuristic search, and serial pattern recognition, which summarize as intelligence, can be used instead of optimality as unifying principles. Just as in economics, the focus will then be on the environment: Given an intelligent human being, the behavior in a certain environment should be predictable without empirical study. This raises the interesting question of whether such individual behavior will be so well-defined and well-contained that it can be aggregated without empirical frequency studies of individual differences.

There is a chance that psychological knowledge may be improved through more intensive study of economic behavior. Most economic behavior is routine behavior. This holds true in the first place for the consumer, but it is also true to a varying extent for business and government. Decisions are mostly made by routine or by default. Katona (1953), who seems to have been the first to make this point, stresses that economic behavior is a propitious area for studying habit formation as well as genuine decision-making.

PROBLEMS IN ECONOMIC BEHAVIOUR
The Renewed Quest for Psychological Explanations

Economic behavior encompasses problems perceived as worrisome, but it also encompasses choices with more positive aspects involving utility and need satisfaction through the procurement of goods. Even the latter can be laden with conflict. Sjöberg (1985) reports that in a random sample of activities over a week for almost 100 adults, 10 percent of the activities could be said to be economic in the sense that the subjects gave economic motives for them. Mostly, they were associated with negative mood.

A consequence of distinguishing psychological from economic rationality is that mood and affect are becoming more and more a focus of interest in the study of consumer behavior (see Pieters & van Raaij, 1988). It is likely that the same will apply in the study of other decision-makers' behavior as well. Interestingly, Simon (1990, p.18) notes:

But we are just beginning to see that, because of the strong dependence of intelligence on stored knowledge, cognitive and social psychology must be brought much closer together than they have been in the recent past. When we have made these new connections solid, the challenge will remain of bringing affect and emotion more centrally into the picture.

To what extent do mood and emotion have effects on investment behavior or behavior in the financial markets that are believed to be characterized by economic rationality? Historians have observed that, because of temporary or more permanent ill health, there have been mood effects on historical decisions like the institutionalization of the Lutheran Church in Sweden and on some well-known peace treaties.

While early economists like Alfred Marshall (1947/1890) devoted considerable space in their discourses to what they conceived of as psychological or biological problems, economic textbooks nowadays rarely mention psychological concepts. There is frequent use of a few concepts like expectation. It should thus be noted that, in context, those are economic concepts and have little to do with psychological science. For example, rational expectations theory, which incorporates the idea of reaction to information, is a pure economic theory based on the rationality concept (Carter & Maddock, 1984).

Let me now give a few examples of economic problems with psychological dimensions.

Psychological Reactions to Economic Policy Measures

A statement like the following one is often found in newspapers and journals that comment on economic developments. "The effect of the Central Bank action has probably mainly come about on the political and psychological levels. The Central Bank has helped politicians and investors to remember the underlying problems and not to overinterpret temporary positive signs."

This explanation is essentially a guess that seems plausible on the basis of earlier experience. It may be correct. For the economist there is no way to test it to see whether it holds in the specific situation and whether some generalizable knowledge can be gained. The mainstream economist shuns the idea of asking people, except maybe experts, about their subjective judgments and behavior.

There is a long tradition in economic psychology, started and pursued for over 40 years by George Katona (1975), that shows how psychologists can contribute to the proper study of such problems. Sample surveys and skilful questioning can provide answers, albeit at some expense for collecting and analyzing data. There is also some theory that can be used to model the problems and possibly improve solutions. Even a psychologist may, however, find it difficult to extract the truth by interviewing decision-makers, especially politicians and investors.

Short-run Self-interest vs. Long-run Collective Interest

The economic development in Eastern European countries is another important area of economic behavior that it is hardly possible to treat adequately using only methods from economics. In the newly established market economies there is impatience to reach a considerably improved standard of living in a short time. Individual short-term self-interest, and collective and long-term interest have to strike a subtle balance after long individual deprivation.

Solving productivity and distributive justice problems at the same time is a rather complex undertaking, and the results so far do not appear to be very successful. The situation is similar to a social dilemma (see Dawes, 1980). Social equity theory also seems applicable. The latter deals with the problem of fair distribution of gains and losses (see, e.g., Walster & Walster, 1975).

In social dilemmas, one of the major issues pertains to how people can be made to give up some short-run individual maximization of self-interest in favor of long-run collective interest (Levine & Moreland, 1990, pp.605; Messick & Brewer, 1983;). Despite the fact that social dilemma research indicates that it is difficult to find good solutions, the research can help structure the problems and furnish ideas for better solutions (cf. Messick, 1986).

Stimulating Entrepreneurship and Innovation

A third example concerns entrepreneurship. Many countries have problems with certain regions that are less developed than the rest of the country. "At their most recent meetings, the European Community Heads of State or Government have underlined the need to develop a spirit of enterprise and to reduce the charges that weigh heavily on small and medium-sized enterprises (SME's)" (*European File*, February, 1988, p.3) What is "a spirit of enterprise" if not psychology?

In some countries, the North has fallen behind, in other countries it is the South. The most common explanation is that there is too little entrepreneurial activity in those regions. The lack of entrepreneurship is attributed by welfare politicians and their advisors largely to lack of opportunities. This gives rise to the problem of providing subsidies so as to create opportunities and incentives. The effects of such subsidies on actual development mostly seem disappointingly low.

Psychological research can contribute with some theory (Wärneryd, 1988). There is, for example, Atkinson's theory of achievement motivation (Atkinson, 1957, 1964) and McClelland's (1961, 1975) work on need achievement and the power motive. According to McClelland (1961) and his followers, entrepreneurs are characterized by high need achievement, implying that they tend to choose tasks (activities) with moderate probabilities of success, in laboratory studies approximated as $p=0.50$. They want to succeed and they want to be proud of their achievements, which they cannot be if the success is too easily won. If, on the other hand, the task is too difficult, they may not be able to succeed without some luck.

According to McClelland and Winter (1969), the need achievement theory, which is based on Atkinson's model, implies that if government can increase the probability of success for business firms from low to moderate, the high-need achievers, who have the highest potential for entrepreneurship, will be attracted to business. So also will the low-need achievers, but not to the same extent. If high fear of failure prevails, however, and if the probability of success increases from low to moderate; the effects will rather be for people to leave business. If the probability of success increases from moderate to high, high-need achievers will find business uninteresting and seek other challenges with moderate levels of success probabilities. Those with high fear of failure will be attracted since they see chances of being successful.

What psychology tells us is that the effects of financial support, that is, of creating opportunities, will depend on the psychological characteristics of the population. Intervening psychological variables are essential for understanding the behavioral outcome of economic policy measures, as Katona (1975) always maintained. Psychology can also provide a model for discussing, predicting, and assessing possible consequences.

The Importance of Policy Credibility

According to rational expectations theory (and certainly to psychological theory), people are sensitive to information on which they can base and revise their expectations (Carter & Maddock, 1984). The theory assumes that people deal with information exactly as prescribed by economic theory. If government institutes a financial policy, a crucial question will be the credibility of the policy. This can be compared to the credibility of a communicator in psychological communication theory. Will business decision-makers, labor union-officials, and consumers believe what is said when government, for example, declares war against inflation?

The effect of the information about a new policy will depend on the properties of the source of the information. The economist usually deals with the credibility question through the use of objective indicators, "proxies," for example, of how earlier government policies have fared (Backus & Driffill, 1985). A psychologist naturally thinks of devising ways of measuring the credibility of an information source by asking people about their opinions. Hovland, Janis, and Kelley (1953) devised ways of measuring credibility, finding causal factors behind it, and estimating the effect of varying credibility.

Psychological Science and the Treatment of Economic Problems

These examples show that, at the societal level, there are important economic behavior problems with distinctly psychological dimensions. There is a tendency not to think of them as being susceptible to psychological research despite the fact that there exist basic psychological theory and examples of applications. Successful applications often presuppose that psychologists show concern for context and for modeling both psychological and contextual variables (cf. Lea, Tarpy, & Webley, 1987, Preface).

If, for a change, a psychologist is invited to participate in a panel discussion about economic problems that have occurred in recent years, such as the so-called stock exchange crises, he or she will probably find that the participating economists freely use psychological explanations. The latter do not derive from analysis of data, but may seem plausible enough. The typical psychologist will have a tendency to be very guarded in his/her attempts at explanation and will refer to paucity of research for an excuse. The psychologist looks for clear empirical data and fails to use a model based on earlier research to elucidate similar phenomena. New situations give rise to demand for new data that refer specifically to the situation. It has been characteristic of much of psychological research that it is reported with little attempt at abstraction, at making it more generalizable and generative (cf. Gergen, 1982). Cialdini (1988) gave an excellent example of what psychologists can do to achieve such purposes. He has distilled six general principles of influence that can be used to analyze compliance situations (from the victim's vantage point). He generously shows how they operate in practical situations.

The economist usually has in the back of his or her mind some abstract model that helps integrate and make meaningful the few data and casual observations that are available. The economist's model is ultimately based on the three important and forceful components of the economic approach to human behavior, as succinctly formulated by Gary Becker (1976): (a) the assumption of utility-maximizing behavior, that is, rationality, (b) the assumption of stable preferences (over broad groups of commodities), and (c) the assumption of market equilibria (market forces tend towards equilibria).

EXAMPLES OF SIMPLE MODELS FOR DEALING WITH ECONOMIC BEHAVIOUR

Towards Macropsychology

George Katona (1979) was convinced that macropsychological concepts were necessary in the study of macroeconomic problems. His basic model posits that economic behavior is a function of ability (mostly measured as aggregate disposable income) and willingness (economic motivation as measured, e.g., by survey data on attitudes) to consume/save. Reactions to macroeconomic stimuli, that is changes in macroeconomic variables, depend on the stimuli and the state of the variables mediating between stimuli and responses. Economists may use intervening variables representing sociodemographic and income groups when data are available for such breakdowns.

In Katona's model the main intervening variables are psychological. This is a stimulus-organism-response model at the macro-level. In a discussion of, for example, the economic consequences of a tax cut, Katona availed himself of his simple model of consumer reactions, combining economic (ability) and psychological (willingness) variables. Katona could then say that if consumers were optimistic about their future income, something that could be estimated through interview surveys, they would spend most of the money received through the tax cut, probably starting long before the tax cut materialized into more money in the pocket.

Next, I propose to present some simple models that follow the basic pattern of Katona's model.

The Psychology of Saving

What can a psychologist say today if asked about how savings in the national economy will develop over the next years and how saving can be stimulated? The reason behind the question is that the role of psychological factors has been repeatedly stressed in the public debate. The question "Why do people save?" accompanied by the politician's question "How can people be made to save more?" has been posed at least since the Middle Ages, when legislation against certain kinds of consumption was introduced in the form of the so-called sumptuary laws. Classical and neoclassical economists devoted a lot of interest to factors that influenced thrift (for a review, see Wärneryd, 1989a and 1989b). It was suggested that impatience and lack of self-control were important factors and it was assumed that such factors were associated with low education, low income, and low age. Some economists provided rather elaborate psychological theories which were quite different from what the contemporary psychologists were busy studying.

In more recent years a few psychologists, starting in the 1940s with Katona (1975), have studied saving behavior. The studies have been based on survey data and have used simple psychological theory, developed specifically for the study of saving and consumption. More recently the idea of saver groups who have different motives for saving and may respond differently to economic stimuli has been introduced. Reasoning from a cluster analysis of survey data, Wahlund and Wärneryd (1987) suggested the existence of four saver types: wealth managers, goal savers, buffer savers, and cash managers.

When something is known about the properties of these saver groups, the potential consequences of a tax incentive plan for stimulating saving can be more meaningfully addressed than if all savers are treated as

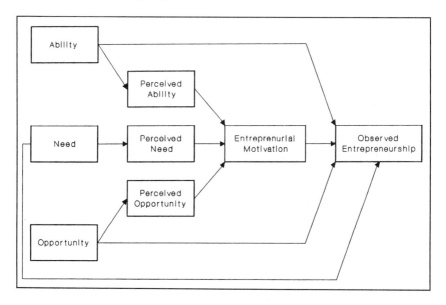

FIG. 1. Factors affecting entrepreneurship.
Source: P. Davidson (1989). Continued entrepreneurship and small firm growth (p.10). Doctoral dissertation. Stockholm: Stockholm School of Economics.

one aggregate. According to a Swedish study (Wahlund, 1991), the wealth managers are the group most responsive to tax incentives for saving.

There is still a need for developing more elaborate theory that deals with the complex behavior of perception of the uncertainties of the future and the will to provide for it rather than buying immediate satisfaction through consumption now. It is the task of the psychologists to study the perceptions and motives that make people save and that have to be influenced if saving behavior is to be encouraged. It is important to explore to what extent the amounts saved and the frequency of saving depend on the degree of uncertainty about the future and the degree of security for the money or other resources saved.

It is already possible to elaborate a little on these ideas. One can consider what factors tend to increase human concern about the future and affect the security of money saved. Examples are, inflation and taxes and how the four saver groups will react. These ideas find support in Marshall (1947/1890), and they have been corroborated by more recent research (see Katona, 1975; Wärneryd, 1989a). This simple model can be used to discuss the problem of stimulating saving behavior, but one should be aware of the ethical implications of suggesting increases in the public fear of the future.

The Psychology of Entrepreneurship and Innovation
There are several types of psychological studies on entrepreneurship, based on (a) the achievement motive according to McClelland (1961), (b) personality theory like locus of control theory or personality inventories (Brockhaus, 1982), and (c) cognitive psychology like risk-taking behavior (Ronen, 1986).

A common criticism is that psychological variables have not proved that they can contribute substantially to explaining variance. It is said that structural variables belonging to the environment are more important. A conclusion that lies near at hand is that variables belonging to the environment, usually called structural or contextual variables, and psychological variables must be combined in the analysis of entrepreneurship. Certain types of motivation that may be related to personality characteristics must be combined with cognitive factors and be assumed to operate under certain situational circumstances.

Davidsson (1989) presents a structural equation model that in its essentials is quite simple and still seems to provide a good structure for an analysis of entrepreneurship problems and policy measures to stimulate entrepreneurship. The model contains three objectively defined factors: ability, need, and opportunity, all of them defined in terms of objective indicators. In the model they are combined with the corresponding subjective variables: perceived ability, perceived need, and perceived opportunity. These variables are measured through some form of subjective report from the individual. Together they influence a fourth subjective variable: entrepreneurial motivation. All of the variables contribute to the dependent variable "observed entrepreneurship." The model mixes objective, structural data with subjective data of cognitive and motivational phenomena.

The model has been empirically tested on what the author calls "continued entrepreneurship", that is the growth of small firms. The empirical tests so far indicate that the model has good explanatory power. The author summarizes (Davidsson, 1989, p.210):

> Objective measures of Ability, Need, and Opportunity are capable of explaining a substantial share of the variation in past growth rates. Need factors appear relatively more important than the other two. The results also leave considerable room for explanations based on the manager's subjectively perceived Ability, Need, and Opportunity.

Fiscal Psychology
Psychological research on taxation has primarily focused on tax evasion (Lewis, 1982). What causes an individual to evade tax? An economic explanation is as follows. An individual can make a gain by evading tax but runs a risk of being caught and punished. The potential loss is

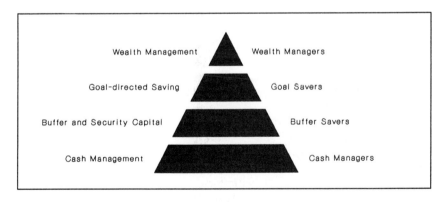

FIG. 2. A Hierarchy of Savings Needs and Saver Groups.
Source: R. Wahlund (1991). *Skatter och ekonomiska beteenden. En studie i ekonomisk psykologi om främst skattefusk och sparande utifrån 1982 års skatteomläggning* [Taxes and economic behaviors: An economic-psychological study on tax evasion and saving with particular emphasis on the Swedish tax system change in 1982] (p.344). With an English summary. Doctoral dissertation. Stockholm: Stockholm School of Economics, Economic Research Institute.

weighed against the potential gain. This deterrence model focuses interest on the level of taxation that affects the possible gain, on the probability of being caught, and on the severity of the punishment. Psychologists have a feeling that this model may be adequate for some purposes but that it misses such important aspects as self-respect and recognition by others. Psychological researchers thus try to combine economic and psychological variables to explain tax evasion.

De Juan (1989) presents a model for tax evasion that seems to summarize earlier findings quite well. She tests it on empirical data from a survey of Swedish youth. She assumes that tax evasion is a function of three sets of factors: (a) propensity to evade, (b) ability to evade,and (c) opportunity to evade. For each set of factors she provides indicators, based on questions posed in a mail survey of people aged 16-35.

The opportunity to evade is based on an index that comprises, among other things, economic situation, self-employment, and risk proneness. The index for ability to evade tax is made up of skills in law, skills in certain trades, and influence from peer groups. The propensity index covers the attitudes towards the tax system and towards tax evasion, to what extent it is shameful to evade tax. De Juan finds that propensity to evade has the highest correlation with reported tax evasion. Her model serves as a convenient way of keeping in mind important variables when discussing tax evasion.

There are more elaborate models and there is an ongoing discussion about the possibility of getting adequate and accurate reports from regular interviews with taxpayers (see Hessing, Kinsey, Elffers, & Weigel, 1988). Still, in a discussion of the psychology of tax evasion, de Juan's simple model may suffice.

Economic Behavior as Studied in Other Disciplines

It may come as a surprise to many psychologists that there exists interesting research in psychology that is never published in psychological journals. Two new, rapidly developing areas should be mentioned for their interest in cognitive psychology. Then there is, of course, the field of consumer behavior.

Behavioral accounting already has a fairly long history, and there are many good review articles (see, e.g. Swieringa & Weick, 1982). Essentially, behavioral accounting is preoccupied with the human use of accounting and auditing reports. In this research human information processing models have met with considerable interest. For many years the lens model in Hammond's version was the leading theory (see Libby, 1981). Many experimental studies have dealt with how judgments are affected by different factors, such as reporting or not reporting certain information in the annual statement of a business firm. The problems studied stem both from accounting and auditing contexts. Judgment and decision theory has inspired a number of studies of how applications for loans can best be handled and has led to attempts to use bootstrapping techniques. Being familiar with modern cognitive psychology can be of some help in this area even without deeper knowledge about accounting.

In financial economics many observations of deviations from economic rationality have led to an awareness of the need for developing new thinking (see Arrow, 1982). There seems to be an increased use for cognitive psychology. Prospect theory, in particular, gives rise to many interesting insights in an area that has been said to come closer than any other economic field to the ideal market where economic rationality prevails. It may even be possible to make money out of one's better knowledge of human nature through so-called arbitrage effects! Knowledge about the regression toward the mean effect, which is well-known from test theory, has been utilized in strategies for buying stock. This principle may also have served other speculators, though inadvertently, making them think highly of their own ability (cf. Hogarth, 1987, pp.24-28).

Certain types of economic behavior, notably consumption, are heavily researched for practical purposes. Some contributions to developing psychological theory have been made by this research. Ölander (1990) counters the assumption that consumer behavior study exclusively serves the managerial purpose of influencing consumers through marketing efforts. A content analysis of the leading journals demonstrates that the approaches have wider application and serve consumer policy interests as well. In economic psychology there is a quest for developing theory of a more basic nature, independent of specific uses in marketing and policy-making (see Ölander, 1990).

There is often a need for a simple, yet sophisticated, model of consumer behavior that can be used for quick structuring of consumer behavior problems and for providing theory-based psychological answers to many pertinent questions both at the macroeconomic level and at the level where marketers work. Howard (1989) presents a model that nicely integrates psychological knowledge about consumer behavior. When, for example, a market researcher is confronted with a client's problem, such a model can be quite helpful.

The model comprises six basic concepts, theory-based relationships between the concepts, and a provision for estimating the relationships by means of multiple regression. The concepts used in the Consumer Decision Making (CDM) model are: 1. information sources (F, or facts); 2. knowledge about the brand (B); 3. attitude towards the brand (A); 4) confidence, the consumer's degree of certainty that she or he is correct about her or his evaluative judgment of the brand (C); 5. intention to buy the brand in some specified time period (I); and 6. purchase of the brand (P).

The influence from information processing theory, decision theory, and the Fishbein-Ajzen attitude theory is easily detected in this model. Howard (1989) summarized much psychological knowledge and fitted it to his model in which he assumes somewhat different properties for the three stages he distinguishes in consumer purchasing processes. The role and form of F thus varies, and F affects the values of B, A, and C differently depending on how far the latter have developed. Particular attention is paid to the development of A, which comprises benefits of the brand or product and the need satisfaction (performance) that the consumer judges the brand to be capable of.

WHAT DOES THE NEW ROLE INVOLVE FOR PSYCHOLOGY?

There is only rarely a listing of anything having to do with economics in the subject indexes of psychological texts. The *Annual Review of Psychology* of 1990 has one entry. It relates to the relevance of studying economic context in connection with personality development (Collins & Gunnar, 1990). According to Collins & Gunnar (1990), variables of the economic system are coming more and more into focus in personality research as impoverished groups develop in welfare societies. This illustrates the point I want to make: Structural (contextual) variables and individual variables must often be combined for a meaningful study of economic behavior. This has also been strongly emphasized by Lea et al. (1987) and is a recurrent theme in their textbook on economic psychology.

The new role for psychology entails more involvement with economic problems in society and participation in attempts to solve problems at the aggregate level. An integral part of this idea is the development of theory through laboratory research on economic behavior. While psychologists have carried out relatively few laboratory experiments relating to economic behavior, experimental economists have conducted many theory-testing and theory-developing experiments (see, e.g., Smith, 1982).

Because economic behavior in the public eye is the domain of economics and because economic research has a kind of birthright, the psychologist's role requires more understanding of what economic theory makes economists expect from the psychological study of economic behavior. Economics is, first, a frame for dealing with economic problems at the national level, and economists may search for help in this context, not for ways of explaining individual differences.

CONCLUDING REMARKS

In a somewhat jocular vein it could be said that what is outlined above are some ways for psychologists to compete with economists for the attention of the mass media and various decision-makers, especially at the policy level. The serious side is that psychologists should participate more in discussions of psychological problems at the aggregate level (both the macrolevel and the mass-market levels). To do this they should develop models that make it possible to use sophisticated (and plausible) reasoning without always asking for new data. It is a question of taking care of and utilizing extant psychological knowledge.

Good psychological knowledge from research exists in many areas. By good is meant that its employment in problem-solving improves the quality of the solution. There is, of course, also theory that is poorly conceived and that should be used with care, if at all. A common deficiency is that the theory does not cover context effects and thus may not serve well in an applied area.

In spite of such qualifications, theory should be used in generative ways. This will, in my view, lead in the long run to better psychology. In the process many instances of "it depends" and some overuse of contingencies and individual differences that psychologists tend to display will be sorted out. This happens when psychological variables are combined with structural variables.

If psychologists become more involved in macropsychology, it may eventually be possible to overcome mainstream economists' doubts about the use of psychology and there will be chances of more cooperation. Otherwise, economists will continue to invent their own psychology. As Schumpeter pointed out: "Economists have never allowed their analysis to be influenced by the professional psychologists of their time, but have always framed for themselves such assumptions about psychical processes as they thought it desirable to make" (quoted from Coats, 1988, p. 215).

REFERENCES

Akerlof, G. A., & Dickens, W. T. (1982). The economic consequences of cognitive dissonance. *American Economic Review*, 72, 307-319.

Arrow, K. J. (1963). Utility and expectation in economic behavior. In S. Koch (Ed.), *Psychology: Study of a science* (pp. 724-752). New York, NY: McGraw-Hill.

Arrow, K. J. (1982). Risk perception in psychology and economics. *Economic Inquiry, 20,* 1-9.

Atkinson, J. W. (1957). Motivational determinants of risk taking behavior. *Psychological Review, 64,* 359-372.

Atkinson, J. W. (1964). *An introduction to motivation.* New York, NY: American Book.

Backus, D., & Driffill, J. (1985). Rational expectations and policy credibility following a change in regime. *Review of Economic Studies, 52,* 211-221.

Becker, G. S. (1976). *The economic approach to human behavior.* Chicago, IL: University of Chicago.

Böhm-Bawerk, E. von. (1912). *Positive Theorie des Kapitales.* Dritte Auflage. Zweiter Halbband. Innsbruck: Verlag der Wagner'schen Universitäts-Buchhandlung. (Original work published 1888).

Boring, E. G. (1950). *A history of experimental psychology.* (2nd ed.). Englewood Cliffs, NJ: Prentice-Hall.

Brockhaus, R. H., Sr. (1982). The psychology of the entrepreneur. In C. A. Kent, D. L. Sexton, & K. H. Vesper (Eds.), *Encyclopedia of entrepreneurship* (pp. 39-57). Englewood Cliffs, NJ: Prentice-Hall.

Carter, M., & Maddock, R. (1984). *Rational expectations: Macroeconomics for the 1980s?* London: Macmillan.

Cialdini, R. B. (1988). *Influence: Science and practice.* (2nd ed.). Glenview, IL: Scott, Foresman and Company.

Coats, A. W. (1988). Economics and psychology: A resurrection story. In P. Earl (Ed.), *Psychological economics. Development, tensions, prospects* (pp. 211-225). Dordrecht, The Netherlands: Kluwer.

Collins, W. A., & Gunnar, M. R. (1990). Social and personality development. *Annual Review of Psychology, 41,* 387-416.

Davidsson, P. (1989). *Continued entrepreneurship and small firm growth.* Doctoral dissertation. Stockholm: Stockholm School of Economics.

Dawes, R. M. (1980). Social dilemmas. *Annual Review of Psychology, 31,* 169-193.

de Juan, A. (1989). *Fiscal attitudes and behavior: A study of 16-35 year old Swedish citizens.* (Research rep.nr. 285). Stockholm: Stockholm School of Economics, Economic Research Institute.

Etzioni, A. (1988). *The moral dimension: Toward a new economics.* New York, NY: Free Press.

European File. (1988 February). *The Community and business: the action programme for small and medium-sized enterprises,* No.3. Commission of the European Communities. Brussels, Belgium.

Gergen, K. J. (1982). *Toward transformation in social knowledge.* New York, NY: Springer.

Herrnstein, R. J. (1990). Rational choice theory: Necessary but not sufficient. *American Psychologist*, *45*, 356-367

Hessing, D. J., Kinsey, K. A., Elffers, H., & Weigel R. H. (1988). Tax evasion research: measurement strategies and theoretical models. In W. F. van Raaij, G. M. van Veldhoven, & K.-E. Wärneryd (Eds.), Handbook of economic psychology (pp. 516-537). Dordrecht: Kluwer

Hogarth, R., (1987). *Judgment and choice* (2nd ed.). Chichester: John Wiley & Sons.

Hovland, C. I., Janis, I., & Kelley, H. H. (1953). *Communication and persuasion*. New Haven, CT: Yale University Press.

Howard, J. A. (1989). *Consumer behavior in marketing strategy*. Englewood Cliffs, NJ: Prentice Hall.

James, W. (1890). *The principles of psychology*. (Vols. 1-2). New York: Henry Holt.

Jevons, W. S. (1911). *The theory of political economy*. (4th ed.). London: Macmillan. (Original work published 1871)

Kahneman, D., Knetsch, J. L. & Thaler, R. (1986). Fairness as a constraint on profit seeking: Entitlements in the market. *American Economic Review*, *76*, 728-741.

Kahneman, D. & Tversky, A. (1979). Prospect theory: An analysis of decision under risk. *Econometrica*, *47*, 263-291.

Katona, G. (1953). Rational behavior and economic behavior. *Psychological Review*, *60*, 307-318.

Katona, G. (1975). *Psychological economics*. New York, NY: Elsevier.

Katona, G. (1979). Toward a macropsychology. *American Psychologist*, *34*, 118-126.

Lea, S. G., Tarpy, R. M. & Webley., P. (1987). *The individual in the economy: A survey of economic psychology*. Cambridge: Cambridge University Press.

Levine, J. M, & Moreland, R. L. (1990). Progress in small group research. *Annual Review of Psychology*, *41*, 585-634.

Lewis, A. (1982). *The psychology of taxation*. Oxford: Martin Robertson.

Libby, R. (1981). *Accounting and human information processing: Theory and applications*. Englewood Cliffs, NJ: Prentice-Hall.

Mandeville, B. (1924). *The Fable of the Bees: or, Private Vices, Publick Benefits: With a commentary critical, historical, and explanatory by F.B. Kaye* (Vols. 1-2). London: Oxford University Press. (Original work published from 1712 to 1732)

Marshall, A. (1947). *Principles of economics: An introductory volume* (8th ed.). London: Macmillan (Original work published 1890)

McClelland, D. C. (1961). *The achieving society*. Princeton, NJ: van Nostrand.

McClelland, D. C. (1975). *Power: The inner experience.* New York, NY: Irvington.

McClelland, D. C. & Winter, D. G. (1969). *Motivating economic achievement.* New York, NY: Free Press.

Menger, C. (1923). *Grundsätze der Volkswirtschaftslehre.* Vienna: Hölder-Pichler-Tempsky. (Original work published 1871)

Messick, D. (1986). Decision making in social dilemmas. In B. Brehmer, H. Jungermann, P. Lourens & G. Sevón (Eds.), *New Directions in Research on Decision Making* (pp. 219-227). Amsterdam: Elsevier.

Messick, D., & Brewer, M. B. (1983). Solving social dilemmas: A review. In L. Wheeler & P. Shaver (Eds.), *Review of personality and social psychology,* vol. 4., pp. 11-44. Beverly Hills, CA: Sage

Murphy, G. (1951). *Historical introduction to modern psychology.* (Rev. ed.) New York, NY: Harcourt Brace.

Ölander, F. (1990). Consumer psychology: Not necessarily a manipulative science. *Applied Psychology, 39,* 105-126.

Parsons, T. (1954). *Essays in sociological theory: The motivation of economic activities.* Glencoe, IL: Free Press.

Pieters, R. G. M., & van Raaij, W. F. (1988). The role of affect in economic behavior. In W. F. van Raaij, G. van Veldhoven, & K.-E. Wärneryd (Eds.), *Handbook of Economic Psychology* (pp. 108-142). Dordrecht, The Netherlands: Kluwer.

Robbins, L. (1979). The nature of economic generalizations. In F. Hahn & M. Hollis (Eds.), *Philosophy and economic theory* (pp. 36-46). Oxford: Oxford University Press (Original work published 1935)

Ronen, J. (1986). *Individual entrepreneurship and corporate entrepreneurship: A tentative synthesis* (Report no.86-8). New York: New York University, Vincent C. Ross Institute of Accounting Research.

Scitovsky, T. (1976). *The joyless economy: An inquiry into human satisfaction and consumer dissatisfaction.* New York, NY: Oxford University Press.

Shefrin, H. M. & Thaler, R. H. (1988). The behavioral life-cycle hypothesis. *Economic Inquiry, 26,* 609-643.

Simon, H. A. (1990). Invariants of human behavior. *Annual Review of Psychology, 41,* 1-19.

Sjöberg, L. (1985). Economical acts and reasons in everyday life. A study of randomly selected acts. In H. Brandstätter & E. Kirchler (Eds.), *Economic Psychology* (pp. 327-335). Proceedings of the 10th IAREP Annual Colloquium. Linz: Rudolf Trauner.

Smith, A. (1982). *The theory of moral sentiments.* Edited by D. D. Raphael and A. L. Mactie. Indianapolis, IN: Liberty Classics. (Original work published 1759)

Smith, A. (1982). *The wealth of nations*. Harmondsworth, Middlesex: Penguin. (Original work published 1776)

Smith, V. L. (1982). Microeconomic systems as an experimental science. *American Economic Review, 72*, 923-955.

Spence, K. (1964). *Behavior theory and conditioning*. New Haven, CT: Yale University Press

Swieringa, R. J., & Weick, K. E. (1982). An assessment of laboratory experimentation in accounting. *Journal of Accounting Research, 20*, 56-101 [supplement].

Tarde, G. (1902). *La psychologie économique* (Vols. 1-2). Paris: Alcan.

Thaler, R. H., & Shefrin, H. M. (1981). An economic theory of self-control. *Journal of Political Economy, 89*, 392-406.

Wahlund, R. (1991). *Skatter och ekonomiska beteenden. En studie i ekonomisk psykologi om främst skattefusk och sparande utifrån 1982 års skatteomläggning* [Taxes and economic behaviors: An economic-psychological study on tax evasion and saving with particular emphasis on the Swedish tax system change in 1982]. With an English summary. Doctoral dissertation. Stockholm: Stockholm School of Economics, Economic Research Institute.

Wahlund, R., & Wärneryd, K.-E. (1987). Aggregate saving and the saving behavior of saver groups. *Skandinaviska Enskilda Banken Quarterly Review, 3*, 52-64.

Walster, E., & Walster, G. W. (1975). Equity and social justice. *Journal of Social Issues, 31*, 21-43.

Wärneryd, K.-E. (1988). The psychology of innovative entrepreneurship. In W. F. van Raaij, G. van Veldhoven, & K.-E. Wärneryd (Eds.), *Handbook of Economic Psychology* (pp. 404-447). Dordrecht, The Netherlands: Kluwer.

Wärneryd, K.-E. (1989a). On the psychology of saving: An essay on economic behavior. *Journal of Economic Psychology, 10*, 515-541.

Wärneryd, K.-E. (1989b). Improving psychological theory through studies of economic behaviour: The case of saving. *Applied Psychology, 38*, 213-236.

ECONOMIC SOCIALIZATION:
Cognitive-developmental and Cross-cultural Perspectives

Organizer: S. H. Ng,
University of Otago, New Zealand
Chair: G. Sevon,
Swedish School of Economics, Finland

Contributors:

A.S. Bombi, S. Cacciamani, A. Pieramico, Universita La Sapienza,
Rome, Italy
Economic conceptions and moral judgement in children 6 to 11 years old

S. Lau, The Chinese University of Hong Kong, Hong Kong
Money: What it means to children and adults

S. H. Ng, University of Otago, New Zealand
F. Cram, Auckland University, New Zealand
Effects of cognitive conflict on children's understanding of public ownership

D. Roker, University of Sheffield, U.K.
The economic socialization of British youth: The impact of different
school types

G. Sevon, Swedish School of Economics, Helsinki, Finland
Economic socialization of children: A cross-cultural study

P. Webley, University of Exeter, U.K.
The context of children's economic understanding and behavior

This symposium presents studies in economic socialization relating to several issues.

1. In what ways are economic conceptions sufficiently different from other conceptions such as moral and political judgments? (Bombi, Cacciamani, & Pieramico, 1990)

2. How adequate is the cognitive-developmental perspective for economic socialization research? (Webley, 1990) What are the roles of social structural and cultural variables? (Roker, 1990; Lau, 1990; Sevon, 1990)

3. How can economic understanding be improved in an experimental setting? (Ng & Cram, 1990)

Bombi et al. regarded children's economic ideas as part of social cognition and summarized two main theoretical approaches to the cognitive-developmental studies of social cognition. One approach considers the development of social cognition in the various domains as a unitary process characterized by the same stages. A second approach regards the domain-specific developments as somewhat separate from each other.

In their Italian study, Bombi et al. interviewed children about criteria of payment for two different jobs and about the fair distribution of resources between two young persons. Results showed that children's reasoning about equity in the economic domain was different from that in directly experienced interpersonal relations, thus supporting the second of the above two approaches. On the practical side, the results suggested that any attempt at "economic education" at an early age should be planned by taking into account the fact that children tend not to perceive the moral implications of certain economic behaviors.

Webley argued that the majority of economic socialization research has been underpinned by three assumptions that have severely limited understanding in this area. The thinking behind most studies is typically (a) acultural—it fails to examine the importance of cultural values in defining the meaning of "economic" acts, (b) afunctional—it fails to provide a functional understanding of the practical importance of "economic" behavior, and (c) parochial—it adopts an adult-centred view of the economic world, thereby reducing the social practice of childhood economics to a stage in the move towards economic maturity rather than casting it as a response to practical problems faced by children in their own worlds.

Against this background, Webley outlined his attempt at constructing a child-centered functional account of the economic life of the child as well as its role in economic development. The account depends first and foremost on defining what is meant by "economic" behavior. For the most part researchers have tended to regard this meaning as given, and the term economic has simply served as a label for the subset of categories and concepts associated with the acquisition, management, and distribution of wealth. Spending and saving, borrowing and lending, withdrawing and depositing, investing and hoarding—all of these, which are conventionally regarded as "economic", have been of interest to cognitive developmentalists. Although there have been studies looking at the development of economic understanding in different cultures, they have therefore generally been concerned with the child's understanding of formal institutions such as the bank. However, the need is to look at the functional significance of economic activity as well as its formal aspects.

The emphasis on the functional aspects of children's economic activity has important implications. Most important, the child is cast as an economic problem-solver, and economic development is defined in broader terms because the functions of economic activity are emphasized along with their form. This encourages one to concentrate on the children's own understanding of their economic world and the problems presented in it. To illustrate this approach, Webley examined the problem of resource allocation faced by British children in their everyday life.

Roker reported research on the way in which British teenagers developed ideas about their economic environments. In contrast to most previous research, which has focused on family influence, Roker focused on the role of educational experience by comparing adolescents in private (fee-paying) and state schools. The subjects were 190 girls aged 15-18 attending the two types of schools. Each subject completed a standardized questionnaire; afterwards, 135 of them from the two types of schools were matched for socioeconomic background and selected for interview. The interview explored a range of socioeconomic and political values and orientations. Results showed significant differences between the school samples. For example, the private school sample had higher career aims, were generally supporters of a right-wing political and economic philosophy, and gave more individualistic attributions for poverty and unemployment. These differences were constant even when controlling for social class.

Lau presented findings of three large-scale studies on money perceptions by Hong Kong Chinese. In the first study, 378 kindergarten children were asked to give free associations to 86 Chinese words. The word *money* elicited numerous associations (ranked 9th in 5-year-olds and 21st in 6-year-olds), indicating that money was not an unfamiliar or disinterested concept even for very young children. Results also showed that children's associations of money were essentially nonevaluative and functional in nature. Evaluative associations, however, became predominant among subjects tested in the second and the third studies. In the second study, school teachers, business people, and high school students were asked to rate what money meant to them. It was found that teachers perceived money to be less good and honest than business people did. Relative to these two professional groups, the student group gave money higher goodness and honesty ratings but lower interest ratings. In the third study, the relation between money attitudes and value orientations was examined in a large group of college students.

Results showed that subjects who endorsed highly the values of enjoyment, security, and achievement rated money as more important than did those who did not endorse these values as highly. On the other hand, subjects who were high on the prosocial and maturity types of values rated money as less important than those who were low on these values.

Cultural effects were highlighted in Sevon's paper, which was based on a cross-cultural study involving 8- to 14-year-olds in ten countries (Algeria, Austria, Denmark, Finland, France, Israel, Norway, Poland, West Germany, and Yugoslavia). The interview topics covered both the understanding of, reasoning about, and attitudes towards a variety of economic phenomena. Specifically, understanding was gauged from subjects' discussion about prices, salaries, savings, and investments. Reasoning was tested by asking subjects to talk about consequences of abolishing taxes, of printing more money, of diamonds or oil found, and of price reductions. Attitudes towards poverty, richness, and unemployment were scaled. Results showed age and culture effects.

Understanding deepened with age, whereas attitudes remained fairly unchanged. Culture effects were complex, and appeared to reflect variations in institutional conditions, values, and experiences with economic affairs across countries.

In the first of two studies, Ng and Cram surveyed New Zealand children's understanding of public ownership. Although the items of ownership (schools, buses) are already familiar to the 5- to 12-year-olds, the ownership itself is embedded in social institutions (e.g., city council) remote from the direct observation of children. Relative to private ownership, which usually involves an identifiable individual owner and is within the children's personal experience, public ownership is more difficult to understand. To understand public ownership, children have to transcend the personalized focus of private ownership, grasp the institutional context of ownership, as well as develop constructs relating to positional power (e.g., boss), social subsystems, and so forth. It was predicted and found that, as the children grew older, the basis of their understanding of public ownership changed from physical to abstract concepts.

The hierarchical levels of understanding established in this study provided a means of measuring the effects due to cognitive conflict to be induced experimentally in the second study. Children were first interviewed about bus ownership. Those who thought that the bus driver owned the bus were selected and formed into friendship dyads. One member of a dyad was shown a video depicting a bus driver receiving instructions from another adult whereas the other member viewed a neutral video. Half of the dyads then discussed bus ownership, the rest discussed a neutral topic. This procedure created four conflict conditions: no conflict, nonsocial conflict, social conflict, and social as well as nonsocial conflict. Results showed that subjects in the social conflict condition progressed the most. In addition, subjects who had talked actively by making rejection or integration statements to resolve the disagreement during discussion made the most progress.

During the symposium, the discussion centered on specific aspects of individual studies and on the three general issues identified at the beginning of the present paper. In addition, a main theme emerged from the discussion concerning the distinction between the personal economic environment (e.g., career planning, budgeting, private ownership) and the general economic environment, which is more detached from individuals and not highly subject to their control (e.g., taxation, inequality, public ownership).

REFERENCES

Bombi, A.S., Cacciamani, S., & Pieramico, A. (1990). *Economic conceptions and moral judgements in children 6 to 11 years old*. Paper presented at the 22nd International Congress of Applied Psychology, July, 1990, Kyoto.

Lau, S. (1990). *Money: What it means to children and adults*. Paper presented at the 22nd International Congress of Applied Psychology, July, 1990, Kyoto.

Ng, S.H. & Cram, F. (1990). *Effects of cognitive conflict on children's understanding of public ownership*. Paper presented at the 22nd International Congress of Applied Psychology, July, 1990, Kyoto.

Roker, D. (1990). *The economic socialization of British youth: The impact of diffent school types*. Paper presented at the 22nd International Congress of Applied Psychology, July, 1990, Kyoto.

Sevon. G. (1990). *Economic socialization of children: A cross-cultural study*. Paper presented at the 22nd International Congress of Applied Psychology, July, 1990, Kyoto.

Webley, P. (1990). *The context of children's economic understanding and behavior*. Paper presented at the 22nd International Congress of Applied Psychology, July, 1990, Kyoto.

VALUES, LIFESTYLES AND CONSUMPTION PATTERNS: International Comparisons Between and Within Countries

Organizer & Chair: E. J. Chéron,
Laval University, Canada

Contributors:

E. J. Chéron, Laval University, Canada
T. E. Muller, McMaster University, Canada
Values, lifestyle and consumption patterns: Comparison between the
Canadian provinces of Ontario and Quebec

I. Schopphoven, Fern Universität Hagen, FRG
Values, lifestyle and consumption patterns: Comparisons between
urban and rural Germany

T. Sugimoto, University of Shizuoka, Japan
Urban and rural cosumption patterns in Japan

E. Tissier-Desbordes, Ecole Supérieure de Commerce de Paris, France,
J. Moscarola, Université de Savoie, France
Values, lifestyle and consumption patterns: Comparisons between Paris
and Annecy in France

Discussant: T. E. Muller, McMaster University, Canada

The conclusion of free-trade agreements in North America and Europe together with the fast-growing economies of leading Asian countries has restructured international trade into a new three trade-bloc configuration. This new triad accounts for two-thirds of world gross production and 85% of world discretionary income. Therefore, consumption similarities and differences both between and within those three major trade partners are of particular interest for the future of international trade.

The overall objective of the symposium was to explore the possible identification of a transnational typology in terms of international intermarket segmentation.The specific objectives of the symposium were to compare values (Kahle, 1983), lifestyles, and consumption patterns across and within four countries in each of the three major trading blocs of the future. Samples of households in three distinct socioeconomic classes (low, middle, and high income) were selected in two different regions in each of four countries—Canada, Germany, France, and Japan. Data was collected on ownership and priority of acquisition of durable products and services, personal value profiles, lifestyles, and socioeconomic background variables.

The same data collection instrument was used among countries and between regions within each country. Countries and regions within countries were compared for differences of ownership and differences in the relative importance of personal values and lifestyles. Values and lifestyles were used as potential predictors of clusters of households with similar priority of acquisition. Finally, ownership patterns were related to socioeconomic demographic and geographic variables.

Measures of ownership obtained from the four samples were validated by comparing the average number owned of 23 comparable durable products and services (see Figure 1) with the Human and Development Index (HDI) published in *The Economist* (1990), which is based on real gross domestic product per head life expectancy, and literacy rate. Average ownership in the samples ranked the four countries in the same order as the HDI measure, with Japan first, followed by Canada, France, and Germany in descending order.

Results from 494 representative households in the provinces of Ontario (Hamilton area) and Quebec (Quebec City) in Canada revealed significant differences in terms of ownership, values, and lifestyles. Clusters of households with similar priority of acquisition could be predicted from lifestyles in Ontario and from values and lifestyles in Quebec.

Correspondence analysis of ownership, values, and descriptive variables indicated that socioeconomic and geographic descriptors differentiated ownership much more than they did personal values.

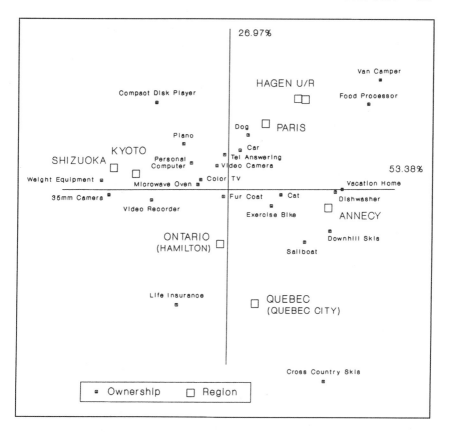

FIG. 1. Comparison of ownership of 23 durable products and services in Japan, Canada, France, and Germany.

Results from 143 households in the urban and rural regions of Hagen in Germany revealed significant differences in terms of ownership. However, only one significant difference between the urban and rural respondents with respect to values and lifestyles was found: There was a higher need for security in the rural area. Clusters of households with similar priority of acquisition could be predicted from values and lifestyles. In contrast to the region of residence, socioeconomic descriptors of all residents were found associated with several significant differences in values and lifestyles.

Results from 363 households in the French cities of Paris and Annecy indicated significant differences of ownership, values, and lifestyles. Values and lifestyles were not found to be good predictors of priority of acquisition. However, sociodemographic variables (age and income) were significantly associated with ownership.

Results from 391 households in the urban city of Kyoto and the rural cities of Shizuoka and Myiazaki in Japan revealed significant differences of ownership. In terms of values and lifestyles, only one significant difference was found between the urban and the rural cities: There was a higher need for a sense of accomplishment and the need to struggle to survive in the urban area. Income was found to be a better predictor of ownership than values and lifestyles.

A correspondence analysis on ownership is included in this summary for the eight regions involved in the study. The first two dimensions accounted for 53.38% and 26.97% of overall variation in the data. As can be seen, there is a lower degree of ownership differences between the two selected regions in Germany and Japan than in the two regions in France and Canada. Similar results were found for values and lifestyles, indicating that Germany and Japan appear more homogeneous than France and Canada.

In spite of the limitations of cross-cultural research (Douglas & Craig, 1984), these findings tend to confirm and extend the research by Rhea, Garland, and Crawford (1989). Persistence of cultural differences appears to prohibit the possibility of international intermarket segmentation. Therefore, marketing strategies need to be adapted to consumption patterns not only within trade blocs but to countries within trade blocs and to different regions within countries.

REFERENCES

Douglas, S. P. & Craig, C. S. (1984) Establishing Equivalence in Comparative Consumer Research. In E. Kaynak & R. Savitt, (Eds.), *Comparative Marketing Systems* (pp. 93-113). New York: Praeger.

Kahle, L. R.(Ed.).(1983). *Social Values and Social Change: Adaptation to Life in America*. New York, Praeger.

The Economist. (1990) May, 80-81.

CONSUMER PSYCHOLOGY:
The Consumer View

Organizers: M. Friedman,
Eastern Michigan University, U.S.A.
F. Ölander, Aarhus School of Business, Denmark
Chair: M. Friedman,
Eastern Michigan University, U.S.A.

Contributors:

H. Akiyama, University of Michigan, U.S.A.
Medical consumerism and self-care among older adults: A comparative
study of the U.S. and Japan

R. J. Faber, University of Minnesota, U.S.A.
T. C. O'Guinn, University of Illinois, U.S.A.
Understanding a problem of compulsive buying

M. Friedman, Eastern Michigan University, U.S.A.
Consumer boycotts and the consumer interest

R. O. Herrmann, R. Warland, Pennsylvania State University, U.S.A
Low involvement and time pressure as barriers to consumer information
search

F. Ölander, Aarhus School of Business, Denmark
S. Gronmo, University of Bergen, Norway
Consumer power: Enabling and limiting factors

Like other fields of psychology, consumer psychology encompasses a
wide range of behavior and experiences that can be studied from many

perspectives. Marketing interests and a stimulus-response paradigm have often led consumer psychologists to a reactive view of the consumer in their research and in their consulting work with marketing managers. By contrast, this symposium assumes a proactive view of consumers both individually and collectively. It examines obstacles to effective consumer decision-making (compulsive buying behavior as well as time pressure and low involvement) along with factors which facilitate it in Japan and the United States.

Finally, the symposium asks what factors influence how individuals in Scandinavia and the United States organize to further their interests as consumers.

The five symposium presentations are listed and summarized below.

CONSUMER POWER:
Enabling and Limiting Factors

Sigmund Gronmo, University of Bergen, Norway
Folke Ölander, The Aarhus School of Business, Denmark

The paper presents a conceptual framework for the systematization and comparison of various cases in which attempts have been made, successfully and not so successfully, to exercise consumer influence at various levels of society. Such comparisons can provide the basis for hypotheses and generalizations about determinants that affect the outcome of uses of consumer power or influence. The inspiration for developing the framework comes partly from the literature on power and influence in political science, sociology, and social psychology, and partly from the authors' own, case-oriented empirical research. In a project supported by the Nordic Council of Ministers, the authors carried out day-long group interviews with representatives from industry, consumer organizations and agencies, and the mass media in four Nordic countries. One of the cases encountered in these interviews will be used to illustrate the framework.

The main components of the framework are:

1. Constellation of Actors and Interests: (a) Actors, (b) Interests.

2. Context: (a) Resources, (b) Culture and norms.

3. Process: (a) Events and arenas, (b) Definition of the situation, strategies, means, and legitimations.

4. Outcomes: (a) Short-term outcomes, (b) Long-term outcomes.

CONSUMER BOYCOTTS AND THE CONSUMER INTEREST

Monroe Friedman, Eastern Michigan University, U.S.A.

American consumer organizations have used a variety of techniques to express their grievances to business firms (e.g., class action suits and letter-writing campaigns), but one technique, the consumer boycott, is perceived by business leaders to be more effective than any other. Yet despite the reputation of the boycott as an effective instrument for organized consumer action, little theoretical or empirical attention has been devoted to its understanding.

This study attempts to fill this gap by developing a taxonomy of boycott actions and by identifying variables believed likely to influence their effectiveness. The analytical framework draws upon theoretical work in psychology and empirical studies recently conducted of national, regional, and local boycotts.

MEDICAL CONSUMERISM AND SELF-CARE AMONG OLDER ADULTS: A COMPARATIVE STUDY OF THE UNITED STATES AND JAPAN

Hiroko Akiyama, University of Michigan, U.S.A.

There was a time when people unquestioningly accepted their doctor's diagnoses. Today, attitudes are changing. Medical consumerism is on the rise. The emphasis is shifting to patients' rights and physicians' obligations. People are taking their health into their own hands, questioning their doctor's advice and challenging their prescribed treatments.

A study of a stratified random sample of 900 persons aged 45 years and over in Japan and 728 in the United States revealed both similarities and differences in the manifestations and explanatory factors of medical consumerism in the two societies. Respondents were asked in face-to-face interviews if they had experienced any of 32 common symptoms of illness in the past 3 months, and if so, what actions they had taken in response, including both self-treatment and professional care. Perceived physician efficacy was assessed by 4 indicators; beliefs about the right to autonomy in doctor-patient relations, preference for physician care, experience of medical error, and the desire of patients for their own medical records. Findings indicate that in both societies, those with less emotional distress were more likely to take care of their ailments themselves rather than consult a physician. Perceived physician efficacy was found to have stronger impact on professional care use among Japanese than Americans. The complete paper presents detailed findings and contains a discussion of possible explanations in terms of variations in health-care delivery systems and in cultural beliefs and their implications for health-care policy and utilization.

LOW INVOLVEMENT AND TIME PRESSURE AS BARRIERS TO CONSUMER INFORMATION SEARCH

Robert Herrmann, The Pennsylvania State University, U.S.A.
Rex Warland, The Pennsylvania State University, U.S.A.

Increasing the availability of product information and making it more understandable have been suggested frequently as ways to help consumers become better informed. These suggestions cannot, however, overcome two major barriers to information use: (a) lack of interest in or involvement with certain categories of information, and (b) time pressures on consumers resulting from excessive commitments for the time available.

As might be expected, low involvement and time pressure reduce consumer search effort. There is evidence, however, that if there is involvement with a product category, search activity is high even under time pressure.

These results suggest the importance of educating consumers about product benefits (e.g., the nutritional benefits of food) and the significance of key evaluative criteria used for judging products. When consumers understand the potential benefits of particular choices, they will be more motivated to seek information on the relative ratings of different brands, even in the face of time pressure.

UNDERSTANDING THE PROBLEM OF COMPULSIVE BUYING

Ronald J. Faber, University of Minnesota, U.S.A.
Thomas C. O'Guinn, University of Illinois, U.S.A.

Compulsive buying has recently been recognized as a severe psychological problem affecting some consumers. Compulsive buyers are people who are impulsively driven to buy and unable to control their urge, which often stems from negative self-feelings.

Through the use of both survey research and clinical depth interviews, the authors have engaged in a systematic study of this phenomenon. The results indicate that compulsive buyers have lower self-esteem and are more prone to fantasize than other consumers. They also have a greater tendency toward compulsive behaviors in general. Although compulsive buying typically first appears in late adolescence or early adulthood, the root cause may be based in childhood experiences.

The motivation for compulsive buying comes more from the psychological benefits received from the process of buying than from the possession of purchased objects. These psychological benefits include feelings of importance and desirability, feelings of arousal and excitement, and positive interpersonal interactions. Ultimately, however, this behavior can lead to severe consequences, including extreme levels of debt, anxiety, frustration, domestic dissension, and a further loss of self-esteem.

ECONOMIC PSYCHOLOGY POSTER CONTRIBUTIONS

THE INFLUENCE OF AFFECT AND INVOLVEMENT ON THE DECISION-MAKING PROCESS

Kazuhisa Takemura, Kohka Women's College, Kyoto, Japan

The purpose of this study was to examine the influence of positive and negative affects and involvement on the decision-making process in consumer behavior. It was hypothesized that the effect of positive and negative affect on decision-making strategy is asymmetrical and that there is an interaction effect between affect and involvement.

Each subject, 81 university students in all, was randomly assigned to one cell of a 3 (positive, neutral, or negative affect) x 2 (high or low involvement) design. A method of monitoring information acquisition was used to trace the information-search process in the decision task, in which subjects were asked to choose among 6 radio-cassette recorders.

In the experiment, the affect states were induced by a report of success or failure in a performance test. In order to manipulate the degree of involvement in the decision task, a method of outcome dependency was utilized. In the high involvement condition, each subject was asked to use the chosen recorder for a few months before the decision task. In the low involvement condition, each subject was not asked to use the chosen recorder.

Major findings obtained were as follows: (a) Subjects in the negative affect condition spent greater amounts of time and searched for information more extensively on the decision task than did subjects in the positive affect condition (see Table 1). Subjects in the negative affect condition were more likely to return to information they had already searched. (b) Subjects searched for information more extensively and rechecked information more often on the decision task in which they had greater involvement. (c) The interaction between affect and involvement was significant. The interaction revealed that affect had a strong effect on the decision-making process in the high involvement condition.

TABLE 1

Mean number of pieces of information searched for on a decision-making task performed under different affect conditions

Level of Involvement	Affect		
	Positive	Neutral	Negative
High	19.54	34.80	38.85
Low	23.62	28.69	24.31

RESOURCE APPROACH METHODOLOGY: LIMITS AND POSSIBILITIES OF ITS USE IN APPLIED PSYCHOLOGY

Igor M. Smorodin,
Leningrad Polytechnic University, Leningrad, USSR

The resource approach, whose conceptual and formal methodology apparatus was initially formed in the sphere of modelling the generalized laws dealing with the processes of production and consumption in economics, is becoming increasingly popular among researchers working in different fields of social and natural sciences. Four essential features of the approach can be distinguished: the realization of the notion of restrictions, the concepts of exchange and interaction, a dual logic for defining basic terms, and the concept of dynamics.

The concept of "resources" is shown to support the idea that human mental and information processing capability is limited in a number of branches of psychology. The initial restriction postulate has given rise to a number of appropriate, debatable questions, and specific patterns of resource allocation and resource scarcity have been discussed elsewhere (e.g., is the pool of resources a single or a multiple unit?) However, the inadequacy of the resource approach, which is based exclusively upon limited human capacities, becomes apparent as soon as the notion of restriction, being itself a means of explaining various empirical effects, turns into an object of a concrete analysis. Therefore some authors deny that the resource approach is efficient and question the very statement that cognitive capacities are scarce, arguing that such limits could be removed through training and practice.

Such contradictions between followers and opponents of the resource approach might be smoothed away if one turned to the idea of trade-off substitution taking place in dynamic systems.

At an operational level of describing empirical evidence, one can observe similar processes in thermodynamics, geography, and especially economics and register them in terms of isotherms, isobars, indifference curves, or equal-utility contours, for example. Not only can the common trade-off itself be observed on the external level of performance (e.g. performance characteristics, ROC curves), but trade-off substitution also occurs in human cognitive processes. This trade-off substitution regulates human activities. The author proposes a description of the scarce capacity of human information-processing, and ways of overcoming human constraints by means of trade-off substitution. This approach makes it possible to use micro-economic models of limited resource allocation and substitution on a wider scale.

EVALUATION OF TELEVISION ADVERTISEMENTS BASED ON BEHAVIORAL DATA

Masashi Ida, Tokiwa University, Ibaraki, Japan

Verbal reports are sometimes unreliable for predicting or describing behavior, thus making it necessary to measure the behavior itself, by using a method unique to the science of behavior. In Experiment 1 an attempt was made to see whether behavioral data can be used as a measure, on the assumption that the time subjects allocate to watching TV commercials corresponds with the attractiveness of the ads or the extent of the viewer's interest. In Experiment 2, the assumption was that the response bias in the matching equation that holds in two-alternative operant choice behaviors reflects the relative "value" (v) of paired commercials, that is, $k_{ab} = v_a/v_b$. Knowing two of three response biases, one can estimate the remaining one. For example, if $k_{ab} = v_a/v_b$ and $k_{bc} = v_b/v_c$, then $k_{ac} = (v_a/v_b)(v_b/v_c) = v_a/v_c$ (Miller, 1976). This transitivity can be tested. If transitivity holds, then relative values of the commercials can be estimated. In experiments, the subjects (15 university students) sat before a TV screen and were asked to operate two kinds of switches, one to switch channels from one commercial to another, and the other to keep the chosen commercial on the screen for two seconds. Two kinds of commercials were run repeatedly on two different channels. The commercials were paired a against b, a against c, and b against c, and the time allocated to viewing each was measured.

It was found that there is a transitivity in the time allocated to the viewing of each commercial. For instance, if $T_a > T_b$ and $T_b > T_c$, then $T_a > T_c$ (whereby T_a represents the time allocated to viewing commercial a). Transitivity was also evident in the total time (TT) allocated to each of the three commercials that is $TT_a > TT_b > TT_c$.

Because a metric nature, a transitivity, was observed in the data of time allocation obtained in Experiment 1, it is possible to evaluate the subjects' preference for various commercials. In Experiment 2, the subjects (8 university students) were presented with three types of TV commercials which they viewed in pairs or under concurrent conjugate reinforcement schedules (see Rovee-Collier & Gekoski, 1979). Each of the three pairs of commercials were shown under the three different conditions. The subjects were asked to choose one of the two commercials by operating the switches as in Experiment 1. The time allocated to each film was measured. The results were that k_{ac} was predicted on the basis of observed response biases for commercial a paired with commercial b, and commercial b paired with commercial c. Closeness of fit was observed between predicted and actual k_{ac}, except for one subject.

It was found that there was a metric nature in the time people allocated to watching television commercials in Experiment 1 and that there was a transitivity among response biases in Experiment 2. Therefore, it is not only possible to evaluate people's preferences for particular commercials but also to predict the amount of time a person is likely to spend in viewing the commercials under certain conditions. On the basis of the two experiments, it is possible to develop methods of predicting how long people view certain television advertisements in ordinary situations.

References

Miller, H. L., Jr. (1976). Matching-based hedonic scaling in the pigeon. *Journal of the Experimental Analysis of Behavior, 26*, 335-347.

Rovee-Collier, C. K., & Gekoski, M. J. (1979). The economics of infancy: A review of conjugate reinforcement. In H. W. Reese & L. P. Lipsitt (Eds.), *Advances in child development and behavior* (Vol. 13, p. 199). London: Academic Press.

THE IMPACT OF INITIAL LETTERS ON BRAND NAME RECALL

Marcus Taft, and Lawrence Ang, University of New South Wales

In 1984, Vanden Bergh, Collins, Schultz, and Adler speculated that a brand that begins with a plosive consonant (i.e., /p/, /b/, /t/, /d/, /k/ or /g/ (Bic, Tide, and Coca-Cola) is better remembered than one that does not. This is because plosives are strong sounding. In their experiment, they found that subjects could recall and recognize plosive nonwords (e.g.,

KE, DICS, BILS, DALLAKS) better than nonplosive ones (e.g., JAF, VADE, VIG, NEMLADS). However, their stimuli had a number of confounds in terms of comparative length and wordlikeness. The experiment reported here is an attempt to redress those confounds. We did this by tightly matching all aspects of plosive nonwords (e.g., CALVOW, TAIVIS, DUSHIM) with their nonplosive counterparts (e.g., RALVOW, HAIVIS, FUSHIM) such that they only differed in their initial letter and nothing else. Furthermore, the 20 matched plosives and nonplosives all had six letters, two syllables, followed basic English orthographic principles, began with a single consonant of the same frequency, neither began with a prefix nor ended with suffix, and did not rhyme or begin with a real word. Each matching pair of plosive and nonplosives was then randomly assigned to a line drawing picture of 20 products comprising 10 physically hard products (e.g., hammer, brick, glassware) and 10 physically soft products (e.g., tissue paper, baby oil, jelly). In keeping with the theory of phonetic symbolism (Newmann, 1933), we predicted an interaction effect by which subjects would be able to recall more plosive nonwords if they were paired with hard products than soft ones and vice versa for nonplosives. This is because, phono symbolically, stronger sounding plosives may be more appropriate for a hard product, whereas softer sounding nonplosives are more appropriate for soft products. This was, therefore, a 2 (plosives versus nonplosives) x 2 (hard versus soft product) factorial design.

Twenty-six tertiary educated subjects were tested individually over three phases. In phase 1, they were presented with a drawing of a product and a nonword written underneath it. They were told to write down the nonword and then rate it for its appropriateness to the product. In phase 2, the procedure was repeated (to optimize retention). Phase 3 was a surprise recall task. Subjects were presented with the line drawings without their brand names and told to write down what its name was.

Only a main effect of the initial letter was found. Recall of the nonwords beginning with plosive consonants was better (mean proportion recalled per item = 45%) than recall of those beginning with nonplosives (mean = 39%), $F(1,19) = 7.728$, $p<.02$. There was no difference in recall between hard products and soft products, $F(1,19) = 2.361$, $p>.05$. The expected interaction effect whereby plosives can be recalled better when paired with hard products and vice versa for soft products was also not found, $F(1,19) = 0.446$, $p>.1$). In conclusion the type of product (hard versus soft) and its pairing with the type of nonwords used (plosives versus nonplosives) did not have any effects on a subject's ability to recall. Only the main effect of plosives versus nonplosives was found, a result supporting that of Vanden Bergh et al (1984), even after possible confounds are controlled for.

References

Newmann, S. (1933). Further experiments in phonetic symbolism. *American Journal of Psychology, 46*, 53-75.

Vanden Bergh, B. G., Collins, J., Schultz, M., and Adler, K. (1984). Sound advice on brand names. *Journalism Quarterly, 61*, 835-840.

BINARY CHOICE IN MULTIALTERNATIVE DECISIONAL TASKS

Kazuya Nakayachi
Japan Society for the Promotion of Science
for Japanese Junior Scientists, Tokyo, Japan

Earlier studies have shown that the process of deciding in a multialternative choice task consists of two steps. In the first step, undesirable alternatives are roughly eliminated on the basis of a few attributes. In the second step, the remaining alternatives are carefully evaluated and a choice is made. The purpose of this study was to determine how many alternatives survive the initial screening.

The subjects, 90 students, were asked to choose the best driving school from one of the choice sets consisting of 3, 6, or 9 alternatives. Subsequently, they were asked to recall the attlibutes of each alternative.

In the 6 and 9 alternatives conditions, the results showed that the mean recalls for the third-ranking alternative were markedly lower than those for the top two alternatives.

Moreover, the difference between the mean recalls for the top two alternatives, one of which was chosen right at the end, was very small.

Within these multialternative conditions, the results suggested that two alternatives survived the screening step, and one of them was chosen in the second step.

Traffic Psychology

ON THE UNIFICATION OF TRAFFIC SCIENCE

JOHN A. MICHON
Department of Psychology and Traffic Research Center, University of Groningen, The Netherlands

THE UNIVERSAL CHARACTER OF TRAFFIC

Mobility and its offspring, transportation and traffic, are universal phenomena simply because it is logically impossible to be in two places at the same time. However, mobility, transportation, and traffic are not universal just because of logical demands.[1] Traffic, broadly defined, plays a decisive role in a great many fundamental socioeconomic processes; processes, for example, that will result in more than 1,500,000,000 motorized vehicles on the world's roads, before the century is out—twice the present number!

One would expect that such a fundamental, universal concern of humankind would by now have given rise to a dedicated and well-organized scientific discipline, one with strong support both from within the scientific community and from without. But this is not the case at all. Traffic science as it exists today is markedly deficient in at least three very important respects. The first shortcoming is that although Traffic has been studied by scientists from many different disciplines, they have failed to define the problems they are tackling in a coherent way. What is even worse, they frequently do not even quite understand what their colleague in the next office is talking about. In other words, Traffic scientists strongly resemble the Five Blind Men, each touching a different part of the elephant but unable to grasp the whole.

A second, related problem plaguing contemporary Traffic science is its lack of direction. Failing a common vocabulary, or what I will call a "context of interpretation," it is really difficult to decide what course to follow, or even to establish that there *is* a course to follow. In other words, Traffic science also resembles the Valiant Young Knight who mounted his horse and rode off in all directions at once.

In the third place—partly as a consequence of the preceding two shortcomings—the results from Traffic research frequently fail to impress traffic authorities. The fact that Traffic scientists hardly ever seem to agree, added to the shotgun approach that is characteristic for Traffic research, cannot fail to arouse strong suspicions in administrators. In other words, to an outsider, and that category certainly includes traffic administrators and politicians, Traffic science is bound to bear strong resemblance to Fawlty Towers, TV's perspective of the service rendered by some hotels.

THE ISIRT ROUND TABLE

Altogether, Traffic science is presently perceived as a marginal undertaking that seems to be incapable of meeting the tremendous challenges posed by its subject matter. This is really a serious problem. It was recently discussed at a Round Table called by ISIRT. ISIRT stands for International Scientific Initiatives on Road Traffic.[2]

This Round Table has made two things very clear to me. First, an improved status for Traffic science depends critically on successful unification. Second, it convinced me that successful unification, in turn, depends on the availability of a suitable context of interpretation—a paradigm, or a "striking image."

The role of "striking images" in science is well known. A familiar example is the remarkable change in the status of organic chemistry as a result of Kékulé's discovery of the cyclical structure of the benzene molecule. An even more dramatic paradigm shift occurred as the result of the visualization of the DNA molecule as a double helix. Unfortunately, the unifying power of a striking image is greater for the natural sciences than for the disciplines that investigate really complex social and technical systems such as the Traffic system.

But perhaps one can learn from the successes of environmental science, certainly an extremely complicated domain for study. Barely twenty years after the Club of Rome published its epochal report, *The limits to growth* (Meadows, 1972), environmental science has become a highly respectable interdisciplinary field of research, with a good deal of coherence, direction, and impact.

Perhaps the various large-scale disasters and near-disasters such as Chernobyl, the Exxon Valdez, or Three Mile Island have contributed to this rapid development. But these highly dramatic events cannot be the only reason for the impact of environmental science. After all, Traffic is replete with disasters, too. Every year half a million people are killed on the road. That amounts to one fatality every minute of the day, day in and day out. Each year 15 million people are injured so as to require medical treatment. About a quarter of these, 4 million people, never quite recover and suffer from residual effects for the rest of their lives. Traffic accidents occur at a rate of 10 per second, and the damage they cause, worldwide, amounts to a staggering 200 billion dollars every year, a sum that is of the same order of magnitude as the entire Savings and Loan scandal in the United States. Seen from this perspective, Traffic not only *has* its disasters, it *is* a disaster, a chronic disaster.

Disasters notwithstanding, the impact of environmental science is more likely to result from an effective way of representing the planetary ecosystem as an interlocking ensemble of dynamic processes. The most thrilling version of the ecological context of interpretation is, undoubtedly, the Gaia Hypothesis. It looks upon the planet Earth as one tremendously complex and delicate organism, the only known exemplar of a threatened species (Lovelock, 1988).

In the face of the short but remarkable history of environmental science, the question arose at the ISIRT Round Table if perhaps a similar striking image could be used to "boost" Traffic science (Michon, 1990). In due course two answers emerged, one optimistic and one pessimistic. They will be referred to as strong unification and weak unification, respectively. In the remainder of this paper both views will be discussed and, for reasons that I will explain, rejected. Instead, a third, theoretically and pragmatically more promising approach to unification will be proposed.

PERSPECTIVES ON UNIFICATION

Strong (Ontological) Unification

The most eloquent defense for a strong unification of Traffic science was put forward at the ISIRT Round Table by Mackay (1990). Strong—or ontological—unification is very serious about the universal character of Traffic: It entails recognition of the fact that Traffic penetrates all human activity. The analogy with environmental science figures prominently, if implicitly, in strong unification. Unfortunately, therein lies its limitation. Environmental science has been amenable to strong unification largely because it is concerned with a natural system. The consequences of any influence on the system translate directly into biological or chemical processes. Tracing these processes may be enormously difficult, but in principle this task does not seem to be more complicated than forecasting tomorrow's weather. In contrast, the Traffic system is, to an overwhelming extent, an *artificial* system. A good many processes and mechanisms do not obey any natural law, and occasionally they may even seem to obey no rule at all. In other words, in spite of its universal character, Traffic is not uniformly governed by natural laws or by logical, lawlike regularities. This effectively rules out the possibility of strong, or ontological, unification.

Weak (Pragmatic) Unification

The second view proposed at the ISIRT Round Table is one that may be called weak, or pragmatic, unification. It was put forward in a remarkably transparent way by Rumar (1990). In this view, any attempt at developing a common paradigm for Traffic science, a paradigmatic image of the Traffic system, is doomed to failure. In other words, intrinsic coherence appears to have no place in weak unification. Instead, the assumption is that coherence is best served by imaginative project management in multidisciplinary projects. Direction, and the quality of research in general, is seen to depend crucially on the creativity and status of recognized specialists within their own disciplines. Finally, it is expected that impact is closely related to the investigators' ability to translate their findings into the idiom of the traffic administrator.

Perhaps weak unification represents a more realistic point of view than does strong unification. Yet, in my opinion, weak unification admits defeat! It does not lead to cumulative insight into Traffic as a universal phenomenon. It offers neither direction nor support in asking the right kind of question. Last but not least, it carries no promise that its results will be used in the best way, or even in an acceptable way. Weak unification maintains the present state of Traffic science, the chaos of Fawlty Towers.

Epistemological Unification

As I pointed out, both scenarios for unification are unsatisfactory, one being too pretentious, the other not being pretentious enough. It has recently occurred to me, however, that there is a third, and indeed more promising road to unification. I will refer to this approach as epistemological unification since it is based on recent views on the nature of scientific explanation.

Let me first illustrate this with the following tasteful example. Cooking may be described in terms of three distinct frames of reference: the dish, the recipe, and the ingredients. The first frame deals with such matters as the appearance and taste of food; the second, with the rules that, when followed, will produce a certain dish; and the third, with the physical and chemical properties of the foodstuffs to which the rules are applied.

These three frames of reference are representative of three fundamental levels of explanation, or stances (Dennett, 1978, 1987; Pylyshyn, 1984). The first is known as the intentional or rational, stance. From this point of view it is acknowledged that it is possible to predict the behavior of a complex system even if one is ignorant about its internal structure. If the purpose of a system and the conditions under which it operates is known, its behavior can be predicted simply by assuming that it is an intelligent or rational system. It does not matter if the system is "really" intelligent or "really" rational simply because no one knows what is really "real" in the first place. The second level of explanation is called the functional design stance. From this point of view the behavior of a system is described in terms of a set of rules or procedures. Together, these rules form a behavioral "grammar" that is capable of generating precisely those behaviors that strike one as intelligent or rational when they are looked at from the intentional stance. The third level of explanation looks at a system from the physical point of view. It will explain the activity of a system in terms of its basic architecture—its hardware—and the natural laws that apply to it.

Incidentally, it should be noted that each level of explanation may be applied to any phenomenon, limited only by practical considerations. Nobody will be stopped from explaining in terms of the interactions between elementary particles *why* some people like to ride a motor bike, although it would seem to be quite cumbersome, to say the least. Conversely, explaining the behavior of a falling stone in terms of its desire to return to earth is ill advised simply because it will not carry one very much farther on the road to understanding the universe than a simple explanation in terms of Newtonian mechanics.

This three-level approach to scientific explanation appears to be reflected in the specific contributions of the three legs on which the body of Traffic science is standing: the social sciences (represented by economics and law), the behavioral sciences (psychology, ergonomics, and, increasingly, artificial intelligence), and engineering (Michon, 1987). Of these three, the social sciences deal mostly, if not exclusively, with the intentional aspects of Traffic, that is, the goals and motives of the actors—travelers and authorities, users and suppliers. The behavioral sciences on the other hand are concerned mostly with the intermediate, functional level of explanation. Finally, engineering is mostly concerned with the architecture or infrastructure.

Striking a Balance

Epistemological unification, as advocated here, is based on the insight that a well-developed Traffic science must depend equally on all three levels of explanation and, consequently, also on a balanced contribution of the social and technical sciences as well as the behavioral sciences.

The coherence and the direction of Traffic research is bound to remain marginal unless all three levels of explanation are intrinsically involved. I claim that the present uninspiring state of affairs is a direct consequence of the relative absence of the functional level.

Why is this so? Conventionally, traffic administrators tend to adopt the intentional stance that is characteristic of the social sciences, and, conventionally, they communicate directly with engineers. That is the simply the way things are conventionally organized. Engineers conventionally rush to their workshops and try to accommodate the administrators' requirements directly in the system's architecture, but, unfortunately, this response leaves them oblivious to the functional relations that govern the behavior of human beings.

I am not suggesting that the conventional approach never works. Frequently, it does work. The more complex the system, however, the smaller becomes the likelihood of success. In terms of my culinary figure of speech, it means that if you put ingredients together without a recipe, you're probably in good shape if you like hodge-podge. But if you try the same strategy while aiming for a *Civet de Canard à l'Orange*, the odds will be overwhelmingly against you.

An Example: Travel Information Systems

An example of this inadequate conventional approach concerns a study of the information needs of public transport customers. Increasing attention is being paid to the development of advanced (electronic) information systems that can provide individualized advice about departure times, connections, and so forth.

The approach to this issue adopted by the transport authority in this particular case was to request (a) a study of "mobility profiles" and thus to achieve a segmentation of the market according to distinct travel patterns as they derive from professional or personal factors, (b) a study to determine the specific information needs of each segment, and all this as (c) a step toward the implementation of advanced systems that would meet the specific demands of each segment or mobility profile.

If I have been understood thus far, it should now become apparent that the segmentation according to mobility profiles is typical of the intentional stance: In each profile different motives, attitudes, and beliefs are attached to people with different aims and purposes. The underlying assumption is that differences in motives, attitudes, and beliefs will affect the way travelers search and select relevant information about, say, the platform from which their train will depart. Similarly, it must become apparent that the second and third requirement are typical for the physical stance: They both refer to the implementation of data bases and equipment that various categories of customers may use for extracting information.

However, the platform from which the traveler's train will be leaving is precisely what the traveler should be able to find out. At this point any other information would be irrelevant, if not outright counterproductive, at least momentarily. What is needed is a careful analysis of the behavioral and cognitive procedures and strategies that enable the traveler—any traveler—to cope with the various critical points of a trip—any trip. The important thing is to find out exactly what information is required at any time during the trip. Why this information is used by the traveler, whether to get to a customer, a lover, or a music teacher is of secondary concern. (Incidentally: what mobility profile is represented if the three coincide?)

Now, if I have really been understood up to this point, it should be evident that these considerations make a crucial distinction between the functional what and the intentional why of information needs that is lacking in the philosophy of the transport authority concerned. And these are precisely the considerations that bring out the special significance of the functional perspective.

A Halfway Summary

I have just outlined a framework for unification. This approach avoids ontological claims about the universal character of Traffic that is implied by strong unification. At the same time it shows that the interactions between the social sciences, the behavioral sciences, and engineering are far more intrinsic and intricate than is suggested by weak unification.

I have also argued that there is a proper division of labor between the three levels of explanation and that more explicit attention should be paid to the intermediate, functional level, which, as it happens, is the specific domain of the behavioral and cognitive sciences.

THE CONTEXT OF INTERPRETATION

Problem-solving as a Context of Interpretation

Is there an appropriate context of interpretation, a paradigm or striking image that is rich enough to carry the full weight of epistemological unification as outlined before?

As I have argued on several occasions, beginning as early as 1974 (see Michon, 1976), an appropriate context of interpretation for Traffic science is found in the general theory of problem-solving that was first formulated by Newell & Simon (1972). This is the computational approach to intelligence. It states that activities of any complex adaptive, or learning, system must be based on a symbolic representation of the situation in which it may find itself, together with the operations that the system can perform on this representation, in order to selected from a set of available alternatives the action or actions that will bring it closer to its goal.

Four Task Domains

Is a formal theory of problem-solving indeed rich enough to serve as a framework for Traffic science? After all, Traffic covers a whole spectrum of human activities or tasks. I think that the answer is affirmative. It is possible to partition the domain into a number of hierarchically ordered task domains (Michon, 1976, 1987), each of which can be studied, in the context of problem-solving, from the intentional, functional, and architectural points of view because independent representations and operations can be formulated for each stance.

In the first and most general task domain the human being is viewed as a goal-directed psychophysical entity whose problems consist of satisfying a range of basic, essentially biological needs. This implies searching for food, shelter, a partner perhaps, and includes the need for exploring the environment. For these purposes the organism can rely on a great many procedures and strategies; the infrastructure in which these problems are solved ranges from trails through nature that will lead the hunter to his game, to the foraging potential of the modern shopping mall. Whatever the needs, in order to satisfy now one and then the other, the organism is forced to move from place to place.

The second task domain covers social intercourse in its many forms. In this domain the human being is treated as a social agent intentionally pursuing a variety of activities. Here, the problem is to organize this activity pattern in a way that will simultaneously satisfy certain spatiotemporal, socioeconomic, and personal constraints. To perform these activities, travel patterns are developed that satisfy these constraints.

The third task domain relates to the role of the individual traveler as a consumer of transport. The problem here is to make a trip in such a way that such constraints are satisfied by selecting, according to some criterion of optimality, the best available transport alternative. In this context, moving between places is subject to the constraints that are imposed by the social activity pattern: going to a meeting empty-handed poses a different problem from traveling with a case full of documents.

Finally, the fourth task domain deals with the active road user, the person who, as pedestrian, cyclist, or driver, faces the task of moving safely and efficiently from A to B, irrespective of the particular purpose for which the trip is made. In this task domain road users have at their disposal a large set of characteristic strategies, procedures, and skills that enable them to keep their lane, to avoid obstacles, and to maintain a certain speed within the constraints imposed by the dynamics of the vehicle they are operating, or their bodies when on foot.

A PRACTICAL EXERCISE: GENERIC INTELLIGENT DRIVER SUPPORT

Unification of Traffic science has come a long way, but how easy is it to press this theoretical framework into concrete action—regulations, interventions, or equipment? I will address this question by briefly reviewing a research project that is presently being carried out under my direction. The project is known as Generic Intelligent Driver Support (GIDS). GIDS involves 13 partners from universities, research organizations, and industry, and it is supported through the DRIVE Program of the European Economic Community (Michon & McLoughlin, 1991; Smiley & Michon, 1989).

GIDS brings social, behavioral, and technical scientists together for a concerted effort to design and build a small in-vehicle knowledge refinery. It is an information filter that is tuned to the intentions of the driver: GIDS should offer its driver adaptive support under a wide range of driving conditions. In spite of the project's rather technical objective, each group of scientists is explicitly addressing the issues that are characteristic for the level of explanation for which they are specifically equipped, without losing sight of the principal objective. Thus, social scientists in the GIDS project are concerned with issues of acceptance and safety, that is, with the impact of a GIDS system on overall driving behavior. The behavioral and cognitive scientists are analyzing and developing formal procedures to represent the knowledge that drivers possess and that the GIDS must share in order to interact with the driver. And, as one would expect, the engineers are developing the architecture that will realize the various intelligent support functions in a reliable way.

To appreciate the purpose of GIDS, imagine that you are traveling to Switzerland for a holiday in the Alps. Upon arrival your rental car is waiting for you at the airport. You insert your personalized GIDS smart card in the little slot on the dashboard, and almost instantly the vehicle will know who you are. It will know, for instance, that you have never driven on winding mountain roads before, and that you have a tendency to brake very briskly. Knowing these and other things, the GIDS system will then take you on the road, guiding you slowly through hairpins and keeping you away from nasty 15-plus-percent down slopes. Moreover, realizing that your knowledge of German, French, and Italian is marginal, it will translate for you all the local traffic information into your native language, including whatever there is to read on the various road signs. GIDS systems are not only useful during holidays. Back home you have to cope with a growing amount of information of an increasingly complicated nature. This is caused by the increasing intensity of traffic, the increasing number of on-board and road-side sources of information, and by the additional equipment with which our vehicles are being equipped, devices such as telephones, fax machines, and dictation equipment. This avalanche of information is likely to exert its influence on almost every aspect of the driving task. It will affect route planning as well as navigation, maneuvering, and elementary vehicle control. And what adds to the effect is that unless something is done about all this information, it will be thrown at the driver in an uncoordinated fashion, irrespective of meaning or urgency. Fortunately, something *is* done about it: GIDS. An important function of GIDS is, indeed, to protect the driver from information pollution.

The most important and innovative feature of GIDS, however, is that it takes into account the intentions, the capabilities, and the limitations of the individual driver. For this purpose GIDS incorporates a knowledge base containing detailed scenarios for driving maneuvers such as overtaking, negotiating intersections, or merging into a traffic stream. These scenarios are then matched with the actual and intended behavior of the driver. The matching is done by a special component of the system, called the Analyst/Planner. *If* a mismatch is found between the actual and the required behavior and *if* the situation in which this happens is critical according to some criterion, *then* the Analyst/Planner will issue a message or a warning. Such messages are communicated to the driver at an appropriate time by means of one of a number of presentation systems, including a touch screen and a voice synthesizer. Messages are scheduled by another component, the Dialogue Controller.

Scheduling involves, among other things prioritizing messages according to urgency and resolving conflicts between messages.

As a behavioral scientist, I find the GIDS concept very close to my heart for several reasons. First, it establishes a protocol for the integration of several important support functions that are representative, not only for the driving task, but also for complex human skills in general.

Similarly, GIDS is concerned with the integration of information across several presentation modes, including visual, auditory, and tactile messages. These two points make it a fascinating exercise in human-computer interaction, especially with respect to the fundamental problem of doing several things at once (multitasking). Third, the GIDS system is a functional design that is able to take individual differences into account. Most important, however, GIDS qualifies as a clear example of unification in the sense of this address: the GIDS system is an intelligent architecture that will, under a range of circumstances, function in a way that is consistent with the goals and intentions of the driver.

SUMMARY AND CONCLUSION

Traffic is a universal phenomenon, but a highly artificial one. It is, in fact, so diverse that it is impossible to build a strongly unified Traffic science. Conversely, weak unification of Traffic science is not a very likely prospect either. To guarantee coherence and direction, more than efficient research management or good faith is needed. With this in mind I have argued for an alternative approach to unification, using the epistemological distinction between three levels of explanation dealing with intentions, functions, and architecture, respectively.

Traffic science has long suffered from dystrophy of the functional perspective. This leads to a symptomatic, somewhat unfocused approach to problems of congestion, safety, and environmental pollution. Epistemological unification should restore the balance between the three essential levels of explanation, thereby creating an opportunity for greater internal coherence and greater direction, and, as a result, greater impact as well.

Epistemological unification should also restore an essential focus on the human being. The essence of epistemological unification appears to be well-captured by Nobel laureate Herbert Simon in the general context of cognitive science:

> Intelligent behavior is adaptive and hence must take on strikingly different forms in different environments.

Intelligent systems are ground between the nether millstone of their physiology or hardware, which sets inner limits on their adaptation, and the upper millstone of a complex environment, which places demands on them for change (Simon & Kaplan, 1989, p. 38).

What I have said is summarized by this quotation if the word *Intelligence* is replaced by the word *Traffic*, and such is indeed my vision of a unified Traffic science.

ACKNOWLEDGEMENT

This paper is based on an invited keynote address presented during the 22nd International Conference of Applied Psychology, held in Kyoto, 23-27 July 1990. The author wishes to thank the participants of the ISIRT First Round Table, held in "De Wipselberg," Beekbergen, the Netherlands, 18-21 October 1989, for their penetrating discussions of the problems of Traffic science. Thanks are especially due to Professor Murray Mackay and Professor Kåre Rumar who, respectively impersonated the Devil and the Deep Blue Sea in between which I initially got caught, until I attained the peaceful state of mind provided by Epistemological Unification.

REFERENCES

Dennett, D. C. (1978). *Brainstorms: Philosophical essays on mind and psychology*. Hassocks, Sussex: Harvester Press.

Dennett, D. C. (1987). *The intentional stance*. Cambridge, MA: MIT Press.

Lovelock, J. (1988). *The ages of Gaia*. Oxford: Oxford University Press.

Mackay, G. M. (1990). Towards a unified traffic science. *IATSS Research*, *14*, 19-26.

Meadows, D. L. (1972). *The limits to growth: A report for the Club of Rome project on the predicaments of mankind*. New York: Universe Books.

Michon, J. A. (1976). The mutual impacts of transportation and human behavior. In P. Stringer & H. Wenzel (Eds.), *Transportation planning for a better environment* (pp. 221-236). New York: Plenum Press.

Michon, J. A. (1987). On the multidisciplinary dynamics of traffic science. *IATSS Research*, *11*, 31-40.

Michon, J. A. (1990). The need for a unification in traffic science. *IATSS Research*, *14*, 12-16.

Michon, J. A., & McLoughlin, H. (1991). The intelligence of GIDS. In Commission of the European Communities (Ed.), *Advanced telematics in road transport* [Proceedings of the DRIVE Conference Brussels, 4-6 February 1991] (Vol. 1, pp. 371-6). Amsterdam: Elsevier.

Newell, A., & Simon, H. A. (1972). *Human problem solving.* Englewood Cliffs, NJ: Prentice-Hall.

Pylyshyn, Z. W. (1984). *Computation and cognition: Towards a foundation for cognitive science.* Cambridge, MA: MIT Press.

Rumar, K. (1990). The impossibility of a unified traffic science. *IATSS Research, 14,* 27-31.

Simon, H. A., & Kaplan, C. A. (1989). Foundations of cognitive science. In M. I. Posner (Ed.), *Foundations of cognitive science* (pp. 1-48). Cambridge, MA: MIT Press.

Smiley, A., & Michon, J. A. (1989). *Conceptual framework for generic intelligent driver support* (Technical Report DRIVE V1041/GIDS-GEN 01). Haren, the Netherlands: Traffic Research Center, University of Groningen.

NOTES

1. For reasons of brevity the triad *mobility, transport,* and *traffic* will henceforth be referred to as *Traffic* (with capital T). When the term traffic is to be understood in the restricted sense of vehicles in motion, it will be printed with a lower case *t*.

2. The ISIRT Round Tables are sponsored by the International Association for Traffic and Safety Sciences (IATSS) of Tokyo. The First Round Table brought together a small, international group of 45 prominent Traffic scientists, engineers, and administrators to discuss the problem of traffic safety in the light of the need for greater unification of Traffic science. The ISIRT Second Round Table (on the environmental impact of Traffic) will be held in Stockholm in May 1991, and the Third Round Table will take place in Toulouse in October 1991. Papers and discussions of the ISIRT First Round Table were reported in 1990 in a special double issue of IATSS Research, *14,* 1-116.

CHANGE IN PERSPECTIVES OF TRAFFIC PSYCHOLOGY

Günter Kroj
Bundesanstalt für Straßenwesen, Bergisch
Gladbach, FRG

FROM ACCIDENT TO SAFETY RESEARCH

In the early stages of motorization, "safety" was not defined, but "danger" was equated with accidents. Today, it is generally accepted that the non-occurrence of accidents cannot be equated with safety. The accident as a result of a certain type of behavior is less significant than the behavior itself. This circumstance has led to the elaboration of a behavioral continuum ranging from normal behavior to the accident, characterized in this order by decreasing reliability. This perspective has ultimately shifted the focal point from accident analysis to the study of normal behavior, with the development of the traffic conflict technique being one important step in this line of research.

FROM RESEARCH INTO PERFORMANCE BEHAVIOR TO ANALYSIS OF RISK BEHAVIOR

In the 1920s and 1930s performance characteristics remained the focus of psychodiagnostic interest. As empirical personality research advanced, the influence of the moderator function of personality traits became increasingly clear, especially with regard to performance characteristics, performance motivation and, hence, personality structure. In this context, one particular form of performance motivation has gained significance for the interpretation of traffic behavior in traffic psychology: so-called high-risk behaviour. Almost all comprehensive theories of traffic behavior published to date refer in some way to high-risk behaviour. Examples are the Model of Subjective and Objective Safety (Klebelsberg, 1971), the Risk Compensation Theory and Risk-Homeostasis Theory (Wilde, 1982), and the Model of Subjective Risk Control (Näätänen & Summala, 1976). From the perspective of traffic psychology, this means that the legal requirement for nonhazardous behavior on the part of the road user (as included in many national traffic codes) is not tenable. Instead, behavior in traffic must be understood as high-risk behavior under risk conditions.

This shift in attempts to explain traffic behavior has given rise to different psychological preconditions for safety measures and safety campaigns. The above-mentioned development of explanatory hypotheses and models in traffic behavior is dealt with in a subsequent section of this paper.

FROM INDIVIDUAL DIAGNOSTICS TO SITUATION DIAGNOSTICS

As early as the first decades of this century, psychotechnics had already focused on the rapid changes in external situations as a specific characteristic of traffic behavior. Thus, the influence of situational behavioral conditions had been recognized in traffic psychology long before the interactivity debate. The question as to what a traffic situation is will not be as easy to assess from a psychological perspective as from the perspective of traffic technology, where physical traffic conditions (e.g., multiple-lane highways and road layout with specific curve radii) serve as adequate determining features. The practical significance of the concept of the situation becomes clear in the question of what a hazardous traffic situation is. In the course of time, the view has gradually prevailed that "hazardous/nonhazardous" are not characteristics of the physical surroundings but of behavior under these external conditions. Thus a "hazardous situation" is characterized by correspondingly hazardous behavior. The danger of a situation is thus a function of the external (physical) *and* the individual behavioral conditions.

Huguenin (1985) attempted to summarize how such interaction between persons and situations can appear. He provided a synopsis of several model approaches (see Figure 1) in which the action should be regarded as the function of situational factors, predispositions, and assimilation processes.

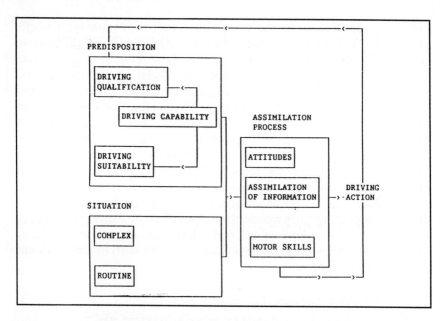

FIG. 1. Connections between predisposition, situation, assimilation process, and driving action (Huguenin, 1985).

FROM DIAGNOSTIC TO PEDAGOGICAL AND ERGONOMICAL TRAFFIC PSYCHOLOGY

The cases for examination and expert opinions fall roughly into the following two principal groups (see Figure 2): drivers reported for functional disorders and drivers convicted for traffic violations. In the case of the drivers convicted for traffic violations (e.g., drunk driving), expert opinions are formulated on the grounds of blatant negative behavior in traffic without necessarily any suspicion of concomitant physical or mental disorders.

In recent years, increasing deviations from the classic form of testing the aptitude of traffic offenders have been observed. There are various reasons for this development, the principal one being changes in the concept of driver ability.

Previously, driver ability was determined by means of a horizontal inventory of a driver's performance ability and personality structure and was primarily perceived as a constant. In the past decade, however, variability in driver ability under different conditions has increasingly been observed and has caught the attention of the scientific community. The identification and prediction of possible changes in living conditions and lifestyles has emerged as a special problem in this context. It became

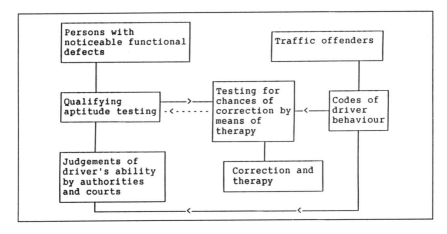

FIG. 2. Model of measures if there are doubts about the ability of licence applicants and drivers to participate in motorised traffic (Müller).

important to consider not only personal characteristics and habits but also, and above all, the situational factors associated with traffic violations and accidents. In view of the low degree of accuracy of the accident and offence criterion, the modest results of follow-up studies on tests to predict driver ability are not surprising. The question of the period of validity of these tests or of the maximum prediction period has remained largely unsolved (Klebelsberg, 1988).

This explains why general, preventive, educational measures or measures with a deterrent effect should be preferred in combating drunk driving and other traffic violations. In a road safety concept of this nature, therefore, expert opinions and tests to predict driver ability are of special importance, especially if considered in conjunction with driver improvement and rehabilitation programs for cases of deviant behavior (Winkler, 1986). Over the last few years, programs for alcohol-impaired drivers have gained special importance not only as a counterbalance but also as an indispensable means of supplementing the disciplinary measures of penalizing the driver and revoking the driver's license (Hebenstreit et al., 1982).

A society with traditionally liberal views on alcohol consumption, the use of the car, and drunk driving offences is becoming increasingly aware of its responsibility to provide the individual with the opportunity for, and assistance in, examining and changing his or her individual attitudes and habits in the light of current trends. The future success of such efforts depends not only on the quality of driver-improvement programs but also on the constellation of all measures affecting traffic violations, particularly alcohol-related offences (Müller, 1987).

However, a considerably greater effect will result from influencing general behavior. This is the key task of ergonomic traffic psychology as taken up recently by the European research projects PROMETHEUS and DRIVE. Especially in recent years, the automobile industry has intensified efforts to find means of making it easier for tomorrow's driver to cope with the progress of technology and obtain a real increase in safety. In this context, social scientists recently presented a highly regarded safety check-list that allows assessment of the reactions of road users to the introduction of high technology in the car and on the roads (Chaloupka, Hyden, & Risser, 1990). Social scientists have hereby given weight to demands for the work of engineers in the safety sector to be linked with psychological know-how or psychological research. After all, engineers do not usually ask how their products will be used by people, for thoughts, attitudes, behavioral tendencies, and visible behavior can be neither exactly measured nor described in millimeters or seconds. This reality relates to the fact that engineers have developed a tendency to avoid having to tackle these matters.

Often, demands are made in the engineering sector for the state and society to establish risk norms that can be expressed in quantitative terms and in technical language. Because it is now theoretically possible to express the risks inherent in technical installations numerically, the setting of such norms should make it possible to use maximum-risk "limits" to assess whether the hazard level of a technical system meets the safety requirements of society.

The technical equipment in road traffic consists mainly of the vehicle and the road. Construction, equipment, and operating specifications were developed for these as motorization increased. Is risk in road traffic determined particularly by the interaction of human behavior and technical equipment?

This question becomes suddenly apparent if one considers the different risks that different people face on a daily basis with the same car in the same traffic environment. This interaction of human behavior and technical equipment is the cause of the actual difficulties, as indicated by the following questions:

- Which methods are to be used to determine the safety requirements imposed by society—particularly when the reduction of risk for one party involves disadvantages for another?
- Who possesses the knowledge to define the scale of these safety requirements?
- Who should use this instrument to ensure more or less risk for society or the individual?

In this context, society is also faced very quickly with the question as to who, ultimately, decides the level of risk at which the individual can no longer be accepted in the car-driving community. Demands for risk norms are presented as being imperative because all verbally formulated ethical and moral requirements imposed upon technology would have to be converted into figures in order to achieve results in practical life. Presumably, it is not implied that only technology can produce results. In this regard the problems of linguistic comprehension between empirical and normative sciences are not underestimated. But does not the judicial system, in particular, strive to determine socially and individually acceptable road traffic norms through the elaboration and evaluation of, say, road traffic codes? From this perspective, society is not only faced with the task of determining or monitoring risk norms but also, in particular, of enabling one to accept and comprehend norms and to use them as a guideline for one's own, responsible behavior. Which role is attributed to sociology or social psychology in this matter? Barjonet (1990, p. 99) made the following comments on these questions:

> Whatever the efficiency of the technical means used to increase road safety, we are compelled to believe that the general safety level of the system depends on the attention granted to it by society. Improving the general safety level implies not only reinforcing the legitimacy of the safety measures but also of safety behaviors. We do have the media tools needed to influence public opinion in favour of safety, to give safety a social value and obtain consensus for it. It is in this indirect way that the involvement of each person in safety will be reinforced.

FROM SAFETY EVALUATION TO SYSTEM EVALUATION

Against the background of dramatic technological developments, far-reaching sociopolitical changes, and the related rapid changes in living conditions, questions directed solely to accident and traffic problems have lost ground. In the 1980s, system components such as mobility, ecology, the economy, and lifestyle have thus attracted increasing attention. Corresponding reorientations in the practical and scientific fields resulted in interdisciplinary scenarios that now cover traffic-related and vehicle-related questions as well as economic cost-benefit considerations. The influence of comprehensive behavioral components such as traffic management, monitoring and penalty systems, and the increasing scarcity of public funds has been recognized and is increasingly being accepted as a guideline for concepts and action in traffic psychology.

It can be seen that research on the "functional structure" of road-users and the findings that can be derived from this on the limitations of and possibilities for the assimilation and processing of information have retained their significance.

Never before has the European automobile industry and the European Community placed such great emphasis on research and development as is currently the case with the PROMETHEUS and DRIVE programs. The aim is not only to make the road traffic system more efficient and more environmentally acceptable but also to offer the individual driver the maximum degree of safety. As the safety aspect had tended to lose significance in vehicle development after the research and development advances in passive vehicle safety in the 1960s and 1970s, these renewed efforts are to be welcomed.

Nevertheless, from the psychological viewpoint focusing on the driver, it should be noted that technological improvements to vehicles do not have a direct effect on accident levels in road traffic. This warning covers terms such as "risk compensation," "risk homeostasis," or the "zero-risk model" (Näätänen & Summala, 1976) or "control of danger" (Hale & Glendon, 1987). In 1989, a group of experts from the OECD took these explanatory models based on traffic psychology and studied them for traffic behavior. They ended by selecting the neutral term *"behaviour adaption,"* meaning that the driver becomes aware of the effect of a safety measure and permanently adapts his or her behavior to it (i.e., not as a one-time, short-term reaction).

The OECD group gathered numerous related research findings that should permit general conclusions to be drawn about the influence of such adaption processes on driving behavior and the level of accidents. In some cases, evidence was found to disprove the reactive adaption theory; in other cases, the validity of this theory was unmistakable. The direction of the adaption processes can be substantiated in general psychological terms and can be summarized in a list of practical questions to the designers of roads and vehicles (see Table 1). In view of

TABLE 1:
List of practical questions to the designer of roads and vehicles

Will the driver be able to perceive the change?

Is the change immediately obvious to the driver while driving?

Does the change increase the subjective safety of the driver, that is, does the driver feel that he has increased control over driving situations?

Does the change allow expansion of the drivers' room for maneuvre?

Does the change fit in with aims related to enjoyment of driving, preference for high-speed driving, thrill, competitive behavior or the like?

From Pfafferott, (1989). Anpaßungsvorgänge im System Mensch-Fahrzeug: Hypothesen, Befunde und Folgerungen. Unpublished manuscript.

the complexity of the processes and the still narrow empirical base, linear relations between changes in vehicle design and construction and behavior adaption should not, however, be expected. Nevertheless, "If work in the field of vehicle-related research and development is accompanied from the outset by these considerations, unfavorable developments can more easily be avoided. Technical innovations would thus be of greater benefit in terms of traffic safety" (Pfafferott, 1989, p. 20).

The so-called cognitive turnaround in psychology, by which the problems and perspectives of gestalt-psychology are eventually experiencing a renaissance in new garb, has a variety of historico-scientific origins. Advances in other scientific disciplines, particularly in cybernetics, computer sciences, linguistics, and biology gave new impulses to psychology, in that psychologists adopted model concepts successful in these other fields and incorporated them in their own theoretical structure, partly as analogies and partly as metaphors. Explanatory models, that were dismissed sixty years ago as metaphysical and at best semiscientific (e.g., the "tendency to good form" [Gestalt]) are reappearing today in different forms, and are increasing in credibility not only because of their reformulation but also because their exponents can point to analogous phenomena in the "reality" of other disciplines. Human beings and animals obviously possess a whole range of "subprograms" (subroutines) that are "called up" under particular circumstances and then function schematically. These routines relate to both behavior and cognitive and emotional processes. However, behavior schemes have not been in the background for some time (Heinrich, 1990).

The feedback principle is the decisive element in the cybernetic control of machines. Here, too, analogies to human behavior were drawn, and some illustrations of behavioral relations that are intended to be psychological in fact resemble drawings of technical regulators. The validity (or its limitations) of modeling of human regulatory behavior analogously to technical regulators is determined by all the above-mentioned distinctions between organisms and constructed machines. Efforts to develop artificial intelligence have given psychology some important impulses for the development of its own models with which to simulate cognitive processes through the use of computer programs (Boden, 1987).

Against the background of recent findings on the limitations and capabilities of human beings, one-sided judgmental assessments and generalizations of responsibility and driving ethics in road traffic have come under increasing criticism. In contrast, empirical studies of conflict situations in road traffic and behavior-influencing methods derived from system analyses are gaining ground. However, the incorporation of several evaluation criteria appears sensible only on the basis of the system principle. But the "system" approach is not particularly new to psychologists. It is very close to the old holistic method of the Leipzig School, the contents of which largely overlap with those of the system concept. Nevertheless, the related methodological problem concerning the recording of psychological totalities also presents considerable difficulties for the system-oriented approach. The key consequence of the holistic or system approach in traffic psychology can be seen in the view that analysis of individual subsystems (e.g., driver, vehicle, and road) and the associated functions (e.g., safety, mobility, economy, comfort, and environment) must always take account of the proper functioning of road traffic as a whole system (Heinrich, 1990).

The methodological difficulties involved in answering these questions are obvious. Strictly speaking, assessment of a safety measure requires the systematic recording of all feed-back to the overall system, a requirement that soon reaches its limits in practical research. In addition, the safety criterion is increasingly being overshadowed by other system criteria in the evaluation process. It no longer suffices simply to ask how much safety is gained through a particular measure.

Instead, the question has to be extended to "What price are we prepared to pay in terms of changes to the other system functions in order to obtain a particular increase in safety?" (Klebelsberg, 1988, p. 148).

With the "reference frame theory of risk," Koornstra (1989) recently took up Wilde's (1982) risk-homeostasis hypothesis and the zero-risk model by Näätänen & Summala (1976) and established a link with the fundamental motivation theory of McClelland et al. (1953). The advantage of this theory is that "it is able to predict the direction and order of magnitude of behavioral adjustments to the otherwise expected risk reduction of safety measures" (Koornstra, 1989).

HUMAN BEHAVIOR IN ROAD TRAFFIC:
Capabilities and Limitations

The question about the causes of incorrect behavior has often led to profound investigations and complicated models of the role of homo sapiens in road traffic. The causes given have often been extreme:

- Humans are "inadequate beings" whose inadequacies cause 90% of road accidents.
- Technology is a monster that constantly overstretches the capacities of these pitiful, inadequate beings.

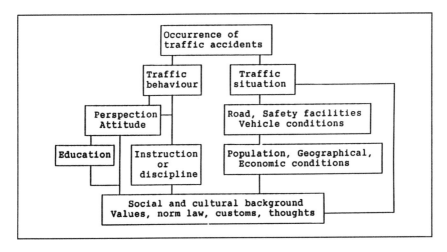

FIG. 3. Relationships between traffic accidents, traffic behaviour, and social and cultural background (Nagayama).

- The consumer society outwits the "dumb mobility lover" with its "hidden temptations" and seduces him or her into taking unintended compulsive actions.

The consequences of these extreme viewpoints provide ample scope for disagreement. But I do not intend to leave it at that. I should like to recall a systematic and, to my mind, well-founded model of the relationships between traffic accidents, traffic behavior, and their technical and social background (see Figure 3).

The advantage of this model lies in the fact that it neither ties the observer down to an excessively narrow "inadequacies model" of the road-user, nor demands from the road-user "cybernetic" powers of imagination in the synopsis of multidimensional interactions. It merely describes the components that influence or determine behavior in traffic, thus providing an incentive for joint consideration of "possibilities for increasing traffic safety" from the viewpoint of the disciplines gathered here. It thus takes account of the shift in emphasis that has occurred in recent years from purely specialist accident research to interdisciplinary safety research.

For example, take the task of driving a vehicle along a road—one of the easiest tasks of all. Technical instruments alone can scarcely cope even during daylight. If the weather is inclement and the road conditions are difficult technology is currently unable to perform the task without the intervention of a driver. By comparison, humans are wonderfully equipped to analyze and formulate complicated visual stimuli in fractions of a second. In addition, they are able to adapt to varied and difficult environmental conditions—including traffic situations, quickly and with a high degree of reliability. In this respect, authors of works published to date have repeatedly expressed surprise that so few accidents actually occur in such an open system as road traffic.

But human beings also have many limitations, and the fact that they are living biological organisms has often been ignored in cybernetic and mechanical models of traffic behavior. From time to time, humans do not function properly, do not react appropriately and, in particular, sometimes make mistakes. "The unreliability of human performance is one of the most reliable of human characteristics" (Rumar, 1989, p. 14).

As far as physiological limits are concerned, I do not need to list them all. It suffices here to mention reduced vision at night, restricted all-round vision, limited capabilities for assessing time gaps and speeds, as well as the general susceptibility of the entire human organism. If the normal decline of the human organism through ageing is added, the limitations of compensation through learning and experience become painfully obvious. The related problems are likely to become only more critical in road traffic in the coming decades, when 30% to 35% of the driving population will be over 60. Nevertheless, this shift in the age pyramid on roads need not lead to a reduction in traffic safety. Indeed, the extensive consideration given in recent years to the problems of young drivers means that the chances for a "pure belief in fitness" in future safety research are not particularly high.

The following fact has emerged as a psychological failing in highly motorized society: Drivers usually receive no direct feedback on whether they have acted correctly or incorrectly. In fact, the opposite is usually the case. People may act incorrectly or contravene regulations throughout their driving lives and may even profit from this behavior. This overall situation results in bad drivers and establishes bad driving habits, a situation that has been known to the behavioral sciences for many years as "negative learning" from bad examples.

Use of in-car and roadside computer technology will be increased in attempts to counteract the overstraining of the driver's visual and psychomotoric capacities. Why should computer technology not be put to the service of enhancing mobility and ensuring safety for the human race? Nevertheless, the question as to what "electronic dreams" can actually bring for the safety of the individual and car-driving society remains open. From the sociopsychological viewpoint, road traffic seriously overstretches the framework of normal human interaction and communication. This has a whole series of counterproductive effects on the behavior of road-users, beginning with the fact that even minor mistakes at the wheel are interpreted as provocations by other drivers.

Cars do not have a sign for "Sorry, it wasn't deliberate!" but they do have horns! In recent years, aggressiveness in road traffic has been the subject of an increasing level of research. The lack of possibilities for communication and the isolation and anonymity of the driver are given as reasons for the total absence of social contacts and for drivers' forgetting their personal responsibility. In wide sections of the population, inconsiderate driving behavior and contraventions of traffic codes and laws are not regarded as violations of common decency and still less as criminal acts.

Psychologists have recognized the close relation between frustration and aggression in the form of the so-called frustration-aggression theory, according to which every type of frustration inevitably leads to aggression in the short or long term. However, psychology also teaches that aggression, like every form of behavior, is subject to a learning process with reinforcement mechanisms. In other words, the model behavior is attributed great significance not only in the general social environment but in road traffic in particular (Böcher, 1988).

This brings me to sociological conditions that include general conditions of life in a society; that is, not only economic and social conditions but also group phenomena and the influences of the mass media. It is against this background that comparative studies of traffic safety are gaining ground in various countries. For example, a pilot study was recently completed in which traffic safety in the Federal Republic of Germany and Great Britain was compared. The surveys indicated that the British are attributed a high sense of social responsibility with regard to driving whereas the Germans are not (Leutzbach et al., 1988).

When considering the particular problems of individual groups of drivers, such as young drivers, it is important to remember that the following categorisation does not lay the blame on a single group of "bad" drivers but rather reflects the weaknesses of the overall system (Böcher et al., 1977). If, for example, inexperience and a greater willingness to take risks are suggested as explanations for the disproportionately high level of incorrect behavior on the part of young male drivers, this only represents part of the overall conditions. Why are young female drivers not so noted for their incorrect driving behavior and not so likely to be involved in accidents? It is precisely in this area that lifestyle analyses and explanatory models based on field-theory offer traffic psychology possible approaches for overcoming stereotypes. Recent studies thus go beyond statistical analyses and traffic surveys and also incorporate general social factors and living conditions under which, say, young drivers "grow into" road traffic (Ellinghaus, Schlag, & Steinbrecher, 1986b; Marthiens & Schulze, 1989; Nagayama, 1989; Rothe & Cooper, 1987).

The last 25 years have not only seen a change in perspective in academic psychology; radical changes have also occurred in wide areas of applied psychology. Having concentrated in the 1960s on questions of the diagnostics of driver aptitude, applied psychologists then turned increasingly to questions of traffic education, training, driver improvement, rehabilitation of drivers, and, in conjunction with other scientific disciplines, the development of system-analytical models for describing and explaining psychological phenomena in road traffic. In traffic psychology it was also inevitably necessary to face up to the social and technological challenges of the 1970s and 1980s. Adoption of the concept of "human failure" so often employed in the technical, legal, and administrative fields was carefully avoided.

While the driver may appear as a regulator in the engineer's road traffic system of the human being, vehicle, and environment, while the costs caused by road-users may be regarded as economic intangibles, and while the legal system may regard "human failure at the wheel" as a cause for blame, psychologists hold that there is nothing more reliable than human unreliability. Even if tomorrow's road-users are highly motorized and drive fully computerized vehicles, they will remain living beings who make mistakes, correct these mistakes, and learn from them. Depending on the interests and/or level of knowledge of the drivers involved, the learning and control capacities that these motorized living beings have at their disposal to deal with such an open system as road traffic—or should I say such "inadequate technology"—are often underestimated or overestimated.

All those who have lost persons close to them or have themselves suffered damage or injury will not, however, be able to consider these inadequacies of the road traffic system in such a calm and detached academic manner. Over the last two decades, traffic psychologists have thus done well to concentrate increasingly on the identification of weak points in the traffic system and the provision of assistance for its victims instead of merely taking the side of those who have escaped damage and singling out "unsuitable" drivers. In the process, obvious weak points in the road traffic system have been discovered and inconsistencies in contemporary car-driving society have been revealed. Traffic psychologists have learned to live with the accusations of ideological bias or lack of reality that their field's approach has earned. Other branches of science are now increasingly experiencing this change in perspective, which is by no means the sole property of traffic psychology. Indeed, this change has led to greater understanding between the different scientific disciplines and to the necessary sensitivity for complex questions, as will be demanded by the safety research of the future.

In the last decade, traffic psychology has advanced far into the field of interdisciplinary accident and safety research and is now actively involved in the development of methods to solve complex problems of modern safety research and practical safety measures. It has developed into a valuable branch of interdisciplinary safety research and is recognized in many fields as a reliable partner in dealing with existing and emerging social problems.

REFERENCES

Barjonet, P. E. (1990). Social structure and the changes in traffic behavior. *IATSS Research*, *14*(1), 95-99.

Böcher, W. (1988). Aggression im Straßenverkehr als Thema der Verkehrserziehung und -aufklärung. *Schriftenreihe Unfall- und Sicherheitsforschung Straßenverkehr*, Heft 68, 54-60. Bergisch Gladbach: Bundesanstalt für Straßenwesen.

Böcher, W., Kroj, G., Pfafferott, I., Spoerer, E., Sogemeyer, H.,& Winkler, W. (1977). Typische Verhaltensweisen von Fahranfängern und Möglichkeiten gezielter Nachschulung. *Schriftenreihe Unfall- und Sicherheitsforschung*, Heft 8. Cologne: Bundesanstalt für Straßenwesen.

Boden, M. A. (1987). *Artificial intelligence and natural man*. London: MIT Press.

Chaloupka, C., Hyden, C., & Risser, R. (1990). Die PRO-GEN Verkehrssicherheit-Checkliste. *Zeitschrift für Verkehrssicherheit*, *36*(1), 28-35.

Ellinghaus, D., Schlag, B., & Steinbrecher, J. (1986). Risikobereitschaft junger Fahrer. *Schriftenreihe Unfall- und Sicherheitsforschung Straßenverkehr*, Heft 58. Bergisch Gladbach: Bundesanstalt für Straßenwesen.

Hale, A. R., & Glendon, A. I. (1987). *Individual behaviour in the control of danger*. Amsterdam: Elsevier.

Hebenstreit, B. v., Hundhausen, G., Klebe, W., Kroj, G., Spoerer, E., Walther, R., Winkler, W., & Wuhrer, H. (1982). Kurse für auffällige Kraftfahrer. *Schriftenreihe Projektgruppenberichte der Bundesanstalt für Straßenwesen, Bereich Unfallforschung*, Heft 12. Cologne: Bundesanstalt für Straßenwesen.

Heinrich, H. C. (1990). Behavioural changes in the context of traffic safety. *IATSS Research*, *14*(1), 85-88.

Huguenin, R. D. (1985). Zur Problematik der Theorienbildung in der Verkehrspsychologie. *Fortschritte der Verkehrspsychologie*, Vol. 1 [Schriftenreihe "Mensch-Fahrzeug-Umwelt"] (Vol. 15, pp. 336-351). Cologne: TÜV.

Klebelsberg, D. (1971). Subjektive und aktive Sicherheit im Straßenverkehr als Aufgabe für die Verkehrssicherheit. *Schriftenreihe der Deutschen Verkehrswacht, 51,* 3-12.

Klebelsberg, D. (1988). Historische Entwicklung und Ist-Zustand für Verkehrssicherheit (Vol. 24, pp. 141-151). Salzburg: Kuratorium für Verkehrssicherheit.

Koornstra, M. J. (1989). *System Theory and Individual Risk.* Unpublished manuscript. Institute for Road Safety Research (SWOV), Leidschendam, The Netherlands.

Leutzbach, W., Buck, A., Kim, H.-S., Allsop, R. E., Hakkert, A. S., Tight, M., Brown, J. D., Biehl, B., Brög, W., Schwertner, K., & Voltenauer-Lagemann, M. (1988). Vergleich der Verkehrssicherheit in der Bundesrepublik Deutschland und Großbritannien. *Forschungsberichte der Bundesanstalt für Straßenwesen, Bereich Unfallforschung,* Heft 183. Bergisch Gladbach: Bundesanstalt für Straßenwesen.

Marthiens, W., & Schulze, H. (1989). *Disco-Unfälle.* Research report, Heft 198. Bergisch Gladbach: Bundesanstalt für Straßenwesen, Bereich Unfallforschung.

Müller, A. (1987). Zweck und Bedeutung verkehrspsychologischer Gutachten im Führerscheinverfahren. *Fortschritte der Verkehrspsychologie,* Vol. 2 (pp. 149-164). [Schriftenreihe "Mensch-Fahrzeug-Umwelt"]. Cologne: TÜV.

Näätänen, R., & Summula, H. (1976). *Road user behavior and traffic accidents.* Amsterdam:

Nagayama, Y. (1989). International comparison of traffic behavior and perceptions of traffic. *IATSS Research, 13*(1), 61-69.

Pfafferott, I. (1989). *Anpasssungsvorgänge im System Mensch-Fahrzeug: Hypothesen, Befunde und Folgerungen.* Unpublished manuscript.

Rothe, P., & Cooper, P. J. (1987). *Rethinking young drivers.* North Vancouver: Insurance Corporation of British Columbia (ICBC).

Rumar, K. (1989). Road user and information technology. *VTI Report,* No. 341a, 12-18. Linköping: Väg-och Trafikinstitutet (VTI).

Wilde, E. J. S. (1982). The theory of risk homeostasis: Implications for safety and health. *Risk Analysis, 2,* 209-255.

Winkler, W. (1986). Aktuelle Fragen der verkehrspsychologischen Fahrereignungsbegutachtung. *Zeitschrift für Verkehrssicherheit, 32,* 163-167.

CROSS-CULTURAL COMPARISON OF TRAFFIC BEHAVIOR AND ATTITUDE

Organizer & Chair: T. K. Cho, Seoul National University, Korea

Contributors:

S. C. Lee, Road Traffic Safety Association, Korea
Cross-cultural differences in driver's traffic attitude: Comparison of Japan, Canada, U.S.A. and Korea

I. Papp, Institute for Transport Sciences, Hungary
K. Ogawa, Osaka University, Japan
Comparison of Hungarian and Japanese children's view of road traffic, based on drawings

K. Renge, Tezukayama University, Japan
International comparison of traffic behaviors: Canada, Korea and Japan

T. Rothengatter, R. de Bruin, Traffic Research Centre (VSC), University of Groningen, Netherlands
E. Carbonell, University of Valencia, Spain
Cultural differences in the appraisal of traffic violations amongst Dutch and Spanish drivers and police

Comparative studies of cross-cultural differences in the attitude and behavior of road-traffic participants could provide valuable information for developing safety measures. Though it is easy to agree that such studies are meaningful, carrying them out is costly and time-consuming.

This symposium, somewhat restricted in its scope because of the limitations mentioned, was composed of three parts, (a) the behavior and attitude while a person is driving vehicles, (b) children's perception of the road traffic situation, and (c) the difference in drivers' appraisals of traffic violations and the appraisals of police officers.

THE BEHAVIOR AND ATTITUDES OF DRIVERS

Speed of travel, the frequency of visual checkings, and road-crossing behaviors in Japan, Canada, and Korea were recorded and analyzed to identify social and cultural factors that might be relevant to those behaviors.

Traveling speed on the highway or freeway in these three countries was recorded and compared. The average speed and homogeneity of speed, as indicated by the coefficient of variation for each city, are shown in Table 1.

The result shows that speed dispersion is low in Canada, though the average speed is high, while speed dispersion is greater in Japan and Korea, showing a higher degree of variation.

The visual checking behavior at narrow intersections without a traffic signal can be seen as one type of active information acquisition to improve safety. Canadian drivers showed more frequent visual checking behaviors than drivers in Japan and Korea did. A visual check was scored when the driver's head turned to the left or right upon entering an intersection from a road. Thus, if the driver's head turned to the left, then to the right, and again to the left, this movement was counted as three checkings. The average number visual checks among 4-wheeled vehicles in Montreal was 3.4 (100 vehicles); Toronto, 3.3 (160 vehicles); Tokyo, 2.8 (155 vehicles); Osaka, 2.5 (233 vehicles); Seoul, 1.6 (389 vehicles); and Pusan, 1.4 (127 vehicles). The difference between the three countries covered by this study was remarkable.

TABLE 1
Travel speed on highway or freeway in three countries

City	Coefficient of (km/h)	Average speed variation
Montreal	99.22	11.39
Toronto	94.82	10.74
Osaka	92.14	12.90
Tokyo	90.74	12.77
Seoul	88.08	14.90
Pusan	87.09	16.70

This part of the symposium also focused on the results of a survey questionnaire designed to identify the difference in drivers' attitudes that may be causally related to traffic accidents. The attitudes that Japanese, Korean, American, and Canadian drivers have toward pedestrians, traffic signals, traffic accidents, and so forth were analyzed and compared. One of the findings was that 68.3% of the Japanese and 78.9% of the Korean respondents viewed pedestrians' behavior as one of the major contributing factors to traffic accidents, whereas only 26.2% of the American and 29.9% of the Canadian respondents thought so.

To the question of whether drivers generally set their vehicles in motion at an intersection shortly before the traffic signal changes to green light, simultaneously with the change of the signal, or one breath after the change, 29.1% of the Korean and 14.4% of the Japanese respondents thought that drivers in their respective societies generally set their vehicles in motion before the signal changes to green, whereas 3.5% of the American respondents thought so. By contrast, 36.5% of the American respondents thought that drivers in general in their society start vehicles one breath after the signal changes to green, while 17% of the Korean and 16.9% of the Japanese respondents considered this to be the case in their respective societies.

A third finding was that 44.9% of the Japanese respondents attributed the cause of road traffic accidents to their own errors, while 72.3% of the American and 40.7% of the Canadian respondents attributed the cause to other external factors. Whereas 35.5% of the Japanese respondents attributed the cause to sheer misfortune, only 9.6% of the American subjects responded in that way.

CHILDREN'S PERCEPTION OF THE TRAFFIC SITUATION

To gain a glimpse of the world of children with regard to road traffic, participants in the final part of the symposium examined the results of illustrations by eighty 8-9 year-old Hungarian children and 29 Japanese children of the same age, all of whom had been asked to draw pictures of what they saw on the street on their way to and from school.

Most of the drawings by the children showed no clear distinction between roadway and sidewalk. Hungarian children tended to over-emphasize crosswalks and gave greater attention to details of traffic-related elements. Differences in the content of the drawings were notable. For example, the Hungarian children drew a total of 72 pedestrians, 53 passengers, and 54 drivers. The Japanese children drew 48 pedestrians, no passengers, and 4 drivers.

APPRAISAL OF TRAFFIC VIOLATIONS BY
DRIVERS AND POLICE OFFICERS

In the third part of this symposium, participants sought to ascertain cultural differences in the appraisal of traffic violations. Participants examined the responses of drivers and policemen in Spain and the Netherlands who had been requested to estimate the seriousness of traffic violations in different situations and indicate the expected likelihood of being apprehended. The subjective estimates of seriousness were compared with the objective seriousness as gathered from accident statistics. Marked differences in the responses between Spain and the Netherlands were found for both drivers and police officers. Though differences could not all be attributed to differences in culture as such, differences in driver population and road situation appeared to have a significant effect in producing the difference in general. The estimated likelihood of being apprehended is related to the estimated seriousness of an offence, a finding that indicates enforcement activities may have an effect on a driver's perception of risk.

CONCLUSION

The cross-cultural study of traffic behavior is still in its infancy. As the foregoing studies suggest, there are differences in attitude, behavior, and perception of road traffic situations across countries. The knowledge derived from studies in this area could improve such things as driver education, traffic safety education, and traffic laws, thus promoting the overall safety of road traffic. It is hoped that this symposium stimulated the interest in studies on this part of life and in the improvement of the related research techniques and methodology.

VISUAL PERCEPTION AND ATTENTION IN AUTOMOBILE DRIVING

Organizer: T. Miura, Osaka University, Japan
Chair: K. Noguchi, Chiba University, Japan
T. Miura, Osaka University, Japan

Contributors:

L. Harms, Swedish Road and Traffic Research Institute, Sweden
Task demands and processing capacity in driving and driving simulation

O. Laya, Institut National de Rechèrche sur les Transports et le Securité, France
Eye movements in actual and simulated curve negotiation tasks

T. Miura, Osaka University, Japan
Visual search under demanding situations: An underlying mechanism

K. Noguchi, Chiba University, Japan
Speed perception on the real road and in simulation

W. A. C. Spijkers, University of Technology, Aachen, FRG
Street environment, driving speed and field of vision

Dicussants: G. Matthews, University of Dundee, U.K.
J. A. Michon, University of Groningen, Netherlands

The aim of the symposium entitled *Vision in Vehicles* was to examine some of the visual factors in automobile driving from both theoretical and applied perspectives. The topics were speed perception, eye movements, and attention. They are important for traffic safety and the stimulation of theories of perception and attention. The general, or theoretical, theme of the symposium was first to examine the relation between laboratory-simulated experiments and field experiments and, second, to examine effects of attentional demands (workload) on driving behavior or information-processing in relation to resource theory. The symposium was organized by T. Miura and chaired by Kaoru Noguchi of Chiba University, Japan and the organizer. Five speakers presented their papers, as introduced briefly below. Discussants were John A. Michon from the University of Groningen, The Netherlands, and Gerald Matthews from the University of Dundee, United Kingdom. The audience participated actively in the discussion. The full papers of the five speakers are to be published in a special issue of the *Journal of International Association of Traffic and Safety Sciences, 16*(1). Please refer to it for details.

Speed perception plays a primary role in deciding what speed is natural, safe, or optimal in relation to the traveling circumstances. In the first contribution, *Speed perception on the real road and in simulation*, K. Noguchi examined psychophysical relations between actual traveling speeds and perceived (estimated) speeds under real conditions and in video simulation. Under both real and simulated conditions, traveling speed was underestimated. Moreover, the underestimation was smaller in a tunnel than on open road under real conditions, and the underestimation was almost negligible under the simulated condition. In simulation, the travel speed on ascending roads was estimated to be slower than on descending roads, and no significant difference between speed estimation on curved roads and speed estimations on straight roads was found. Underestimation poses a problem for traffic safety, and the difference between field and simulated experiments and revealed characteristics of speed estimation, especially under simulation, raises issues to be clarified in theoretical research. Noguchi also made recommendations concerning the legal speed for traffic safety.

In a contribution entitled Eye movements in actual and simulated curve negotiation tasks, O. Laya of INRETS-LPC, France, attempted to clarify characteristics of eye movements in curves. In driving, the negotiation of curves raises difficulty, as shown by accident records. Laya posed questions about how drivers perceive curves with different radius and angles, and how drivers adjust their driving speed according to their perception of relevant curves. He tried to examine the anticipatory and perceiving phase in the negotlation of curves through scan path, distribution of fixations, and duration of fixation, under real and simulated conditions for subjects with different levels of driving experience.

The first two contributions, which focused partly on the effect of road geometry on perception in driving were followed by three contributions on the effect that the situational complexity of the traffic environment has on perception and attention. In a contribution entitled *Street environment, driving speed, and field of vision*, Will Spijkers of the Institute of Psychology, University of Technology, Aachen, Germany, examined eye movements under different conditions of street complexity (urban, urban freeway, and rural) and driving speed in real driving. He found that drivers look at objects relevant to the driving task much more frequently on urban streets than on rural streets and urban freeways and that, with the increase of driving speed, drivers look at relevant objects much more frequently and with greater concentration on urban streets. Such a tendency was not found on rural streets and urban freeways. Thus, he demonstrated the interactional effect of street environment and driving speed on visual behavior in driving. This was interpreted by an attention distribution model.

The attentional state in driving was examined by the elaborate contribution entitled *Task demands and processing capacity in driving and driving simulation* by Lisbeth Harms of the Swedish Road and Traffic Research Institute, VTI, Sweden. She adopted a dual-task method and at the same time measured driving speed in order to assess coping strategy in real and simulated driving. In real driving, with a secondary task of simple calculation, it was clearly found that drivers respond to increasing complexity of the traffic environment by both reducing their driving speed and allocating more attentional resources to the driving task itself, changes assessed on the basis of the reaction time on the secondary task. In simulation, the same method was used and the attempt was made to assess driving performance directly through detection of visual targets. Similar results were obtained. The one exception was that task difficulty did not influence performance on the secondary task as remarkably in simulation as it did in real driving. This finding suggests that task priority differs between simulated driving and real driving. Harms thereby demonstrated that persons driving under demanding conditions allocate more resources to the driving task itself and reduce driving speed.

What kind of coping strategy is involved in the acquisition of visual information while driving? In Miura's contribution, *Visual search under demanding situations: An underlying mechanism*, an eye-movements method and dual-task method were combined to assess the variation of size of the useful field of view and the detectability of targets in real driving. It was clearly shown that the useful field of view becomes narrower and that the reaction time for detection of peripherally presented targets becomes longer as the complexity of the traffic environment increases. The results are well interpreted by a resource allocation model of trade-off between depth and width of processing at each fixation point. The results reflect an underlying mechanism by which the allocation of processing resources is optimized (a mechanism Miura calls "cognitive momentum") for coping with demanding situations.

With regard to road geometry, Noguchi revealed several features characterizing the underestimation of driving speed and made recommendations for traffic safety. Laya gave suggestions for research on perception of curves, one of the most relevant road geometries. With regard to the driving situation under relatively demanding situations, Spijkers demonstrated that drivers look at relevant objects more frequently, Harms demonstrated that drivers cope both by allocating more resources to the driving task and by reducing driving speed, and Miura demonstrated the decrease of peripheral vision performance, which reflects an optimization of allocation of resources.

Discussions revolved around the validity of simulated experiments and the dual-task method. There are several kinds of merits and demerits of simulation and dual tasks in each experiment. The merits and demerits should be clarified, both methodologically and theoretically. This symposium offered stimulating and fruitful points for future research on visual perception and attention and gave pointers for traffic safety.

ALCOHOL AND DRIVING

Organizers: E. Spoerer, Gesellschaft für
Ausbildung, Fortbildung und Nachschulung,
Köln, FRG
Y. Suzuki, Ibaraki University, Japan
Chair: E. Spoerer, Gesellschaft für Ausbildung,
Fortbildung und Nachschulung, FRG

Contributors:

M. Jensch, Gesellschaft für Ausbildung, Fortbildung und
Nachschulung, FRG
Fear, sex and alcohol: Experiences with multiple drinking-and-driving
offenders

G. Kroj, Federal Highway Research Institute, FRG
Diagnosis and rehabilitation of drinking drivers

M. Sheenan, University of Queensland, Australia
A theory based drink driving education program

Y. Suzuki, Ibaraki University, Japan
Attitudes and Mores Underlying Drinking-driving in Japan

The consumption of alcoholic beverages before or while driving a motor
vehicle is one of the major causes of traffic accidents. The high number
of alcohol-related accidents is a continuous challenge not only for
legislators, law enforcement officials and judges but also for researchers
in the field of behavioral sciences. This symposium tried to reflect
substantial aspects of the problem: basic understanding, education,
deterrence, diagnosis, rehabilitation, and therapy.

In her contribution, *A theory based drunk-driving education program* Mary Sheehan described the development of a drunk-driving education intervention aimed at addressing two points of criticism of existing alcohol and drug education programs. The first weakness identified in these programs is that they are not based on established theoretical models for understanding behavior and effecting behavioral change. Additionally, it was noted that very few program users evaluate whether the intervention actually reduces recipients' later involvement in road accidents.

The search for a model predicting drunk driving by adolescents finally focused on Ajzen and Fishbein's (1980) theory of reasoned action, according to which behavior is determined by intention which, in turn, is determined by the weighted contribution of attitudes towards the behavior and subjective norms concerning the behavior. For their part attitudes are determined by beliefs that the behavior leads to certain consequences and the individual's evaluation of these consequences. Subjective norms are determined by beliefs that significant others think the person should or should not perform the behavior and the individual's motivation to comply with these others.

The application of this theory involved the definition of the following program objectives: separation of drinking from driving by use of counterstrategies; rejection of passenger status; developing or reinforcing the intention to use counterstrategies; practicing the social skills needed to carry out the intention.

To achieve these objectives, educational strategies were designed: to raise students' expectations of the likelihood that drunk-driving behavior would lead to negative consequences, to increase the negative valence of these consequences, to lessen students' estimates of the likelihood of positive consequences, to decrease the perceived attractiveness of these consequences, to increase belief that significant others would disapprove of their drunk-driving or involvement as a passenger, and to increase the perceived importance of this disapproval.

Because it was established that students believe their own personal invulnerability protects them from negative consequences, the decision was reached to place a major emphasis on strengthening students' awareness of consequences that research showed they already viewed as somewhat likely, rather than stress those seen as relatively unlikely. The educational material was therefore focused on raising students' estimates of the likelihood of "being picked up by the police," "damaging a parent's car," or "getting into trouble from parents" rather than the consequence of "being killed" or "being in a car crash." Teaching methods included providing positive models of who uses the strategies and allowing for reinforced practice by role playing counterstrategies in small-group settings. Increasing positive evaluations of the use of counterstrategies was more tied to interpersonal reinforcement through group discussions, teacher feedback, and the processing of relevant video stimulus material. One of two videotapes was presented at the symposium. Currently, research indicates that the drunk-driving education program has been able to change self-reported intentions and attitudes in the short term.

The *diagnosis and rehabilitation of DWI* (drivers who have been operating a motor vehicle while being impaired by alcohol or intoxicated) was the topic of Gunter Kroj. He pointed out that the traffic authority in the Federal Republic of Germany can require applicants to undergo medical and psychological tests before issuing or reissuing a driver's licence. These tests, however, are only required if the licencing agency has reason to doubt an applicant's competence as a driver.

About 100,000 tests are conducted every year at medical and psychological testing institutes of the Technical Inspection Agencies (TÜV). A set of guidelines specifies the nation-wide regulations for testing. They set the national standards for the physical and mental ability required for the operation of motor vehicles. There are different examination procedures, depending on the individual problem under consideration. The information gained in the course of testing determines the manner in which the examination is to continue.

Cases for examination fall roughly into two categories, that of drivers reported for functional disorders and that of drivers convicted of traffic violations. Besides the qualifying outcome of an examination, there are also expert opinions with a supportive and therapeutic orientation. At the present time, they usually pertain to drunk drivers, focusing on the question of whether it is advisable for a driver to participate in a relevant rehabilitation program.

For novice drivers who have comitted a drunk-driving offence in the two-year probationary period a special re-education program was designed in 1986. Instructors are psychologists with special qualifications. Besides programs for reducing the length of time that DWI first offenders lose their driver's license there are DWI rehabilitation courses for recidivists. Having decreased the recidivism rate by about 50 percent they are very successful.

Yukio Suzuki entitled his presentation *Attitude and mores underlying drunk-driving in Japan*. He dealt with four aspects: the present state of affairs, public opinions and attitudes, legal sanctions, and methods of education for prevention.

In Japan only 0.67% of all accidents and 6.05% of all fatal accidents are caused by drunk drivers. In a roadside survey in 1983 drivers of about 70,000 vehicles underwent a breath test. In 2.46% of all cases alcohol was detected. About one third of this subpopulation (35.3%) showed a breath alcohol figure that exceeded the legal limit of 0.25 mg/l.

From case studies dealing with imprisoned drunk drivers, three types were found. The P-type drunk driver has many serious personal problems other than drunk driving. He or she has experience with hospitalization for alcoholism, alcohol-related diseases, brawls and vandalism while drunk, and has many personal debts or fines to pay. The H-type or *h*abitual drunk-driver can hardly separate drinking from driving, does not greatly regret his or her alcohol-related traffic violation, and lives in a community in which social sanctions against drunk-driving are lenient. The A-type or *a*ccidental drunk-driver committed the violation of driving under the influence of alcohol and caused a fatal accident. He or she has no problems in daily life and arouses people's sympathy.

According to other studies drunk driving in Japan is regarded as one of the most criminal of all traffic violations. Nevertheless, 64% of the male drivers, 28% of the female drivers in one survey (52% in all) admitted that they have driven a car during the past five years after having more than one drink.

Examining the mores of drinking in Japan, Suzuki mentioned the tradition of group drinking, the relatively high respect that the heavy drinker is accorded among youths, the conclusion of business talks by the consumption of alcoholic beverages, and the relatively lenient social sanctions against such deviant behavior of drunkards as brawling, blundering or vandalizing.

Finally, Suzuki outlined the Danshukai program, an attempt to cure alcoholics through regular group meetings where members confess and discuss their failures, sufferings, anxieties, and troubles based on drinking frankly with each other.

The symposium's last presentation was given by Markus Jensch. His paper dealt with fear, sexuality and alcohol. He discussed the relationship between fear, feelings of inferiority, the fiction of superiority, the creation of illusions with the help of alcohol, and the finality of uncontrolled drinking.

The cases that he had taken were from long-term rehabilitation programs for multiple drunk-driving offenders. They clearly showed that alcohol is a multi-functional helper in dealing with fear. By clouding the perception of reality, it enables an illusionary compensation of deficits, creating the feeling of narcissistic omnipotence. At the same time, alcohol also eliminates inhibitions and affords temporary courage and self-confidence. Equipped with pseudostrength provided by alcohol, the drinker is able to break sexual taboos.

Uncontrolled drinking is thus neither a coincidental aberration in drinking behavior nor the result of incorrect drinking habits. On the contrary, it is a systematically pursued protective mechanism of final rather than of causal nature. It allows pent-up rage to be released deliberately and methodically.

The logical conclusion is that drinkers must learn to make a fundamental change in their disturbed and limited every-day behavior. He or she must understand the psychodynamics of their drinking and dispense with neurotic perfectionism and striving for personal superiority.

REFERENCE

Ajzen, I., & Fishbein, M. (1980). *Understanding attitudes and predicting social behavior.* Englewood Cliffs, NJ: Prentice Hall.

RESEARCH ON DIFFERENT ROAD USER GROUPS AND COUNTERMEASURES

Organizers: H. Häcker,
University of Wuppertal, FRG
Y. Nagatsuka, Niigata University, Japan
Chair: H. Häcker, University of Wuppertal, FRG

Contributors:

H. Häcker, University of Wuppertal, FRG
Methodical remarks to the research on different road user groups

R. D. Huguenin, Swiss Council for Accident Prevention, Switzerland
Behavior analysis of young drivers

M. J. Kuiken, University of Groningen, Netherlands
Adaptive messages to novice drivers

S. Nishiyama, Hiroshima University, Japan
A countermeasure for young drivers

M. W. B. Perrine, Vermont Alcohol Research Center, U.S.A.
Countermeasures for Alcohol-impaired Drivers

The interaction between driver, vehicle, and road (person-machine interaction, driver-highway-vehicle interaction) has become more and more important in describing road-user behavior and reducing the number of traffic accidents (O'Day, 1968; Marek & Sten, 1976). Because risk behavior in road traffic is one of the most dangerous behaviors in highly mobile and highly technological societies, much research is done to reduce human injuries (e.g., Rothengatter & de Bruin, 1988; Rumar, 1991).

In investigation of the driver-highway-vehicle system, human factors—often described as "human error"—may be regarded as the main component in the causation and prevention of traffic accidents (Shinar, 1978: Brown, 1979).

In the search for ways to reduce the number of road accidents many attempts have been made over the decades to develop adequate theories to analyze the accident process (Munsterberg, 1912; Marbe, 1935; Smillie & Ayoub, 1976; McKenna, 1982). There are many different and sometimes independent approaches and different issues, and different strategies for countermeasures are recommended. Because the road-vehicle-environment system must be seen as very complex, the different approaches should therefore complement each other.

For this reason, "different accident involvement" (McKenna, 1982) is the most important issue for an understanding of the fact that the effectiveness of accident reduction programs depends on many factors.

In addition to the "different accident involvement" concept, however, the differential aspects must be extended to include the person and the situation and, consequently, to the interaction between person and situation (Magnusson & Endler, 1977; Näätänen & Summala, 1976; Klebelsberg, 1982). In keeping with the topic of this symposium, different groups of problem drivers, specific countermeasures, and safety programs were examined. Effective accident safety programs require a great deal of research, to describe, predict, and modify unsafe behavior. But the present state of research-based knowledge cannot subdue the problems of all traffic conflicts in countries with high accident rates. In addition, there are specific continental and local characteristics in technical, judicial, and social systems. Relevant aspects include significant problem groups and relevant research activities in different countries.

Because the habit of drinking alcohol and driving a car are often correlated and are often the cause of injuries or accidents, M. W. Perrine (Vermont Alcohol Research Center in Burlington, Vermont, USA) explicated measures to deal with alcohol-impaired drivers in the United States. The nationwide accident statistics show some reduction in alcohol-related accidents. It is being assumed that countermeasures contributing to this broad, general reduction are primarily of a legislative nature (e.g., regulation of the drinking age, limitation of permissable blood-alcohol concentrations, the suspension of the driver's licence by police officers and the courts, and increased control). On the other hand, psychologically based and carefully evaluated driver improvement programs (weekend intervention programs) are found to be effective. Technological countermeasures (critical tracking task, ignition interlock device) have been found to be only minimally effective.

In the Japanese highway system young drivers are problem drivers, as in Europe and the United States. Nishiyama (Hiroshima University, Hiroshima, Japan) presented a study in which he explored by questionnaire relevant habits and attitudes of young drivers (students). This study was based on the hypothesis that young drivers can be educated to be safe drivers because of the high flexibility in their driving habits.

To improve the driving performance of young student drivers, the specific baseline of habits, skills, and attitudes must be considered. When taking these facts into account, one may found it useful to analyze sex differences. Male and female student drivers differ in many skills and habits for safe driving.

Huguenin (Swiss Council for Accident Prevention, Bern, Switzerland) summarized the results of a series of studies analyzing the specific attitudes of young drivers in the German-speaking parts of Europe. In these studies a multifactorial design was used. In European studies the hypothesis is tested that the pattern characterizing behavior and attitudes of young drivers is the key to modifying behavior.

Novice drivers are not always young drivers, but accident data show a considerable number of accidents involving novice drivers. M. J. Kuiken (Traffic Research Center, University of Groningen, The Netherlands) reported the results of a study in which a driver support system had been developed. Data relating to situational information about accidents and errors were gathered on samples of inexperienced and experienced drivers respectively. The results showed that the types of errors and accident situations differ depending on the level of experience and that these differences can be attributed to differences in error perception.

Professional drivers (bus drivers, truck drivers, taxi drivers) represent an interesting subgroup of drivers with regard to the relation between a given accident criterium and personality dimensions. Häkkinen (1958), for instance, was able to show that the accident criterion of reliability is high when accident rates were included systematically over a relatively long period. Rather high correlations have also been found between accidents and various psychomotor, psychometric personality variables, and biographic data. C. Steenkamp (Human Sciences Research Council, Pretoria, South Africa) has been able to replicate this person-related approach with a study on black bus drivers. Scores on an eye-hand-coordination test and 16 PF scores were used to predict driving success with a reasonable degree of certainty.

During the long history of traffic psychology there have been periods in which traffic psychology has had a fruitful influence on contemporary psychology. But traffic psychology is becoming dissociated from the mainstream of contemporary psychology. H. Hacker (University of Wuppertal, Germany) outlined the essentials of the person-situation debate and discussed important repercussions in the field of traffic psychology. The analysis of human behavior in driving a car leads one to consider the complex interaction of the person and the situation during the driving task.

Another impact comes from modern evaluation research. Many improvement programs can demonstrate that the treatments are effective, but it is not known why the intervention strategies are effective. According to Scriven (1980), research on the so-called "intrinsic evaluation" must be increased.

REFERENCES

Brown, I. D. (1979). Can ergonomics improve primary safety in road transport systems? *Ergonomics*, *22*, 109-116.

Häkkinen, S. (1958). *Traffic accidents and driver characteristics*. Helsinki: Finland's Institute of Technology, Scientific Researches No. 13.

Klebelsberg, D. (1982). *Verkehrspsychologie*. Berlin: Springer.

Magnussen, D., & Endler, N. S. (1977). *Personality at the cross-roads: Current issues in interactional psychology*. Hillsdale, N.J.: Lawrence Erlbaum Associates Inc.

Marbe, K. (1935). The psychology of accidents. *Human Factor*, *9*, 100-104.

Marek, J., & Sten, T. (1977). *Traffic environment and the driver*. Springfield, IL : Thomas.

McKenna, F. P. (1982). The human factor in driving accidents: An overview of approaches and problems. *Ergonomics*, *25*, 867-877.

Münsterberg, H. (1912). *Psychologie und Wirtschaftsleben*. Leipzig: Barth.

Näätänen, R., & Summala, H. (1976). *Road-user behavior and traffic accidents*. Amsterdam: North-Holland.

O'Day, J. (1968). Systems analysis and the driver. Driver behavior: Cause and effect. Proceedings of the Second Annual Traffic Safety Research Symposium of the Automobile Insurance Industry, pp. 83-99. Washington DC: Insurance Institute for Highway Safety.

Rothengatter, J. A., & de Bruin, R. A. (1988). *Road user behaviour: Theory and research*. Assen: van Gorcum.

Rumar, K. (1991). Risk behaviour in road traffic. In A. Kuhlmann (Ed.), *Proceedings Weltkongress für Sicherheitswissenschaft. Leben in Sicherheit* (pp. 103-117). Cologne: TÜV Rheinland.

Scriven, M. (1980). *The logic of evaluation.* Point Rayes, CA: Edgepress.

Shinar, D. (1978). *Psychology on the road: The human factor in traffic safety.* New York: Wiley.

Smillie, R. J., & Ayoub, M. A. (1976). Accident causation theories: A simulation approach. *Journal of occupational accidents, 1,* 47-68.

PROBLEMS OF APTITUDE TESTS FOR DRIVERS OF MOTOR VEHICLES

Organizers & Chairpersons:
H. Ohta, Tohoku Institute of Technology, Japan
T. Matsuura, National Research Institute of Police Science, Japan

Contributors:

N. Fukazawa, National Organization for Automotive Safety and Victim's Aid, Japan
Driving aptitude tests today in Japan

K. Ogawa, Osaka University, Japan
Study on norms based on Japanese data which were collected by using the driver aptitude tests device ART-90

C. J. Steenkamp, Human Sciences Research Council, South Africa
Aptitude testing and driver selection

U. Wenninger, B. Bukasa, Austrian Road Safety Board, Austria
Validation study on the relation between computerized traffic psychological tests carried out by means of ART-90 and driving behavior

Discussants: S. Yoshida, Tohoku University, Japan
T. Ishida, Waseda University, Japan

Many types of motor driver aptitude tests have been developed in recent decades. Although the goal of these tests is the same, namely, the reduction of traffic accidents, the ways in which they are used differ according to country and a variety of social factors. In general, tests are used primarily for the purpose of driver selection and driver education. A central purpose of this symposium is to exchange knowledge of how tests are used in various countries and to discuss their applications, functions, and utility. Another important concern is the refinement of the tests themselves. Aptitude tests require a high degree of accuracy in the prediction of drivers' behavior, that is, tests must have both validity and reliability. In recent decades, many studies have been conducted to investigate the relation between accident rate and aptitude test scores. It is, however, difficult to ascertain quantifiable relations clearly.

There could be several reasons for this. For example, different factors other than the psychological ones measured by the tests can be instrumental in driving accidents. By using tests alone, one finds it difficult to predict with certainty whether a driver will cause an accident. Furthermore, accident records may not necessarily be suitable as a dependent variable because traffic accidents occur relatively infrequently. At this symposium four speakers reported on their own research in this area, focusing on validation as well as on the applications, functions, and utility of psychological tests for drivers.

U. Wenninger reported on her study on the relation between computerized traffic psychology tests carried out by means of ART-90 and driving behavior. According to Austrian law, the selection test is required if there are doubts concerning driver reliability in traffic and/or signs of serious deficiencies in visual perception, concentration, reactive capacity, intelligence, or memory.

The traffic aptitude test developed by the Austrian Road Safety Board (ART-90) is administered in the process of driver diagnosis.

Validation studies have been carried out for the purpose of refining this test. In these studies, U. Wenninger and her colleagues investigated correspondences between the traffic psychology test battery and various criteria of driving behavior. One hundred nonvolunteer applicants to whom driver aptitude tests were administered drove for about an hour on a standardized route while being viewed by two observers recording their behavior. Visual perception, concentration, and personality dimensions were examined by means of the ART-90.

Correlation coefficients ranged from .30 to .68. Comparisons of the mean values groups determined according to various criteria of driving behavior showed significant differences in their test results. Regression analysis proved that the test battery covers approximately 2/3 of the variance of the main driving criteria. The validity of performance tests compared to personality tests is essentially higher.

Mr. Ogawa reported on his study on norms based on Japanese data collected by using the driver aptitude test device ART-90. In this research the diverse diagnostic personality and skills tests currently being administered in Japan were discussed, as was his current work on the standardization of the ART-90 for Japanese use.

Aptitude tests in Japan were originally used for driver selection. Accident rates have been employed as a dependent variable in criterion-related validity studies. Many studies have been made to investigate the relationship between drivers' characteristics and accident rates. Three kinds of test are widely used by Japanese driver-training organizations: the Speed Anticipation Test (Maruyama, K., & Kitamura, S. 1961), the Discriminative Reaction Test of Multiple Performance Type (Nagatsuka, Y., & Kitamura, S., 1961) and the personality test. Those who receive low marks on the tests are not only told that they are prone to accidents but are also given specific information regarding problem areas of which they should be aware during actual driving. It is necessary, therefore, to grasp the relation between the test results and actual driving behavior clearly.

Now developing an apparatus which will make it possible to record actual driving behavior under natural circumstances, Maruyama et al. (1975) have been examining the relation between the tests and driving behavior. Nagayama & Renge (1989) have recently developed a test for improving driver risk perception. Fukazawa (1983) also developed a similar type of test. The purpose of these tests is not to identify poor drivers but to educate drivers. In Japan, at present, the aptitude tests are being utilized primarily for driver education.

Steenkamp reported on his study entitled *Aptitude testing and driver selection*. A few decades ago, he noted, emigrants gradually began to move into urban areas in search of a higher standard of living. One of the most popular occupations among the new emigrants was that of professional driver. Signs of a problem common elsewhere in Africa began to be seen. The traffic volume increased drastically. The death rate in the Republic of South Africa rose to more than 24 per 100 million kilometers, exceptionally high by First World standards. Bus and transport companies, research institutes, and the National Road Safety Council began to investigate the possibility of using driver selection techniques, with the aim of reducing accidents.

In this report an aptitude test battery developed by Terre Blanche (1988) was used for a validation study. The study was carried out on 221 bus drivers. The experimental battery existed of a biographical questionnaire, a cognitive aptitude test, an eye-hand coordination test, an accuracy test, a depth-perception test, a reaction test, and two personality tests (16 PF and TAT). The drivers were divided into four groups according to accident rates. Study results revealed that psychological factors, such as intelligence, age, experience, and reaction time, correlated significantly with accident rates.

Mr. Fukazawa reported on his driver improvement program, *Driving aptitude tests today in Japan*. The program has been developed with the aim of enhancing driver risk perception ability. At present, about 60% of the Japanese population is licensed to drive. The improvement of driver education methods is a higher social priority than is research in the area of driver selection. Fukazawa examined test validity in two phases: test scores studied in relation to accident rates, and test scores studied in relation to actual driving behavior, visual search behavior in particular. The correlation coefficient between numbers of accidents and test scores was –.36, indicative of a significant relation between test scores and accidents ($p < .01$). In observations of visual search behavior, the number of drivers turning their attention to various objects, rear-view mirrors, and sideview mirrors was recorded. The results of the regression analysis indicated that the correlation coefficient was $r=0.71$, with a high level of reliability ($p < .05$). Through examination of the effect of education by means of the driver improvement program, it was concluded that it would be possible for any driver to enhance his or her risk perception ability, especially through participation in a program that would enable the person to recognize the need for personal improvement in this area.

After the presentations by four speakers, Mr. Ishida and Mr. Yoshida commented. Ishida raised the issue of sampling distortion and asked about procedures for driving observation.

Yoshida pointed out that more intensive research on construct validity is needed. It is important to know the relation between the three points of the triangle (represented by tests, behavior, and accidents.

REFERENCES

Blanche, T. (1988). Driver Selection. The Construction and Validation of a Computer-based Method. HSRC-Report PERS-426. Pretoria: HSRC.

Fukazawa, N. (1983). *Kiken Kanjusei Sindan Test (TOK)*. Kigyo: Kaihatsu Center. (In Japanese)

Marayuma, K., & Kitamura, S. (1961). Speed Anticipation Test: A Test for discrimination of accident proneness in motor driver. *Tohoku Psychologica Folia, 20*, 13-20.

Maruyama. K., Matsumura, M., Kato, T., & Komatsu, H. (1975). A Driver Recorder of Equipment-Free Type (DREFT) and its application to analysis of Natural Driving Behavior Including Eye Movement. *Tohoku Psychologica Folia, 34*, 110-123.

Nagatsuka, Y., & Kitamura, S. (1961). Discriminative Reaction Test of Multiple Performance Type: A test for discrimination of accident proneness in motor driver. *Tohoku Psychologica Folia, 20*, 21-34.

Nagayama, Y., & Renge, K. (1989) (in Japanese). *Kiken Kanjusei Sindan Test (TOK)*. Kigyo Kaihatsu Center.

TRAFFIC PSYCHOLOGY POSTER CONTRIBUTIONS

GENERIC INTELLIGENT DRIVER SUPPORT (DRIVE PROJECT V1041)

J. A. Michon, University of Groningen, The Netherlands

The Aims of GIDS

Generic Intelligent Driver Support (GIDS) is studied in project V1041 of the DRIVE Program of the European Economic Community. GIDS is bringing together 12 partners from 5 EEC countries and the EFTA country of Sweden.

The stated goal of GIDS project is to determine the requirements and design standards for a class of intelligent co-driver systems that will be maximally consistent with the information requirements and performance capabilities of the human driver. Essential for the GIDS is that it brings together behavioral and technical scientists in an equal effort to design and build an in-vehicle "knowledge refinery" that will filter, integrate, and present information in a way that is tuned to the intentions of the driver under a range of driving conditions.

The Approach of GIDS

In GIDS the question of how intelligent driver support ought to be structured is stated in terms that are consistent with the present state of the art of RTI and behavioral science methodology. The proposed solution embodies a limited, but realistic and important, set of features:

1. Environmental conditions. These have been integrated into a coherent "small world" that allows a driver to negotiate a relevant subset of frequently occurring situations, including a traffic circle, T-junctions, an intersection, and curved roads. The "small world" will guide much of the empirical research in GIDS because it can be implemented in the real world as well as in driving simulator studies and computer simulators.

2. Subsets of the driving task. The entire driving task being far beyond the scope of the present GIDS project; a subset of driving tasks has been selected. They are geared to the constraints imposed by the

"small world," including entering and exiting a traffic circle, turning, merging, negotiating an intersection, following a curve, following a car, and overtaking.

3. Support functions. The support functions to be incorporated into the GIDS prototype derive from the GIDS aim to provide driver support at each of the principal levels at which road users must cope with their task: planning (navigation), maneuvering (obstacle avoidance), and handling (steering and accelerator control). In addition the role of instructional feedback to novice drivers and the effect of some in-vehicle tasks (carrying on a telephone conversation) are studied.

4. System architecture. Functionally, the system architecture consists of an analyst/planner accepting inputs from a series of special purpose applications (sensors), a repertoire of "situations," a data base containing information about the driver, and a dialogue controller that is responsible for scheduling the intersections between the system and the driver.

5. Presentation systems (MMI). The driver will interact with the GIDS system by means of a variety of displays and controls, including voice input and output, touch screen, switches, and intelligent controls (steering wheel and accelerator).

6. Driver characteristics. GIDS systems will have to adapt to various states and traits of drivers. A limited number of driver characteristics will be studied, especially age and driver experience.

The Motivation of the GIDS Consortium

The GIDS concept constitutes an original and innovative step towards the development, implementation, and acceptance of advanced RTI systems. The project is taking great care to ascertain:

1. the generality of the approach, so as to facilitate its application by a broad spectrum of users, including manufacturers and road traffic authorities;

2. the specificity of the approach, culminating in the development of an operational prototype that will demonstrate the essential features of the GIDS concept in a realistic, if limited, environment for a realistic, if limited, set of functions within a realistic time frame set by the present phase of the DRIVE Program;

3. the integrative character of the GIDS design, providing multifunctional support to drivers on the basis of presently available and, supposedly, future driver information systems in a variety of situations; and

4. the complementarity of the project with other, related programs. The GIDS project is special in the sense that it provides an essential

link in research on the interface between humans and machines, pursuing a systems approach with a strong behavioral component.

SIMULATIVE EXPERIMENTS ON THE CONTROL OF BEHAVIOR IN MONOTONOUS AND HASTENED CONDITIONS DURING DRIVING

Yasuhiro Nagatsuka, Niigata University, Niigata, Japan

Drivers are often compelled to be in prolonged and/or hastened situations when driving. They can come to feel monotony, drowsiness, or haste that will lead them to show deteriorations in performance. From the point of view of traffic psychology, it is important to identify the conditions under which these deteriorations are avoided. In the simulation task of a choice reaction (CR) experiment, these conditions cause deteriorations in performance, including delayed choice reaction time (CRT), increase in errors (Es) and an increased coefficient of variation (CV). It was hypothesized that such deterioration will be reduced by active rest (doing a subsidiary task during a rest period between the reactions) and correct motor programming (CMP), that is, a motor set for correct reactions. Two simulation experiments were conducted to examine the hypotheses.

The main task of Experiment 1 was a prolonged CR task lasting 120 min. Ss performed a subsidiary task: uttering their own CRT fed back orally by an experimenter as knowledge of results (KR) at each rest period (interstimulus interval, ISI: 10.5 or 30 sec.). Control Ss performed the main task only. Shortened CRT and smaller CV were found in the experimental group. Few Es arose in both groups.

In Experiment 2, the main task was choice reactions to 3 stimuli under a hastened condition (ISI: 1.5 sec.). Before the main task, Ss made another kind of choice reaction to 2 stimuli for 15 min. The experimental Ss were informed of the correctness of their reactions. To mold CMP, a worsening of Es and CV in the main task were found in the CMP group.

AN ANALYSIS OF CAR-FOLLOWING BEHAVIOR IN DRIVING

Hiroo Ohta, Tohoku Institute of Technology, Sendai, Japan

This study was conducted to determine what factors contribute to individual differences in the driving distance headway. A field experiment was performed with two cars. The experimenter drove the leading car while a subject drove the second car. The following instructions were given to the subjects by 2-way radio at set temporal intervals while driving: (1) "Follow the car ahead at a distance that seems comfortable" (2) "Approach the car ahead until you begin to feel the distance is dangerous." (3) "Follow at a minimum safe distance." (4) "Follow at the distance that you feel to be neither too far nor too near." Each subject carried out the same sequence of instructions at speeds of 50 km/h, 60 km/h and 80 km/h. Subsequent to the field experiment, personality tests and driving attitude tests were administered to each subject.

The main findings were as follows:

1. In each of the four stages, the subject adjusted his distance headway relative to velocity. However, the time headway calculated from the relationship between the velocity and the distance remained constant. This result gives evidence of a generally high level of ability in drivers' time perception.

2. Drivers subjectively feel safe and comfortable even when the distance between themselves and the car ahead is too small to be safe.

3. In some cases, individual differences in distance headway could be associated with personality factors, as evidenced in personality test results. For example, drivers following the car ahead at a short distance tend to be introversive, depressive, and uncooperative.

DRIVING BEHAVIOR OF YOUNG DRIVERS

Satoru Nishiyama and Mieko Fujikawa,
Hiroshima University, Hiroshima, Japan

The purpose of this investigation was to ascertain (a) the percentage of college students possessing a driver's license, (b) the ratio of regular drivers to occasional drivers, (c) men's and women's driving techniques and/or manners, and (d) the attitude of the subjects toward observance of traffic laws, safety awareness, and other aspects of road safety.

On the basis of data gathered from questionnaires completed by 606 college students, we can conclude the following:

1. 93.6% of the men and 45.9% of the women possessed driver's licenses; 67.7% of the subjects were so-called "paper drivers"—those who had a driver's license but did not drive regularly. These facts may account for dangerous driving performance due to lack of experience.

2. The differences between male and female drivers were found as shown in Figure 1.

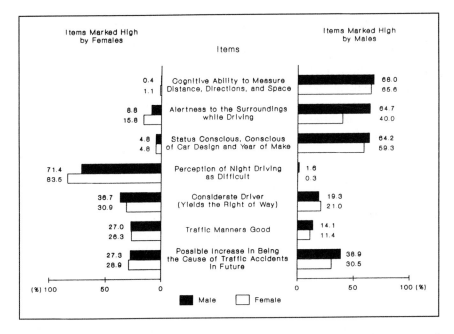

FIG. 1. Differences between male and female drivers: Their driving performance and their strengths and weaknesses

We found the obvious differences between male and female drivers in (a) cognitive ability, (b) attentiveness, and (c) night driving. By contrast, it was difficult to judge whether the percentage among the male and female subjects was high or low in the following items: (a) considerate driver (yield the right of way), (b) good or bad traffic manners, and (c) possible increase in being the cause of traffic accidents in future.

To reduce road accidents, the mentality and/or behavioral traits of young drivers must be recognized and taken into account in many aspects.

WHY ARE OLDER DRIVERS GUILTY PARTIES IN ACCIDENTS?

Liisa Hakamies-Blomqvist, University of Helsinki, Finland

The accident risk of elderly drivers has three characteristics: (a) Elderly drivers have more accidents than younger drivers, (b) accidents in which elderly drivers are involved have more severe consequences than the accidents caused by younger drivers and (c) elderly drivers are more often legally responsible for the causation of the accident (Hakamies-Blomqvist, 1990). Elderly drivers are likely to be involved in accidents because they fail to yield the right-of-way or ignore road signs, especially in complex traffic situations (OECD, 1985). The aim of this study was to see how aspects of the traffic situation that theoretically should complicate the driving task for the elderly are connected to the risk of causing an accident. This was done by comparing key variables of accidents for which older drivers were held responsible and accidents for which they were not held responsible.

The material consisted of 367 in-depth, on-site accident reports filed by the Finnish Multidisciplinary Road Accident Investigation Teams organized by the Traffic Safety Committee of the Insurance Companies, that is, all fatal accidents in Finland from 1975 through 1987 in which one of the drivers involved was 65 years or older. Corresponding accident reports ($n = 1,589$) of drivers aged 26 to 64 years were used as comparison material. The distribution of responsibility and the role of alcohol intoxication in accident causation were calculated for all the material. For the sake of clarity, the comparison was thereafter restricted to vehicle collisions that did not involve alcohol. The chi-square frequency test was used for statistical analysis.

Of all the evaluated accidents the aged drivers had a 79.1% share of driver-attributed responsibility. The traffic situation was the main difference between the accidents for which elderly drivers were held responsible and accidents for which they were not held responsible. The share of guilty drivers was disproportionately high at intersections, especially when left-turning maneuvers were involved. There were no differences in the external circumstances of the accidents, such as time of day, type of road, and light conditions. Guilty and nonguilty drivers were also equally often alcohol-intoxicated.

The risk of being involved in an accident as a guilty party is higher in difficult traffic situations than in comparatively uncomplicated ones, but it is not increased by conditions generally considered risky for older drivers, such as bad light or alcohol intoxication. This observation supports the notion that older drivers are able to compensate for subjectively felt difficulties. Safety measures for elderly drivers should therefore be concentrated on difficulties that cannot be avoided or compensated for. An example would be simplification of the most difficult spots in the traffic environment. Such development would be helpful not only for older drivers but for all road users.

References

Hakamies-Blomqvist, L. (1990). *Deadly collisions of elderly drivers* (in Finnish). General Psychology Monographs No. B 10). Helsinki: University of Helsinki.

OECD (1985). *La sécurité des personnes agées dans la circulation routière.* Rapport préparé pour l'OCDE et l'OMS. Paris.

NEW MALE AND FEMALE DRIVERS' CONCEPTIONS OF RISKS IN TRAFFIC AND OF THEIR OWN DRIVING SKILL JUST AFTER PASSING THE DRIVING TEST

E. Keskinen, M. Hatakka, A. Katila, and S. Laapotti,
University of Turku, Finland

As the first part of a research project for evaluating the effects of the new driver training system in Finland, 82 driving licence applicants answered a questionnaire just after passing the driving test. The questionnaire included four subscales dealing with problem-causing things (16 items); strong and weak components of one's own driving skill (19 items); risks in traffic (13 items); and risks depending on one's own character, habits, and skills (11 items).

The results show that new drivers in general estimate the risks in traffic to be quite low. Males saw fewer risks than females. In addition, males found more strong components in their driving skill than females did in theirs.

This low subjective risk level and overestimation of one's own driving skill is not an ideal attitude to promote safe traffic behavior (Näätänen & Summala, 1976; Finn & Bragg, 1986; Matthews & Moran, 1986).

References

Finn, P., & Bragg, B. (1986). Perception of the risk of an accident by young and older drivers. *Accident Analysis and Prevention, 18,* 289-298.

Matthews, M., & Moran, A. (1986). Age differences in the male driver's perception of traffic risk: The role of perceived driving ability. *Accident Analysis and Prevention, 18,* 299-313.

Näätänen, R., & Summala, H. (1976). *Road User Behavior and Traffic Accidents.* Amsterdam: North-Holland.

AN EXPERIMENTAL VIDEO-ANALYSIS OF DRIVER BEHAVIOR WHILE INTOXICATED

Shinya Yoshida, Tohoku Gakuin University;
Masato Furukawa, Showa Women's University;
Kinya Maruyama, Tohoku University, Sendai, Japan

The purpose of this study is to examine the effects of alcohol on driver behavior using a car equipped with devices with which almost any driving performance, including eye movements, can be videotaped (Maruyama, Matsumara, Kato, Yoshida, & Komatsu, 1975). Six subjects participated in Experiment 1 on two separate days. Their 2 runs while intoxicated in the test course were compared with their 5 sober runs in the equivalent courses and 2 runs on streets. In Experiment 2, 8 subjects completed one run in the test course, after which half of them re-ran the same course while intoxicated. The rest of the subjects re-ran it in the sober condition. The behavioral items used in analyzing the changes were selected with reference to the license test in Japan. The effects of alcohol were inspected by controlled experimental methods and case-study methods.

Behavioral changes that were identified with the effects of alcohol in this study were disadvantageous to driving. The following functional or mental changes were deduced: (a) reduction of attentional fields and/or shortening of cognitive processing, which were inferred when subjects failed to react to exchanged road signs in the test course, (b) impairment of speed control, (c) reduction of motor control, (d) deterioration of memory register, which was inferred when subjects forget what had just been done, (e) production of motor-dominated premature responses, (f) loosening of self-regulation, and (g) loss of objective self-awareness or monitoring functions. Although there were large individual differences among the subjects, each behavioral change was characterized by one of the above functional effects or combination thereof (Yoshida, Kato, Furukawa, & Maruyama, 1984).

References

Maruyama, K., Matsumura, M., Kato, T., Yoshida, S., & Komatsu, H. (1975). A driving recorder of equipment-free type (DREFT) and its application to analysis of natural driving behavior including eye movements. *Tohoku Psychologica Folia, 34*, 110-123.
Yoshida, S., Kato, T., Furukawa, M., & Maruyama, K. (1984). An experimental video-analysis of driver behavior while intoxicated. *Japanese Journal of Applied Psychology, 9*, 1-14. (In Japanese)

THE REACTION TIME VARIABILITY AND THE PERSONALITY TYPE OF ACCIDENT-PRONE DRIVERS

K. Matsunaga, T. Kito, F. Kitamura, K. Shidoji, and T. Yanagida
Department of Psychology, Kyushu University, Hakozaki, Fukuoka,
Japan

It was hypothesized that driving accidents are caused by a combination of an increased fluctuation in reaction time accompanied by insufficient distance between vehicles. Therefore, the differences in reaction-time variability between accident-prone and non-accident-prone drivers were analyzed. In addition, the Yatabe-Guilford (Y-G) Personality Inventory was administered to the drivers.

The measurement system was composed of a personal computer: green (G), yellow (Y), and red (R) light emission diodes (LEDs); and two button switches. Each of the three LEDs was turned on for 3 seconds alternately in random order and at random intervals under a limitation of between 3 and 60 seconds. The G-LED was switched on 20 times, and the Y-LED and R-LED were each switched on 15 times during one session, which lasted for 5 minutes.

Each subject was required to press a button on the right (R-button) with his right forefinger (F-finger) while all the LEDs were turned off and to remove the finger as soon as possible from the R-button when the Y-LED was switched on, or to press a button on the left (L-button), instead of the R-button, as soon as possible when the R-LED was switched on. The time (named R-reaction time) between the Y-LED coming on and the R-button being released, and the time (named L-reaction time) between the R-LED coming on and the L-button being pressed were measured.

Using standard deviations of R- and L-reaction times, and the Y-G components, such as cyclical tendency and lack of cooperativeness (which correlate with high reaction-time variability), and general activity (which correlates with insufficient distance between vehicles, we found that accident-prone drivers (at the rate of 94%) could be significantly separated from non-accident-prone drivers (at the rate of 81%).

TRAIN DRIVERS' ACCIDENT LIABILITY AND SIMPLE CALCULATION TASK PERFORMANCE

Shigeru Haga, Hiroyuki Abiru, and Hiroaki Shiroto,
East Japan Railway Co., Tokyo, Japan

In the Japanese railway industry, train drivers are screened with the Uchida-Kraepelin Test, developed by Yuzo Uchida (1923), in which testees are required to perform simple additions continuously for 30 min with a 5 min break in the middle. Task performance is evaluated based upon the amount of calculation solved every minute; low estimation is given when performance level is low or performance "profile" is bad.

The authors examined the test results of 3,914 train drivers and their accident records for two years, from April 1987 to March 1989. Statistical analyses of the data showed that the accident liability did not differ between the drivers who had scored well on the test and those who had scored poorly.

The outcome was inconsistant with previous studies, most of which confirmed the empirical validity of the test. Factors that might produce the difference in the results were examined, and the effectiveness of the test for accident prevention was discussed.

THE INFLUENCE OF PARKED VEHICLES UPON ACCIDENTS INVOLVING PEDESTRIANS CROSSING THE STREET

Tsuneo Matsuura, National Research Institute of Police Science, Tokyo, Japan

The influence of parked vehicles upon accidents involving pedestrians crossing the street was assessed with accident analysis and computer simulation. First, 263 accidents between crossing pedestrians and vehicles moving straight ahead were classified according to their paths, the presence of parked vehicles, and their positions in relation to the pedestrian. The classification revealed that parked vehicles affected about half of the accidents; the most common accident pattern influenced by parked vehicles was that involving a crossing pedestrian, a parked vehicle on the right-hand side, and a vehicle coming from the right (i.e., type P1 accident).

To establish the factors that intensify the influence of a parked vehicle masking the sight of the pedestrian, an additional 42 accident reports of P1 accidents were analyzed. It was ascertained that the size of the parked vehicle, the pedestrian's height, and the distance between the pedestrian and the parked vehicle were such intensifying factors.

With the intensifying factors as independent variables, computer graphics was used to calculate the greatest distance at which the driver of a moving vehicle could see the pedestrian's head behind a parked vehicle (i.e., discovery distance); the factors substantially increased the distance. Through comparison of the discovery distance and the driver stopping distance, the attempt was made to clarify whether each P1 accident could have been avoided. In many cases the discovery distance had been too short to avoid a collision.

Psychology and Law

EYEWITNESSES, EXPERTS, AND JURORS: Improving the Quality of Jury Decision-making in Eyewitness Cases

Steven D. Penrod,
University of Minnesota, Law School,
Minneapolis, MN, USA
Brian L.Cutler,
Florida International University, USA

In recent years it has been increasingly common for criminal defense attorneys to challenge the reliability of eyewitness identifications by introducing expert psychological testimony concerning problems of eyewitness identification. The acceptance of expert psychological testimony on issues associated with eyewitness memory is a source of heated debate (McCloskey & Egeth, 1983). Much of the debate centers around three issues raised by lawyers and psychologists who oppose the introduction of expert eyewitness testimony: (a) Is there an adequate scientific base of knowledge upon which to base expert testimony; (b) Is psychological knowledge about eyewitness memory beyond the ken of the jury; and (c) What are the effects of expert psychological testimony on jury decision-making? In this essay we report the results of several studies we and our colleagues have conducted in an effort to answer these questions.

THE QUALITY OF THE RESEARCH ON
WHICH EXPERT TESTIMONY IS BASED

Some psychologists doubt that the existing body of research and theory on human memory is sufficient to draw valid conclusions about eyewitness memory (Konecni & Ebbesen, 1986; McCloskey, Egeth, & McKenna, 1986). The primary issues raised by these psychologists are that the body of scientific research examining eyewitness reliability is not sufficiently large to provide a basis for scientific conclusions; that there is disagreement among psychologists about memory processes and about the consistency of the research findings; and that the research techniques and subject populations used (i.e., college undergraduates) do not justify generalization of the findings to actual crime settings.

Of course the consistency of research findings and the extent to which memory and eyewitness testimony research generalizes to actual criminal cases are ultimately empirical questions. One way to examine the consistency and coherence of the research findings is to use existing research as a data base for further, secondary study. Shapiro and Penrod (1986), for example, conducted a quantitative "meta-analysis" of 128 eyewitness identification and facial recognition studies, involving 960 experimental conditions and 16,950 subjects. Two analytic techniques were employed. The first was an "effect size" analysis, which combined the effect sizes of eyewitness factors across studies in which a particular factor was manipulated. An effect size (indexed by d) reflects the magnitude of differences between two means (e.g., the mean correct identification rate for male witnesses versus the mean rate for female witnesses) in terms of the number of standard deviations separating their means. A d of zero would indicate that two means are identical, while a d of .3 (or –.3) would indicate a difference in means that, in the context of this study, is worthy of note.

The variables examined included such eyewitness factors as context reinstatement (efforts to mentally reinstate the conditions under which observations were originally made), transformations in the appearance of faces (such as disguises and changes in pose), depth of processing strategies (the memorial strategies employed by witnesses during the original viewing), target distinctiveness, exposure time, cross-racial identification, the length of the retention interval, and a number of others. Shapiro and Penrod (1986) found that many variables operating at the encoding and retrieval stages did, in fact, produce significant and sometimes substantial effects on performance (see Table 1, which summarizes the impact of factors on correct identification rates). These variables had typically been examined in a half-dozen or more separate studies, and in one instance, 29 studies involving nearly 1,800 subjects.

TABLE 1
Manipulated Variables

Variable	Studies	S's	d	SD	D	Z	P
				Hits			
Context reinstatement (yes vs no)	23	1684	1.91	1.87	1.39	17.54	***
Subject age (young vs old)	9	603	1.10	0.68	0.78	13.34	***
Transformation (none vs disguise)	19	2682	1.05	0.83	0.67	13.46	***
Face was associated with rich vs poor elaboration at exposure	10	362	1.00	0.67	0.98	8.15	***
Encoding instructions (high vs low)	29	1868	0.97	1.32	0.63	9.87	***
Target distinctiveness (high vs low)	22	2174	0.76	0.79	0.67	12.53	***
Exposure time at study time (long vs short)	8	990	0.61	0.74	0.38	4.48	***
Same vs cross race identification	17	1571	0.53	0.56	0.40	6.99	***
Pose at study (¾ vs front or profile)	10	1266	0.53	0.87	0.30	5.37	***
Mode of presentation at study time (live or videotape vs still)	5	896	0.50	0.80	0.18	3.92	**
Retention interval (short vs long)	18	1980	0.43	0.61	0.27	8.03	***
Race of target (white vs minority: black or oriental)	18	1894	0.24	0.55	0.10	2.05	*
Training in facial recognitions (yes vs no)	8	534	0.18	0.58	0.08	0.54	ns
Same vs cross sex identification	13	1197	0.14	0.19	0.23	3.18	***
Knowledge of recognition task	5	703	0.10	0.12	0.05	0.42	ns
Mode of presentation at recognition phase (live or video vs still)	13	1807	0.07	0.28	0.14	3.13	*
Sex of target (male vs female)	19	2052	0.02	0.38	−0.08	1.88	ns
Grand means for entire data set	443	44301	0.47	0.85	0.32	25.57	

* < 0.05   ** < 0.001   *** < 0.0001

Shapiro and Penrod's second analytic method was a "study characteristics" analysis, which integrated the results from all studies to examine the influence of study characteristics (the techniques, settings, and experimental conditions under which the studies were conducted) on performance. For these analyses the identification conditions of more than 950 experimental cells (involving more than 16,000 subjects) were coded for analysis. In brief, Shapiro and Penrod (1986) found that almost all study characteristics accounted for statistically significant portions of variance in eyewitness performance.

In all, eleven sets of variables accounted for a highly significant (and, one could easily argue, a forensically significant) 47% of the variance in hit rates.

It was especially noteworthy that, after the effects of study characteristics had been controlled for, a variable that reflected whether a study was a laboratory or a field study accounted for only 3% of the variance in performance. In contrast, when considered separately, study type had accounted for 35% of the variance. This result underscores that the laboratory/field distinction is almost entirely confounded with variables that systematically predict identification performance—indeed, nearly 75% of the variance in laboratory versus field study outcomes could be accounted for by variables measuring attention, knowledge about the identification task, mode of presentation targets, exposure time, number of targets studies, and target race. Stated another way, the argument that laboratory results may not generalize to performance under naturalistic conditions is substantially weakened by these results. Furthermore, the variables that account for laboratory versus field differences also mirror natural variations in witnessing and identification conditions that exist in real-world eyewitness situations. Laboratory, field, and real eyewitness situations all vary along dimensions such as focus of witness attention, load at study and recognition, opportunity to view, and same- versus cross-race identifications. Knowledge about the effects of these variations on eyewitness performance should, in principle, be of value to anyone (police, district attorneys, judges, jurors, and psychologists) trying to evaluate the reliability of an identification made under a particular set of circumstances.

LEGAL ISSUES CONCERNING EXPERT TESTIMONY

That mistaken identifications occur, when considered alone, is not necessarily troublesome (insofar as the identification procedures were fair). Mistakes are worrisome, however, when juries convict defendants on the basis of erroneous identifications. The criminal justice system is designed, in theory, to provide safeguards against mistaken identifications—safeguards such as exclusion of eyewitness identification evidence in some instances in which counsel is absent from the identification proceeding, rigorous cross-examination of identifying witnesses, and the use of instructions to the jury on factors they should consider when evaluating eyewitness identification. However, from a psychological perspective, serious questions can be raised about the effectiveness of traditional safeguards.

As noted earlier, defense attorneys now seek to supplement these traditional safeguards with expert psychological testimony. A central proposition used to support the admissibility of expert psychological testimony is that jurors are not fully sensitive to the factors that influence eyewitness memory. Lack of sensitivity, in this context, refers to: (a) poor knowledge about factors that influences memory and (b) the inability to integrate or use that knowledge when making an inference or judgment about eyewitness accuracy. If jurors are not adequately sensitive to factors that influence the accuracy of eyewitness identifications, they cannot effectively evaluate eyewitness evidence. Opponents of expert testimony doubt that jurors need or will benefit from expert testimony.

JUROR SENSITIVITY TO EYEWITNESS EVIDENCE

Do laypersons effectively use identification evidence such as witnessing factors and identification procedures to draw appropriate inferences about the accuracy of identifications? A few studies have addressed this question. These studies generally use one of three methodologies: a multiple-choice questionnaire method in which laypersons are queried about factors that influence eyewitness memory (e.g., Deffenbacher & Loftus, 1982), a prediction method in which the witnessing conditions of an eyewitness experiment are described to the subject and the subject predicts the identification accuracy-rates (e.g., Brigham & Bothwell, 1983), and a mock-jury method in which mock-juries (or jurors) try a case involving eyewitness evidence (e.g., Lindsay, Wells, & Rumpel, 1981). While each methodology has its advantages and disadvantages, the studies have converged on the conclusion that empirical findings are often inconsistent with lay-knowledge of and assumptions about factors that influence the accuracy of eyewitness identification—particularly with respect to eyewitness confidence. These findings led Wells (1984) to recommend that "the lay person, as trier of fact, be counseled on these matters."

Even though previous research has yielded consistent findings, most studies can be criticized on the grounds that subjects have not actually been called upon to evaluate eyewitness testimony. The extent of the impact of eyewitnessing factors on jurors' inferences can be better estimated by simultaneously examining the effects of multiple witnessing factors and by closely approximating actual criminal cases—that is, by increasing the external validity of the experiment. In a series of studies (Cutler, Penrod, & Dexter, 1989, 1990; Cutler, Penrod, & Stuve, 1988), we have investigated the juror's use of eyewitness evidence. The primary concern of these experiments was to examine the lay person's knowledge about and critical consideration of the variables that influence eyewitness memory, and the lay person's belief in or skepticism about eyewitness memory *per se*.

Methods

Undergraduate and experienced jurors served as subjects in Cutler et al. (1990) and Cutler et al. (1988). These mock jurors viewed a videotaped trial of a defendant accused of the armed robbery of a liquor store. The videotaped trial lasted approximately 45 minutes and conformed to the format of an actual trial. To maximize the realism of the videotaped trial, practicing trial attorneys assumed the roles of attorneys.

The primary source of evidence in the trial was the positive identification of the defendant by the victim of the robbery. The victim was the first trial witness. She testified about the witnessing conditions and the conditions under which she identified the defendant as the robber. The second witness was the police officer, who testified about the conditions under which the identification was made. The third witness was a character witness for the defendant. The fourth witness was the defendant, who denied all allegations.

Approximately 20 witness and identification factors were discussed in the trial, all of which surface in the examination and cross-examination of the first two witnesses. Ten of these variables were systematically manipulated in a complex factorial design. The ten manipulated factors were all presented in high versus low forms: perpetrator disguise (i.e., the perpetrator was either disguised or not disguised); a weapon used or not; the robbery was violent or not; there was a long or short retention interval between the crime and the identification; mugshots were searched by the victim or not; biased versus unbiased line-up instructions were given to the witness; large or small line-ups were used; voice samples were given to the victim or not; the witness was 80% versus 100% confident about her identification. The manipulated variables were chosen because of their forensic relevance and their demonstrated varying effects on identification accuracy. Testimony was also offered about additional factors, but these were held constant across experimental conditions. For example, the witness testified that she was able to view the robber for approximately 90 seconds (the duration of the robbery).

Results

The major dependent measures included verdicts, estimates of the probability that the eyewitness identification was correct, and the strength of the prosecution and defense cases. In addition, subjects rated the probability that the average person could make a correct identification given the circumstances described. A set of free recall questions tested subjects' memories for the testimony and eyewitnessing conditions.

Results indicated, first, that jurors remembered the evidence quite well—in particular, recall of the witnessing conditions was generally over 90% accurate. However, despite the excellent recall, none of the variations in eyewitnessing conditions had a significant effect on student juror's verdicts or assessments or the accuracy of the eyewitness identification. Overall, only witness confidence influenced verdicts—54% of jurors convicted if the eyewitness was 100% confident compared to 39% convictions if the witness was 80% confident. Estimates of the probability that the identification were correct were 69% and 60%, respectively.

Experienced jurors and undergraduates differed only minimally in their assessment of trial evidence. Among experienced jurors, weapon presence did have an appreciable effect on probability ratings and on verdicts, with the former being statistically significant. This effect, though, was not in the expected direction. These jurors were more likely to find the identification correct (66%) and to convict (46%) in the weapon-present condition than the weapon-hidden condition (54% and 30%, respectively). Also, experienced jurors in the mugshot-search condition gave significantly lower probability ratings ($d = .39$) and (nonsignificantly) fewer guilty verdicts ($d = .25$) than jurors in the no-mugshot-search condition.

Although these experiments represent a substantial step toward greater external validity, they still support the conclusion of previous, less externally valid research. Of the ten factors that were manipulated, only one, witness confidence, had a consistent, statistically significant, and substantial effect on subjects' perceived probability that the identification was correct, and on verdict. The finding that witness confidence predicted verdict and probability ratings was expected, given previous similar findings (Bothwell, Deffenbacher, & Brigham, 1987). Factors that have been shown to affect identification accuracy—such as disguise—had trivial effects on probability ratings and on verdicts.

It is crucial to note that in our manipulation checks subjects demonstrated superior memory for the manipulated variables. There is little doubt that subjects attended to and understood this evidence during the trial, but they basically did not use the information when making judgments about the accuracy of the identification, culpability of the defendant, strength of the prosecution's and defense's case, or credibility of the witness. We also found no evidence to support the proposition that juror's take witnessing factors into consideration if the witness is less confident but not if the witness is highly confident.

Most important, the findings lend support to the argument that jurors *may* benefit from expert psychological testimony about factors that influence eyewitness performance.

THE EFFECTS OF EXPERT'S TESTIMONY ON THE JURY

Commentators have offered a variety of hypotheses about the effects that expert testimony on eyewitness issues may have on jurors. Proponents of eyewitness testimony argue that expert testimony will serve precisely the function envisioned in Federal Rule of Evidence (FRE) 702 in that it "will assist the trier of fact to understand the evidence (and) or to determine a fact in issue." In light of the earlier discussion of research showing that jurors appear to be insensitive to probative evidence concerning the impact of eyewitnessing factors on eyewitness performance, this hypothesis suggests that expert testimony will *sensitize* jurors to the effects of various factors on eyewitness performance and enable them to evaluate evidence more effectively. Clearly this would be a desirable effect. Sensitivity refers both to the knowledge of how a given factor influences eyewitness memory and the ability to render decisions in accordance with that knowledge. For example, a juror might know or believe that disguise makes it more difficult for a witness to identify a perpetrator but may fail to make use of the knowledge/belief when actually assessing the accuracy of an identification. This juror might be described as knowledgeable but possessing poor integration skills.

Critics of eyewitness expert testimony sometimes argue that expert testimony will either have no effect on jurors and will therefore be a waste of time or, if there is an effect, the testimony will simply *confuse* jurors and make it difficult for them to sort out and evaluate the evidence: "there is always the possibility that the testimony will affect the jury in some unanticipated and undesirable way. Jurors may misinterpret, overgeneralize, or misapply the information presented by the psychologist, and so may come to unwarranted conclusions" (McCloskey, Egeth, & McKenna, 1986, p. 6).

Clearly it is possible that expert testimony will have no effect on the judgments of jurors. Though pessimistic, this hypothesis is reasonable in light of research indicating that jurors have difficulty in understanding and evaluating mathematical and statistical evidence (Thompson & Schuman, 1987). Similarly, jurors are known to draw inappropriate inferences in trials in which multiple, loosely-related charges against a defendant are joined (Tanford & Penrod, 1984).

Critics of eyewitness expert testimony also argue that expert testimony may be prejudicial because it will simply induce *skepticism* about eyewitness testimony generally. They contend the testimony will induce jurors to give insufficient and therefore inappropriate weight to such testimony. Woocher (1986) observed that: "[the] experimental psychologist's impressive credentials might lead the jury to rely too heavily on her opinion and therefore undervalue the weight of the eyewitness evidence". Though it is agreed that improved juror sensitivity is a desirable effect of expert testimony, there is considerable disagreement as to whether jurors should be made more skeptical of the accuracy of eyewitness identifications. Some argue that jurors place too much weight on identification evidence (Loftus, 1986), whereas others point out that there is little evidence in support of that claim (McCloskey & Egeth, 1983).

RESEARCH ON EXPERT PSYCHOLOGICAL TESTIMONY

It is possible to examine skepticism and sensitization effects independently, and it is possible to detect juror confusion as well. Unfortunately, the procedures designed to test the effects of expert testimony in previous jury simulation research have confounded skepticism and sensitization effects and thus made it quite difficult to determine exactly how jurors are affected by expert testimony. For example, in a study of expert testimony effects, Wells, Lindsay, and Tousignant (1980) found a main effect for expert testimony such that jurors who heard expert testimony were less likely to believe the eyewitnesses than jurors who heard no expert testimony. There was also a main effect for witness condition indicating that jurors were somewhat sensitive to the witnessing conditions. Though there was a trend toward improved sensitivity with expert testimony, the interaction term was not statistically significant. Thus, the study yielded a skepticism effect and a nonsignificant sensitizing effect.

In Loftus's (1980) mock-jury study, expert testimony significantly reduced the number of convictions, and, in direct contradiction to the eyewitness research findings, violence of the crime increased the number of convictions. The trend toward increased convictions associated with the violent crime was weakened by the expert testimony, though the interaction term was not tested for statistical significance. These findings suggest that the expert testimony produced some sensitization.

Hosch, Beck, and McIntyre (1980) exposed subjects to a videotaped trial and manipulated the presence of expert testimony. Juries who heard the expert testimony rated the identification as significantly less important to reaching a verdict than did juries who did not hear expert testimony. Maass, Brigham, and West (1985) examined the impact of several forms of expert testimony on jurors' perceptions of the defendant's guilt. Expert testimony led to more lenient pre- and post-deliberation judgments.

Fox and Walters (1986) exposed undergraduates to videotaped segments of eyewitness testimony and expert testimony. The witness expressed either high or low confidence. Three conditions of expert testimony were tested. In all expert testimony conditions, the expert psychologist discussed the weak relationship between confidence and accuracy. Results showed that jurors who heard expert testimony were significantly less likely to believe the witness than were jurors who did not hear expert testimony. A main effect was also found for witness confidence. There was no trend toward improved sensitivity to the weak confidence-accuracy relationship associated with expert testimony.

These studies indicate belief of eyewitnesses is reduced and fewer convictions are obtained if expert testimony is presented. However, it is not clear whether this reduced belief is due to skepticism (which it may appear to be on first examination), to improved sensitivity to factors that might have impaired the witness's ability to make a correct identification, or to both. Fox and Walters, 1986; Hosch, Beck, and McIntyre, 1980; Maass, Brigham, and West, 1985; and Katzev and Wishart (1985) did not independently vary the presence of expert testimony *and* witnessing and identification factors that would influence eyewitness performance. Therefore, skepticism and sensitivity are perfectly confounded. Fox and Walters (1986) did vary the presence of expert testimony and eyewitness confidence simultaneously, but there was no substantial improvement in juror sensitivity to the weak relationship between confidence and identification accuracy.

The only experiments that simultaneously and independently varied witnessing factors that influence identification accuracy and the presence of expert testimony were those by Loftus (1980) and Wells, Lindsay, and Tousignant (1980) and both studies showed trends (albeit weak ones) toward improved sensitivity. Unfortunately, the two studies were weak in realism and external validity. Another problem with this general body of research is that the choice of dependent measures is unsystematic. None of the experiments attempted to determine whether jurors remembered the eyewitness testimony and the expert testimony. Furthermore, in experiments in which sensitivity and skepticism effects were not confounded, expert testimony had weak effects on juror sensitivity. Expert testimony may have improved juror knowledge about memorial processes and the factors that influence memory, but the effect might have been attenuated because of poor integration skills. These experiments did not attempt to assess knowledge and integration separately.

ASSESSING THE EFFECTS OF EXPERT PSYCHOLOGICAL TESTIMONY

In light of existing research, the concerns over the effects of expert testimony are valid but speculative. The next study in our series (Cutler et al., 1989) explored in detail the influence of expert testimony on the cognitive process of jurors in an effort to disentangle the effects of expert testimony.

Method

Cutler et al. (1989) improved on earlier experiments in a variety of ways. First, witnessing and identification conditions, witness confidence, and the presence of expert testimony were varied orthogonally, which allowed for independent tests of sensitivity and skepticism. Second, the study reflects Well's (1984) recognition that it is important to examine the influence of expert testimony on variables in addition to final (or predeliberation) verdict: "There are other effects . . . such as the effect of expert testimony on the *process* by which jurors reach a verdict. . ." To determine the stage(s) at which expert testimony has effects on juror sensitivity, Cutler et al. (1989) explored juror memory, knowledge, inference, and decision-making.

In that study we used 538 undergraduate subjects who saw the same trial materials seen by the subjects in the earlier studies, except that expert psychological testimony was introduced. The expert testimony proceeded as follows. First, the witness's expertise was established, and the judge explained to the jury that the expert was qualified at a previous hearing. Next, the expert described to the jury the case-relevant documents that he had studied before the trial. Then, in full accord with FRE 702, the expert testified about the reconstructive nature of memory and the factors that affect memory at the perception, encoding, storage, and retrieval stages. In response to the defense attorney's question, the expert discussed how the factors of the crime and of the identification procedure might have influenced the witness's memory for the perpetrator. In all trials the expert discussed the effects of stress and violence, the presence of a weapon, the passage of time, suggestive lineup procedures, and the relation between confidence and identification accuracy. The expert discussed the effects of disguises only in trials in which the witness testified that the robber was disguised during the robbery.Immediately after the defense's examination of the expert, the prosecution mounted a rigorous cross-examination. Both direct and cross-examination were based on actual trial testimony.

Four factors, each having two levels, were manipulated: witnessing and identification conditions (WIC), witness confidence, the form of testimony, and whether or not the expert gave an opinion about the likelihood that the witness's identification of the perpetrator was correct (lack of space prevents discussion of the latter two factors in this paper). In view of the established findings that jurors are insensitive to the factors that influence eyewitness identification accuracy, several factors were combined to form a powerful manipulation of WIC. In the "poor WIC" the witness and the police officer offered the testimony associated with the disguise, weapon-present, 14-day-retention-interval, and suggestive-lineup instruction conditions. In the "good WIC" the witness and the police officer offered testimony associated with the no-disguise, weapon-hidden, two-day-retention-interval, and neutral-lineup instruction condition.

As in the earlier studies, the witness's confidence in the accuracy of her identification was varied. In half of the trials, the witness testified that she was 80% confident; in the other half, she testified that she was 100% confident.

The orthogonal manipulation of expert testimony, confidence, and WIC allowed independent tests of sensitization effects and skepticism effects. A skepticism effect would appear as a main effect for expert testimony such that jurors would be less likely to believe the identification if there is expert testimony than if there is no expert testimony. A sensitization effect would emerge as a statistical interaction between WIC and expert testimony or between witness confidence and expert testimony. This interaction would show that WIC are more predictive of jurors' judgments if there was expert testimony than if there was no expert testimony. Witness confidence, on the other hand, would show a stronger relationship with jurors' judgments if there was no expert testimony than if there was expert testimony.

The dependent measures addressed four domains of interest. *Memory* for the witnessing conditions and for the expert testimony (for those who viewed expert testimony) was assessed. Jurors were asked to recall the four stages of memory. *Knowledge* about the effects of witnessing factors was assessed. For factors manipulated and held constant, jurors rated the extent to which the factor was likely to contribute to a correct identification in the specific case they were deciding and in eyewitness cases in general. To obtain measures of the jurors' *inferences* drawn from the eyewitness evidence, subjects rated the credibility of the eyewitness and the strength of the cases as argued by the prosecution and the defense. Also assessed were *decisions* about verdict and ratings of the probability that the defendant committed the crime, the probability that the witness correctly identified the robber, and the probability that the average person could make a correct identification under the circumstances.

Assessments of juror memory, knowledge, inference, and decision-making were designed to ascertain the point in the inferential chain where jurors go awry in evaluating eyewitness evidence. Is it that jurors do not remember the evidence, that jurors do not think the evidence is important, or that jurors fail to integrate effectively the information in their inferences or judgments? The answer to this question might vary as a function of the factors being examined. It was clear from the previous experiments that jurors, for the most part, recall the evidence and that the evidence does not influence their judgments. It might be that some factors are believed to be unimportant. Other factors might be viewed as important but are not given sufficient weight to be reflected in the jurors' judgments.

Results

As in the earlier studies, jurors demonstrated superior memory for the evidence surrounding the crime and the identification. This finding indicates that memory cannot be blamed for any lack of effects for WIC on jurors' judgments. In light of the high recall rates, it is also probably the case that expert testimony does little to improve memory, as there is little room for improvement. Overall memory for the expert testimony was also very good, although over half the subjects incorrectly reported that the expert discussed mugshot searches and the effects of the size of the lineup. This latter finding suggests there was an appreciable response bias toward reporting that the expert discussed a given factor, although accuracy-rates were much higher for factors actually discussed by the expert.

WIC, witness confidence, and the various forms of expert testimony were examined for their influences on juror knowledge, inference, and decisions. Analyses centered on how expert testimony (collapsed across form of expert testimony and expert opinion) influenced juror knowledge, inference, and decision-making, as compared to the control group.

In discussing the results of this study we again make extensive use of d, a standardized measure of effect sizes. A d of zero would indicate that two means are identical, while a d of .3 (or –.3) would indicate a difference in means that, in the context of this study, is worthy of note.

Juror Knowledge

Juror knowledge refers to the juror's view of how an eyewitness factor influences identification accuracy. Consider, for instance, the ratings for the role of disguise. If jurors in both the good and poor WIC conditions rated the impact of disguise as 5 on a 9-point scale anchored at one end by "produces false identifications" and at the other end by "produces correct identifications" this would indicate that jurors failed to recognize a differential impact of disguise on identification accuracy. If juror knowledge was improved by expert testimony we would expect to see ratings of impact to spread apart in the good and poor WIC conditions. Similar spreading might also be observed in the ratings of the effects of weapon visibility, retention interval, or lineup fairness and a narrowing of differences in the ratings of the impact of witness confidence.

In fact, the WIC manipulation had a large effect on ratings of the role of *disguise* (d = 2.30), indicating that jurors were well aware that disguises affect identification accuracy. It is therefore not surprising that expert testimony did not improve juror knowledge for the effects of disguise (i.e., all interaction terms were statistically nonsignificant).

WIC had a trivial and nonsignificant main effect on weapon visibility ratings (d = .13), indicating that jurors were unaware of the effects of weapon focus on identification accuracy. But, WIC had a larger effect on weapon visibility ratings among jurors who had heard expert testimony (d = .41) than among jurors who had heard no expert testimony (d = –.03). This finding indicates that expert testimony improved juror knowledge for the effects of weapon focus.

WIC had a large effect on the knowledge ratings for retention interval (d = .78), indicating that subjects were aware that person recognition accuracy declines over time. WIC also produced a large main effect on ratings of importance of lineup instructions (d = 1.70), indicating that jurors considered lineup instructions to be important in assessing identification accuracy. Even though jurors were aware of the effects of lineup instructions, one form of expert testimony improved juror knowledge in comparison to the other (d = 2.22 and 1.39, respectively).

Witness confidence had an appreciable main effect on knowledge ratings for witness confidence (d = .72), indicating that jurors believed confidence is a good predictor of identification accuracy. Confidence was viewed as less relevant among jurors who had heard expert testimony ($d = .52$) than among jurors who had heard no expert testimony ($d = .84$).

These analyses show that jurors believed that disguise, retention interval, and lineup instructions all have appreciable effects on identification accuracy, but jurors were unaware of the effects associated with weapon visibility. As in previous experiments, jurors felt that witness confidence was an important determinant of identification accuracy. The presence of expert testimony improved juror knowledge of the effects of weapon visibility, lineup fairness, and witness confidence. Of course, knowledge of these factors is no guarantee that the knowledge will be successfully employed when making inferences and judgments.

Juror Inferences

Inferences refer to the juror's perceptions of the credibility of the eyewitness and the strengths of the prosecution's and defense's cases. Ratings of credibility varied directly with the witness's confidence level ($d = .37$), but confidence was given less weight in determining witness credibility if the expert testified ($d = .11$) than if no expert testified ($d = .52$). WIC also affected eyewitness credibility ratings to a greater extent if the expert testified ($d = .34$) than if no expert testified ($d = -.01$), indicating that expert testimony improved juror sensitivity to WIC effects.

The prosecution's case was perceived as stronger in the good WIC ($d = .30$), but WIC had more of an effect on the perceived strength of the prosecution's case if the expert testified ($d = .54$) than if no expert testified ($d = .15$). The prosecution's case was perceived as stronger if the witness was 100% confident ($d = .20$). The defense case was perceived as stronger in the poor WIC ($d = -.30$) and if the expert testified ($d = .23$). WIC had a stronger influence on ratings of the strength of the defense's case if the expert testified ($d = -.53$) than if no expert testified ($d = -.13$).

In sum, although jurors indicated that they believed several of the factors included in the WIC manipulation would influence eyewitness performance, without expert testimony, WIC had negligible effects on juror inferences. When the expert testified, however, jurors demonstrated significant sensitivity to WIC when drawing inferences about the credibility of the eyewitness and about the strength of the prosecution's and defense's cases. The presence of expert testimony also reduced juror's heavy reliance on witness confidence. The presence of expert testimony also increased the apparent strength of the defense's case but did not increase juror skepticism about the eyewitness's credibility.

Juror Decision-Making

WIC had an appreciable effect on jurors' judgments about the accuracy of the identification (d = .30). Jurors were more likely to judge the identification accurate in the good WIC rather than in the poor WIC. However, WIC had a large influence on jurors' judgments if the expert testified (d = .53) but a negligible effect if no expert testified (d = .12). Expert testimony produced trivial main effects on probability ratings. Thus, there was no evidence for a skepticism effect.

WIC had a main effect on verdict such that more convictions were obtained with good WIC (d = .29). Once again, WIC had a stronger influence on verdicts if the expert gave testimony (d = .37) than if no expert testified (d = .20). Expert testimony and form of expert testimony produced trivial main effects on verdicts, again indicating no skepticism effect.

The Problem of Knowledge versus Integration

It is clear from the above analyses that jurors do indeed possess some knowledge of the effects of disguise, retention interval, and suggestive lineup instructions. However, jurors are unaware of the influence of weapon visibility and are unaware that confidence is not a powerful predictor of identification accuracy. Thus, poor knowledge is partly responsible for the lack of juror sensitivity. Evidence for problems of integration skills emerges from the findings that WIC, without expert testimony, had a trivial influence on inferences and decisions (all d's were no greater than .20). Thus, it is both lack of appropriate knowledge and poor integration skills that jointly contribute to produce poor juror sensitivity to eyewitness evidence.

This experiment indicates that expert testimony improved juror knowledge. Expert testimony increased the juror reliance on witnessing and identification conditions and reduced the reliance of jurors on witness confidence when they draw inferences about the credibility of the eyewitness and the strength of the prosecution's case. There was no evidence to suggest that expert testimony promotes skepticism toward the eyewitness's credibility, the accuracy of the identification, or the defendant's culpability (all d's were less than .10).

SUMMARY AND CONCLUSIONS

Proponents and opponents of expert testimony disagree over (1) whether there exists an adequate scientific foundation for the presentation of such testimony, (2) whether the evidence provided by the expert is beyond the ken of the jury, and (3) whether expert testimony is likely to improve jury decision-making. We have reported a series of studies designed to examine these three issues empirically.

The first study was a quantitative "meta-analysis" of a large body of experiments conducted by researchers interested in facial recognition performance. This study indicated that factors investigated by researchers have substantial and reliable effects on eyewitness performance and that experimental laboratory findings do not differ significantly from findings produced in field settings.

In a second set of studies mock jurors were shown realistic videotaped criminal trials in which the primary evidence was the identification of the defendant by an eyewitness. The evidence surrounding the crime (e.g., the disguise of the perpetrator, the extent to which the witness was threatened) and the identification procedures (e.g., the time delay between the crime and the identification, the procedures used to construct and conduct the lineup parade) were manipulated via the testimony of the eyewitness and the police officer in charge of the investigation. These studies examined the extent to which juror decisions were influenced by the variations in the crime and the identification. The studies indicate that jurors were uninfluenced by the factors that normally influence identification accuracy—with the exception that judgments were influenced by the confidence of the eyewitness. Unfortunately, a number of studies indicate that confidence is only weakly related to the accuracy of the identifications.

In the third set of studies the videotaped trials included expert psychological testimony. In the first study of this set, expert testimony improved the sensitivity of jurors to eyewitness evidence. If expert testimony was presented, jurors took the witnessing and identification factors into consideration to a greater extent, and the confidence of the witness to a lesser extent, than if no expert testimony was presented. The study also showed that expert psychological testimony did not increase juror skepticism about eyewitness evidence.

Overall, these studies indicate that expert psychological testimony can improve jury decision-making by assisting jurors in the task of appropriately evaluating eyewitness evidence and that the improvements in juror sensitivity can be secured without increasing juror skepticism.

ACKNOWLEDGMENTS

Much of the research described here was supported by National Science Foundation grant SES-8411721 to Steve Penrod.

REFERENCES

Bothwell, R. K., Deffenbacher, K. A., & Brigham, J. C. (1987). Correlation of eyewitness accuracy and confidence: Optimality hypothesis revised. *Journal of Applied Psychology, 72*, 691-695.

Brigham, J. C., & Bothwell, R. K. (1983). The ability of prospective jurors to estimate the accuracy of eyewitness identifications. *Law and Human Behavior, 1*, 19-30.

Cutler, B. L., Penrod, S. D., & Dexter, H. R. (1989). The eyewitness, the expert psychologist, and the jury. *Law and Human Behavior, 13*, 311-332.

Cutler, B. L., Penrod, S. D., & Dexter, H. R. (1990). *Juror sensitivity to eyewitness identification evidence, 14*, 185-191.

Cutler, B. L., Penrod, S. D., & Stuve, T. E. (1988). Juror decisionmaking in eyewitness identification cases. *Law and Human Behavior, 12*, 41-55.

Deffenbacher, K.A. & Loftus, E.F. (1982). Do jurors share a common understanding concerning eyewitness behavior? *Law and Human Behavior, 6*, 15-30.

Fox, S. G., & Walters, H. A. (1986). The impact of general versus specific expert testimony and eyewitness confidence upon mock juror judgment. *Law and Human Behavior, 10*, 215-228.

Hosch, H. M., Beck, E. L., & McIntyre, P. (1980). Influence of expert testimony regarding eyewitness accuracy on jury decisions. *Law and Human Behavior, 4*, 287-296.

Katzev, R. D., & Wishart, S. S. (1985). The impact of judicial commentary concerning eyewitness identifications on jury decision making. *The Journal of Criminal Law and Criminology, 76*, 733-745.

Konecni, V. J., & Ebbesen, E. B. (1986). Courtroom testimony by psychologists on eyewitness identification issues: Critical notes and reflections, *Law and Human Behavior, 10*, 117-126.

Lindsay, R. C. L., Wells, G. L., & Rumpel, C. M. (1981). Can people detect eyewitness identification accuracy within and across situations? *Journal of Applied Psychology, 66*, 79-89.

Loftus, E. F. (1980). Impact of expert psychological testimony on the unreliability of eyewitness identification. *Journal of Applied Psychology, 65*, 9-15.

Loftus, E. F. (1986). Experimental psychologist as advocate or impartial educator. *Law and Human Behavior, 10*, 63-78.

Maass, A., Brigham, J. C., & West, S. G. (1985). Testifying on eyewitness reliability: Expert advice is not always persuasive. *Journal of Applied Social Psychology, 15*, 207-229.

McCloskey, M., & Egeth, H. (1983). Eyewitness identification: What can a psychologist tell a jury? *American Psychologist, 38*, 550-563.

McCloskey, M., Egeth, H., & McKenna, J. (1986). The experimental psychologist in Court: The ethics of expert testimony, *Law and Human Behavior, 10*, 1-13.

Shapiro, P., & Penrod, S. D. (1986). A Meta-analysis of the Facial Identification Literature. *Psychological Bulletin, 100*, 139-156.

Tanford, S. and Penrod, S. (1984). Social inference processes in juror judgments of multiple-offense trials. *Journal of Personality and Social Psychology, 47*, 749-765.

Thompson, W. C., & Schumann, E. L. (1987). Interpretation of statistical evidence in criminal trials: The prosecutor's fallacy and the defense attorney's fallacy, *Law and Human Behavior, 11*, 167-187.

Wells, G. L. (1984). How adequate is human intuition for judging eyewitness testimony? In G. L. Wells & E. F. Loftus (Eds.), *Eyewitness testimony: Psychological perspectives*. New York: Cambridge University Press.

Wells, G. L., Lindsay, R. C. L., & Tousignant, J. P. (1980). Effects of expert psychological advice on human performance in judging the validity of eyewitness testimony. *Law and Human Behavior, 4*, 275-285.

Woocher, F. D. (1986). Ethical responsibilities governing the statements experimental psychologists make in expert testimony. *Law and Human Behavior, 10*, 101-115.

NEW HORIZONS IN LAW AND PSYCHOLOGY

Organizer & Chair: G Davies, University of Leicester, U.K.

Contributors:

R. H. C. Bull, Glasgow College, U.K.
P. Horncastle, Austin Knight Selection, U.K.
Evaluation of police officer training

G. Davies, University of Leicester, U.K.
Psycho-legal research: The necessity of a two-pronged attack

D. Hessing, Erasmus University, Netherlands
Application of psychology to tax evasion

G. Köhnken, University of Kiel, FRG
Establishing the validity of witness statements

F. Lösel, Universität Erlangen-Nürnberg, FRG
Law and psychology: Plotting a position in the face of new horizons

J. C. Yuille, University of British Columbia, Canada
Eyewitness research with police trainees

Discussant: D. M. Thomson, Monash University, Australia

This symposium was the first to be organized by the newly constituted Psychology and Law Division of the International Association of Applied Psychology and was convened and chaired by G. M. Davies (University of Leicester, U.K.). The aim of the symposium was to illustrate the range of problems studied and methods employed in contemporary studies of psychology and law.

F. Lösel (University of Erlangen-Nuremberg, Federal Republic of Germany) opened the proceedings by noting the flowering of legal psychology under such pioneers as Sterne, Munsterberg, and Jung in Germany at the turn of the century and its recent re-emergence as a growth area within the discipline. It was still a minority interest but was growing in importance, whether measured by conferences or book and periodical publication.

This rapid growth has been associated with confusion as to the range and diversity of problems to be studied. He identified a number of discrete areas, including (a) conditions and causes of criminal behavior (e.g., delinquency, murder, child sex abuse), (b) expert witnessing: the provision of in-court advice on such issues as credibility and criminal responsibility, (c) features of the legal process (jury decision-making; sentencing), and (d) the impact of punishment and treatment regimes.

He cautioned that the nature of psychology and of the legal process meant that conflict and debate were inevitable. Jurisprudence aimed at a normative approach where information was precisely codified and categories of behavior were absolute and distinct (e.g., the insanity defence). Psychology, on the other hand, was an empirical science that talked in probabilistic terms. Moreover, interest by psychologists in legal issues seemed highly selective, with some areas (eyewitness testimony) receiving disproportionate attention and others (civil law) being largely ignored.

Davies's paper focused on the debate over the applicability of psychological research to legal issues in witness behavior. He highlighted four different methodologies that had been used to study witness identification: a laboratory-based experimental approach, simulated criminal incidents, field studies, and single case studies. Claims had been made for the superiority of each of these techniques as a guide to understanding and predicting witness behavior.

Davies argued that all methods had strengths or weaknesses; all offered different compromises between forensic realism on the one hand and scientific precision and control on the other. Successful prediction of the behavior of real witnesses would only come through looking for convergence among a range of studies using different techniques. He offered cross-racial identification and the utilization of contextual cues to facilitate witness recall as successful examples of convergence in action, though the subsequent discussion suggested that there were others (e.g., effects of stress on recall) where results were far from consistent.

J. Yuille (University of British Columbia, Canada) presented the results of a major study of long-term eyewitness recall. In this study, police cadets recalled incidents from their training 1 or 12 weeks later. The incidents involved were either emotionally neutral (questioning a person seen acting suspiciously) or moderately stressful (the same incident, but the person queried their authority and refused cooperation).

Accuracy of recall for the role play declined significantly over time for the stressful but not for the nonstressful incident. The impact of stress on recall was more marked for participants who questioned the suspect than for onlookers. Police cadets who recalled at both 1 and 12 weeks showed superior memory to those who had recalled only after 12 weeks. Yuille contrasted these findings to those from a case study involving witnesses to an actual violent crime. In both instances details (height, weight, age, and clothing color) were poorly remembered over time but the main actions were well retained, particularly by those subjects who had been interviewed shortly after the event.

A very different approach to the problem of witness memory was illustrated in the paper by G. Köhnken (University of Kiel, Federal Republic of Germany). Experimental studies may provide guidelines on trends of recall over time but, from the lawyers point of view, say nothing about the reliability of a specific individual's recollection. Köhnken described methods of detecting veracity through direct observation of witnesses and their behavior while testifying, which he characterized as unreliable and inconsistent. He contrasted this approach to truth determination with statement credibility assessment, a technique long practiced in Germany but now formalized and subject to rigorous empirical scrutiny both in Germany and North America.

Statements by witnesses are analyzed for 19 different criteria that are said to be indicative of truthfulness. Köhnken explained that this technique was particularly useful with juveniles who would be otherwise vulnerable to cross-examination in court. Debate ensued as to the ubiquity and value of the various criteria and the extent to which they were natural products of discourse or of particular methods of questioning.

R. Bull (Portsmouth Polytechnic, U. K.) in his paper illustrated the way in which psychology could be applied effectively in the evaluation of policing skills. Following widespread concern over the effectiveness of traditional training methods in human relations, the Metropolitan Police had introduced a new program (Human Awareness Training, or

HAT), which included role-play exercises with video feedback. Bull explained that he had been brought in to evaluate this program using a number of different methods in an effort to gather an overall impression of HAT's effectiveness.

A questionnaire study of officers in training had indicated that there was a significant reduction in anxiety over social interactions during the course of training but that this was accompanied by a growing negative attitude toward racial minorities. However, a study of official complaints indicated a significant reduction for HAT-trained officers compared to those who had enrolled under the earlier scheme. Moreover, observational study of the newly trained officers on duty indicated that members of the public were generally satisfied with their interactions with the officers concerned. Bull argued that police training could only benefit from such multileveled evaluation.

A final paper from D. Hessing (Erasmus University, The Netherlands) illustrated the application of psychology to tax evasion. A group of tax payers who had consistently evaded taxation in two consecutive years were identified from their records and a similar comparison group assembled who had no record of evasion. When questioned as to their honesty in filling in their tax returns, no significant relation emerged between actual behavior and verbal reports despite documented evidence of the recovery of the evaded dues in the case of the evaders. Attitudes toward taxation and evasion predicted verbal reports but not actual behavior. Documented status, however, was predicted by various personality measures such as alienation and a self-serving orientation, which, in turn, had no relationship to verbal statements.

Hessing's work raised again the general issue of methodology, one of a number touched on by the discussant, D. Thomson (Monash University, Australia), a psychologist who is also a qualified barrister. He shared Lösel's concerns regarding the differing goals and methods of psychology and law but looked forward to a challenging future for this fledgling discipline.

DRUG ABUSE PROBLEM AND ITS MEASURE IN THE EAST AND WEST

Organizer & Chair: M. Tamura, National Research Institute of Police Science, Japan

Contributors:

B. S. Brown, National Institute of Drug Abuse, U.S.A.
Outreach to stop the spread of AIDS among intravenous drug users

V. P. Hans, University of Delaware, U.S.A.
Psycholegal attitude toward corporate responsibility for wrongdoing

W.-K. Jhoo, H. K. Lee, E. C. Shim, H. C. Kim, Kangweon National University, Korea
Drug use among Korean adolescents (1989)

T. Koyanagi, Ichihara Prison, Japan
Current trends and treatment methods for stimulant drug offenders in correctional institutions in Japan

M. Tamura, National Research Institute of Police Science, Japan
Family role for preventing relapse of stimulant abuse

Discussant: T. Kubo, Ministry of Justice, Japan

In this symposium, during which sociocultural factors and cross-cultural differences were taken into account, effective prevention, law enforcement, and rehabilitation measures for drug abuse were considered and ways that psychology and other social sciences can contribute to the solution of the problem of drug abuse were explored.

In a presentation entitled *Outreach to stop the spread of AIDS among intravenous drug users*, Brown pointed out that the most rapidly growing population of AIDS cases in the United States is intravenous drug users (IVDU). To confront this problem, the National Institute on Drug Abuse (NIDA) organized a national outreach research project in 55 cities across the United States. The program provides outreach intervention including counseling, skills training, peer support systems, didactics, and HIV testing for out-of-treatment IVDU and their sexual partners.

Outreach activities for IVDU are available on the streets, at criminal justice facilities, and in emergency rooms and health-care facilities. Sexual partners can benefit from the program through Ob/Gyn clinics, baby clinics, social service clinics, shelters for homeless/battered women, launderettes, beauty parlors, health-screening vans, and housing authorities.

Data on 16,000 IVDU and 2,000 sexual partners who participated in the program shows that intervention resulted in decreased IV drug use frequency and increased the use of bleach and condoms. Kubo, the discussant, pointed out the importance and difficulty of identifying and locating the target population, and the process of motivating actual utilization of preventive procedures.

Jhoo, a pharmacologist interested in psychosocial aspects of drug abuse, presented his survey, *Drug use among Korean adolescents* (1989). A NIDA-type prevalence survey was conducted with 6,240 high-school seniors in 17 Korean cities. Jhoo's findings showed that alcohol and cigarettes are the most prevalent drugs (cigarettes used by 84.2% of males, 52.1% of females; alcohol used by 58.0% of males, 16.1% of females). After cigarettes and alcohol come inhalants and marijuana, but user rate was found to be small (2.3% and 3.0% for males respectively, and 2.2% and 1.3% for females).

Self-reported delinquents have a higher prevalence rate than nondelinquents for all of the drugs surveyed. In terms of social attitude, drug users were seen to be less satisfied than nonusers with themselves and their friends, family, school, and society. It was also pointed out that, owing to the enforcement of drug regulations, drug problems in Korea have decreased. The necessity of a nation-wide survey of drug abuse among adolescents was indicated as well as the need for studies on causes and measures to deal with drug abuse.

In her presentation entitled *Psychological attitude toward corporate responsibility for wrongdoing,* Hans noted that business corporations are increasingly facing both civil lawsuits and criminal charges in courts in the United States today. However, psychologists have conducted little research on how corporate responsibility for wrongdoing is judged. An important factor to be considered is the attitude toward business and the role business should play in compensation for harm. In addition, it is necessary to note differences between corporations and individuals that have an important effect on judgments of wrongdoing. These include types of violations (diffuse economic harm versus focused bodily harm), the potential that corporations often possess to harm large numbers of people, and the financial and other resources business corporations command.

The elaboration of the judgment model and factors included in the model were discussed, and the application of quantitative statistical techniques such as confirmatory factor analysis was suggested. The similarity of research design to studies done by several criminologists and the possibility of collaboration were mentioned along with a discussion on how theories of public perceptions of corporate wrongdoing could be enriched by international research on the topic.

In a presentation entitled *Family role for preventing relapse of stimulant abuse,* Tamura insisted that the family role was an essential for rehabilitation of drug users in Japan. The strength of the family bond was said to be a key factor for maintaining a low Japanese crime rate.

A total of 157 probationers who were ex-users of stimulants were sampled. The effectiveness of family factors in quitting the use of drugs was analyzed by comparing the differences between success and failure samples in probational supervision. The best index to identify a drug-free law-abiding life among males was the presence of regular work. For females, the index was the absence of promiscuous sexual relations with drug abusers. The family role for the prevention of relapse into drug abuse is to provide a drug-free environment and to pay close attention to the probationer's daily behavior. Probationers need to adjust to family expectations and show improvements in daily behavior in order to re-establish desirable family relationships that had undergone disintegration at the time of drug abuse and to succeed in rehabilitation.

Discussions centered on the need for a structural model of drug abuse and on family and causal analysis through application of recent statistical techniques. The family bond in Japanese society within the frame of control theory in the field of criminology was also discussed.

In a presentation entitled *Current trends and treatment methods for stimulant drug offenders in correctional institutions in Japan,* Koyanagi pointed out characteristics of stimulant abusers and methods to educate them. Education for drug dependents in correctional institutions is organized at three points in time: upon entry, midway through custody, and at the time of discharge. The aim of education is to enable drug dependents to give careful consideration to the conditions that led to their dependency, to recognize the significance of the effects of drugs on mental and physical well-being, and to consider the damage caused by drug abuse to family and friends. Cumulatively, these factors may bring the abuser to reject involvement with drugs.

The need for study of the effectiveness of various treatment methods was pointed out. Separate grouping differentiation of treatments for inmates willing and those unwilling to participate in the treatment course was also discussed.

PSYCHOLOGY AND LAW POSTER CONTRIBUTION

CRIMINAL BEHAVIOR AND MASCULINITY: THE GENDER-ROLES IDENTITY OF MALE OFFENDERS

Keiko Ishihara, Hachiohji Medical Prison, Tokyo, Japan, and Masahisa Kodama, Waseda University, Tokyo, Japan

The purpose of this study was to investigate gender-based personality theories about male offenders and to present a critical overview of the theories of the Masculinity-Femininity hypothesis.

The subjects were 63 male prisoners of first admission (mean age: 35.6) and 99 male recidivist prisoners (mean age: 38.2). The control groups consisted of 152 salaried men working at general enterprises in Tokyo (mean age: 43.6) and 236 male university students (mean age: 21.3).

The gender-based personality of the subjects in each group was investigated with questionnaires (in Japanese) based on the Sex-Role Inventory developed by Bem (1981). Their rating score on 45 items of the scales was calculated through an F test and X2 test among the groups. The group of salaried men recorded the highest average score per item (4.37) and per subject (65.97) for masculinity items. By contrast, the group of recidivist prisoners showed the highest average score per item (5.31) and per subject (75.64).

The characteristics of the recidivist prisoners shown by the high score on femininity contradict the popular version that masculinity is one of main factors of criminal behavior. These facts suggest the necessity of considering criminal behavior as referring not to the Masculinity but to the Femininity.

Reference
Lipsitz Bem, S. (1981). *Bem Sex-Role Inventory—Professional Manual.* Consulting Psychologists Press.

Origin and number of participants at the 22nd International Congress of Applied Psychology

Region	Country	No. by Country	No. by Region
Asia	Japan	924	
	Taiwan	10	
	South Korea	9	
	India	8	
	China	8	
	Hong Kong	8	
	Singapore	6	
	Philippines	2	
	Indonesia	1	
	Pakistan	1	
	Thailand	1	
	Total		978
Oceania	Australia	52	
	New Zealand	4	
	Total		56
Middle and Near East	Israel	24	
	Iran	3	
	Iraq	1	
	Turkey	1	
	Kuwait	1	
	Total		30
Africa	South Africa	7	
	Ivory Coast	1	
	Total		8
North America	USA	270	
	Canada	50	
	Total		320
Central and South America	Mexico	9	
	Brazil	6	
	Trinidad	2	
	Venezuela	1	
	Puerto Rico	1	
	Bolivia	1	
	Total		20
Europe	Holland	50	
	West Germany	50	
	England	30	
	Finland	28	
	Sweden	27	
	Italy	24	
	Belgium	19	
	Spain	17	
	France	17	
	Austria	8	
	Norway	8	
	USSR	7	
	Portugal	7	
	Switzerland	6	
	Denmark	4	
	Ireland	4	
	Hungary	3	
	East Germany	3	
	Yugoslavia	2	
	Poland	1	
	Total		315
GRAND TOTAL			1727

359

Author Index

Note: this is a cumulative index for all three volumes of the Congress proceedings. Page numbers preceded by 1: appear in volume 1; those preceded by 2: in volume 2, and so on.